WARNE...

Praise for *Sylvia Townsend Warner*

'A living and revelatory biography, as passionate and truthful,
elegant and enchanting as its subject. Claire Harman restores
Sylvia Townsend Warner to her real place as, in her best works, second
only to Virginia Woolf among the women writers of our century'
George D. Painter

'A fascinating and moving tale, told with
insight, sympathy and objectivity'
Times Literary Supplement

'Harman skillfully weaves Sylvia's stories and letters into the
biography, and the brilliance of the samples on display
constantly takes you aback . . . Outstanding'
John Carey, *Sunday Times*

'Really interesting and totally gripping. It evokes a person and
a period and a whole world in a very effective way'
Victoria Glendinning

'As lively and perceptive as this idiosyncratic,
rewarding writer deserves'
New Statesman

Praise for *Robert Louis Stevenson*

'A delight from beginning to end . . . Stevenson has
found a worthy biographer at last'
John Carey, *Sunday Times*

'Superbly readable'
Evening Standard

'Full, rich, intelligent and smooth . . . a continuous pleasure to read'
Allan Massie, *Literary Review*

'It takes real skill to preserve a sense of overall shape,
as Harman's excellent biography does. Her judgements
are crisp yet unobtrusive . . . she allows Stevenson to bring
h...

'Both the life and the writing are irresistibly entertaining'
Theo Tait, *Daily Telegraph*

'Vivid and engaging . . . Stevenson emerges from her pages
as a vital, courageous, contrary and exhilarating figure'
Times Literary Supplement

ABOUT THE AUTHOR

Claire Harman is the award-winning biographer of *Sylvia Townsend Warner* (1989), *Fanny Burney* (2000) and *Robert Louis Stevenson* (2005) and the author of the bestselling *Jane's Fame: How Jane Austen Conquered the World* (2009). She writes regularly for the literary press on both sides of the Atlantic and was elected a Fellow of the Royal Society of Literature in 2006. Her most recent work is *Charlotte Brontë: A Life* (2015).

Sylvia Townsend Warner

A Biography

CLAIRE HARMAN

PENGUIN BOOKS

PENGUIN BOOKS

UK | USA | Canada | Ireland | Australia
India | New Zealand | South Africa

Penguin Books is part of the Penguin Random House group of companies
whose addresses can be found at global.penguinrandomhouse.com.

First published by Chatto & Windus 1989
Published by Minerva Press 1991
Published in Penguin Books 2015

001

Printed in Great Britain by Clays Ltd, St Ives plc

A CIP catalogue record for this book is available from the British Library

ISBN: 978-0-241-96443-9

www.greenpenguin.co.uk

MIX
Paper from
responsible sources
FSC® C018179

Penguin Random House is committed to a
sustainable future for our business, our readers
and our planet. This book is made from Forest
Stewardship Council® certified paper.

To A.M.P.

CONTENTS

Illustrations

Acknowledgements:
5, Harrow School Archives; 10, 14 and 15, Janet Pollock; 21, Joy Finzi; 22, John Miles; 1, 2, 3, 4, 6, 7, 9, 11, 12, 13, 16, 17, 18, 19, 20, Dorset County Museum.

Acknowledgements

The author and publishers would like to thank the following for permission to reproduce copyright material: Susanna Pinney and William Maxwell, Executors of the Estate of Sylvia Townsend Warner, and Chatto & Windus Ltd. for extracts from *Letters* by Sylvia Townsend Warner (1982); the Estate of Sylvia Townsend Warner and Carcanet Press Ltd., for extracts from *Collected Poems* by Sylvia Townsend Warner (1982); Susanna Pinney and William Maxwell, Executors of the Estate of Valentine Ackland, and Chatto & Windus for extracts from *The Nature of the Moment* by Valentine Ackland (1973) and *For Sylvia: An Honest Account* (1985); the Estate of Robert Frost and Jonathan Cape for extracts from *The Letters of Robert Frost to Louis Untermeyer* (1964); The Collection of American Literature, Beinecke Rare Book and Manuscript Library, Yale University (as owners only) for extracts from letters of Sylvia Townsend Warner to George Plank and to Leonard Bacon, extracts from the journal of Alyse Gregory and from the letters of Valentine Ackland to Alyse Gregory in their possession; Chatto & Windus for extracts from letters of Sylvia Townsend Warner to Charles Prentice in their archive at Reading University; Harry Ransom Humanities Research Center, The University of Texas (as owners only) for extracts from letters of Sylvia Townsend Warner to Nancy Cunard and to Alyse Gregory.

I would like to express my thanks to Susanna Pinney and William Maxwell who gave me full access to the Sylvia Townsend Warner and Valentine Ackland papers in the Dorset County Museum and permission to quote from the published and unpublished writings of both Sylvia and Valentine. Without their generous help and encouragement, and that of the trustees of Sylvia Townsend Warner's estate, Joy Finzi and Peg Manisty, I would have been unable to write this book.

I must record my gratitude to Janet Pollock, Bea Howe, Peg Manisty and Angela Pitt for their invaluable help and friendship and to Jean Larson, Mary Dene, Steven Clark, Julius Lipton and all of the above for kindly allowing me to quote from material in their possession. The late Rosemary Manning was particularly generous in loaning me Valentine's letters to Alyse Gregory, now at Yale University, and the late Hilary Machen was as generous with his time, reminiscences and encouragement.

I would like to thank Roger Peers, of the Dorset County Museum, for his help and interest in my research, and also Michael Bott, of Reading University Library, and A.D.K. Hawkyard and J.S. Golland of Harrow School.

Many people have spoken or written to me about Sylvia, and significantly increased my understanding of my subject: Sybil Chase, Marchette Chute and the late Joy Chute, the late Vivien Elgood, the late David Garnett, the late Kenneth Hopkins, Colin House, the late George Howe, Peter Jones, J. Lawrence Mitchell, George D. Painter, O.B.E., Trekkie Parsons, the late Mrs Lucy Penny, the late Edgell Rickword, Ruth and Antony Scott, the late Norah Smallwood, Janet Stone, the late Grafin Antonia von & zu Trauttmansdorff, Mrs Elizabeth Warner and Elizabeth Wade White.

I would also like to thank my editor at Chatto & Windus, Jeremy Lewis, a model of patience, my family and Jacky Quigley and Nancy Stenhouse.

I

1893—1917

I

On 5 December 1893, the bell of Harrow School Chapel was tolling for one of the school governors, a Professor Tindall, who had died the day before. Only thirty feet away from the bell-tower, across the road, lived George Townsend Warner, an assistant master at the school, and his young wife Nora, who fell into labour at the alarming sound of the knell. She was expecting their first and, as it turned out, their only child, who was to be called Andrew, a name associated with the landed side of Nora's family. Old Doctor Stiven was called out to the Warner's house and at six o'clock the next morning, Wednesday 6 December, the baby was born, plump and healthy. And female.

News of the birth reached Rickmansworth by wire before breakfast time, where Nora's three orphaned siblings and three unmarried aunts kept house together. Aunt Annie, leading family prayers, burst into tears at the thought that Nora's parents, both dead that year, had never seen their first grandchild. Purefoy, Nora's fifteen-year-old sister, took a more cheerful view. The birth of a niece was the brightest spot in a year draped in mourning, and she bounded round the garden joyfully despite her black dress.

The baby was renamed Sylvia Nora.

George Townsend Warner and Nora Hudleston had been married

for sixteen months before Sylvia's birth. They had met in Newton Abbot, Devon, where George's father was headmaster of Newton College, a school for boys, and Nora's father was retired from the Indian Army, a colonel on half-pay. Nora (whose full name was Eleanor Mary) had been born in 1866 and brought up in Madras, where as the eldest of four surviving children she enjoyed longer than any of the others the years of her parents' prosperity. She had a pony, a devoted ayah, extravagant clothes, extravagant tastes, and by the time the family moved back to England, their fortune lost by the collapse of an Indian bank, Nora was unwilling and unable to be disciplined by either parent. She was 'an extraordinarily pretty girl' and 'very fascinating',[1] as her sister said, and indulged many flirtations, although she also developed 'an efficient way of boxing the ears of married men' – a business-like attitude. Even when money was short, Nora's social activities were not subdued. She made her own evening dresses, ingeniously copied from the French fashion papers, and went to all the best Newton Abbot parties and dances. Perhaps it was at one of these that Nora, looking supremely confident, haughty and conspicuous, met Mr Warner's son George and fell in love with him fiercely and for his lifetime.

George was an engaging young man with a deep-set, intense regard, moustaches and very long legs. When he met Nora, he was still up at Cambridge with a scholarship to read history, studying under Cunningham and Creighton in what was called the new 'scientific' method. His seven years at the university were gloriously successful: he gained the senior place in the Historical Tripos in 1887, the first Whewell Scholarship in International Law in 1889 and a fellowship at his college, Jesus, in 1890. 'Landmarks of Industrial History', which Warner was to publish later as a book, caused some 'confusion of face'[2] among the Tripos examiners, for this alarmingly direct young man with the low, clear voice had covered fully all the questions that could then be set on his subject, and done so in a concise two hundred and fifty pages.

On leaving Cambridge, George accepted a job at Harrow School as an assistant master, thereby continuing his family's long connection with the famous public school. He and his father were both Old Harrovians and his grandfather, the Reverend George Townsend Warner, had been a master there from 1846 to 1853 under Dr Vaughan. The Reverend George's most notable achievement was the consolidation of two villas into one house, West Acre, known as 'Warner's long range', after a contemporary laughing-stock, a long-range missile for use at sea invented by a Captain Warner. 'I was foolish enough at Harrow to think my prosperity would last forever', the Reverend George lamented in 1861 to his son, also George Townsend Warner (known to his parents as 'Townsend'), then expensively idling at Trinity College, Cambridge, and showing more enthusiasm for racquets than for Classics. When the Warners moved from Harrow to Torquay, where the Reverend George took over the running of Highstead School, their fortunes turned and never recovered. Bad health, money worries and a touching, if rather overwhelming concern for his son's spiritual welfare, dogged the ageing headmaster, whose own devoutness was solemn and simple. Contemplating the dangers to which young Townsend was exposed at Cambridge was an agony: the opera, the ballet, drink, the summer months 'perilously full of cricket', Bishop Jowett's view of Thessalonians ... and his son did nothing to reassure him, writing back to renewed pleadings that he should study, 'I have a strong aversion to Plato in any shape'.[3]

The Reverend George died in 1869, the year after Townsend received his M.A., having given him a job as tutor at Highstead in anticipation of his son being unemployable elsewhere. Townsend had taken holy orders and a plain, lively, highly intelligent Scots wife, Flora Jane Moir, who was almost four years his senior. The couple had to make do with rather modest accommodation in Torquay, a far cry from Flora's native Edinburgh and the stimulating, literate circle in which she had grown up. But they did not have to stay there long, for in 1875 Townsend, who was far better suited to teaching than his father would ever have supposed, was offered the headship of Newton College in Newton Abbot. The Warners settled there with their young son George, born in 1865, and his younger siblings Flora (Sissy), Robert (Bertie) and Euphemia (Effie).

One of the boys at Newton College, Arthur Quiller-Couch,

wrote later in his memoirs of how the new headmaster 'did actually and at once revolutionise the place for its good'; 'under Warner's hand miracles began and continued to happen'.[4] Warner brought with him from Highstead the best of the staff there and raised standards in the school so rapidly that Newton (an unendowed establishment, relying on its reputation) could soon afford a new chapel, laboratory, fives court, squash court, cricket field and pavilion. A lazy scholar himself, he had become an admirable pedagogue; strict and energetic on one side, fatherly and essentially pleasure-loving on the other, 'a gentleman with every attribute of a good headmaster', as Quiller-Couch noted, 'save a sense of justice, of which he had scarcely a glimmer'.[5]

This man who was 'our Prospero' to the boys of Newton College was known to his children as 'the Chief'. Photographs show him most often in a sea of family and friends, wearing a cricketing cap and a grey, wedge-shaped beard. They are always on holiday, in Argyllshire or Ettrick. Flora, a rather well-upholstered lady in a plaid, is seated on a chair; Townsend is lounging on the grass or leaning one foot on a wall. Their children look healthy and happy: young George is holding a shotgun and a spaniel, and around the edges of the group stand numerous ghillies, exhibiting the bag.

George, writing to Nora Hudleston, re-created the conversation on one of these holiday shoots, the members of which were himself, 'the Chief', Bertie, a lugubrious guest called Harry, and Murray, the ghilly:

> – Now we must go on after that bird ... I know exactly where he is ...
> – Did you see him down?
> – No, but I know exactly where he is ... you saw him Murray?
> – Eh, I couldna mark him. He went oot a ma sight round yon bit knowe ... He'll no gang far ... Maybe he might reach the bottom ...
> – Good Lord!
> – Come on
> – Sam you're a very nice dog, but I don't want you; you

smell; go away to your master. Mr Warner will you kindly call Sam?

– Here Sam come here good dog ... Good heavens how you do stink ... What a misfortune it must be to a dog to stink like that ...

– He certainly *is* high this morning.

– Now we'll just go straight for that bird .. He's dead .. I know exactly where he is – in that glen where the bracken is so thick ... Hullo, where's the whip? .. I've lost it ... I know where I left it.

– Eh I've got the wheep Maister Warner. Ye dropped it jist where we were pickin' up the burds. Eh syne ye promised me saxpense whenever 'a found it we hae na lost ane eh afore d'ye mind hoo' many ye lost at Drumelgier. Eh a ken ...

– Good heavens Murray don't make such a row. Why you're enough to frighten every bird off the place. I wonder there's anything left between here and Cnoe Moy – *Murray*!

– Yes Sir.

– Don't make so much noise.[6]

George was at Cambridge, finishing his M.A., when he wrote this. Nora, his fiancée, attended the graduation ceremony in 1891, thinking when she saw him enter the theatre that 'immediately everyone else looked shapeless and uncouth'[7] by comparison. In August 1892, when George had completed his first year as assistant master of one of the Modern Side fourth forms at Harrow, he and Nora were married at St Paul's Church, Newton Abbot. 'The Chief' officiated at the ceremony, as he did at the baptism in the same church twenty months later of his grand-daughter Sylvia. By the time the young Warners could get down to Devon, the baby was already strong and curious, and held on to Townsend's wagging beard so fiercely during the christening that he was distracted and named her Cynthia by mistake. But it was put right later in the register.

II

Dame Armstrong's House, Harrow-on-the-Hill, where Sylvia was born, was a square, light-stuccoed Georgian building. The ground floor windows on the west side looked onto Church Hill, exactly opposite the spot (commemorated by a plaque) where Anthony Ashley Cooper saw the pauper's burial and turned his mind to social reform. The ground floor windows on the east side of Dame Armstrong's looked down a drop of almost fifteen feet to the pavement of High Street, so steep was the fall of the hill under the house. The Warners shared this home with E.M. Butler, another master at the school and the baby's godfather, but did not stay there long after Sylvia's birth. Together with the nursemaid, the baby, the rocking-horse and the spaniel, George's beloved Friday, they moved to a tall semi-detached villa at the top of Waldron Road, Radnor Lodge.

Harrow in the 1890s was still a small town in Middlesex, surrounded by countryside and innocent of the Metropolitan Line. From her nursery window Sylvia was possessor of 'a most entrancing view [...] endless, rich and classically handsome: meadows, and the enormous solitary elms of that clay soil, belts of woodland, here and there sober pale-faced eighteenth-century houses showing through their baffle of trees; and the Thames Valley mists thrown over it like a gauze.'[8] Down the steep stairs from Sylvia's nursery were the dining room and the drawing room, down further were the kitchen and scullery and, in a semi-basement, George's workroom, with half a view of the rockery. This room was long and divided by George's interests; at one end were his books, the fireplace and a dhurry-draped wicker settee, creaking under Friday; at the other end was a carpenter's bench, a rack of smooth, oiled tools and the enormous rocking-horse, ten hands high, which had come from Newton Abbot and his youth, and on which he still rode, book in hand, rocking to the metres of Keats, Elizabeth Barrett Browning, or the Border ballads. Sometimes Sylvia was hoisted up in front of him; the soft voice and the melancholy words made her throat swell, she did not know why. The horse creaked and juddered in the dusky room.

Sylvia's favourite place in the house was the attic boxroom.

Here lived a dome-topped trunk, hat boxes, her father's old-fashioned opera hat, an alarming dressmaker's dummy and numerous dresses with large sleeves and tight waists, rustling mysteriously. It was the oddness of the assortment that appealed to her, and the privacy of the room, for she was a lone child who did not mix easily with her peers, but whose imagination was always at home in a boxroom. Other places were not so congenial, such as the den by the coal-cellar where knives were sharpened and the scullery, which the child also disliked, but on the whole Radnor Lodge was a bright and interesting house, enlivened by Nora's Indian print curtains and gay eiderdowns, by the carved lion-legs of a table and the shining painted knobs of a chest of drawers. It was the Warners' first and last unshared house, and Sylvia was especially happy in it. Between her father in his workroom and her mother in the drawing-room, playing Heller studies on the grand piano, Sylvia lacked little. The woman played, and the little girl danced round in a rapture. And from this verse, which George composed, it would seem her parents were happy there too:

How well-contented in this private grange
Spend I my life, that's subject unto change;
Under whose roof with moss-work wrought, there I
Kiss my brown wife, and black posterity.[9]

According to her aunt, Sylvia was 'an abnormally intelligent child, even at an early age',[10] eager, observant and self-possessed. 'Sylvia has early attained to the dignity of her first dining-out,' wrote George to his mother at Christmas 1898, 'and though she will be torn away by inexorable fate in the shape of her nurse and perambulator at seven, I daresay she will contrive to cram as much amusement into her one glorious hour as grown-ups do into a whole evening. More perhaps than they gain where pork chops and turnips on silver plate form the second entrée.' Sylvia's earliest memories are all happy, even ecstatic; the superlative joy of rolling down a daisied slope, eating butterballs out of the larder, running away from her nurse through the scented shrubs of the nursery garden and the forbidden rapture of licking her finger and squeaking it gently across a window-pane. Dressed in blue serge and wearing a sailor-hat and the name of a warship, the little black-haired girl bowled her hoop down the lanes between Harrow and Roxeth, making up tunes and peering into ditches with passionate longing to take home the discarded objects she saw there: old kettles, single boots, blue enamelled saucepans. Her nurse, nasty Florence, always thwarted these enthusiasms and considered her charge to be *very* unrefined, 'a child with low tastes'.[11]

'Art thou whirly, Hilly Warner, art thou sore detest?' was Sylvia's childish rendering of the hymn 'Art thou weary, art thou languid, art thou sore distrest?' and another revised version, 'Fawny was the clown, and he said –' for 'Thorny was the crown on His head' remained obscure to her parents for so long that George made her a book about Fawny the Clown and added periodically to his adventures, thinking it was 'Sylvie's' invention. The first hymn she knew by heart was 'The spacious firmament on high', which she loved, as she did the words 'When in the sultry glebe I faint' from the paraphrase of a psalm. She was 'an impressionable small child'[12] and used to scream at the Oxo posters of the day which showed a bull rising out of a teacup, though her favourite toys were an ill-favoured family of dolls, Mr and Mrs Marks and their daughter Kitty, carved for her by her father, who recorded their low-life adventures in an endless poem, 'The Marksiad'.

At about the age of six Sylvia was sent to a local kindergarten, but only stayed one term. She was a mimic, unwittingly disrupting the children and irritating the teachers so much that her parents withdrew her. Her report at the end of term was very unsatisfactory, 'only one kind word in it, and that was Sylvia always sings in tune'.[13] Subsequently, it was Nora who gave Sylvia her early lessons. In the small yellow-painted attic room which Nora used for her needlework and painting, Sylvia sat down to Reading Without Tears. Without reading, too, for she had a phenomenal memory and 'was thought a promising scholar till the day when I maintained that NAG spelled "horse", or at least "pony"'.[14] Nora took up the Bible next and by the age of seven, Sylvia was reading from it and making its vocabulary her own: 'So when our old fat spaniel trotted into the butcher's shop and scavenged a gobbet out of the scrap bucket, it was with a clear conscience and a sense of saying the right thing that I exclaimed, as I dragged him away, "Friday! Thou shalt not commit adultery!" Yet it was all wrong, somehow. [...] When I was asked to explain myself, I took my stand, rather aggrievedly, on reason. Had I not asked my mother what adultery meant? Had she not explained that it was the sins of the flesh? I could not understand why there should be all this fuss.'[15]

The lessons in the attic proceeded from the Bible to geography, history, French and Shakespeare. Some arithmetic was attempted, but informed innumeracy was a family failing, and Nora not the best teacher of this subject. Most educative of all to the young girl were Nora's stories of her distant girlhood in Madras. The Hudlestons, an old and distinguished Cumberland family with a seat near Penrith called Hutton John, had a history of service in the East India Company – the seventh Andrew Hudleston retired from it in 1830, and his forebear John had been Director in the late eighteenth century. When Nora's father Colonel Josiah Hudleston and his wife Fanny were living in Madras they were well-respected (Josiah's cousin William had been sometime Governor) and prosperous, and Nora recalled those days vividly:

> She began to unpack this astonishing storehouse, full of scents and terrors, flowers, tempests, monkeys, beggars winding worms out of their feet, a couple of inches a day, not more, or the worm broke and you had to begin again, undislodgable holy men who came and sat in the garden, the water carrier's song – and as she talked as much for her own pleasure as mine, and made no attempts to be instructive or consecutive, I never tired of listening. [...] My mother's recollections of her childhood in India were so vivid to her that they became inseparably part of my own childhood, like the arabesques of a wallpaper showing through a coating of distemper.[16]

Sylvia was never 'read down to' either by Nora and George or by her grandmother Flora, another gifted story-teller and frequent visitor to Radnor Lodge, who would take the child on her knee and read from *The Song of Roland* or *Sir Gawain*. Before anything else, Sylvia learned to be a superlative listener. The three most important adults in her early life each pleased her by pleasing themselves. She was treated as a rational being, and though this set her apart from others – 'I was [...] solitary and agnostic as a little cat, and mistrusting other children to a pitch of abhorrence'[17] – it preserved in her a capacity for delight and a freshness of response few people are lucky enough to escape childhood with.

'The Chief' retired from Newton College in 1895 and moved to the living of Alfold on the Surrey–Sussex border. The rectory of St Nicholas Church, a twelfth-century foundation restored in the 1840s, was a comfortable and congenial house to visit and the Warners went there frequently. Flora was energetic in Alfold, battling against draughts in the church, installing a new organ, even causing a telegraph office to be established in the village, following a series of misadventures which befell Sissy returning from India. Her influence was pervasive, if sometimes arcane: 'My grandmother, a theologically inclined unbeliever, wrote all my grandfather's sermons. He got quite a name as a preacher, and afterwards people used to say that it was difficult to reconcile the Mr Warner they met in society with the Mr Warner they heard in the pulpit.'[18] Townsend is still remembered in the parish as the rector who was interested in cricket, though the memorial window to him steers clear of the subject.

Flora was a natural writer. Apart from enormous correspondences with her children, her sermon-writing and volumes of memoirs, she was a collector of anecdotes and 'true stories', which she retold with effortless clarity. 'I loved her next to my father,' wrote Sylvia, 'and she loved me next to him. And her father loved her beyond all others.'[19] Her father was George Moir of Charlotte Square, Edinburgh, a short, ugly, highly cultured man, 'a German scholar like all the fashionable intellectuals of his date'[20] (the 1820s and 1830s), whose translation of Goethe's *Wallenstein* was at the printers when Moir heard that Coleridge was engaged on the same task, and so withdrew. Carlyle called him 'kind, lively, very ingenious' – they were neighbours in Edinburgh – 'with whom I am growing very intimate';[21] and Moir also knew the painter Constable, who was married to his cousin. Flora Moir was a charming and quick-witted young woman with a 'quiet dignity'[22] of which even her father-in-law approved. At the end of a dinner party Matthew Arnold once said to her 'I see that good taste means a great deal to you, and morality very little.'[23] Her grand-daughter admired and adopted the same standards and loved her visits to Alfold, where she and Flora would sit together on the bank of white violets in the paddock, or in the snuffy, comfortable sitting-room where one day, quite suddenly and unexplained, Flora threw Sylvia to the floor and began to play rough-and-tumble 'with reckless, burning abandon'.[24] A moment later she was sitting down, brushing back a piece of hair with her hand and perfectly composed before Nora came into the room.

Flora's younger sister Anne was married to Ponsonby Moore (later Earl of Drogheda) and lived at Moore Abbey, County Kildare, a large gloomy, castellated building with more gothic about it than simply the shape of its windows. 'Aunt Tenny' wore massive rings, drank – water – from a jewelled chalice and was a friend of Lady Augusta Gregory and the Abbey Theatre group. Sylvia visited Moore Abbey with her parents in the summer of 1900, seeing this rather extraordinary branch of her family for the first time. The Warners were met at Monasterivan by a barouche landau, complete with coachman, footman and a separate vehicle for the luggage. Sylvia found a great deal to enjoy at Moore; a royal suite, a Georgian dolls' house, gardeners in traditional Irish dress and chimney-pot hats and a mildewed sedan chair in the hall which became her special retreat. There were also elaborate meals, which absorbed Sylvia's full attention, inducing her father to write the following verse, 'Moore 'abbiness':

> You must not spear each Individual Pea,
> Altho', my Child, your fork may be four-pronged,
> Because if you attempt this feat, you see
> Your parents' dinner will be too prolonged.[25]

But the house was plagued by ghosts, the noise at night being sometimes insupportable. Nora, who had heard bare-footed people in the dressing-room and what sounded like a sighing horse over her bed, vowed on the boat back to Holyhead never to stay there again.

Other holidays were more modest and comfortable. For several summers the family stayed at Camber, Kent, in lodgings run by a Mrs Dive. Sylvia loved the marshes and the sea, and pined so much on her return to Harrow that her father bought a black kitten, her first, as a consolation. He had a very short stumpy tail, and Sylvia named him Mister Dive, causing a misunderstanding the following year at Camber when the landlady thought she overheard Miss Warner praying fervently for her husband. Feline Dive was sent prawns in matchboxes through the post and Sylvia used to put her ear to telegraph poles to hear him purring distantly, until someone commented on this, and she stopped doing it.

When Sylvia was very young, it had occurred to Nora that they ought to attend more closely to the Christian year. She told Sylvia the story of the three kings; the star standing over the stable, the kings entering and seeing the ox, the ass, the woman and the baby. Sylvia, captivated by the narrative, interrupted 'and did they KILL it?'[26] Children, she maintained later, are born humanists, and check all moral assertions against what they observe in the adult world. Her parents were not given to moral assertions but Florence, the nurse, was. Florence had devised a punitive bogey who, she claimed, looked out of the nursery chimney-place when the sinful Sylvia's back was turned. The child, thinking the goblin's way of going about things odd, declared that she didn't believe it. 'As I slept in my nursery, this entailed an anxious night, since I had of course been assured that if I didn't believe in him, he would soon pop out and show me I was wrong. But by the morning he hadn't done so, and I got up an agnostic.'[27] This was more of a definition than a decision, as she had never had a great deal of Christianity thrust upon her, though she had had, in the usual course of things, a great deal of Church. All her life she deplored the idea that fear, guilt and self-abnegation can be in any way a means to salvation and thought back gratefully on Florence's goblin — 'what infinite blessings have been emptied out on us from what were certainly intended as vials of wrath'.[28]

Soon after this incident, Florence was replaced by a young

woman of Westmoreland stock called Grace, a benign creature who introduced Sylvia to mushroom picking and taught her one Wordsworth sonnet and one page of Bewick's *Birds* each week. Sylvia, at the age of ten, needed all the companionship she could get. She had grown very lanky and thin. Her black hair was long and rather messy, her knees were always dirty and her face was changing from its sweet childish oval to what threatened to be a Hudleston jaw. She was about to be a terrible disappointment to her mother.

III

Looking back on the falling-off of her mother's love for her, Sylvia, then aged seventy-seven, wrote in a letter, 'for the first seven years of my life I interested her heart; and I was an amusing engaging child and she enjoyed her efficiency in rearing me. But nothing compensated for my sex.'[29] Nora's ill-feeling was many-faceted; Sylvia was not a son, she was not going to be a beautiful daughter, she was rather off-puttingly clever and rapidly becoming the apple of her father's eye. Also, as can be seen in many later pastimes, Nora did not persist in anything she had lost interest in or been thwarted by. Child-rearing and childbirth presumably came under this heading, for it was often intimated to Sylvia that her mother had suffered much.

Sylvia admired her mother for much the same reasons as did George, who loved his wife steadfastly, though sometimes with an ironic detachment which Nora failed to perceive. She was an exciting but intimidating woman, 'brilliantly witty, autocratic, mocking, with several areas of her heart as hard as a stone. I wrote cold, and amended it to hard. Nothing about her was cold. She was intensely, savagely loyal, very hard-working and with a hand that could turn to anything.'[30] Nora was also vain and impervious to the giggles of schoolboys as she launched down Harrow High Street in her latest creation in mauve and black. Indeed, Nora caught every fashion so newly off the pages of the papers that she always appeared eccentrically dressed. She had few women friends, but many men found her intriguing and she knew how to use her charm to maximum effect. Flirtations, though, were undertaken in a spirit of conspicuous waste, for she was devoted to George. He on his part was neither intimidated nor embarrassed by his wife. He was a single-minded man. What may have appeared to others as volatility, eccentricity or downright bitchiness was to him high-spirited individualism, and unflawedly admirable.

Following the death of 'the Chief' in November 1902, Flora moved to London, to a house on Eaton Square near her younger son Robert, who had gone from the Middle Temple to a job on the legal side of the Board of Education. In 1903 George was appointed Master of the Modern Side at Harrow and the Warner family moved from Radnor Lodge to 1, Grove Hill, an even taller and steeper house in red brick with a garden which fell away downhill at an alarming angle. Sylvia, being almost ten years old, had outgrown a nursery and had a bedroom on the first floor and schoolroom at the top of the house. But Nora barely had time to turn the drawing-room over to rose-patterned chintzes before they were on the move again, for George had been made housemaster of 'High Street', the house now called Bradby's.

High Street was a large, elegant, early-Victorian house built of yellow brick with a recently-constructed wing for the forty or so boys (of ages fourteen to eighteen) who lived there. The Warners' side had a very grand entrance hall, large rooms, a spacious, irregular-shaped garden, central heating, a fire-alarm system and a cook. At first their furniture seemed quite inadequate for the increase in space and elegance; they bought, they borrowed and they gradually settled in. Where the rocking-horse lived at this date is not clear; certainly not in George's study, which was a business-like room on the first floor, looking onto the street and the entrance to The Park. This room formed a physical link between George's home and school life, a door at one side leading out into the family quarters, at the other into the boys' wing. He was often in his study. The responsibilities of housemastership brought extra work to a man who was already going at full tilt and who had books to write as well. His time, his drawing-room, even his family holidays were now at the disposal of the boys.

Warner was, by all accounts, a brilliant teacher, 'one of the most inspiring [...] that the public schools have known'.[31] He had not only a remarkable knowledge and understanding of his subject – history – but wit, imagination and intellectual energy, a youthfully eager mind which challenged his pupils to respond and to think for themselves. 'It may not be well-known', wrote an ex-pupil, 'in what high regard he was held at the two universities. The pupils of Warner were no little gratified to find that they went thither as marked men. Behind the scenes, where dons young and ancient discuss the teaching of history, his work at Harrow was recognised as the greatest in the land, his advice sought and opinions accepted without discussion.'[32] Strict with the younger boys, he gave considerable latitude to his sixth formers and Head of House, and his history students formed a 'family' whose loyalty to and affection for Warner lasted well beyond school years. His influence on these boys was great, but never overpowering, for it was not his desire to impose ideas. 'I do not know,' wrote the same pupil, 'that any of his "school" turned into philosophers; but in most of them there was something of the poet.'

Clear style was of utmost importance to Warner. His little book *On the Writing of English*, used in schools for many decades, gives some indication of his teaching method and the pleasure he took in it. Part 2 (paragraph 8), 'On "Succulent Bivalves"', begins:

> This, you remember, is what the Bad Journalist called the Oyster. I use the term to denote the tribe of commonplace phrases, the 'arm-in-arm' companions which go about together, and the hackneyed quotations. Luckless creatures these last, torn from their king's houses and led into captivity; poor degraded slaves, you will find them in the gutters of English – ill-used, pathetic and bedraggled, yet with remnants of their dignity still clinging to them. 'A thing of beauty is a joy for ever.' So wrote Keats; but all joy has left that hapless line. 'On the light fantastic toe' comes dancing by, but with the steps of the music hall. 'A ministering angel thou' … yes, once upon a time. But she and another poor lady lack that repose 'which stamps the caste of Vere de Vere'. Let these poor things be; they are at every man's 'beck and call'. Don't you drag them, shrinking and ashamed, into the light.

Warner indulged his aptitude for satire in the criticism of pupils' essays, but never humiliated a boy on account of bad work. He went through each essay sentence by sentence with its author, exposing all the faults and even the smallest virtues of style. Sometimes a boy would find on his paper a scorecard of how often a favourite adjective had been pressed into service on each page, or he might find a little drawing of a cannon belching smoke at the side of a purple passage, and the words 'pom-pom!' in Warner's small, exceedingly neat handwriting. Another pupil, the novelist L.P. Hartley, recalled how 'when one made a blunder he forebore for the moment from comment; perhaps he was thinking it out, for it was generally devastating when it came. But in more genial moods he would remark, "If you ever say that again I shall fall on you with my teeth and my umbrella" [...] The most irrepressible among my contemporaries held him in awe. Nor was G.T.W. to be trifled with; he was a man of moods, and one could not always please him simply by trying to. But he was a teacher of the first order and he got more out of his pupils than it seemed in their power to give. He was a genius.'[33]

He was also a 'poet of no mean order' (a description from a gazetteer which became a family joke) and had a facility for turning verses and writing skits, as the pages of *The Harrovian*, which he edited for fourteen years, show. According to one friend, Warner's verse was 'capricious [...] but at its best it had an elfin delicacy';[34] he excelled at satiric and comic verse, the more specific the occasion the better. Left without an argument, his muse rapidly became emotional, which Warner could not handle so well. His was a polished and useful talent and had the distinguished young music master, Percy Buck, been a more school-song-minded man, there would doubtless have been many more collaborations in the style of 'You?', written two years after the end of the Boer War and still, occasionally, sung today:

> You go forth where your brothers went,
>   And the shadows gather round;
> With last lights out, and the camp-fires spent,
>   From the veldt dead voices sound,
> Voices that ask 'Is it well with the Hill,

Now as in the days that were?
Is it well?' And phantom sentries still
Challenge you 'Who goes there –
You? –
Pass, Friend – All's well.'[35]

Warner was an excellent fives player, 'the most brilliant and dazzling exponent any of us have known',[36] and vastly improved the standard of fives in the school, occasioning great satisfaction at Harrow when a pair of fives players, trained by him, won all the major public school matches two years running. One of these boys, Ronald Eiloart, the captain of the first eleven, was a particular favourite of George's and had no sooner left the school to train as an architect in 1906 than he began to spend holidays twice a year with the Warners. It was said of George that 'what he wanted and what he got in his House was a set of good clean fellows, playing the game.'[37] 'Ron' was just such a fellow: a wholesome, willing public school man.

'Playing the game' was paramount. George Warner abhorred sham and affectation and was quick to sniff them out. When an old acquaintance wrote to him 'If you have a fault it is that you do not suffer fools gladly,' he readily agreed; it was a characteristic he was most proud of. E.M. Butler, who had shared Dame Armstrong's house with Warner and knew him from boyhood, described 'a certain personal exclusiveness which made him formidable to the casual acquaintance. [...] He was not intelligible to all; he had no love of popularity; at times a brusqueness of manner, a seeming want of interest in his surroundings, an apparent absent-mindedness with regard to those with whom he happened to be made him misunderstood. He had strong opinions and expressed them freely.'[38] Brilliant intellectual, athlete, sportsman, artist and carpenter, hard-working, 'clean' and with a sentimental streak, Warner must have seemed to the boys an adult model of that unicorn, the 'all-rounder'. And though no beak is ever spared a schoolboy's humour, and all have nicknames, George Townsend Warner held the respect of most of his pupils and the adoration of many.

Sylvia was, of course, excluded from the school life to which her father gave himself so wholeheartedly. He was up at 6.45 a.m. for

First School, back with the family for breakfast, off again for the day, and often in his study at night. He and Nora took their responsibilities very seriously, and any boy who was looking peaky or troubled could be sure of a visit from one or the other of them. To have one's parents so thoroughly *in loco parentis* to forty young men in whom one has little interest, and over whom no sway, must be galling to any twelve-year-old girl. In a story Sylvia wrote many years later, an elderly woman meets a former pupil of her adored schoolmaster father:

> It had touched her to meet this grey-haired man who still remembered his teacher with such living piety. But for all that he had been one of them, one of those special pupils who came thronging between her and her birthright, whose voices rose and fell beyond the study door, who learned, who profited, who demanded, who endeared themselves by their demands, who were arrayed for the ball while she, her father's Cinderella, went barefoot like the cobbler's child in the adage.[39]

Whether this is wholly a fiction or based on her own feelings, the resentful – almost splenetic – note rings true and jars sharply with all the other evidence of what was certainly a secure and happy childhood. Her father's time may not have been hers, but his affections were: 'there is a bull's-eye gravity about the way these people love'.[40] When the voices were rising and falling beyond the study door, Sylvia was not ravaged by jealousy or rejection. She was looking forward to a time when she and her father, so alike in mind and manner, so admiring each of the other, would have themselves to themselves. The story was written in 1961. The spleen is retrospective, the echo of loss.

IV

She was too tall, she was too skinny, said Nora, herself very short and rounded, and even those terrible glasses didn't stop her peering short-sightedly at music. George on the other hand applauded his daughter's excellent playing. He also admired the long legs, wading in and out of the March Burn at Ettrick, and had the good sense to tell her so. After 1904 the Warners went every winter to Lenzerheide in Switzerland, where George taught Sylvia to skate, and every summer to the Tushielaw Inn in the Ettrick valley. They took Friday's successor Pooloo with them, an enormous blue-black poodle with a lion cut. George was a keen dry fly fisher and Nora a watercolourist. Each would spend whole days at these pursuits, for holidays were sacrosanct: there was to be no work and no fluster. Sylvia was by this time old enough to spend the day alone walking. It was a landscape familiar to her from the Border ballads and legends Flora and her father loved. She would walk along the Ettrick admiring the peculiar clarity of the water and the look of the stones under it and, above the clamour of the river, the sound of curlews. When it was fine she would lie for hours on the heathered side of Craig Hill, watching sheep on the slope of Cacrahead opposite. And when it rained – it often rained – she would go bathing or sit under a waterfall on the reasoning that it was better to be wholly than partially wet. 'It was the first hill-landscape I knew; and though I have loved other, grander landscapes since [...] it is still the authentic country of my mind.'[41]

The young men who came on these holidays for a week at a time came to be with George, to fish, walk or sketch with their old teacher, and Sylvia had little or nothing to do with them. It was the same at Harrow, where only formal occasions called out masters' families. Speech Day would see her in her best dress – often a utilitarian one, as Nora's ideas about high fashion did not extend downwards to daughters – and school concerts saw her wincing under the blows of a treble solo. She made no friendships among the boys (not that it was encouraged) while she was their contemporary, indeed she disdained them. Vivien Elgood, the longest-surviving Harrovian from the pre-war generation, was Head of House at High Street in 1906 and sat next to Sylvia at certain house meals. They found each other dull – conversation began and ended with the salt – but even through this adolescent fog, Elgood perceived that his neighbour was self-possessed, isolated and 'unusual'.

As she grew up, Sylvia's education became more diverse and even less formal. Nora still read with her – mostly Dickens (whose works Nora's family all loved and knew backwards) and the newly-translated novels of Tolstoy, Dostoievsky and Turgenev. She also taught Sylvia to sew skilfully and, by observation, to become like her an accomplished and exotic cook. A French governess came twice a week, taught grammar and conversed with Sylvia on a wide variety of subjects, discovering in the girl a natural aptitude for the language. Early attempts to teach Sylvia German had not come to much and George was reduced to sending her to chapel with the German Bible. If anything would drive her to attend to German, he maintained, the Harrow School chapel sermons would. But apart from the discovery that Samson's name in German was Simson, and that God said let the earth bring forth cabbage, she did not progress far by that method. Later she had tuition in German from Constantine Moorsom, a colleague and friend of George's, who was amazed at the speed with which she learned and at her intelligence. He used to say that he had never had a better pupil.

It was George, though, who was most completely responsible for the shaping of Sylvia's intellect; he 'made' her. 'To receive from him a private lesson in history or literature', wrote a pupil, 'was an illuminating privilege, long to be remembered'.[42] All Sylvia's lessons were private lessons and, being unconstrained by time-table, examinations or schoolroom discipline, allowed full scope for George's imaginative and fanciful side. It was a conversation rather than a lecture which took place between 'Ruzzie' and Sylvia in the drawing-room, over the breakfast table, on a walk or working together on one of his meticulous maps intended for the classroom. The cobbler's child in this case was very well-shod. By the age of seventeen or so, Sylvia's erudition was both phenomenal and perfectly natural. In the opinion of some, she was 'the cleverest fellow we had',[43] to others she was known – somewhat disparagingly – as the best boy at Harrow.

The last item in the appendix to George Townsend Warner's *On the Writing of English* is a short essay called 'Upon the Quality called "Romance"'. It is the latter of two pieces included by Warner as examples of youthful essay-writing, the other piece being the work of a sixth former at Harrow, N.A. Walton. 'Upon the Quality called "Romance"' is kept deliberately anonymous, both in the text and in the contents pages, and a prefatory note by Warner avoids revealing the author's sex or station: 'Here, finally, is an even younger piece of stuff, the work of a fifteen-year-old. Its writer would now criticise it ferociously on the ground that it is altogether too elaborate or fanciful: might even condemn it as sentimental. But it serves my purpose to illustrate two or three things [...]' This is the first paragraph of the essay that follows:

> It is difficult to define Romance; it is like attempting to describe the air, it is so universal, so all-embracing. In everything done alone, and out-of-doors there is much Romance. It lies in walking alone over the broad curving moors, in the tracking of a stream, in the discovery of some narrow rocky hollow, hidden away in the cleft of the hills: in a lesser degree, in the opening of a new book. Romance comes upon one suddenly in the friendly buffeting of the North Wind, in the tinkle of flowing water heard far off, in the sailing of a cloud's shadow down the opposite slope, across the valley between, and up the hillside where one stands watching.[44]

'Upon the Quality called "Romance"' could very well be Sylvia Townsend Warner's first appearance in print.

Music was increasingly important to Sylvia. Her early piano lessons had been uninspiring: 'My hands were set on the keyboard and coerced into playing scales in unison – a hateful proceeding – and in contrary motion which was enjoyable.'[45] A later teacher 'took me by the scruff of the neck and dropped [me] into a Haydn sonata' and Sylvia never looked back. Once she had 'discovered' music, she became completely bound up in it, went to every concert, opera and ballet available, and got up at 7 a.m. to practise the piano. When she was sixteen she began to study music with Dr Buck; piano and organ (at both of which uncomplementary skills he was expert) and also the history and theory of music, and composition. By 1911 she was composing regularly, setting favourite poems to music and writing among other things a set of piano variations.

The fact that music was an area into which neither parent could follow far may have influenced Sylvia, but it is unlikely that she would have chosen to specialise in music without the encouragement and example of Percy Buck. He was an urbane and witty man with a remarkably wide-ranging mind, more than a match for George Warner, whose close friend he became soon after joining the staff at Harrow in 1901, aged thirty. He had previously been organist at Wells, then Bristol and later held two chairs of music, one at Dublin, where he was non-resident, and the other at London. The master who introduced Buck to Dr Wood, the headmaster, for the first time had said, 'Don't you think Dr Buck is the best-looking man you've ever seen?'[46] He had prematurely silver-grey hair and an easy, placid manner and soon became a school favourite, despite a marked preference for spectating rather than partaking in sports. Apart from playing in chapel, Buck gave an organ recital every week and played the piano at High Street's regular house-singing, rather rollicking, informal occasions where the house song, 'Rome was not Built in a Day', written by Warner and Buck, provided a final flourish before 'Forty Years On' and the National Anthem. To Sylvia he was both a family friend, known by the nickname 'Teague' on account of his Irish blood, and her personal mentor, one of the few people she could talk to as an equal.

Sylvia's closest friends at this time were among people of her parents' age. Maud Moorsom, the wife of Constantine, was a woman with a caustic wit, rather like Nora Warner in temperament, only without the sting of the blood-tie for Sylvia, who was always very close to her. Ruth, Maud's young daughter, was in much the same situation as Sylvia had been; an only child, and a girl-child, living on the fringes of a world given over to Boys. Though Sylvia had many closer friends in her life, she retained a uniquely protective and maternal affection for 'Puss', as if the conditions of childhood they shared provided more than just cementing memories, provided a bond of sympathy too. Ruth had piano lessons from both Sylvia and Dr Buck: Buck would play for her – or himself – rather than for her tuition while Sylvia, the lesser pianist, was the better teacher for a small child. Sylvia explained herself clearly, though Ruth found her expression, squinting and angular, as off-putting as Percy Buck's chain smoking.

In 1911 and 1912 Sylvia was at an age when all good upper middle-class girls should 'come out'. Her long hair was now dressed and worn 'up', her shoulders were exposed at suitably grand dinner engagements and one or two dances were attended. This was the absolute minimum, but somehow even modest šocial adventures were sabotaged by Sylvia not adjusting her demeanour in the least to the requirements of coquetry. Her coiled hair only emphasised an angular jaw, at the grand dinner she would turn the conversation round to theology and at her first ball she was only happy when dancing with Ruzzie, and then she was in heaven. To Nora, this must have been extremely galling. On every count which she held dear, her daughter did worse than fail; she deliberately refused to take part.

To Sylvia, as to Lolly Willowes, the heroine of her first novel, 'coming out' was really the beginning of 'going in', and the process ended in marriage, an institution towards which she had no inclination whatever. A passage in Lolly Willowes nicely describes the redundant position of young men in the life of a girl who adores her father:

> Laura compared with her father all the young men whom otherwise she might have accepted without any comparisons whatever as suitable objects for her attentions, and she did not find them support the comparison at all well. They were energetic, good-looking, and shot pheasants with great skill; or they were witty, elegantly dressed, and had a London club; but still she had no mind to quit her father's company for theirs, even if they should show clear signs of desiring her to do so, and till then she paid them little attention in thought or deed.[47]

Being unmarriageably intellectual was not completely a comfort to Sylvia, for she still had unwanted admirers to deal with, some of a particularly unwantable stamp. On one occasion, at a dinner, Sylvia became impatient of the repeated advances of a cleric (she was fatally attractive to elderly clerics) and his sepulchral breath chilling her shoulder. Nora had boxed the ears of married men; Sylvia attacked with erudition. She unloosed an astonishing flow of language at the hapless man, making some chance remark of his the occasion for a closely-argued exposition of the life and work of Aloysius Beza, jurist of the Counter-Reformation. She must have done this in part to entertain Buck – who was also present – and no doubt he was entertained.

Despite, or perhaps because of, Nora's policy of non-cooperation on the matter of clothes, Sylvia became, as soon as she had an allowance, a young woman of fashion. Often her choice – of hats especially – emphasised her extreme individualism and soon made her as much of a joke among the boys as Nora had ever been. More, indeed, for Nora was considered to be a very good-looking woman and Sylvia was not. Once Sylvia appeared in the Hen-coop – the transept of Harrow School chapel reserved for masters' wives, daughters and other stray women – in an almost unbelievable hat from which protruded an artificial lily on a tall stem, inspiring joy in many schoolboy hearts that morning, and as a fashionable bridesmaid she wore a 'tea-tray' hat so wide that she could only get into the car by holding her head on one side and letting it in vertically. She remembered herself at this time as being 'in outline like a kite, an immensely wide hat and a skirt measuring four inches round the ankles, or wearing one of those cache sex muffs that hid my young form from waist to knees. It was the largest muff in Harrow, and Oh! how I fancied myself: and a very amiable man who was then engaged in making love to me asked me tenderly if I curled up in it at night.'[48]

The very amiable man was Percy Buck and he succeeded. A love affair between them began in 1913, when Sylvia was nineteen. The considerable difficulty of keeping this secret in the closed society of the Hill was partly assuaged by the satisfaction Sylvia derived from conducting such an affair (Buck was married, had five children and was twenty-two years her senior) under her mother's nose. Sylvia remained Buck's mistress for the next seventeen years, during which time he was, in his unassuming way, immensely influential over her, and though she had several other lovers as a young woman, none was so much her equal as 'Teague'.

V

Ronald Eiloart, now qualified as an architect, still came to Ettrick every summer with the Warners, who usually set out from Harrow on or near 30 July, Nora's birthday, and stayed in Scotland until the middle of September. George would go out fishing immediately, and kept tallies of his total holiday catch, comparing year with year. In 1913 Ron was nearly outdoing him with the dry fly and when not fishing was off on enormous walks across the moorland with Sylvia and the somnolent Pooloo, who being the least hardy of the three had to be lifted over fences on the way home. Other guests came and went, including the Sturts – family friends of whom Sylvia was particularly fond – but it was Ron who stayed longest and at the end of the day was 'hobnobbing in the pub' with Sylvia. Nothing would have pleased George better than to see that particular young couple in each other's company, though he can hardly have thought that the hobnobbing would lead to anything permanent. The holiday continued in the accustomed way; they all picnicked in Peter's Wood on curries and risottos heated over a spirit-lamp, went bathing in the burn (where a bathing-tent collapsed on Nora and Sylvia) or wandered round the Yarrow Show, snuffing up the smell of wet wool. On a couple of occasions, however, George had to stay indoors and rest, which often meant working on the articles and books and proofs of books he had constantly in train. He was feeling, he said, 'rather seedy'. What appeared to be bad digestion had been troubling him for several years.

On 22 September 1913, a week after their return from Tushielaw, the Warners received a telegram at High Street. Sylvia heard a noise like an animal howling and hurrying to discover what had happened found that the howling animal was her mother. George was rigid and silent: the telegram said that Flora had been run over by a taxi in Sloane Square and was dead. The shock of the news did not register so powerfully with Sylvia at that moment as did the inhuman noise it had called out of her mother.

Flora was buried with her husband at Alfold four days later. She had been a model matriarch, combining very strong maternal affections with a lively-minded independence, and the family was never so united again. For her part, Sylvia, the last Warner, held to her grandmother's example of right-thinking and doing, and appreciated increasingly throughout her life Flora's subtly admirable character. 'It all stemmed from her, all the high-minded good sense and latent wild emotion of the family, all the force and direction and sense of romance mixed with realism and contempt of balderdash – the impetuosity with which she would stamp on nonsense or pettiness, and the melancholy that underlies love.'[49]

Early the following year, 1914, George bought a piece of land and a piece of river at the edge of Dartmoor, possibly using some of the money inherited from his mother. He wanted to build a house which could be used for holidays and at the same time nurtured towards his retirement. South Devon was home ground for both him and Nora, the moor had all the wildness of landscape he loved, and there was room for a large garden, gardening being a passion neither had ever been able to indulge sufficiently in Harrow. There was no debate over who should be the architect – it was just the job to help young Ronald along.

The result, Little Zeal, was a comfortable Georgian villa with half-panelling in the hall, 'rational' cupboards and exclusive fishing rights. It was also damp, had no electricity and was isolated from even the inadequate shops of South Brent, but if that was the price for not having neighbours, the Warners were prepared to pay it. George and Ronald together did much of the carpentry for the house, dynamite was applied where Nora wanted a rock garden and a local man patrolled with a gun in their absence to establish order on land that was already home to countless rabbits and moles. There were to be no servants, for Little Zeal was undertaken by George and Nora in the spirit of adventure.

Sylvia, who in 1914 was in her twenty-first year, was not expected to be one of the permanent fixtures at Little Zeal, although she had a room of her own there: 'I was young, sullen, exalted, lay awake with toothache and La Cathedrale [presumably *La Cathédrale engloutie*, one of Debussy's 1909 *Préludes*], and dressed my hair like a Velasquez infanta by candlelight.'[50] She had planned to leave home that year for the Continent, where it is said she was to study composition with Arnold Schoenberg. It is intriguing to speculate on what might have come of her career as a composer under the influence of this challenging teacher, whose pupils included Webern, Alban Berg and Bax, but the opportunity was lost in the course of events of 1914. Sylvia continued composing, probably under the supervision of the Royal College of Music, where she was well-known through her association with Buck, and she began at the same time to study the music of the fifteenth and sixteenth centuries. She was trying her hand at writing stories and sketches at this time, and the earliest poem in her first book *The Espalier* (published in 1925), 'Hymn for a Child', is of this date. The story of Jesus and the elders in the temple is treated not as an example of virtue, but of consummate canniness and the last stanza is typical of Sylvia's barbed wit:

> Teach me, gentle Saviour
> Such discreet behaviour
> That my elders be
> Always pleased with me

It is unlikely that this is the only poem of that period. 'Morning', also in *The Espalier*, but undated, could be:

> The long, long-looked-for night has sped
> 'Tis time we should arise
> Out of this tossed and blood-stained bed
> Where a dead woman lies.

In 1914 the whole family went up to Ettrick as usual at the end of July. The news from Europe was bad, but only on 1 August did George note in his holiday diary, 'serious risk of war', and that certain friends were not coming up to join them. Germany declared war on Russia the next day. In their sitting-room at the inn, Sylvia listened to the men discussing the news: '[Geoffrey Sturt] sat, his eyes burning, saying we must fight or France would be lost – it was France, not Belgium; while my father and Philip Wood, almost as theoretical in knowledge of war as he, sat by, grievedly consenting to the burden of the young men.'[51] On the 3rd, George went out fishing; the water had been very low for days but now was rising. He came home and 'devoured' the papers, but was dispirited by 'our folk hesitating'. On the 4th the papers, which had to be fetched from a couple of miles away, were suggesting that something was going to be done, which heartened George, and in the evening came the news of Britain's ultimatum.

News that war had been declared came through on 5 August. 'Good egg', wrote George, 'now or later, and now is better.' Geoffrey Sturt went off to enlist on the 6th. The Warners' holiday went on as before, the walks and fishing and outdoor lunches, with little to disturb it but an alarm about the availability of petrol. George finished and despatched his book *On the Writing of English* and followed what scant and confused news there was of the war; the invasion of Belgium, the beginnings of a Belgian Resistance, the loss of the *Amphion*. It was all 'anxious and depressing', on top of which George had been smitten by a 'Mysterious Plague', a chronic pain which forced him to lie down. Then the first letters began to arrive from ex-pupils joining up: Ron Eiloart had joined the R.A.M.C. during the first week of the war. August 12th came and went and was particularly disappointing that year at Tushielaw – not a shot. They left for Harrow early, 'and that was the end of our summers at Tushielaw, and of the world I was born into.'[52]

By the time school reconvened in September, the country was plunged into one of the most anxious periods of the war, a situation 'so acute, so swiftly changing and so menacing that years seemed to have passed instead of eight weeks', as George wrote in an article for the *Cornhill Magazine*. 'One wondered, as the train brought one back, whether Harrow could be the same. And on walking up the hill it was almost a shock to find no obvious change in the familiar surroundings.'[53] Rumours, which had reached as far as Ettrick, that the school had been taken over by the army, all proved false. The greatest noticeable difference was that a number of members of staff were absent and that the school rifles had been removed and replaced with a few carbines (later replaced in turn by wooden dummies).

The idealism which flooded the recruiting-stations, though much the same in spirit as was instilled in his boys at school, obscured, in George Warner's opinion, an important issue, 'that armies cannot in a moment be bought with money, that brave men are not soldiers, and that what is needed is not so much the will to fight as the will to make ready'.[54] 'Improvised Armies' was the subject of the first of an influential series of articles by Warner which appeared in *Blackwood's Magazine* during the war. The topics he chose – civilian control, divergent operations (in answer to the debilitating quarrels among our own leaders over the multiple fronts), recruiting, compulsory service, blockades and the neutrality of the United States – show how closely he followed the strategic developments in the war and how quick he was to react to them. His essays for *Blackwood's* were startling because not overtly opinionated: his arguments were taken from historical precedent, thoroughly researched and clearly presented. He was amused to see how the newspapers in January 1916 were 'all gradually taking up my Blackwood article ['Recruiting in Wartime'] and quoting its facts as if they had known them all their born days'.[55] They were read with interest at the War Office too.

In the first few months of the war Sylvia had attached herself to an organisation in Harrow which had been thrown together under the ambiguous name of War Help. Much of its activity was concerned with fund-raising for the Red Cross, but when the first Belgian refugees began arriving in London, the War Help committee applied itself to find homes for them. Sylvia, whose mind was essentially practical, thought it would be less disruptive to the Belgians (and the people of Harrow) to house the refugees together. First one, then two empty houses were lent her and the local tradesmen and householders provided fittings. One of the refugees, a young Belgian woman, remained in affectionate correspondence with Sylvia for the rest of her life and it is clear that Sylvia's youthful concern and curiosity heartened the refugees, if only by providing a talking-point.

Both Sylvia and her father kept up a flow of correspondence to Old Harrovians at the front and heard their first-hand accounts of conditions in this new, peculiarly ungentlemanly type of warfare. From a military hospital in Boulogne, Eric Milner-White wrote of how he and one of George's best pupils, Geoffrey Hopley, passed the time by talking of Harrow and the man who had been housemaster and history teacher to both of them. White was an army chaplain, Hopley a Grenadier guardsman dying of wounds, alternately bored by inactivity and furious at '"those damned Germans" who have put his year at Harvard in such jeopardy'. 'Greetings from your history school here assembled!'[56] wrote White cheerily. Hopley could not write. His arm was wounded, his thigh shot through. He was plagued by nightmares of legs and died after three months' feverish pain. *The Harrovian* was given over more and more to obituary notices of young men such as this. The roll of honour read out in School chapel every Sunday, a mangled form of previous years' class lists, lengthened steadily.

At the start of the war, the atmosphere at the school had been excited; maps, flags and charts of ships and losses on both sides were put up around the place. There was no great rush into the O.T.C. because 470 out of 500 boys were already in it. George delivered a series of special lectures to them which were collected in book form as *How Wars Were Won*. The Warners did not go to Ettrick again, but spent every holiday at Little Zeal, where much basic garden work was still to be done. Nora looked on critically as George resorted to a chemical mixture to kill ribbon grass, while Sylvia tarred the gate – 'and everything else'[57]. When they went back in the summer of 1915 the ribbon grass was still there, but this time George watched while Nora darted to and fro, as if the weeds were trying to escape. The hay was still standing in the fields in September: the old and garrulous labourer, whose only available assistant was the local idiot, stood with his scythe on the Warner's porch and declared he'd never seen the like. As soon as the first heavy garden work was over, the Warners were planning a new project, diverting the stream which ran along their ground: 'If we are lucky enough to see Ron home again we will turn him onto this job: He and N. shall design it; and he and I will make it.'[58] Ron was writing regularly from the front and sending little gifts back to Nora – bulbs from Flanders, lace from Valenciennes.

Late in 1915, Sylvia saw a notice in the paper about a scheme to train women of the leisured class in munition-making to relieve the regular hands, as factories were now working non-stop. She applied to join it and received a pamphlet instructing her that 'low-heeled shoes are advisable, and evening dress is not necessary.' A few weeks later, Sylvia was living in dismal lodgings in Erith, south of the Thames, and making her way to Vickers' factory for a night shift as a shell machinist:

> Through the open doors of the workshop came noise and
> light and warmth: it looked as gay as a ballroom. Once inside
> it, the place wrapped me round like a familiar garment. Up in
> the roof the big driving-belt slid over the rollers: I thought of
> them going on shift after shift, day after day like a waterfall
> sliding over the top of a crag. Shell-cases, 4.5s and
> 18-pounders, were piled high against the walls and stacked
> on every spare foot of floor, with numbers and hieroglyphics
> chalked on their grey sides and sleek faces. [...] All the
> driving belts in motion dazzle the eyes like a mist, and
> looking across row after row of machines, the other side of
> the shop seemed a mile away. Last of all one notices the
> workers, inconspicuous, inconsiderable – mere human beings
> among these infallible Titans of iron and belting.[59]

In this noisy, stifling and intimidating environment Sylvia worked
an eight-hour shift with a half-hour break, along with the other
'lady-workers' – the members of the dilution scheme – whom the
regular hands referred to as the Miaows. Her work was mostly at
base-facing shells, that is, paring down a steel shell-case the size of
a large jam-pot to the correct length, ascertained by gauges and
scales. It took about fifteen minutes to complete the process for
each shell and the work was both monotonous and difficult: 'After
a while it begins to flatten one into the essential dough: every shell
thieves a little of one's pride of self,' Sylvia observed, and though
dead tired herself at the end of a shift, she realised how much
worse things were for the 'regulars', men and women 'bone-weary,
working the long hours of necessity, living in the vitiated air of the
shop, where the noise eats them like a secret poison'.[60]

The regular factory girls were surprisingly young, vigorous and
high-spirited, and their hair was noticeably healthy. 'Comparing
them with the anaemic and toothless young women that I had seen
bicycling listlessly in country lanes, I thought – Gone is the rustic
mirth with the rustic junketings. Allegra has painted her cheeks
and come to town.'[61] Talk among the women was not of the war –
a taboo subject – but of their work and, most commonly of all,

food. Sylvia, vainly searching the streets of Erith for a pie shop, behaved in a way unthinkable in Harrow. She approached a policeman and said, 'Policeman, I'm hungry.'

Undertaking factory work, when any work was considered unsuitable for a young lady of Sylvia's class, must have endowed her with an aura of oddity and daring in the eyes of her own society; certainly it was meant to. Thinking ahead to the time when she could look back on it all was one way of passing the time: 'Like Stevenson combatting the sensitive plant at Valima, standing at my lathe I talked wittily and at length with my friends that were not there.' Or she would follow in imagination the whole process of shell-production: 'the molten steel being poured out, statelily, like cream: the shell-cases tumbled out on the workshop floor all rough and clumsy, to pass through process after process till, slim and polished, they went off to be filled, discreet of curve, demure of colour, Quakerish instruments of death: and that one day when, alive and voiced at last, they would go shrieking over the trenches.'[62] Sylvia was only part of this scheme for a few months. A longer-serving Miaow pointed out to her colleagues, shivering in their hut during the seven-minute break allowed at 4.30 a.m.: 'When you've been at it longer you won't think of your shells as so many dead Boches or live Tommies, but as so many pre-destined objects that you want to get through before you go off work − so many dead weights to be heaved up and slipped on a gauge − so many inches of backache.'

George encouraged Sylvia to write an article about her experiences at Vickers and the result was an eight-thousand word piece called 'Behind the Firing Line' which *Blackwood's* accepted in January and published in February 1916. Sylvia's name did not appear: it was attributed to 'a Lady Worker', but she was paid handsomely for it, sixteen guineas, as compared with the six shillings, including bonus, she earned per shift in the munitions factory. It was the only published work of Sylvia that her father ever saw.

The war was going badly in 1916. The Battle of Jutland, a near-disaster, was the nearest thing the British had had to a victory. On 5 June Lord Kitchener died in a mine explosion off the Orkneys and Lloyd George, who took over the War Office, began the thankless task of trying to impress a new strategy on Haig and Robertson, his Chief-of-Staff. The newspapers were full of maps showing every movement of the Allied forces on the Western Front and alongside the grim lists of losses in the ranks – thousands every day – published advertisements for 'war' products which could in many cases be despatched from a London store straight to the trenches: the luminous 'Active Service' watch, bullet-proof jackets (officer type only) and Dr Miller's Nutrient for 'the prevention of nervous breakdown by timely "nourishment of the nerves"'.[63] On 1 July the Battle of the Somme began and was to last more than four months, with unprecedented British losses. It was during this summer that George Warner was asked by the Foreign Office to undertake 'a work of national importance' – what work remains unknown, but he accepted, and arranged for his form work at Harrow to be suspended. Nora's brother Frank Hudleston, who was Principal Librarian at the War Office and a military historian, was also engaged on secret war work. His youngest sister Purefoy guessed as much, for suddenly Frank had no holidays or spare time, but 'naturally I was never told anything'.[64] After the war, the French Government made him a Chevalier de la Légion d'Honneur. On hearing that George Warner was going to be working for the government, a pupil wrote to him from France: 'It is a real recognition and tribute, and it has all come about so quietly and naturally out of the even, hidden labour of days and years.'[65] Undoubtedly George felt honoured, but he was not complacent and went down to Little Zeal after a fortnight of nationally important work with a great deal on his mind.

Looking round the flourishing house and garden on a beautiful day when Sylvia was absent, Nora said to George that Little Zeal was to her 'like a dream of her childhood come true'.[66] Hard work and long effort were beginning to be rewarded; the Foreign Office job alleviated Nora's thwarted ambition for George to become a headmaster (something he never wanted himself), and she, disburdened of a daughter, was free to throw her violent energies into building up their future home. Aged fifty, Nora was as attractive to George as she had ever been and a constantly amusing companion. They shared countless small, weak private jokes; for instance, everything at Little Zeal had a name, from the morning ritual of George stalking marauding rabbits – Bunfire – to all parts of the garden – entrances called Ma'gate, Rams-gate and Moor-gate and beds called Accursed Spot and the Apple Pie Bed. Nora was also, unintentionally, a source of entertainment. Sylvia described to her father Nora's method of having a good tidy-up in the store cupboard: 'All the things on the left she moved to the right. All the things on the right she moved to the left. In the middle there was a sort of neutral zone where she just took things up and put them down again.'[67] Towards the end of Sylvia's stay, George noted a fragment of conversation:

G. It's always irregular.
S. I wonder if that's sense ... I think it's impossible.
G. Well, if always irregular isn't possible, then never regular is impossible too.
N. (*crushingly*) Never regular happens so often that it's always possible.[68]

Sylvia had spent part of the spring in Edinburgh at a musical function, probably with Percy Buck. George was amused to learn that she had been 'quite a little lioness' there. Father and daughter corresponded regularly when apart and Sylvia was in the habit of sending him small presents through the post. At Little Zeal, in the summer, Sylvia was working on a story referred to by George as 'the "Monolith"', which he admired and suggested she should send to the *Cornhill Magazine*. He was writing poems, another *Blackwood's* article and was also collecting characters (one was an old soldier called Major Hellebore) for the novel he hoped to write one day and which he and Sylvia often talked over in a leisured way.

Though everyone kept an eye on Pooloo, who was considered to be faint-hearted and like to die on the slightest gradient, it was George who slipped in the river, who had renewed attacks of 'waistcoatitis' and felt enervated all day. The strains of 'a tumultuous day' in London in mid-August – hastily summoned by the Foreign Office – were exacerbated by lack of sleep due to stomach pain. On 19 September George and Nora began to pack for Harrow. In some respects it had been a disappointing holiday; fishing had been hampered by the bad weather which had also rotted the harvest, alarms, excursions and two telegrams had disturbed their peace and most of all George felt his low spirits to have been a nuisance.

> [19th] I slept very badly and disturbed N: both weary in the morning. We had the usual clearing up to do and N did almost all of it. I was a damn dispirited body [...] Better night, praise be, and so on next day 20.
> (Weds) we were rather fitter for the journey, though N seemed to have got my complaint: must be some common cause.
> Excellent time here, but the catastrophe of the last three days was regrettable.

They got back to Harrow at about six o'clock, but an hour and a half later George was taken ill and was in acute pain. Two and a half days later he was dead, having refused morphia to the last. He wanted to retain consciousness as long as possible.

VI

News of Mr Warner's death travelled swiftly down the High Street. School was going in to chapel at the time: it was the first Saturday of term and the new boys' first service. The news was passed along, whether by a 'fez' or a 'blood', surprised and subdued by it, or a new boy, privily wondering what was 'G.T.W.'. The air of shock had dissipated by the following day when the Headmaster, having quoted the first verse of 'You?' as a conclusion to his address to the new pupils, continued his sermon, 'And it is of him who wrote those feeling lines that I would speak tonight, one to whom every stone of Harrow was dear, every link with the past sacred, every adventure for the future brave and full of hope.'[69] George had passed irrevocably into history. At The Times's printing-works his obituary was set up in type, waiting for Monday's edition.

His long body was lying at 162 Grove Hill, where he had been removed during his illness. His face was wearing 'a queer *secret* look' in Sylvia's eyes. '"Behold, I will show you a mystery", those unmoving lips seem to say.'[70] The two days of George's illness had been ravelled up in fear and vain solicitude. The rapidly changing demeanour of the doctor and nurses, the presence of a black oxygen cylinder at George's bedside – which he waved away – his unremitting pain, were steps to a conclusion neither Sylvia nor her mother could face. There was no time for leave-taking, no time to give or receive comfort. Sylvia may not even have been at home when her parents arrived back from Little Zeal that evening, may only have seen him dying.

The cause of death was entered on the death certificate as chronic gastritis, acute dilatation of the stomach and heart failure. The symptoms seem rather like those of a burst stomach ulcer. Sylvia used to say that her father had died of 'so-called Nervous Indigestion', 'the sickness that destroys people who have constant worries',[71] and that he 'broke his heart'[72] in the war. Her father's death was, to Sylvia, a total calamity, exacerbated by deep shock, the effects of which hung over the next fourteen years of her life as palpably as any veil, for if the blow to her hopeful outlook on life was great, the damage done to her heart was much greater, and she began to build up layers of caution around it as any deeply wounded person will. She hardly ever wrote or spoke of his death or the miserable year which followed it. What statements exist are stark ones: 'My father died when I was twenty-two, and I was mutilated.' 'It was as though I had been crippled and at the same moment realised that I must make my journey alone.'[73]

Nora made it all much worse. She felt not only abandoned but cheated, and looked around for someone to blame. Very soon after the death, Sylvia sat mutely by a washstand while Nora poured out a torrent of reproaches, regrets, woes. Sylvia remembered her wailing 'Now you are all I've got left,'[74] the accent probably on the second word. It was 'a cry of angry desolation'. If Nora had howled for her mother-in-law, one imagines her grief for George must have been blood-curdling. Sylvia had no respite from it even at night, for Nora took it for granted that Sylvia would sleep with her. This was a misery, not least because Sylvia had to take her father's side of the old four-poster.

The funeral took place in the school chapel on 26 September and George was buried down the hill at Pinner Road Cemetery, in a plot Nora had bought to fit them both, appending explicit instructions to its use: 'I do not wish any other member of my husband's family or mine to be buried in this grave.'[75] Tributes, obituaries and letters of condolence came pouring in, many from young men at the front who would be dead themselves within a year or two. 'Extraordinarily brilliant', 'an inspirer', 'an exceptionally good teacher', 'for ever a deep part of many lives',[76] came the voices from the other side of the study door. This multiplicity of chief mourners and Nora's lack of feeling forced Sylvia's grief underground. Sylvia's loss was as private as the sympathy between her father and herself had been, 'true minds', as much their shared secret as the rides on the rocking-horse years before.

High Street had to be vacated for the new housemaster and his family, and Sylvia and Nora stayed at Grove Hill until they had arranged where to live permanently. The prospect of living together, the widow and her spinster daughter, down at Little Zeal, was repulsive to them both, but seemingly unavoidable. George's estate, though healthily endowed with savings and share-holdings, had been set up in such a way that his family got more trouble from it than money. In his will George left Nora a legacy of a thousand pounds, all his chattels and a life interest in the rest of the estate, which was to be managed by two trustees, Robert Townsend Warner and a friend called Henry Byng. On Nora's death, all the income from the estate (which the trustees were asked to invest and pay out at their discretion) would be payable to his children, i.e. to Sylvia, but until then she was dependent on her mother. This invidious situation aggravated the bad feeling already rife at Grove Hill and the complex nature of George's estate made it difficult to administer. Nora's income was fluctuating and irregular. Sylvia's income amounted to an allowance of £100 a year.

Nora made it plain that an uncongenial, unmarried daughter was no comfort to her, but gratefully accepted the support of any male visitor. What Sylvia later identified as Nora's 'devouring femaleness' and her iron will were almost overpowering and Sylvia lived in fear of them. Nora's despair had a vindictive edge to it and impressed on her daughter 'that helpless bruise of being unavailing and a nuisance'.[77] One day Nora declared that she wanted 'only anchovy toast, and for the rest I could manage the housekeeping, adding that it was high time I did something useful.'[78] Sylvia was tossed this responsibility at a time when food shortages were acute and money was short. There were no potatoes in 1917 and the nation was urged to eat carrots instead. Interesting though it was to have a patriotic reason for not eating carrots, the two women and their Cockney cook had to eat something, and Sylvia conscientiously scanned the papers' helpful hints on cooking in wartime. A letter in *The Times* suggested boiled rhubarb leaves as an alternative to boiled spinach, but when Nora saw the resultant mess she refused to eat it. Sylvia ate it, out of pride, and became very ill. A correction in next day's paper pointed out that rhubarb leaves contain high levels of oxalic acid and are inedible. 'This discouraged my housekeeping,' Sylvia wrote. 'We gave our meat ration to the cook and to the poodle, both of whom led active lives and needed it, and subsisted on home-grown lettuces and water-biscuits.'[79]

What happened next was so timely and fortunate for Sylvia that it is hard to believe that Percy Buck did not engineer it, seeing, as he would have done, the strain under which Sylvia was living with Nora. At the Royal College of Music it was well-known that American money was available almost for the asking if a worthy project was put forward, the Carnegie (U.K.) Trust's charter stipulating simply that it should 'benefit music' – a wide brief. Sir Charles Stanford, who was then Professor of Composition at the College, had work published by the Trust and R.R. Terry, the Director of Music at Westminster Cathedral, was considering applying to it to fund an ambitious and important project, the collection, editing and publication of the great wealth of Elizabethan and Henrician church music which until then existed only in hand-written form in cathedral part-books. When the Carnegie Trust gave the project its blessing and its dollars, and a committee was formed of Terry, E.H. Fellowes, the Reverend Arthur Ramsbotham and Percy Buck (although early music was not his speciality), Sylvia was asked to join them. Sylvia said later that it was owing to good luck and 'the discerning worldly-wisdom'[80] of the eminent musician Sir W.H. Hadow that she was chosen above a number of other possible editors, including Cecil Stainer, 'all with as good or better qualifications'. She could be relied on 'not to fall out with Terry – indeed to get on very well with him',[81] but that was the least of her credentials. Buck once said that the ideal musicologist 'combines historical aptitude with a love of music', and Sylvia possessed both these attributes. Though her colleagues may have thought her a surprising, even unsuitable, choice as co-editor – she was 'unknown', young and female – she turned out to be an excellent one.

By the autumn of 1917 the memorial tablet to George was in place in the Old Harrovians transept of the school chapel. It read, 'To the dear memory of/George Townsend Warner/Faithful Friend/Beloved Companion/To Young and Old/Wise in Counsel/ Incomparable Teacher'. Nora was preparing to move down to Little Zeal permanently, with a number of distracting projects in mind, for she was still completely overset by George's death and quite unbearable. On the anniversary of 23 September she had just steeled herself to look at George's personal papers for the first time and was plunged back into a state of helpless turmoil, which manifested itself in renewed and bitter outbursts against her daughter. But Sylvia did not now have to go down to Devon with Nora. The Tudor Church Music project ensured her a salary of three pounds a week, little enough to live on, but enough to escape with, and she was negotiating for a flat in London in Queen's Road, Bayswater. A few months later she was lying awake there, alone, apprehensive and vastly relieved, surveying her few belongings by street-light and listening to the milk lorries crashing down the road outside.

2

1918–1930

I

On Armistice Day, 11 November 1918, Sylvia was in Norwich on Tudor Church Music business. On the train back to London, which was packed with soldiers, she sat thinking about the news. The war which had destroyed old Europe and in which ten million young men had died was over. But it seemed hard to celebrate anything – even peace.

The Carnegie U.K. Trust allowed for first-class travel expenses, but the flat Sylvia got home to, above the furrier's at 125, Queen's Road, was not in the same category. It was small, draughty, separated from its bathroom by a flight of stairs and a common landing, and it was not cheap. With £150 from Carnegie and her allowance of £100, Sylvia's annual income amounted to £160 after the rent had been paid. Her great-aunt Mary died in 1918, leaving Sylvia a small annuity, but prices were rising steeply all the time and were 125 per cent higher than in 1914. Food was still rationed and hard to get and Sylvia had to exercise even more ingenuity than she had done as Nora's housekeeper. 'From time to time I felt hungry, and in winter I often felt cold. But I never felt poor.'[1]

Living in London delighted Sylvia. She loved Kensington Gardens and adored Cockneys, so there was seldom lack of entertainment. The British Museum provided warmth during the day and the Westbourne Grove Public Library did the same service in the evenings: 'If I wished to feel ennobled, I had the Wren Orangery at hand. If I needed amusement, London is rich in public statuary, and if the weather wasn't suitable for that, I could sit indoors reading *Tom Jones*. [...] Every little advantage I filched from circumstances, every penny I stretched into three halfpence, every profitable abstention, every exercise of forethought, every stratagem and purloined opportunity made me feel as gay as Macheath.'[2] But thrift did not always suffice. In 1918 Sylvia was summoned to her bank at Harrow one day to discuss the matter of £19 0s 3d by which her account was overdrawn. The bank manager was concerned, having known George Warner and his balance for many years. Sylvia, feeling powerless to help, but not wanting to let the man down, wrote him out a cheque.

When the Church Music project began it was expected to last for five years or so and Terry had originally thought he could do all the work alone. In the event it took five people twelve years to complete. Gathering the material was extremely time-consuming; every major library, cathedral and minster archive had to be searched for manuscripts. Then the long business of editing began: misprints and mistakes in the copying of the music were identified and removed, parts had to be traced, scored and collated, variants weighed and argued over, the whole brought together in a publishable and, most importantly, a singable form. Hard work and high standards of meticulousness were necessary – and a good deal of patience too, as the committee's work resolved itself into a series of conjectural readings. 'There we sat round a table, saying But if; or with a gleam of hope, But why not? And the tugs on the river hooted, clearer & clearer, as the traffic quieted, till the Almoner's house in the Charterhouse (where we sat) became almost as hushed as when it was part of the real Charterhouse, in the clayey Moorish fields.'[3] The composers whose work was finally represented in the ten volumes of *Tudor Church Music* were John Taverner, William Byrd, Orlando Gibbons, Robert White, Thomas Tallis, Thomas Tomkins and three less prolific composers, Hugh Aston, John Marbeck and Osbert Parsley, though the committee were still arguing about inclusions and exclusions as late as 1928.

Dr Terry's health was poor and a few years after his project got under way a collapse forced him to all but abandon it. He disappeared from the list of editors in 1925, long after he had actually ceased to participate in the editing. The driving force behind the committee which remained was Buck, whose powers of organisation and faultless manners held the group together far more effectively than had Terry. The Reverend Arthur Ramsbotham, known as 'Ram', was a gentle and scholarly man with a sense of humour ideally suited to appreciate Sylvia's wit. There was not the same rapport with Edmund Fellowes, although Sylvia had the highest respect for his work as promulgator and promoter of the English Madrigal School. In committee she could find him 'sleepy' or 'absurd', probably because he did not devote the same amount of time to church music as did she, Ram and Buck.

If anyone thought that Sylvia was going to assume a lowly position on the committee, acting as a sort of secretary-cum-dogsbody, they were soon disabused of the notion. She put all her youthful energy and tenacity into the work, knew the material better than any of them and always insisted on her status as co-editor. If this required nerve to begin with, it paid off, and when Sylvia took more work home than did the others it was because she saw how much there was left to do. She always attacked a chore head-on.

Sylvia's musicological work was not confined to her job, for she had done a great deal of original research on sixteenth-century notation, contributing a chapter to the Oxford History of Music on that subject. In February 1919, when she was twenty-five, Sylvia lectured to the Musical Association on 'The Point of Perfection [a notational mark] in XVI-century notation', suggesting that the 'point', which was already known to have a half-dozen or so uses, had an additional, extra-mensural use. One of George Warner's perjoratives had been 'Il y a de la mystique là dedans' and from him Sylvia had learned never to substitute the workings of 'la mystique' for those of human nature when assessing a historical problem. This gave her the insight behind her assertion about the 'point', which though it could not be argued conclusively was argued most persuasively, citing Marinetti and the Futurist poets as examples of 'innovators [...] who do not invent their innovations' and concluding 'I do not put forward this surmise as to the origin of the extra-mensural use of the dot in the flippancy of despair, as one who can find no more reasonable explanation. I offer as a serious contribution to the philosophy of music the suggestion that notation throughout its development has reflected the mingled traditionalism and improvidence of man – man, who has never yet put in a new boot-lace till the old one was broken in two places.'[4] Percy Buck, who was in the chair, said in his vote of thanks: 'I think the best we professional people can do when we find an amateur like Miss Warner [...] who knows far more about her subject than we do, is simply to adopt the attitude of learners.'[5]

Committee meetings for Tudor Church Music usually took place in the evenings, at the Charterhouse, the Guildhall, or sometimes Sylvia's flat, since she had no family to be inconvenienced. For the same reason she did more travelling than the other editors, a joyless undertaking for the most part, involving long hours in trains and modest hotels, where she accumulated a vast stock of speculations and imaginings about the people she observed, the lone and lonely characters who haunt her short stories. At the end of the journey would be a day in the Bodleian, listening to the rain beat down outside, or a dusty room in a provincial church, where she would be undisturbed for hours at a time, her head full of music which had remained unsung for centuries:

> The patient organist
> Who scrolled this clef;
> The boy who drew him horned
> On Gibbons in F;
> Singers and hearers all
> Are dumb and deaf –
>
> 'Dumb and deaf, dead and dust,'[6]

The solitary life which this work imposed suited Sylvia. At home in London she developed a foolproof method of repulsing unwanted company. Whenever the bell rang, she put on her hat, 'so that in case of bores I could mendaciously exclaim, "Oh, how unfortunate! I am just going out", and walk as far as the Underground with them – a mere hundred yards and well worth it.'[7] The bores were usually adjuncts to a group of young men from Harrow among whom she had made friends in her last few years at the school and who were now, when not up at university, as often as not down in London taking advantage of Sylvia's hospitality and sofa-bed. They were centred around one brilliant and unhappy young man, Stephen Tomlin, who was of the type characterised by L.P. Hartley in his memoir of Harrow as 'non-conformers', 'who treated the school as a kind of hotel, useful as providing a night's lodging, but quite inadequate as a stage for the drama of their lives.'[8] This sort of boy did not sprint enthusiastically down to the football fields; there was more irony than gusto in his rendering of 'Rome was not Built in a Day'. He was the antithesis of Ronald Eiloart: highly-strung, sexually ambivalent – not George Warner's sort of boy at all. Sylvia, generally viewed as eccentric and outcast at Harrow, seven or eight years their senior and now embellished with a London flat, appealed strongly to Tomlin and his friends as a mentor. They conceded little to her femininity, nothing to her youth, but if Sylvia was prepared to offer them food, shelter, intelligent conversation and advice, they were more than happy to take it.

In 1918 Stephen Tomlin (always known as 'Tommy') was up at New College, Oxford reading Greats and being miserable. There was a great deal of pressure on him from his father, a successful K.C. soon to be a judge, and later a peer, to keep his nose to the grindstone, to apply himself and to enjoy neo-Gothic architecture, but after a term Tommy had had enough and ran away to Cornwall. There he decided to chuck up his degree and become a sculptor, a decision which met with fierce opposition at home but, once digested, was paid for handsomely; and Tommy, who had considerable talent, became a student of Frank Dobson.

Sylvia was his mainstay throughout this period of trauma and soul-searching. She loved his regard, 'so serious, and so open',[9] his mature intellect and mordant wit. He had a devious mind and loved to argue with Sylvia, or, by making some carefully placed remark, set her off on an imaginative flight of her own. This was the benign side of an ability to manipulate people which Tommy habitually misused. He was not conventionally handsome; short, with a sallow skin, deep-set grey eyes under a prominent brow and a crooked nose, yet he held an almost mesmeric charm over men and women alike. In David Garnett's words, 'there can never have been a young man so much run after and so unfailingly charming to all of his pursuers', and 'there was no one [...] whose laughter expressed a wider range of the emotions. Tenderness, indulgence, confession, apology, accusation, forgiveness, criticism: all such states of mind were expressed in laughter: besides which he would laugh long and merrily, or with tragic bitterness.'[10] But long before he became the most intimate friend of everyone in Bloomsbury, Tommy and Sylvia were walking miles at night in the country together, or sitting up late at 125, singing duets from Purcell, composing songs of their own – words by Tommy, music by Sylvia – or reading the poems of Blake, which moved Tommy more than any others. He was an easy weeper.

One day in 1919 Tommy brought another Old Harrovian, George Howe, and George's elder sister Bea to Sylvia's flat. Bea, a charming and beautiful twenty-year-old, was struck by Sylvia's appearance: carelessly dressed, angular, excessively thin and gawky, they could hardly have been less similar. Bea was observant rather than critical and felt that the young men from Harrow 'treated her more like the Universal Provider that Mr William Whiteley called himself down her road than as a young woman of intellect and unusual looks'.[11] It also seemed to Bea that Sylvia lived off cups of black coffee and cigarettes, as indeed she did, bar a few winkles and the odd scrambled egg. Bea, who had Latin blood, English manners, the colourful background of being recently transported from Chile, and an affectionate heart, seemed to Sylvia a personification of all kinds of elusive feminine virtues and became lodged in Sylvia's imagination as a 'nymph'. A mutual interest soon grew to liking, and liking to a deep, long-lasting friendship. Sylvia, Tommy, Bea and George formed a convivial group, whether they were fashionably exploring the East End and Dockland together or jaunting off to the country for the day. The only reason which would make Sylvia send them away was if 'Doctor Buck' was coming.

One day in 1919 Ronald Eiloart turned up at Queen's Road to see Sylvia. He had survived the war and come back to take up architecture again, with moderate success. Now aged thirty-one, he was as amiable as ever, tall, easy-mannered and still slightly dull. George's death had shocked him profoundly, for he had been virtually a member of the Warner family for years, and the disintegration of the household which had been his support left him feeling homeless and lonely. Over tea he came to the purpose of his visit and asked Sylvia formally for Nora's hand in marriage.

Whether Sylvia had wind of Ronald's intentions before then is impossible to say, but she quickly and delightedly accepted the proposition. Ronald's family, however, disapproved deeply of the match. A bossy fifty-three-year-old widow was not their idea of a hero's welcome, and Nora did nothing to ameliorate their impressions, quarrelling with Ronald's female relations one by one until all of them were cut off. At the wedding, which took place in September 1919 at St Petroc's, South Brent, the Eiloart side of the church dressed in black.

When Ronald went to live at Little Zeal, Nora supported him and there was no need for him to practise as an architect. He led the life of a leisured countryman and George's fishing tackle and carpentry tools were brought back into use again. He set up a small poultry farm in the field adjacent to the house and assisted Nora in her latest enthusiasm, which was for chow-breeding (Nora, like her father before her, was a 'besotted dog-worshipper').[12] If Nora depended on Ronald, she didn't let it show, at least not to Sylvia, and was widely assumed to have had him under her thumb from the first. Sylvia said later of her step-father that he was 'gentle, affectionate, rather dunderheaded, inexhaustibly kind. She [Nora] scorned him in her heart, and had no kindness for him, and no respect for him, and he wasn't so dunderheaded that he didn't know it.'[13] Nora's burial instructions remained unchanged, undersigned 'E.M. Eiloart, September 1919'. In some ways, what Nora and Ronald were espousing as well as each other was the absence of George.

Relations between Sylvia and her mother began to improve almost immediately. Sylvia, apart from being genuinely pleased at the marriage, was vastly relieved to have had the problem of Nora shifted from her shoulders. All the time while Nora had been being brave at Little Zeal by herself, she had not managed to be pleasant, and visits to Devon had taken on the aspect of a dreaded duty. But now there was Ronald, and several dozen hens, ducks and chows to visit as well.

There was still no prospect of Sylvia getting married, though she was now in her late twenties. Her relationship with Buck was predominant over a number of more casual affairs, one with Geoffrey Sturt, the old family friend. Like Buck, he was older than her, had been a friend of her father and had a wife with whom Sylvia was on very friendly terms. It has been suggested[14] that had not Sylvia – and Percy – been so fond of Mrs Buck they might have brought their affair out into the open. As it was, Sylvia was constrained to behave with absolute decorum veiled as indifference. With Tommy, though, there was no need to conceal her feelings and possibly as a result of this, and because of his open manner and charm, Sylvia fell in love with him. Tommy admired her very much and valued her as a uniquely entertaining and affectionate friend, but did not return Sylvia's feelings. Sylvia's adoption of a rather sentimental maternal tone when talking of him – 'the dear boy' and 'the poor child'[15] – is perhaps a measure of how she appreciated the situation and was trying to come to terms with it.

In the Easter of 1921, Tommy, Sylvia, George and Bea went on a holiday together to the Weld Arms, an inn at East Lulworth. Dorset was new ground for all of them and they fell in love with the beautiful coast, the rolling chalk downs and a cove at Arish Mell Gap where Sylvia surprised George Howe by stripping off in front of them all and wading into the sea. Tommy, who was to a greater or lesser extent in love with each of his three companions, was particularly charming and lively during the holiday and it was with regrets that they left him to explore Dorset further by himself as they wobbled off to Wool station in the back of a wagonette.

What Tommy found was a village about five miles west of Lulworth called Chaldon Herring, or East Chaldon. The village lay in a fold of the downs, separated from the vast expanse of Winfrith Heath to the north by a ridge on which stood five ancient tumuli, the Five Marys, and to the south separated from the steep cliffs at the sea by a mile and a half of incomparably beautiful downland. Tommy, approaching along the valley at night, knew he had found the ideal spot for a retreat, and set about finding a cottage to rent. He approached the vicarage first and found it occupied by a lady called Mrs Ashburnham and a number of scottie dogs. She suggested a couple in the village who had a half-cottage to spare and after some delicate preliminary negotiations, Tommy came to an agreement with Mr and Mrs Wallis to rent their two-bedroomed cottage at a pound a week.

In September Tommy was back in London packing up his sculptures and farewelling his friends. He was going to spend the winter working in Chaldon. There was, he told Sylvia, a remarkable man who lived on the outskirts of the village: a recluse and a philosopher, with a very fine head, who was thought to be a writer. Sylvia did not attend very much to this news. 'I had known so many of Tommy's swans – indeed I had been one myself.'[16] Every village in England had its 'Dostoievsky Corner', inhabited for the most part by bores. Chaldon Herring was unlikely to be an exception.

But enthusiasm for his recluse bulked Tommy's letters from Dorset and Sylvia, stung into action, bought the only available work by the man, Mr Theodore Francis Powys, *Soliloquies of a Hermit*, which begins:

> Am I a fool? Is not a fool the best title for a priest? And I am a good priest. Though not of the Church, I am of the Church. Though not of the faith, I am of the faith. Though not of the fold, I am of the fold; a priest in the cloud of God, beside the Altar of Stone. Near beside me is a flock of real sheep; above me a cloud of misty white embraces the noonday light of the Altar. I am without a belief; – a belief is too easy a road to God.[17]

The book's odd mixture of rhetoric and candour, its exposition of the amoral 'moods of God', and the author's intriguing self-portrait, written in the third person, excited Sylvia's curiosity. At Tommy's suggestion, she sent Powys a short play she had been writing – on what subject is unknown – and a correspondence began, Powys's first letters being supremely cautious and artful. *Soliloquies of a Hermit* had been published in 1918 and Powys's only other published work, *An Interpretation of Genesis*, was privately printed in 1911, but he had been writing short stories and novels steadily since 1916 and putting them away, unread, in cupboards and drawers. One by one they were taken out and lent to Tommy, whose company and encouragement brought Powys out of a slough of disillusionment and depression. Soon a parcel arrived at Sylvia's flat addressed several times over in Theodore's small spidery hand, and contained a manuscript, 'Mr Tasker's Gods', for Sylvia's opinion. 'As I read on, though I grew more and more enthralled I also grew more and more frightened and oppressed by this genius – I knew it was genius – which for all its creative power could see in Creation nothing but the blackening of an ancient curse, a curse which dooms all creatures to destroy or to be destroyed.'[18] She was shocked – it was a bleaker version than the finally published one – and she was intrigued.

In March 1922 Sylvia went to Chaldon to stay with Tommy and meet Mr Powys. They arrived at Beth Car, the Powys's small redbrick villa, after a walk in the rain over the Five Marys and round by West Chaldon. They stood dripping in the parlour while Theodore and his young wife Violet, a local woman, assessed this latest of Tommy's visitors from London. Once she had dried her glasses, Sylvia was able to do some observing of her own: 'I know that I must have expected him to look like something hagiological – a hermit or a prophet consumed with the fire of God's word, because the first thing that struck me about him was that his beauty was of a pagan and classical kind, and that instead of a hermit or a prophet I was looking at a rather weather-beaten Zeus.'[19] Stories had gone before Sylvia of her great learning and intellect, and Powys gently teased out of her responses to a number of exaggerated claims of this sort. It was a polite form of cross-examination, and Sylvia stood up to it well:

– I daresay you can read Hebrew quite easily, my dear.
– I can read no language but English and French.
– Violet, do you hear that? Sylvia says she can read French. And astronomy … I'm sure you must know a great deal

about the stars, for you are not afraid of walking in the dark.
– I know nothing about the stars. Perhaps that is why.
– Yes, my dear, I think that is very likely.[20]

Two days after this Theo was standing behind the eagle at St Nicholas's Church, Chaldon Herring, assuring the congregation at evening prayer that 'he shall come unto us as the rain, the latter rain that watereth the earth', as near a reference to Sylvia as he could decently get (Tommy being the former rain, Sylvia the latter), having searched the Apocrypha to no avail for 'a passage about a young lady coming down from London'.[21] Despite the fact that Sylvia and Theodore were fairly mercilessly exploiting each other for entertainment and despite, also, Powys's extreme caution about strangers and Sylvia's high, loud voice, a genuine and immediate friendship sprang up on this first visit to Chaldon. Sylvia was wildly enthusiastic about the village and before she left had evolved a plan for living at Rat's House, a tiny cottage appended to a barn and sheepfold on Chaldon Down, lacking any amenity but an outdoor tap. It came to nothing more than a few after-dinner conversations at Queen's Road, but Theodore perversely encouraged the idea for months afterwards.

Braced by these draughts of urban air, Powys was soon writing again and the new story, 'Hester Dominy', was brought up to London by Tommy and discussed with Sylvia. They agreed that a publisher ought to be found but that one story alone might not excite publication. Sylvia was left with the manuscript and the task of taking it to Tommy's only influential acquaintance in the literary world, David Garnett, who ran the Nonesuch Press and a bookshop on Taviton Street. There went Sylvia to do battle on Theodore's behalf:

> In the bookshop I found an extremely young-looking man whose hair was long and thick and untidy and whose suit was so blue that I felt he might blow up his horn at any moment. When I entered he retreated behind a desk, like some innocent wild animal that has never seen man before but who knows by the promptings of instinct that man is something to be mistrusted.[22]

What the innocent wild animal was fleeing from was this:

> an alarming lady with a clear and minatory voice, dark,
> dripping with tassels – like a black and slender Barb
> caparisoned for war – with jingling ear-rings, swinging
> fox-tails, black silk acorn hanging from umbrella, black
> tasselled gloves, dog chains, key rings, tripped lightly in and
> speaking to me in sentences like scissors told me … it was
> you, dearest Sylvia.[23]

The warm reminiscence is of a cool meeting. Sylvia left 'Hester
Dominy' with misgivings, but Garnett, who very much liked the
story, sent it on to Charles Prentice of Chatto & Windus, a man of
great intelligence and culture. When two more stories were ready,
'The Left Leg' and 'Abraham Men', Prentice prepared to publish
them under the title 'The Left Leg'. The stories were dedicated in
turn to Sylvia, David Garnett and Tommy; Powys' trinity.

II

In July 1922, Sylvia bought a map of Essex in a sale at Whiteley's,
attracted to it 'because I had never been there'.[24] The names
intrigued her – Willingdale Spain, Willingdale Doe, Old Shrill and
Shellow Powells – and so did the colouring of the map. On the
August bank holiday she set off to explore. Walking out from
Great Wakering, she turned off the track onto the marsh and
found a creek beyond which was a low green shore: 'I stood there
for a long time, watching the slow pushing water, and an old white
horse grazing on the further shore. I followed the creek, foolishly
supposing there would be some way across. It curled either way,
and I began to realise that the low green shore was an island. And
this again was marvellous to me, and I stood for another long
time, and letting my mind drift with the tidal water.'

Sylvia had left the map at home by mistake and after her confusion
over the island was fairly thoroughly lost. A storm gathered as she
was trying to make her way back by the sun, and 'the marsh
instantly darkened into an alarming flatness'. When the storm

broke she took to her heels in a panic, being the only object for miles tall enough to be struck by lightning. To add to the day's odd experiences, she heard a voice calling to her from a cattle shed as she ran past it in the rain. Some farmworkers were sheltering there and took her in. 'We watched the lightning stabbing at the marsh. It was a considerable storm.' The man with the voice took Sylvia home, where her dripping clothes were hung in a back-kitchen and she was given a great deal to eat. Sitting in the parlour wearing a rough-textured dress lent by the daughter of the house and listening to a very loud canary, Sylvia was supremely happy. She went home in her own clothes, still wet, and the daughter's woollen bloomers, determined to go back to the marshes as soon as possible and stay the night at an inn.

She remembered the map next time she got on the train from Fenchurch Street, but omitted to notice that there were no inns on the part of the marshes she had chosen to visit – the Blackwater marsh near Southminster. She walked all day (seventeen miles was nothing to her) and at one point saw the sail of a boat behind some trees, seeming to move on land. She was so enraptured by the landscape that she resolved to sleep out if necessary, but a boy on the road told her of a Mrs May who would put her up and Sylvia walked back to find the house and a tall, thin woman picking runner beans. When Sylvia woke next morning in Mrs May's spare room she remembered where she was and dashed to look out of the window: 'I could see nothing but an intense blue sky and a thick white mist, a mushroom mist, from which the thatched roof of the barn and some low tree-tops emerged. This melting veil over my new landscape pleased me more than any clear sight could do. I watched it thin, and become stained with the presence of a barn, and some sheds, and the bean-vines in the garden, and some apple-trees, and the green of the marsh beyond. Going downstairs, I found Mrs May, and at once asked her if I could spend another night at Drinkwaters.'

Sylvia was in a 'solemn rapture'. She went out onto the marsh with Villon's *Testament*, found a sheltered place, and sat there reading all day. 'The nest of tall grass gave onto a little bank of shingle, the ripples clinked over it, the sun shone. I knew that mysterious sensation of being where I wanted to be and as I wanted to be, socketted into the universe, and passionately quiescent.' On her way back to Drinkwaters, she decided to stay on indefinitely.

The visit to the marshes marked a change in Sylvia; she felt, as she was to say later, that she had become properly her own person, having been till then 'the creature of whoever I was with'. She was twenty-eight – *en l'an de mon trentiesme aage*. Her first youth, with its peculiar oppressions, was over, as were the most difficult and lonely years of her bereavement. In Essex that hot August she drew breath, took stock and in her mood of 'passionate quiescence' was surprised by 'the discovery that it was possible to write poetry'.[25] Her stay lasted a month, but the poetry continued to be 'possible' all the rest of her life. Sylvia had discovered a new country – one whose maps she had been studying for years.

Clothes, books and Bea were all requested by post from London and all, in due course, arrived, but no other friends were asked out to share the beauty of the marshes, for it was too private a pleasure. Later in the year she returned to Blackwater for a day with David Garnett. His view of the landscape was less lyrical than Sylvia's and his objection to mud was greater, but he at least acknowledged that 'the grey marshes had a melancholy eerie beauty that was all their own.' He paid more attention to his new companion's behaviour and the turns her frenetic mental energy could take: 'Sylvia gave an extraordinary display of verbal fireworks. Ideas, epigrams and paradoxes raced through her mind and poured from her mouth as though she were delirious [...] But by late afternoon, when we had climbed in the dark into another empty, badly-lit railway carriage and were being trundled half-frozen from Nowhere back to London, Sylvia was silent and exhausted. Brilliance and shyness were alike forgotten.'[26]

1922 was the year in which the first volume of *Tudor Church Music* appeared, William Byrd's *English Church Music, Part 1*. In 1923 it was followed by the first of three John Taverner volumes. The impact made by these authoritative and fascinating books on the musical world was considerable, and the editors began to enjoy a muted celebrity. Sylvia was in one way more professional about her job than previously – she was not working all hours at it. Among the things she brought home with her were dozens of smooth, blank rotographs which would otherwise have been thrown away as wastepaper. On these she wrote poems – about one a week in 1922 – with a delicious sense of indulging a secret vice.

Poetry was not her only self-indulgence. In 1921 she had sent a play to Powys, and in 1922 she wrote another one while at Drinkwaters, a morbid one-act piece called 'The Sin-Eater'. It was Tommy who had told her of sin-eating – the consumption of a collection of cold scraps, peelings and bits of hair by a vocational 'eater' to dispose mystically of a dead man's sins – and with Theo, Tommy had concocted a one-act play of his own on the subject. Sylvia's play shows evidence of her growing admiration for Powys's work in the depiction of the ranting, thuggish Craddock and the kindly Sin-Eater, Abel Morgan. There is a generally malevolent air to it which was not repeated so crudely in any later work, and which attempts to be imitative of Powys, but the rest is all Sylvia trying hard not to be amusing, and succeeding. Her heroine, Hester, has just stifled her husband with a bolster, only to be reviled by the man for whom she did it, who is suspected of the murder. Her passions thwarted, Hester denounces him and freely confesses to adultery and murder. She poisons the scraps, her husband's 'sins', and intends to eat them herself, narrowly preventing the Sin-Eater, a gentle and contented man, from getting there first. The hypocrisy of the local Chapel congregation prevents them from accepting Hester's confession – she is taken to an asylum – and the Sin-Eater is arrested for the murder.

'The Sin-Eater' is dramatically neat and economical, observes the unities and encompasses in its fifty-one small, handwritten pages several convincing portraits and a complex plot. There is also room for some of Sylvia's favourite ironies and her preoccupation with the distribution of innocence and guilt, her most persistent theme:

> *Hester*: Tell me, is it hard to take away sins?
> *Abel*: I can hardly say, ma'am. I've done it for so long, I hardly think about it now.
> *Hester*: Do you suffer with all the sins you take on you?
> *Abel*: No ma'am. I'm a very healthy man.

This will remind any reader of Sylvia's poetry of the argument of 'The Scapegoat', written in 1924 (and, incidentally, a sort of joke about Sylvia's own position on the Church Music committee):

> See the scapegoat, happy beast,
> From every personal sin released
> And in the desert hidden apart
> Dancing with a careless heart.[27]

Tommy and Theo's version of 'The Sin-Eater' had been written the previous winter, to while away the long evenings at Chaldon. Tommy's life was dividing quite sharply in two: in Chaldon he worked hard, was thoughtful, charming and footloose, sleeping under hedges if he wished. Theodore's brother, John Cowper Powys, had noticed the changes wrought at Beth Car by 'Mr Tom Tomlin the Sculptor, a bewitching gipsy-like young William Blake, with the most caressing respect for Theodore, who he calls "Theo" and makes the old rogue laugh and chuckle till he's red in the face.'[28] In London on the other hand, Tommy was becoming well-known in Bloomsbury, owing partly to his friendship with David Garnett and partly to Frank Dobson's connections with the London Artists' Association, run by Maynard Keynes. During the Twenties and early Thirties Tommy sculpted some of the leading Bloomsbury figures; Lytton Strachey, Duncan Grant, David Garnett and Virginia Woolf, who alone of the four did not find Tomlin attractive. Frank Dobson painted a quasi-Futurist portrait of Sylvia in 1921, but Tommy never used her as a model, though Bea Howe did sit to him. By 1923 Tommy was a predictable guest at the most fashionable parties in London, had been nominated by *Vogue* as the most promising young sculptor of the month and was enjoying a certain notoriety as a promiscuous lover. He did not take Sylvia with him into this higher sphere.

After Tommy had been young and promising for a while he began to be depressive and was psycho-analysed by an expensive and well-known consultant, Edward Glover. In one way it did not help him, because his subsequent tendency to talk at length about his own mental states inhibited the workings of his charm, at least for those onto whom he unburdened himself, Sylvia among them.

The importance he set by Bloomsbury friendships, many of which were sexual and emotional as much as intellectual or artistic, indicates that he derived a comfort from them which the real achievements of his own work and his nurturing of Theo's failed to provide. In his third volume of autobiography, *The Familiar Faces*, David Garnett tells an odd story of Tommy disguising himself as a beggar to tell fortunes at a party held by Garnett. From behind his disguise, Tommy was able to tell the guests, all of whom he knew well, a few home truths, but afterwards he seemed 'subdued and ill at ease [...] for his friends had spoken about him to each other in his presence with such callous indifference to his feelings, and had adopted an arrogantly patronising tone in speaking to him, which convicted them of an unforgivable lack of delicacy.'[29] Such sensitivity might have been appropriate had not Tommy preluded it with his own 'callously indifferent' deception. That he did not judge himself but was ready to 'convict' others shows a large capacity for being offended.

In May 1923, *The Left Leg* was published. It had already excited interest through the advance copies, and by the end of the year, when Chatto & Windus published Powys's novel *Black Bryony*, Theo had acquired a group of admirers, some so keen and forward-looking that they were able to spot progressions in Powys's art, although *Black Bryony* had been written several years before *The Left Leg*. In December, when Theo and Violet were coming on a rare trip to London, seeing off their elder son Dicky to Kenya, Tommy took the opportunity to arrange a party in Theo's honour. The party was to be the culmination of several days' activity. On the first day, which happened to be 6 December, Sylvia's thirtieth birthday, both Theo and Violet were silenced and exhausted by tea-time and Sylvia felt it 'a rather painful afternoon'.[30] Her dinner party later in the week was more of a success, for when funds allowed it Sylvia was an excellent cook, and Theo was deeply impressed by the *marrons glacés* served as a sweetmeat: 'It was a moral victory, for I don't think he liked the taste of the one he ate. Certainly when I offered him another he refused it with a grave gesture as though I had pressed him to a second sacramental wafer.'[31] The grand party at Tommy's studio, just off the Fulham Road, got off to a bad start because the host –

Tommy – wasn't there. He and Sylvia arrived late and anxious, to discover the guest of honour handing round the sandwiches and the party in full swing. Theo, 'perfectly and unaffectedly at his ease',[32] had melted the constraint of the guests as soon as he entered the room. This was the man who, in Chaldon, would go to almost any lengths to avoid the mild social challenge posed by Mrs Lucas the postwoman, or Mrs Ashburnham out walking the scotties. He once lay at full length in a field of stubble, hoping that lady might not spot him as she passed, only to hear her saying quizzically, as she stood over him, 'Communing with Nature, Mr Powys?'[33]

Tommy had made a large cake embellished with a left leg sculpted from pink icing. Theo cut the cake with a nib, the pen being mightier than the sword, and thanked all his friends profusely for their hospitality, leaving London the next day 'unassailably determined never to come back to it'.[34]

At about this time Sylvia moved from her flat on Queen's Road to a much more comfortable one on the road parallel to it, Inverness Terrace. The ground floor of Number 121 'pandered to every bourgeois gene in my being; not only was it self-contained, it was positively genteel.'[35] In the flat she chose bright colours for her cushions and covers, all sewn, patchworked or appliquéd expertly by hand, and she brightened up the curtains in her tall windows by adding a large figure to each, which became known as 'Duncan and Vanessa'. The bathroom was an ex-conservatory with 'decency arabesques' painted over its glass walls. 'A scrupulously modest person might have judged them insufficient, but I was not obsessed with modesty, and at that time there really wasn't enough of me to make a fuss about. Besides, there would be steam; and in the summer, trees';[36] sycamores, in the small back garden. Here, too, Sylvia acquired a Cockney charwoman, Mrs Florence Keates, and a black chow from her mother's kennels, called William. These two objects of affection significantly improved the quality of Sylvia's daily life.

At 121 Sylvia began to entertain more regularly and drew a more select circle of Old Harrovians than previously; Victor Butler, the son of the Governor of Burma and a brilliant and witty mathematician, Tommy, the brothers Angus and Douglas Davidson and a friend of theirs from Cambridge, Geoffrey Webb, known as 'Wobb'. The only close friendship with a woman, apart from Bea, which Sylvia developed at this time was with Dorothy Wadham, the secretary to one of the London orchestras, who was, with Sylvia, a member of the Bach Choir. She had spotted Sylvia on the bus after a rehearsal, a tall thin figure swaying in time to unheard music, abstracted and blissfully happy. 'Doffles' followed Sylvia off the bus and introduced herself.

Sylvia saw her aunt Purefoy frequently, and they often played piano duets together, the more taxing and vigorous the better. Purefoy had married the writer Arthur Machen in 1903 and they lived in Melina Place, St John's Wood, with their two young children. The Machens kept open house for their friends every Saturday night, a motley assortment of artists, journalists, musicians and theatre people – both Arthur and Purefoy had been members of the Benson Company in the early years of the century. Frank Hudleston was often there, a lively, lonely character and perfectly eccentric: 'he was totally detached from his environment.'[37] Frank wore his clothes until they dropped – quite literally – from his back and used to attempt to throw a banana skin across the Edgware Road every morning on his way to work at the War Office. Once inside the office, however, he was regarded as 'the most ponderously reliable of authorities'.[38]

In the summer of 1923 or 1924 Sylvia was commissioned to meet Purefoy's son Hilary on the train from Paddington to Newton Abbot. Hilary was a young schoolboy at Merchant Taylors, off to spend a holiday at his Aunt Nora's house. Ronald Eiloart was at South Brent station to meet them with the Model T Ford which took them the mile or so to Little Zeal, and Hilary was greeted by Nora's voice from an upper window quoting from one of the novels of Somerville and Ross: 'Is that my darling Major Yates? Thanks be to God! I have someone to take my part at last.' The expansive mood could soon wear off, but it was a sign of approval if Nora talked – sometimes entirely – in quotations. Hilary had been schooled in the major source, Dickens, by his parents, who had the same habit of extravagant quoting. He could answer back appositely, but was still young enough to come a cropper at other hurdles. Looking at his aunt's tiny hands, he remarked that Uncle Frank had warned him to be careful because 'your Aunt Nora's got a fist like a leg of mutton.' A stony silence was broken by Nora's reply, 'Oh he *did*, did he?'[39]

The house was not spotless. Behind the curtains in Hilary's room lay a quantity of dead flies and there was dust everywhere. Nora's cooking was excellent, but to the boy the servings seemed disappointingly small. Seeing an earwig in the curry one evening, Hilary exclaimed excitedly. The look Nora gave him could have killed several small boys, but Sylvia threw her head back and cackled. When it was her turn to be served, Sylvia said, 'No really darling, I don't think I *could*,' and ostentatiously ate a little rice.

Hilary was very much in awe of his aunt and cousin, but for the latter awe was tempered with admiration. On walks over Dartmoor together, Sylvia did not adapt her pace to his and went ahead at a lick, jumping over streams and bounding up hills, while he was left to make the best of it. Nora hired a baby grand piano for Sylvia's longer visits in the summer, and in the evenings she was expected to play and Hilary sing. The boy disliked this, naturally enough. It was just one element in a generally uncomfortable holiday, for he noticed that Aunt Nora 'never passed by an opportunity to scorn'.

III

In 1923 Sylvia had begun to write a novel alongside the poems which she now considered part of her life. It was called 'The Quick and the Dead', but did not develop satisfactorily, and she abandoned it in favour of another story she wanted to try out, that of a contemporary witch. She had read Margaret Murray's book *The Witch-Cult in Western Europe* when it was published in 1921 and, more recently, Pitcairn's *Criminal Trials of Scotland*. In Pitcairn's account of witch trials 'the actual speech of the accused impressed on me that these witches were witches for love; that witchcraft was more than Miss Murray's Dianic cult; it was the romance of their hard lives, their release from dull futures.'[40] At first she wrote a poem – lost or unidentifiable – on the theme of vocation to witchcraft. Later she began a novel, titled 'Lolly Willowes'. 'One line led me to another, one smooth page to the next. It was as easy as whistling [...] I told nobody. I barely told myself. I felt no obligation to go on, let alone finish.'[41] In this leisurely manner, the novel spun itself out for almost a year and in the autumn of 1924, when she answered an advertisement for a cottage to let in Idbury, Oxfordshire, she took the manuscript with her and read most of it aloud to Edie Sturt, Geoffrey's wife, who had come to stay.

It seems that by this time in her life Sylvia had all but given up composing. She was to say later, to Ralph Vaughan Williams, 'I had come to the conclusion that I didn't do it authentically enough, whereas when I turned to writing I never had a doubt as to what I meant to say.'[42] Of the very few pieces of her music which survive, 'Memorial', a rhapsody for solo voice and string quartet written between 1918 and 1920, is the most ambitious. It is a setting of parts of Walt Whitman's 'A Sight in Camp in the Daybreak Grey and Dim' and 'Memories of President Lincoln', and the music, dark, brooding and uncertain in key, is sensitive to Whitman's words, a hymn to death. It is interesting that the work contains discords 'of a wilful nature'[43] and that 'whenever it seems about to lift into the light it falls back – or, on occasions, surges back – into the dark.'[44] Even the ending, lifting through a long diminuendo, is not wholly consolatory; it is quiet rather than peaceful. As with many of her poems and, later, her stories, a deliberate friction is set up between the form and the tone.

In one sense, Sylvia never gave up composing, for all her writing is musical in nature and shows not simply a fine ear for cadences and the lyrical effects of language, but a keen interest in form and structure. 'I really learned all my ideas of form from studying music',[45] she said late in her life. Many of the poems Sylvia had been writing since her visit to the marshes ended on a sombre note, a dying fall. Even in the most straightforward of them there could be a quiet key change, often subtly disturbing, as in 'Match me, O Rose!':

> A red rose shining in the sun
> Told me of summer new-begun.
> I smoothed each petal, and kissed each petal,
> And counted them one by one.

Eighteen – and I had two years more.
'Match me, O rose!' I said; and tore
In half two petals, two crimson petals,
To bring them to a score.

Just at that moment the wind blew –
Petal by petal away I threw,
And turned to the rose-bush, the lovely rose-bush,
Where other roses grew.[46]

Plain diction in Śylvia's poems does not always convey plain meaning, but can be complicated and counterpointed by the 'music' of the poem. As the critic Denis Donoghue has written, 'Poetry consisted, for Sylvia Townsend Warner, in the turning of an experience, real or so fully imagined as to be real, toward the decisiveness of song.'[47]

In the autumn of 1923 David Garnett had been reading Sylvia's poems and said he would like to send them to Charles Prentice, and that they were very good. Sylvia was unusually nervous while the poems were being 'considered': 'I felt like a cat whose kittens are taken away and she goes anxiously leaning about the house and as her hope fails her mew grows harsher and more imperative.'[48] In November she heard with amazement that they had been accepted.

Sylvia went to meet Charles Prentice at the Chatto & Windus offices in St Martin's Lane, 'feeling sick and highly-strung': 'I was shown into a small room and presently a stranger came in and looked at me without a word. I transferred a great many bus tickets from my right hand to my left and we shook hands and sat down. After a very long pause I said Are you Mr Prentice? and he said: Yes. After another long pause we both began to speak at once. It was like a nightmare, or a religious ceremony. But he said such praising things about my poems that I soon felt quite at home with him.'[49] The book was to come out in the spring of 1925. In the course of conversation, Prentice asked if Sylvia had written anything else and she promised to send him her novel.

It took Sylvia a number of weeks to choose a title for her poems, but she finally hit on 'The Espalier': 'it seems to me expressive – a naturally rather straggling plant such as the mind is – mine at any rate straggles – deprived and formalised into producing fruit.'[50] When the book was published it attracted a creditable amount of attention from reviewers, most of whom noted what Charles Prentice had singled out in Sylvia's poetry, its objectivity. *The Nation* spoke of its 'quality of freshness, of spontaneous feeling' and the author's 'un-Victorian mind'. Part of the book's impact was made by the un-Victorian mind expressing itself through forms which were not simply traditional but almost quaint in 1925; the ballad, the epitaph, the pentameter quatrain; the bathos with which gipsies, sextons and country maids are treated; and a frame of reference which stretches from Pyrrhon to Mother Goose – not, in Sylvia's mind, a necessarily large step. There are several poems which are Chaldon-based, notably 'Nelly Trim', Sylvia's most anthologised poem, and many which reflect the enthusiasm she shared with Powys for wanting to make your flesh creep, but there is no attempt at consistency in the collection, not even consistency of surprise. As the book settled down, she began to acquire a few influential admirers; A.E. Housman, Louis Untermeyer, who did much to promote her work in the United States, and Sir Arthur Quiller-Couch, her grandfather's old pupil, who was later to write that 'the writings, especially the poems of [...] Miss Sylvia Townsend Warner, perpetuate – with a curious turn as often happens – the mental distinction of a family.'[51] The only person whose response was a slight disappointment was the dedicatee, Percy Buck.

Sylvia's novel, 'Lolly Willowes', which had been submitted at the same time as the poems, was accepted by Charles Prentice with only one demur. The version that he saw ended at page 244 with Lolly burying the apple bag and smoothing the earth over. Prentice felt that in the light of the preceding conversation between Lolly and Satan this was too strong an intimation of death. Sylvia therefore added the last three and a half pages and handed it back, later regretting that she didn't tidy the whole book up more. It was scheduled for publication in 1926. Meanwhile Sylvia was writing two short stories very different in tone from 'Lolly Willowes'; 'The Son' and 'Some World Far From Ours', an extraordinarily delicate story about the bed-maker of a *chambre d'accommodation*, which is at once both worldly and lyrical, reminiscent of Colette, whose writing Sylvia admired. In this year she also began a story written in the first person, 'Elinor Barley', based on the folksong 'The Brisk Young Widow'. It was a rather deliberate exercise, and after a few months began to drag. At the end of the year advance copies of *Lolly Willowes* were ready, but Sylvia was apprehensive about the book, as she indicated to David Garnett: 'Your letter has given me a great deal of silent joy. It has given me the assurance I wanted, and if it comes from you I can believe it. Other people who have seen *Lolly* have told me that it was charming, that it was distinguished, and my mother said that it was almost as good as Galsworthy. And my heart sank lower and lower.'[52]

Laura, 'Lolly', Willowes is a twenty-eight-year-old spinster when her adored and adoring father dies and leaves her dependent on the hospitality of her two older brothers and their wives. For twenty years she lives the life of a spinster aunt, familiar and negligible as the furniture in her brother's London home. Then she decides to break away and live by herself in the country, thinking that her capital, administered by her brother, will enable her to be free. Despite the discovery that she has very little money to call her own, Laura takes a room in a small Bedfordshire village, Great Mop. In the company of her landlady, Mrs Leak, and a gentle poultry-farmer, Mr Saunter, she leads a released and happily aimless life, only slightly disturbed by intimations that there is a secret in herself she has yet to uncover. The arrival in the village of her self-important nephew, Titus, havocs Laura's peace, and in a perturbed state of mind she realises that the only further escape for her is into witchcraft, and that she has had a vocation for it all along. A vicious and ugly kitten appears, her familiar, as confirmation of her compact with the Devil and Laura understands that most of the villagers – including the parson – are witches too. With her landlady as chaperone, she attends her first Sabbath, but is bitterly disappointed by its semblance to any other social occasion, calling out skills she has never possessed. Thinking that witchcraft, too, might prove inadequate, Laura wanders off alone, only to meet Satan in the guise of a kindly gamekeeper and have her faith in him restored. Her nephew is subsequently bedevilled by a series of plagues which drive him out of the village and Laura, meeting Satan again, is able to come to an understanding of his character and her own which frees her to live undisturbed, 'a hind couched in the Devil's coverts'.

The story was really an elaborate way of presenting the same thesis as Virginia Woolf did in *A Room of One's Own*, published three years later, except that where Virginia Woolf's woman wants a room in which she can write fiction, Lolly Willowes's vision is of women being able to 'sit in their doorways and think':

> When I think of witches, I seem to see all over England, all over Europe, women living and growing old, as common as blackberries, and as unregarded. I see them, wives and sisters of respectable men, chapel members, and blacksmiths, and small farmers, and Puritans. In places like Bedfordshire, the sort of country one sees from the train. You know. Well, there they were, there they are, child-rearing, house-keeping, hanging washing from currant bushes; and for diversion each other's silly conversation, and listening to men talking together in the way that men talk and women listen. Quite different to the way women talk and men listen, if they listen at all. And all the time being thrust further down into dullness when the one thing all women hate is to be thought dull. [...] It sounds very petty to complain about, but I tell you, that sort of thing settles down on one like a fine dust, and by and by the dust is age, settling down. [...] And they think how they were young once, and they see new young women, just like what they were, and yet as surprising as if it had never happened before, like trees in spring. But they are like trees towards the end of summer, heavy and dusty, and nobody finds their leaves surprising, or notices them till they fall off. If they could be passive and unnoticed, it wouldn't matter. But they must be active, and still not noticed. Doing, doing, doing, till mere habit scolds at them like a housewife, and rouses them up —[53]

To be struggling for privacy, not power, is still not a very common view of the feminist ideal and the retiring nature of the heroine, Lolly, perhaps persuaded readers that it was not a very serious one either. The book seems ultimately comfortable on that score, though it was much wittier and crisper than most women's fiction of the period. The novelty of the theme, and the author's apparent imperviousness to received wisdom, ensured the book a high oddity value. Though *Lolly Willowes* set out to overturn 'the bugaboo surmises of the public' about witches, and about the single woman, that too common phenomenon of the post-war years, it amused people more than it startled them.

The novel was a great success. The Chatto & Windus press cuttings book alone include over ninety notices for *Lolly Willowes*, many of them lengthy, and all favourable. 'I have felt what it is to be famous,' Sylvia wrote to Charles Prentice. 'A friend of mine was sending her silver to the bank, and I helped her to wrap it up in newspapers. Suddenly I discovered I was wrapping up forks in my own name.'[54] The American reviewers were predominantly reminded of Jane Austen, the British reviewers of David Garnett (whose fantasy novel, *Lady into Fox*, had been a bestseller in 1924). *Lolly Willowes* was 'one of the "smart" things to read this season'.[55] Sylvia was written up as 'the girl who is responsible for the sudden interest in witchcraft that has seized on London'[56] and in interviews was asked a lot of foolish questions about black magic, which she answered with a mixture of candour and flippancy, at one time suggesting that modern witches might use their vacuum cleaners instead of broomsticks for flying. There was speculation, too, as to whether Sylvia herself, like Lolly, was a witch, and Sylvia dined out on it for some time. She also encouraged the notion in her own fancy. As a child, she had repeated spells to her cat, Mister Dive, 'feeling a black hope that they would work',[57] and had persuaded the cook to perform the cauldron scene from *Macbeth* with her in the Radnor Lodge kitchen. Sylvia had always kept an open mind on religious questions. A month after *Lolly Willowes* was published, she took tea with Margaret Murray, whose study of witchcraft had been so influential. Miss Murray, an imposing elderly lady, liked the character of Lolly 'though she was doubtful about my devil', Sylvia wrote to David Garnett. 'I wish I were in her coven, perhaps I shall be. Round her neck she wears a broad black velvet band probably for a good reason. She said things that would make the hairs of your head stand bolt upright.'[58] Sylvia also had dinner with Virginia Woolf, summoned by fame and mutual friends, at which Mrs Woolf asked how she knew so much about witches. 'Because I am one,'[59] Sylvia replied.

The sales of the book were very high. Chatto & Windus reprinted twice in one week in February 1926 (the book came out in January) and the U.S. sales 'leapt the 10,000 fence'[60] by June. *Lolly Willowes* was selected as the first Book-of-the-Month choice of the new American book club and nominated for the Prix Femina (which was won that year by Radclyffe Hall). Sylvia had written to Charles Prentice at the end of January acknowledging receipt of an 'incredibly magnificent cheque' for £16 5s 6d, more than five times her weekly salary, but such sums became so familiar that by September she was able to receive a cheque for £233 without comment. In 1926 she earned £437 from *Lolly Willowes* and in 1927, from Lolly and her next novel *Mr Fortune's Maggot*, an amazing £1284, eight and a half times her Tudor Church Music income. It was the only time at which Sylvia could be considered a bestseller, and *Lolly Willowes* remains the book by which she is imperfectly remembered.

Following the interest in *Lolly Willowes*, Sylvia began to contribute articles and book reviews to a number of magazines, *The Nation*, *Time and Tide*, *Eve*, *The Forum*. There was a widening gulf between Tommy and herself – he was now often in the company of the painter Dora Carrington, Lytton Strachey and Lytton's brother Oliver. Sylvia had made new friends at Chatto & Windus: Charles Prentice, who became her devoted escort, and Prentice's junior at the firm, Harold Raymond. Raymond and his wife Vera lived on Launceston Place, only a few steps across Kensington Gardens from Sylvia's flat in Inverness Terrace. Vera, though only a little older than Sylvia, indulged her husband's authors in a maternal spirit and Sylvia was often present at her select Christmas and birthday parties. Sylvia called Harold 'Chatto'; they called her 'Lolly'.

Charles Prentice was almost exactly Sylvia's contemporary, although he looked older. He had joined Chatto & Windus in 1914, straight from Oxford, only to leave it almost immediately for the front line in Flanders. In 1926 he succeeded Percy Spalding as senior partner in the firm and his former place as typographer was taken by the young Ian Parsons. Under Prentice's guidance, Chatto & Windus 'maintained what was possibly the most distinguished list in London, both in content and appearance',[61] for he was a scholar and acute businessman as well as a publisher 'of exact judgement'.[62]

His looks were undistinguished. He was of medium height, with a round, bespectacled face, a balding head and 'the quietest voice of any man I've met', according to Bea Howe. He was 'a man of silences' and 'a genius in eiderdown clothing',[63] inspiring confidence and admiration in his authors, many of whom, like T.F. Powys, became his friends. From 1926 until the early Thirties, he was devoted to Sylvia.

Sylvia and Charles Prentice often went down to Chaldon together (along with William the chow, a seasoned traveller) to visit Theodore, Sylvia staying at Beth Car, Charles in Mrs Way's spare bedroom at the other end of the village. Theo had finished a long novel in 1925 which he said would be his last and which had, for the time, exhausted his fervour to write. The title, 'Mr Weston's Good Wine', was taken from Jane Austen's *Emma*, appropriately enough, for Sylvia opined that 'Mr Woodhouse talks *exactly* like Theo.' Powys was in high spirits, no longer fretted by poverty, and enjoying a certain celebrity, much of it in Chaldon itself, for the village had changed since Tommy retreated into it. Betty Muntz, another of Frank Dobson's students, had heard of Tommy's unspoilt country workplace and followed him there. In the mid-Twenties she was taking Mrs Wallis's cottage regularly, and later began to buy up a row of cottages which she turned into a studio and summer school, attracting a succession of arty young Londoners and Americans on short, possessive visits. Theodore was not the only literary attraction. His brother Llewellyn, the 'earth-philosopher', and sister-in-law Alyse Gregory, the American novelist and woman of letters, had a cottage at White Nose, a mile or so further along the coast from Chydyok, where Gertrude and Katie Powys, both remarkable and talented women, lived in one of two very isolated downland cottages. A tall betrousered young woman from London, Mrs Molly Turpin, was one among many visitors suffering from 'what we knew as "Powys

Mania" [...] everything all of them said was beautiful and wise and true.'[64] Theodore's more famous callers included Augustus John, Lady Ottoline Morrell and Lawrence of Arabia, whom Theo mistook for a tax inspector and treated with extreme caution. 'Theo used to invite them to go for little walks with him,' Sylvia recalled, 'so that Violet could wash up the tea-things in peace.'[65] The only person missing from the scene was Tommy, who had bought himself a cottage in Swallowcliffe, Wiltshire, and saw little of the Powyses any more.

In 1926 there was a crisis between Sylvia and Tommy and an irrevocable, deeply wounding break. The cause is unknown, but it seems to have been inextricably bound up with two things: the imbalance in their affections for each other, and Tommy's confused state of mind. Psycho-analysis had encouraged him to hunt out explanations for his behaviour, a habit which aggravated his strict conscience. Possibly, analysis made him irresponsible, shifting the blame for his actions onto the past, much in the way that he had shifted the charge of insensitivity from himself onto Garnett's guests at the party. He was a coward in difficult personal situations, and may have put off for years telling Sylvia what he readily told Bea, that he found Sylvia's open affection for him embarrassing and her person physically repulsive. Once his best and most admired companion, by the mid-Twenties Tommy had relegated Sylvia to a lowlier position, calling on her when in the grip of one of his partially-demented attacks of self-disgust, ranting and railing with ghastly lucidity. Sylvia bore all this out of love and the impulse to support him, but perhaps on one of those disturbing evenings he turned on her and told her what he felt.

In the winter of 1926, Tommy ran off to Paris with his friend Oliver Strachey's daughter Julia, whom he married the following July. Virginia Woolf, who was at the wedding, was amused to see Judge Tomlin locked into his pew, having mistaken the hinge for the latch, but wrote to her sister Vanessa, 'I repeat for the thousandth time: I cannot see the physical charm of that little woodpecker man.'[66] The marriage degenerated fairly quickly. Julia was a bright and naive girl, not Tommy's match intellectually and perturbed by his drinking, infidelity, depressions and remorseful guiltiness. She was later to think he had a 'daemon' and 'an illness of the soul',[67] and that he lacked a capacity for ordinary human affection. His work did not attract the attention it deserved and he became increasingly bitter. It is interesting to note that the piece which is considered his best, a head of Virginia Woolf, was never officially finished, as Mrs Woolf 'took a shudder at the impact of his neurotic clinging persistency'[68] and would not complete the sittings. In the tiny cottage in Wiltshire, Julia Strachey saw Tommy's hold on his talent loosen: 'every day Tommy would come out from his studio, where perhaps he had been working, perhaps sitting motionless, simply staring desperately ahead. Perhaps weeping. When he emerged, he would stand about, looking out of the kitchen window, but soon stray back into his studio, shutting the door behind him.'[69] From 1927 onwards, Sylvia did not speak of him.

Early in 1927, Sylvia finished her second novel, 'Mr Fortune's Maggot', 'in a state of semi-hallucination'. 'I remember writing the last paragraph, and reading the conclusion and then impulsively writing the envoy, with a feeling of compunction, almost guilt, towards this guiltless man I had created and left in such a fix.'[70] Sylvia had had the idea for the book in the winter of 1925 in the form of a vivid dream: 'A man stood alone on an ocean beach, wringing his hands in an intensity of despair; as I saw him in my dream I knew something about him. He was a missionary, he was middle-aged and a deprived character, his name was Hegarty, he was on an island where he had made only one convert and at the moment I saw him he had realised that the convert was no convert at all. I jumped out of bed and began to write this down and even as I wrote a great deal that I knew from the dream began to scatter; but the main facts and the man's loneliness, simplicity and despair and the look of the island all remained as actual as something I had really experienced.'[71] In the evening Duncan Grant came to dinner, but as soon as he had left, Sylvia went back to writing. What she wrote that day remained the beginning of the book 'with hardly a word's alteration'. There was a break between this first inspired spurt and the main effort of writing, which was during the latter half of 1926, 'Elinor Barley' having been shelved. Sylvia was suspicious of the book flowing so obligingly. In August 1926, she wrote to David Garnett: 'My missionary is an impossible length, fatally sodomitic, alternately monotonous and melodramatic, his only success is an *aigre-doux* quality which will infuriate any reader after the third page. I love him with a dreadful uneasy love which in itself denotes him a cripple,'[72] but she remained completely engrossed in her story. In the middle of writing the storm on the island, she took William the chow out for his midnight walk and had got half-way down Inverness Terrace under a raincoat and umbrella before she noticed that in Bayswater it was a mild autumn night.

Mr Fortune's Maggot is the story of a conscientious missionary, Timothy Fortune, trying to convert the laughing, naked inhabitants of a South Seas island to Christianity. When Mr Fortune discovers that his sole convert, a young boy named Lueli, is in fact still worshipping an old wooden idol in secret, he sets out to persuade him to destroy it:

> For a good hour Mr Fortune talked on, commanding, reasoning, expostulating, explaining, persuading, threatening. Lueli never answered him, never even looked at him. He sat with downcast eyes in utter stubbornness and immobility.
>
> The night was sultry and absolutely still. Mr Fortune dripped with sweat, he felt as though he were heaving enormous boulders into a bottomless pit. He continued to heave his words into silence, a silence only broken by the hissing of the lamp, or the creak of his chair as he changed from one uneasy position to another, but the pauses grew longer between each sentence. He was weary, and at his wits' end. But he could see nothing for it but to go on talking. And now he became so oppressed by the silence into which he spoke that he could foresee a moment when he would have to go on talking because he would be afraid to hold his tongue.[73]

In the end, it is the priest who loses his god. He leaves the island in a state of utter disillusionment. Little wonder that Sylvia felt 'compunction, almost guilt' towards him, for she did not intend the book to have such a sombre undertow. She began the story in a comic vein and with a note from the O.E.D. on the second meaning of 'maggot', 'a whimsical or perverse fancy; a crotchet', but it is the first meaning which persists through Timothy Fortune's tragedy, with its implications of infection and decay. The ultimate message of the book is extremely bleak:

> For man's will is a demon that will not let him be. It leads him to the edge of a clear pool; and while he sits admiring it, with his soul suspended over it like a green branch and dwelling in its own reflection, will stretches out his hand and closes his fingers upon a stone – a stone to throw into it.[74]

Like *Lolly Willowes*, *Mr Fortune's Maggot* is an appealing blend of cleverness, oddity and pathos, and as such seemed to fit into the voguish Twenties genre of the 'fantasy novel', typified by Garnett's *Lady Into Fox*. But there is much more to Sylvia's two novels than their oddity. Both books are rich in imagery and extraordinarily sensual descriptive prose; the author's imagination is wayward rather than whimsical. But probably her greatest achievement in the two books is her handling of the central characters; Lolly, the woman fleeing from her fate of ordinariness and Timothy Fortune, the mild man brought down by love, both mute, middle-aged English failures – the most unpromising material. Without laughing at them, glorifying them or sentimentalising them, Sylvia opens these characters up to the reader's sympathy, and in the process they acquire a reality which overflows the books which were meant to contain them.

Mr Fortune's Maggot was received enthusiastically by a public – especially an American public – whose appetite had been whetted by *Lolly Willowes*. The reviews were sometimes embarrassingly enthusiastic, the sales again good, again Sylvia just missed a prize – this time the James Tait Black – and was selected by an American book club, the Literary Guild. Sylvia now thought of herself as a writer, though it is doubtful that her colleagues on Tudor Church Music noticed, as they were working hard on William Byrd and Thomas Tallis at the time. Oddly enough, Sylvia found it soothing that Buck remained unimpressed by her literary achievements. It was a relief 'to be reduced to my common denomination again and to be treated just as an ordinary accustomed Sylvia and to have my life-long convictions recognised as extempore'[75] – every now and then.

Buoyed up by her success as a writer, Sylvia conceived an ambitious project in the summer of 1927: a study of Theodore Powys. It was intended to be more of a portrait than a biography, for the phenomenon of Theo fascinated her, not his outwardly uneventful life, of which he himself said, 'I did nothing, I went nowhere, I met nobody.'[76] In his reply to Sylvia's proposition he wrote encouragingly: 'You have written about Satan so I daresay to write about Theodore would not be amiss. You won't waste your time, if you wrote about a swallow's course you would write well [...] You may say anything you like. I approve of everything you could ever say here or here-after.'[77] But Sylvia needed neither advice nor encouragement. This was ground she felt absolutely sure on.

David Garnett wrote of Theodore that he 'created works of art which have practically no *direct* representational relationship to the reality of the country life which inspired them, but which have a convincing reality of their own.'[78] It was the creator of the works of art who was Sylvia's subject, and in the seventy-six pages of her typescript which survive, she never writes about his environment, East Chaldon, 'straight', but always humorously or ironically, to fit in, as it were, with Theo's tone. She had only ever known Chaldon as an adjunct to Theodore and the oblique original of his fictional villages, Madder, Dodder, Maids Madder, Dodderdown. She 'wrote it up' out of enthusiasm and as a compliment to him. But the enthusiasm was too much, and burdened the seventy-six pages with the most whimsical and fanciful prose she was ever to compose, shouting down several passages of supreme percipience and subtlety about Theodore's character.

Mrs Way, Mrs Wallis, Granny Moxon, old Mrs Pitman (at whose request Theo grew a beard, shaving it off when she died), Mr Goult the carrier, Mrs Hall the driver, Billy Lucas the village drunk and intellectual, Florrie Legg at the inn and Mrs Lucas the postwoman were 'characters' to Sylvia at this time, purposely viewed two-dimensionally, and romantic because they moved about in Theo's element. Nomenclature encouraged it, for in Chaldon the farmers were called Child and Todd and there was a shepherd called Mr Dove – exactly as if Theo had had a hand in the font.

Sylvia had a manner which, though it may not have countered her eccentricity in the eyes of the village, excused it. As Bea Howe has said, '[Sylvia] had this extraordinary, this very cultured voice, but she never altered her talk when she was speaking either to her daily or a roadmender, or anybody she wanted to have a talk with.'[79] Possibly the inhabitants of Chaldon took the influx of newcomers less amiss than one imagines. Business at the post office had increased dramatically since Theodore became a published writer (Sylvia thought his correspondence with Charles Prentice wholly responsible for the introduction of a letter-box at West Chaldon), and the flow of wealthy young Londoners to the village's empty cottages, sure that 'a woman would cook for us',[80] caused no displeasure. And it was at least diverting to watch the town-dressed lady with the lolloping walk calling across the green in a high voice to a dog which some of the village children thought was a small black bear. Indeed, Sylvia was treated like royalty when the first village bastard of 1927 was named after her.

There was one person at least, however, who took pains to avoid her and this was the young woman who had come to Mrs Wallis's cottage in 1925 as 'Mrs Turpin' and was now known as Valentine Ackland, Ackland being her maiden surname, Valentine an adopted Christian name. She was a young poet and friend of Theodore, six foot tall with smooth, straight, Eton-cropped hair, a quiet melodious voice and reserved manner. The hair, the height and the trousers, which she always wore in the country, made her look like a handsome youth and on more than one occasion visitors to Beth Car had supposed her to be one of the Powyses's two sons. Throughout the winter of 1925 'Molly' spent the evenings with Theo and Violet, talking, reading aloud, borrowing and lending books and sharing their meals. She was a good typist and helped Theo prepare the typescript of 'Mr Weston's Good Wine' and, later, correct proofs. Sylvia first heard about her from Violet, and heard too that the cottage in Chaldon was in effect a bolt-hole from an unhappy marriage which had ended in annulment early in 1927, when Valentine was still only twenty years old. And one day when Sylvia was at Beth Car having tea, Valentine came in.

The meeting was not a success. Although very much impressed by Valentine's slender and romantic figure, her elegance and self-containment, and her scent, Sylvia felt that she was not herself making a favourable impression at all, and this was a blow to her pride. Valentine, who had bought *The Espalier* before Sylvia was someone to be reckoned with, had read it often and thoroughly and with a young poet's professional eye, had come to meet the respected poetess, not an 'aggressively witty and overbearing'[81] woman, and was disappointed. Sensing a failure and also conscious that Valentine was 'young, poised and beautiful, and I was none of these things',[82] Sylvia decided to be dismissive and was in effect rude.

On subsequent visits to Chaldon, Sylvia heard of Valentine's movements – off to her mother's in Norfolk, to her Bloomsbury flat, to the Continent, but was relieved that they never seemed to meet at the Powyses' any more. Little did she realise what use Valentine was making of Beth Car's back door.

IV

In October 1927, Sylvia began the diary she was to keep, with few breaks, for the next fifty years. It is a long, detailed and remarkably unself-conscious account of her life, beginning in 1927 as a busy, entertaining record, a writer's way of salting down experience, developing into a part of her life, her soul's debating-ground and one of the most moving personal diaries ever written.

It shows Sylvia in 1927 leading a very diverse London life. She dined out two or three times a week at least, usually with a single partner – Charles, Wobb, Victor, 'Bunny' (David) Garnett, her uncle Robert, her young friend William Empson – and she had developed an aversion to parties. One party at Edith Sitwell's house made her feel 'degraded': 'The room full of young male poets and old female *rastas*'; at another, 'first I was bored. Then I was disgusted by the sight of Nina Hamnett in a black shiny belly-fitting dress, looking as though she had just swum the Channel [...] I fled with Cecil Beaton to the shelter of the cloakroom where we sat on the bed and I read aloud from *The Fairchild Family*.' Beaton, another Old Harrovian, admired Sylvia very much and made several photographs of her the following year, her hair fringed and cut in a bob, her look imperious, posed against one of his characteristic shiny backgrounds.

Her evenings were very often spent at concerts and recitals, at the Royal College or the BBC or the Philharmonic Hall, where she and Buck were familiar figures. Buck had retired from teaching at Harrow in 1927 and taken the position of Musical Adviser to the London County Council, while still lecturing at the Royal College, editing *Tudor Church Music* and writing books. Once a week he would spend the evening at Sylvia's flat, ostensibly on music business. She found him as surprising a character as ever, with 'a mind so queerly stored with such queerly assorted riches I cannot expect it to have told me everything, although it has been telling me for eighteen years'.

Hers was a life of comparative leisure now, as her income from writing so far outstripped her Carnegie salary. She was writing poetry steadily and had also begun a third novel, this time a love story set in the Essex marshes in the late Victorian period. Having no tie but William, Sylvia was able to depart with her manuscripts into the country to various cottages, one at Idbury, another at Wayford in Somerset, and her favourite, The Barn at Lavenham, Suffolk, where she would stay for weeks at a time, inviting Bea, the Raymonds and Charles Prentice up for visits. Vera Raymond, a keen matchmaker, doubtless thought something ought to come of Sylvia's and Charles's friendship and invited them as a pair to numerous dinners and weekend jaunts. At this time Sylvia saw more of Charles than of anyone else – even Buck – but despite a deepening of their friendship, which could now support as much silence as talk, there was a reservedness on Charles's part which precluded intimacy. One evening in December when Charles was leaving Inverness Terrace after supper he turned faint and collapsed: 'His hands were icy cold, his eyes went quite black, but his politeness was like the moon behind a cloud. When the cloud had cleared a little, I took him back to Earl's Terrace. Poor moon, I wanted to warm it, and put it to bed, but it must sink behind its decent hill alone.'

Sylvia's circle of friends included at its edges people interested in cinematography, literary journalism, architecture and science. She was always interested in a new subject and attended with intelligence, becoming so stimulated by James Jeans's new quantum theory that she entered into a correspondence with him. This was at Buck's suggestion, because he had not been able to answer her query himself, and it niggled him. Conversation with Buck remained one of Sylvia's great pleasures. Their debates were intense and energetic, although Sylvia's incomprehension of algebra was irritating and, like Mr Fortune with Lueli, Buck spent many fruitless hours trying to teach algebra to Sylvia, substituting the words 'Aunt Mary' for the symbol 'x', 'since "x" bewilders you'. On one occasion when Sylvia argued at length about the impossibility of having an idea of infinity, Buck threw up his hands and exclaimed, 'If only I had got hold of you earlier, and made you learn mathematics!'

The preparation of the last volumes of *Tudor Church Music* was in its final hectic stages, with the Carnegie Trust prodding the editors towards completion. Three volumes appeared in 1928 alone: Thomas Tallis, Thomas Tomkins and the third volume of William Byrd. Proof revision and tidying were tiresome and time-consuming jobs, throwing up more work in their wake. Sylvia was still taking on the most irksome jobs, such as searching hundreds of pages of a score for an unidentified part. She did it still in a spirit of her superior effectiveness, though she tried her best to get out of proof correction, attempting to hand Buck concealed packages of Byrd as he left her flat. Unfortunately, he was always sufficiently alert to refuse them.

At committee meetings there was 'the usual slight clash' between Ramsbotham and Fellowes and often the discussion was conducted entirely by Sylvia and Buck, who was sometimes openly irritated by Fellowes. An afternoon's entertainment for Sylvia at this time was often a specialised conversation about medieval music with a visiting parson or academic over tea, or a lunch at the Royal College, where she was on advice-giving terms with Malcolm Sargent. But a feeling that she was growing grey in its service, and that its service paid poorly, was discouraging Sylvia from musicology. When *Tudor Church Music* was just about to 'pay off' and could have secured her a lifetime's further jobs, she chose to cut down her commitments in that field.

In November 1927 Sylvia's uncle, Frank Hudleston, was dying of diabetes in a London nursing home. Nora came up from Devon to see her brother, but went home two days later, even though Frank was sinking fast (and died within twelve hours), because she didn't want to change some arrangement she had made about her dogs – not returning, it seems, for the funeral. Sylvia arranged a wreath of roses and pussy-willow and re-jigged a hat and dress for the funeral, thinking of Frank's persistent charm and good manners the last time she had seen him. In the War Office a memorial tablet (an unprecedented honour for a civilian) was raised to him which read 'Scholar, Historian and Wit'.

A fortnight after Frank's death, Purefoy and Arthur Machen had to move from Melina Place, following a change of landlord, to 28, Loudoun Road, also in St John's Wood – 'excessively refined', Sylvia noted, 'with an airy basement full of black beetles. Whenever Arthur went to fetch another shovelful of coal we heard him crunching.' The Machens were a cheerful, improvident family, and rather unlucky. At Loudoun Road they were particularly badly-off and had to remove Hilary from Merchant Taylors School and put him into an apprenticeship at Walker's, the organ builders, a job arranged by Percy Buck. The schooling of the Machen's other child, ten-year-old Janet, had ground to a halt for a year until it was noticed and she was sent back, paid for by Aunt Nora. Sylvia admired Arthur Machen for his connoisseurship of the morbid and the unusual combination of a vivid and free imagination with an unillusioned, professional approach to the job of writing. Admirers have often depicted him as a Welsh seer of the cloak and staff variety, but Machen was more of a Londoner than anything else, and knew only a few words of Welsh. Almost all his writing was done under pressure of bread-winning, not composed in a trance on a hillside. He worked hard and was rarely satisfied. His wife Purefoy was the most congenial of all Sylvia's relations. She had the delightful part of the Hudleston oddity with none of its drawbacks of temperament. She was generous and magnanimous to a fault and completely lacked affectation. But Loudoun Road quelled even Purefoy's good spirits, for the 'Saturdays' which had been her delight had not moved with them and she began to speak sorrowfully of 'the Melina ghosts'.

One of their 'ghosts' who was also an acquaintance of Sylvia was the composer John Ireland, who set three of Sylvia's poems from *The Espalier* as songs: 'The Scapegoat', 'The Soldier's Return' and 'Hymn to a Child', and who in 1928 had recently composed a sonatina with a last movement based on the witches' Sabbath in *Lolly Willowes*. He was also considering writing an opera based on *Mr Fortune's Maggot*. Sylvia liked Ireland, while finding him 'a trifle con molto sentimento' at times, but a bad experience in March 1928 was to put her off knowing him better. They had gone back to Ireland's studio after a dinner and he was about to play her the sonatina when he suddenly launched into an angry catalogue of his woes and an account of his miserable early marriage: 'with a ghastly exactitude he recalled one quarrel, the girl sitting on the piano and swinging her legs and singing a ragtime. He stopped, musicianly, to give a rather incorrect musician's revision of "I Want To Be Happy" and how he had wanted to murder her. He raged across the room strangling a ghost and then when I jumped up and told him to have done with such tormenting nonsense he stood quite still and dazed.' The worst aspect of this 'evening out of D.H. Lawrence' was its painful similarity to others she had striven to forget: 'he was like Tommy on the worst evening: speaking like an automaton, a rather sentimental automaton, and saying the same thing over and over again. Perhaps he was a little drunk. I tried to think so.'

She dined with him a few weeks later when the sonatina was performed at the BBC and, finding him perfectly normal and unabashed, persuaded herself that it had indeed been the fault of drink. But she made no attempt to see him again.

In the late spring Sylvia's second collection of poetry, *Time Importuned*, was published. It was dedicated to Victor Butler. Sylvia was enjoying a great ease in writing poems and had written in her diary the previous November 'I want to read and write nothing but poetry'. On the day before the typescript for *Time Importuned* went off to Chatto & Windus, she was finishing one poem, 'The Visit', 'and then went mad and wrote "The Mortal

Maid"'. The proofs came through astonishingly quickly by today's standards, in eight days, and Percy Buck looked over them and asked 'if I knew that these were a great deal better than *The Espalier*.' The favourite forms and themes were there and the same characteristic flattening of the end of many poems, but if anything had changed it was the tone rather than the style, and though Buck said in praise that her latest poems were 'better-oiled', Sylvia felt that a truer judgement would be that they were 'more-vinegared'.

A list which Sylvia made a year or so later (having just read I.A. Richards's *Practical Criticism*) indicates the aims of her own poetry:

I am prejudiced:
against poems that are
in *vers libre*

express soul-states and interior
   rumpuses
talk much about love, unless
   sub-acidly
go on for a long time
are verbally rich

sonnets if petrarchan

end on a soul-stirring note
ask questions and exclaim
describe

in favour of poems that are
formally tight in thought and
   construction
evoke frames of mind, mention
   death,
contain conceits, and intellectual
   stresses
look neat
use few images, especially visual
contain references to christian
   faith and mythology
end cynically
appear very self-controlled
state[83]

These lists represent prejudices, not judgements. Sylvia was thinking seriously about her poetry, trying to define it, but still composed primarily for her own pleasure.

Many of the poems in *Time Importuned* 'evoke frames of mind', but one is particularly odd. 'Triumphs of Sensibility II' dramatises in the first person narrative a state of psychosis difficult to link with Sylvia in any way other than through Tommy. The strong and deliberate echoes of Blake enforce this idea, as does the poem's spleen:

Sometimes my friends and lovers come
Like trippers to the Aquarium;
They peer, they tap upon the pane,
And presently they're gone again.

I know they are alive because
I see their breath besmirch the glass;
But be it sigh or be it scoff
It takes the same time to fade off.

And I am glad when they are gone;
For Hug Me Tight will come anon,
And all their looks and all their sighs
Dismember and anatomise

Till they as I are cold and vile,
Guttering friendship to beguile
An itch of self-complacency.
Only my fiend is true to me.[84]

Early in 1928 Sylvia had a notice from the Ecclesiastical
Commission that she would have to leave 121 Inverness Terrace,
as they wanted to turn the flats back into one house. She was
deeply averse to the idea of moving, feeling that it would disrupt
the benign routine life had taken on. However kindly Vera
Raymond flitted about unsuitable flats in Mayfair and Kensington
on her behalf, Sylvia could not bring herself to be grateful, saying
'my bowels long to stay in Inverness Terrace and walk over the
same paving-stones to the same shops.' After a dismal couple of
months' house-hunting, a solution presented itself in the form of
Mr Oliver Warner, the reader at Chatto & Windus, and his wife
Dorothy who were also looking for a house and who, being young
and expecting their first child, could not afford a whole one.
Together with Sylvia they put in an offer on an early-Victorian
house only a few doors away at 113 Inverness Terrace. In the
middle of March an agreement was signed for it at a price of
£1,150. Mr and Mrs Oliver moved into the top part in May, Sylvia
into the basement and ground floor in July and the house was
immediately dubbed 'The Warnerium'.

Sylvia's part of 113 included 'a magnificent Victorian kitchen and two period coal cellars',[85] one of which she converted to a rose-pink bathroom at considerable cost and effort but which kept trying to revert to its original state. Her sitting-room was decorated in vivid colours; the walls were terracotta and yellow, the cushions bright red and 'Duncan and Vanessa' still drew together on her curtains at night. Louise Morgan, in an interview conducted with Sylvia in 1929, said of the flat that 'one would say it belonged to a painter – a painter who had lived a great deal in the south of Europe and loved the sun'.[86] There was also a garden at 113, so small and urban that, in Oliver Warner's opinion, 'the works of nature appear almost as miracles.'[87] Here Sylvia was able to enjoy a garden of her own for the first time. Weeding and digging provided a 'debauch of emotion'. She often gardened at night and never stopped on account of bad weather, even though a gale once blew the trowel out of her hand.

Sylvia soon became very fond of the young Warners and found an unverifiable link in their pedigrees – an aunt called Mary Esther – to substantiate the fancy that they were all, indeed, of one family. Dorothy was a passionate young woman with haunting grey eyes and an undisciplined but acute intelligence which found an ideal tutor in Sylvia. For a writer to be as generous with time as Sylvia was with hers, sitting up late into the night with Dorothy discussing books or listening to problems, is a true mark of affection. To Dorothy, Sylvia was 'a free Greek spirit' and the only one of her friends 'that she could find nothing to pity in', a pleasing compliment, if hard to live up to. Sylvia also loved Oliver, a very different character from his wife: a literary man, quiet, self-effacing and infinitely patient. Sylvia had been painting her flat one day when Dorothy came in for 'an afternoon of amateur metaphysics'. Oliver came back hot and tired from the office in the middle of this to be greeted with '"Sylvia says –"' – as Sylvia said in her diary – 'and then the whole of Bishop Berkeley. My heart bled for Oliver, but no, in a moment he was down talking about the absolute.'

The Warnerium was a civilised and domesticated place. In the darkening evenings the three young people would take it in turns to choose a book for reading aloud: Oliver chose *Paradise Lost*,

Dorothy *Sanditon* and Sylvia *Mr Weston's Good Wine*. They dined out together too, at the Raymonds' or at favourite restaurants – Boulestin's, Martinez and Mrs Diver's oyster bar – and it was pleasant not to come home alone, to sit drinking tea on Dorothy's bed, a cultured, un-intimate family group portrait.

Dorothy's baby was due in October, but she had made little provision for it. When Vera Raymond asked if she was ready for her confinement, Dorothy said certainly, for she had a pot of Vaseline. On the appointed day, Sylvia accompanied her to the nursing-home, wearing a wedding-ring (bought, presumably, to deal with hotel visitors' books), in order to 'throw my womb about if the matron was uppish'. It was not necessary. As Sylvia wrote that night in her diary, 'We crawled upstairs like criminals. She [the matron] said "I suppose you are ready for bed." Dorothy turned a wild eye on me. "Bed?" said I, in a voice that strove to be confident. "Bed?" We were left alone in a room with an empty cradle and a large box full – it said so on the lid – of umbilical pads. While we were striving to put a good face on it, the light went out. But it was only a bulb bust, fortunately, not prison discipline as we thought. Home sad.'

The baby, a girl, was born the next day. Dorothy, as psychologists would now say, 'failed to bond' with her: she behaved exactly as before and her involvement with the child was minimal. When Sylvia brought a seed-pearl necklace to the home a few days later, Dorothy said without irony to the baby, 'Don't cry, you've got a pearl necklace.' 'Fortunately,' Sylvia observed, 'there will always be Oliver to mitigate our detachment and leaven the child's life with a little foolishness.' It was Sylvia's first baby too, and though she was to grow very fond of little Bridget, babies as a class rather alarmed her. During her life she frequently wished for an heir, but never regretted not having had a child.

In the preceding weeks, Sylvia had been struggling with the ending of her latest novel, 'The True Heart', writing, she thought, 'like a verbose guinea-pig'. While Dorothy was still in the nursing-home, Sylvia finished the epilogue at a gallop. Sukey Bond, the 'true heart' of the title, is lying in bed, awaiting the birth of her first child:

It is the childbed, and not the marriage-bed, that changes women. With the first child is born the mother, a new, a different being, who, even should she seek to do so, can never more re-enter the habitation of her maiden self. For a while yet, in the glimmering room where the clock ticked and the light fingered this and the other, the former Sukey watched with her, a faithful presence, a sister; but even now she was unsure of her tenure: at each pang she covered her face, and at the sound of Mrs Lucy's step on the stairs she hid under the bed; at the child's first cry she would vanish like a ghost at cock-crow.[88]

Sylvia finished correcting the proofs of the book in December and sent them off sighingly: 'Goodbye, my dear Sukey; first child of my middle-age'.

Sylvia had an elaborate birthday party on 5 December, the eve of her thirty-fifth birthday. With a few exceptions – Dorothy Wadham, George Howe (Bea was travelling abroad), Edie Sturt and Angus Davidson – the guests were made up from her newer publishing friends. On New Year's Eve, unwillingly facing the prospect of having to leave William and her comfortable flat to go to New York – she had been invited there as guest editor of the *New York Herald Tribune* – she looked back on 1928 as 'a kind year in which I have felt safe and serene, and I think at last forgiven the hurt heart of other years'. Safe, serene and 'middle-aged'. Charles Prentice was 'domesticated kind and peaceful'. Percy Buck was as reliable – and as cool – as a rock. She had finished her third novel, had almost finished with *Tudor Church Music*, and her book on Theodore was ticking along nicely. All was calm, all was bright. Sylvia stood alone in the open doorway of 113 at midnight to let the old year out. In Wiltshire, Tommy, in pyjamas, was leaning out of a window, listening to the Tisbury bells.

V

I woke with a thud to discover the gale over, the ship speeding. A sunny, blowing day. Elling Aanestad and I picnicked, leaping up with sandwiches and claret to see land, the high French coast-line. Presently we saw towers, buildings, a beech-clump, a hay-rick and were at Cherbourg. There was a smell of land in the wind, sea-gulls flew round us, weed and wisps bobbed in the water, fishing-boats were around, the sun shone on the yellow limestone breakwaters and remembering the word "jetty" I had a sudden sensation that I was in some way returned to my native language. We sighted England about 5.30 – Dartmoor a grey dome, with hairy rain-clouds streaking up from it.[89]

The *Aquitania* was coming in to the Solent, rolling like a drunk, bringing Sylvia home from seven weeks in New York City. She shuffled along with the crowd coming off the boat, feeling like 'a dreg trying to escape down a blocked pipe' and temporarily farewelled Elling Aanestad, a young editor with the American firm of W.W. Norton, whom she had met on the boat. She arrived back in London just after midnight on 9 March 1929, to William's ecstatic welcome.

Sylvia's stay in New York had been an endless social round. Her only commitment to the *Herald Tribune* had been to write them four articles during her stay; for the rest she had been fêted mercilessly. She had met and made friends with Dorothy Parker, Elinor Wylie, the novelist Anne Parrish and Louis Untermeyer's wife Jean, a literary hostess who introduced Sylvia to her circle. Everyone wanted to meet her. Anne Parrish was worried that 'anyone so famous and sought-after wouldn't want to be bothered', and was astonished when Sylvia asked her to tea. Recalling these beginnings of their friendship in a letter to Sylvia years later, Anne Parrish wrote 'the publicity lady was young, pretty, well-dressed, and not shy of anyone, and I wished she would take her cup and her plate and go and have her tea in Jericho. You had on a dress, dark, sprigged with little flowers, with a full skirt. Later, another day and without publicity lady, we went up a high building and talked about Jane Austen and the back view of tulips and the look of falling snow.'[90]

Sylvia found herself a celebrity in New York, for her novels had been 'taken up' by some weighty trend-setters. Alexander Woollcott, who is said to have been the highest-paid book reviewer ever, liked to cite Sylvia's evocation of the South Seas in *Mr Fortune's Maggot* as a great imaginative triumph, and Christopher Morley, another influential reviewer, could hardly find superlatives enough to express his enthusiasm for her work. Morley had been one of the judges who chose *Lolly Willowes* as the Book-of-the-Month Club's first selection, and his opinion of the novel, though absurdly worded – 'that most pungent and cordially satisfying kind of thing that one hugs to one's tenderest ribs ...' – was nonetheless so valuable that it was reprinted on Sylvia's American publications for ten years. In New York in 1929 *Lolly Willowes* had gone through numerous reprintings from the Viking Press, who published most of Sylvia's books in America, and a first edition had a rarity value four times that of its original published price.

Nothing puzzled Sylvia more than the disparity between her fame at home and in America. Buck accounted for it in economic terms: narrative is for the prosperous, although the Wall Street crash in October of the same year did not seem to have any marked effect on Sylvia's sales. The most seductive reason for going to New York had been financial, 'having once tasted the decency of having enough to spare for good manners, it is hard to contract again into a careful dowdy', and Sylvia made at least $400 from the *Herald Tribune*. In September she received £542 in royalties from the Viking Press for *The True Heart*, a book which in England had earned her half that sum. It had some very mixed reviews at home and seemed to excite either pious admiration or puzzlement. No one really knew what to make of it.

The True Heart, which had come out while Sylvia was away, is a re-telling of the story of Cupid and Psyche, but as the original was not generally recognised, a great deal of ingenuity in transposing names and characteristics from Apuleius to Victorian England was wasted. Sukey Bond, a young orphan, has just gone into service with a farmer's family in the Essex marshes when she meets and falls in love with Eric Seaborn, a well-bred simpleton and a victim of fits, who, being a social impediment, is kept there by his parents, a rector and his beautiful, haughty wife. This lady, Mrs Seaborn, does all she can to thwart the match between Sukey and Eric, but Sukey's true heart triumphs, after a long separation and adventures which include an interview with the madam of a brothel (Juno) and an audience with Queen Victoria (Persephone). The theme is pure love between two simple souls, and Sylvia could hardly have chosen a more difficult one:

> This love was not a thing to be trifled with, or to be weighed against duties, or to be put off with a pretext, with a *presently*: one might not request it to dance attendance on a bad leg, to cool its ruthless heels until a funeral had been tidied away and a trunk packed. Looking at love in the lane between Chelmsford and Halfacres, Sukey had seen all her scruples and vanities of obligation vanish like a handful of dust thrown in at the open door of a furnace.[91]

David Garnett was not among the book's admirers. He wrote to Sylvia in May, deeply critical of the latter part of the story (the part which Vita Sackville-West especially liked) and of Sylvia's characterisation of Sukey: 'You do a very dangerous thing: you invite the reader to feel superior to your heroine. You hand him a stick and say: squail it at her – she's only an aunt sally and a half-wit.' 'Lord knows how you'll take it after all your maple sugar,'[92] he added, contemplating the lunch he'd arranged with her. Their friendship did not suffer in the least. At the lunch, Sylvia listened attentively to Garnett's criticisms and said she had been convinced of her sin. This was far from saying that she repented of it.

Sylvia was hardly home from America when Percy Buck announced that he would have to go to South Africa for a few months to his son's fruit farm, which was in difficulties. These two long separations were harmful to the intimacy between Buck and Sylvia at a time when both were entertaining doubts about it anyway. Earlier in the year, Sylvia had 'a niggling conviction that love is impossible between equals. One must have a little condescension or a little awe.' Buck was vulnerable to feelings of jealousy and insecurity for all his apparent composure. When Sylvia had by accident posted an empty envelope to him, he replied by sending her a blank postcard; but on reflection – and the infrequency of their meetings left too much time for reflection – felt it could have been a deliberate signal to him that all was over. On another occasion he turned up at the flat unannounced to find Sylvia about to entertain Harold Raymond to dinner. A third chair was drawn up, and Buck was very sociable, but put out. Sylvia, who was probably enjoying the situation, set her guests to acts of domesticity after the meal: Chatto was sent to work in the bathroom with rawl-plugs, Teague to bottling chutney in the kitchen. Chatto's efforts were fervent and unsuccessful, but Buck stuck to the chutney despite appeals for help, saying to Sylvia with meaning, 'I should be sorry to succeed where he had failed.'

In 1929 Sylvia was beginning to feel dowdy and ageing, and this was exacerbated by the uncertainty she felt about her relationship with Buck and the unlikelihood of there being anything comparable to replace it. Her figure had changed, her hair displeased her, looking 'like Disraeli in middle-age, so oily and curly' and she decided to let it grow, against the fashion. Also, it had struck her suddenly that 'what was wrong with my face was that the orders had been mixed. Such a comfort to have a name for it, at any rate.' This mood of low confidence was noticed by a young French friend of Sylvia's who, having spoken of her own lovers, 'enquired when we were going to hear about mine. So I said I should require a little notice in order to beat the moth out of them.' Nora was making a few enquiries too. At Little Zeal that summer, in the middle of a conversation about account books, she drew Sylvia's attention to a cousin who was able to extract offers of marriage from young men on only three meetings. Sylvia was on her mettle and replied that 'ingenuity could do anything, though personally I diverted my ingenuity to ward them off from doing it. Still, said she, the third time. O said I, that's nothing. I have often had young men who didn't propose to me the third time they met me.'

Charles Prentice had met Sylvia so often and still not proposed that they seemed doomed to eternal friendship. His devotion to Sylvia grew steadily, and as a result Sylvia began to take him somewhat for granted. Staying with the Garnetts at Hilton Hall in the winter of 1928, Charles had taken dog William off on a long walk to save Sylvia from the cold: 'Hearing footsteps ringing on the frozen road and snorts I said "It is difficult not to treat Charles like a dog, he is so obliging." Bunny remarked "He is a great deal more obliging than most dogs."' Prentice was an acutely observant man, and perhaps an awareness of being watched by him affected Sylvia's behaviour. After a dinner with Charles, she made an interesting note in her diary: 'He knows me very well, I think, and perhaps I scarcely know him at all [...] That extreme gentleness excites me and I find myself behaving with him as though I were alone out of doors. It's almost unnerving to be so freed of self-consciousness. What he thinks of me I cannot imagine, because I know myself apart from my books. I do not see them as integrally part of myself. But I fancy he is giving the peach to Lueli, taking Mr Fortune in the taxi, picking up Nelly Trim's handkerchief. Yes, I feel sure of this; that accounts for my lack of self-consciousness. As an artist I am not self-conscious, and when I am with him my mind flows as though I were my full artist-self, not the naked Sylvia that wears clothes and is met by people. Suddenly I do something clumsy or idiotic and Sylvia is in torment. But I soon forget her again, she is no more to me than the woman reflected in the mirror opposite.'[93]

Seeing the works as integrally part of the man is exactly what Sylvia herself was doing to Theodore Powys. Her book about him, though not progressing very fast and stooping under the working title 'Eikon Animae', was still a serious project and her diary is full of the raw material for it, anecdotes about Theo, his *bon mots*. Sylvia was freed by Charles's attentions into her 'full artist-self', but Theo did not thrive under scrutiny and was driven further into self-consciousness. When he had requested and read the first section of Sylvia's book, his response had been so evasive that Sylvia immediately began to have doubts: 'He praises the writing so much that I can't help wondering what he won't disclose about the matter', but she was not deterred from publishing a section in *A Chatto & Windus Miscellany 1928*, and the project only ground to a halt in 1930. At Easter 1929, when Sylvia was down in Chaldon with Charles, she was still observing the village for her book: Billy Lucas's drunken singing and Mr Child's coughs ringing through the lanes at night were rendered quaint by being part of Theo's context. Theo himself had 'flu and, having finished *Kindness in a Corner*, had begun work on his last novel, *Unclay*.

When it appeared in 1931 *Unclay* was Powys's twenty-fourth publication since *The Left Leg* in 1923.

In the spring of 192 Sylvia began a novel, 'Early One Morning', with every expectation of success. It was, in outline at least, the most Powys-like story she had ever conceived, which perhaps explains why she was unable to finish it:

> Arthur Clay lives in Rebecca's cottage and feeds her hens. He preaches sermons explaining the stock exchange and giving tips to investors. Mr Spider becomes extremely rich and seduces Sheila. The Gillespies open an Agapemone. Mr Clay abets all these doings, with his success as a pastor he becomes more and more cold-hearted, till he thinks he is possessed by the devil. He takes Sheila to live with him, and subjects her to a torment of chastity. The Bishop steps in __? The communion service in Hebrew, the Bishop fails to understand the language. Mr Clay must turn out the Gillespies and live in the rectory himself. He goes into the empty house and hangs himself.[94]

It was a summer of false starts. She had too many ideas for stories, and none of them had time to settle. Some galling disappointments resulted, such as when the *Atlantic Monthly*, which had begged to take her next novel in installments, rejected a long story called 'This Our Brother'. Sylvia, who hated to waste work almost as much as she hated to be rejected by a magazine editor, touted the story round to a small press and in the summer, in her first really cynical move as a writer, re-modelled and completed the story 'Elinor Barley', begun in 1926, purely because she had found a well-paying publisher she did not particularly respect willing to do a signed limited edition.

The writing which gave her most real pleasure at this time was poetry, in which she felt she had found a new manner. 'My fingers drop myrrh', she wrote in September, and when she began her long narrative poem 'Opus 7', she found it scandalously easy to write. On one occasion she was so carried away with writing a poem that she almost forgot a dinner engagement with Charles Prentice: 'I was dressed by the time he came, but perfectly demented, and told him I was like the Victorian ladies who hurry home from a lover to meet a husband's eye and pour out the children's milk, still quivering, with not a grain of powder to veil their shameful radiance.'

A poem which Sylvia wrote in July, when she was in Lavenham trying to distract herself from Percy Buck's absence in Africa, was read in a magazine later in the year by Valentine Ackland, and aroused her curiosity:

How happy I can be with my love away!
No care comes all day;
Like a dapple of clouds the hours pass by,
Time stares from the sky
But does not see me where I lie in the hay,
So still do I lie.

Like points of dew the stars well in the skies;
Taller the trees rise.
Dis-shadowed, unselved, I wander slow,
My thoughts flow and flow
But whither they tend I know not, nor need to surmise,
So softly I go;

Till to my quiet bed I must undress –
Then I say, Alas!
That he whom, too anxious or too gay,
I torment all day
Can never know me in my harmlessness
While he is away.[95]

Valentine had time on her hands and a speculative nature. She admired the poem, but wondered who the lover could be whose absence was received so equivocally. Some months before this, when she was driving down Inverness Terrace (she had a flat of her own very near by at 2 Queensborough Studios), Valentine had caught sight of Sylvia looking 'haunted and despairing'[96] – a private face, very different from that presented at Violet's tea-party. She felt an immediate impulse to help and wrote to

Sylvia offering the use of her rented cottage in Chaldon, specifying dates. Sylvia was not able to accept it, but appreciated the disinterested generosity of the gesture and the faultless manners of the young woman she had snubbed so pettishly.

Sylvia's planned summer of distractions was too full for spare cottages. She invited a stream of friends to Lavenham and went on from there to stay at Elsworth with Wobb, from whom she was alarmed to hear that Tommy still asked after her. She visited the Machens in their new house at Amersham, which she had helped them to find, and on one occasion took with her a young American woman she had met at a party in New York, Elizabeth Wade White. She went to stay with the Raymonds at Wayford, then on for a week at Beth Car, where Theo gave her his opinion of his brother John Cowper's new book, *Wolf Solent*: 'he thought John kept teasing his characters, not like "an honest Sadist", but lecherously.'[97] But all this jaunting did not shake off Sylvia's melancholy and on a walk over Chaldon Down, when Theo was decrying the unattractive manner of a female relation, Sylvia said she was no better herself:

> Theo faced round. 'You will never be like that, Sylvia. You could not be.' 'Why Theo?' 'You are broad-minded. You are interested in the stars.' He thought it better for the wife to be much younger, for one can make allowances to [sic] a child. With my mind on my own affairs I said, What happens when the child is grown into a disappointing woman like another. 'But she will always keep some childish tricks, some absurd way of behaving. He will recognise that.' Then we came into the sheepfold at Rats Barn, full of fat young lambs like impudent cherubs, and I wondered if to any shepherd a sheep kept some lamb's tricks.[98]

Sylvia went on to Little Zeal for a month, during which several problems connected with her father's estate came to a head with an enormous tax bill which had been laid on his book royalties. The family appealed against the assessment but lost, and the trustees became liable for tax against all the royalties since 1916. Mr Sudbury, a tax lawyer, arranged for the Revenue (known to the Warners as the Income Poop) to be paid and the estate adjusted to prevent the same thing happening again. Sylvia had for some time been one of the trustees of the estate (after the death of Mr Byng) and had been in the invidious position of having to countersign her mother's cheques. Now an arrangement was made whereby Nora had free access to her own money and Sylvia received half the current royalties on her father's books and some invested royalties' dividends. On 4 September, Nora handed her a statement, neatly compiled by Ronald, of her inheritance: £320 per annum allowance, £250 per annum marriage settlement and £195 as her share of the dividends. This gave her a secured income of almost four times her salary, plus dividends, to add to her already substantial income as a writer. She was rich. 'I had no idea it would be anything like this, and felt flabbergasted and rather distressed. In fact I didn't like the prospect of being a wealthy old lady at all. But I must buy a sealskin coat and take lessons in riding a bath-chair and prepare myself, I suppose.' Sylvia invested a large part of the new money and, as always after a windfall, bought presents for all her friends, thinking 'how scandalously easy it was to be kind, when one had money to spend.'

She had been back in London for three weeks when, coming through her front door, she found Percy Buck standing in the hall, having got in with the laundry. Sylvia was uncombed and unprepared, but the greater surprise was to discover 'how massively intimacy can just sweep one on as before. And there was the reflecting piano-top, accepting the umbrella, calm as a glacier, and it was only when he said Kiss me, that absence – his share of it – reared in my ears for a moment.' She decided to dismiss her misgivings, her feeling that his love was less than before, and they settled back into the old pattern.

There were, however, new circumstances. *Tudor Church Music* was finished, the last committee meeting ravelled up and, in early October, the final meeting took place with the Carnegie Trustees, who 'made no foolish pretences of not being delighted to wash their hands of us'. The same group of editors had undertaken to edit William Byrd's *Cantiones*, but the funding of the work was limited and necessitated economies which Sylvia objected to on grounds of inefficiency. She had just finished preparing William Wooldridge's *Gradualia* for Oxford University Press – a job which had taken years and paid only £25. 'Never mind,' she wrote in her diary, 'Virtue shall be its own reward: for never again will I undertake anything of this sort.' One must assume that the offer she accepted soon after to edit the 'Eton Manuscript', Henrician church music, for the Plainsong and Medieval Music Society was better paid.

Musicology may not have brought many benefits, but it did bring pleasures. In May 1929, Sylvia had gone to Newcastle with Ram to hear Tallis's forty-part motet, 'a glimmering uncountable tissue' and in June there was a service at Westminster Abbey to commemorate the work of Robert White, for which Sylvia had prepared all the music. She went alone to hear it. 'It was entertaining to hear my added cantus part careering about that roof on 18th-century wings.' To many people she was still better known as a musicologist and composer than as a writer. Meeting Herbert Howells at a concert, Sylvia was asked which she was doing, 'Music, or t'other thing'. She had to tell him that she had given up composing, not adding that she had also destroyed most of her music. 'Perhaps you will be composing again when you're 85,' said Howells. Sylvia replied that at eighty-five she should be taking up monumental sculpture.[99]

By the end of 1929 nothing had happened in Sylvia's personal life to assuage the feelings of gloom and resignation which had been building up all year. Nervousness and depression did not come naturally to Sylvia, and she took them badly, but resignation was the worst-fitting mood of all, and almost her undoing. Despite Mrs Keates's assurances that 1930 would be an especially lucky year for her, Sylvia only wished for it to pass unobtrusively, perhaps in the country. Walking in Kensington Gardens with William she wondered 'if I could ever get back into the queer inhuman world I inhabited in my salad days. But I can't.' Everything was changing away from her. On 15 January 1930, Bea was married to a young composer and conductor, Mark Lubbock. Sylvia had gone to say 'goodbye to my nymph' and saw the wedding-dress 'spread in her bedroom – an enormous rectangular ghost – like an aeroplane, shrouded in tissue-paper and dust-sheets.' After the wedding she went back to 113 and wept by the gas fire.

Something had to be done about Buck, and in her heart she knew what:

> For since loves have their date
> Why should we seek to renew
> Ours for a year or two
> That must die soon or late,
> When we, my dear, of all the many
> Conclusions, now chose the best and kindest of any?[100]

On the evening of 22 January, after a day of trying to keep her mind made up, Sylvia let Percy Buck into her flat, 'to the slaughter'. She said her piece, staring at some dead freesias, then sat down sweating and trembling. 'He talked for a very long time, very slowly and gravely, and I couldn't make anything out. My own theory of his Freudian distaste he scotched, but there was something that kept mounting; and presently he was saying words like "complementary" and "incompatible" [...] It was beyond all – the feeling I had – that I had torn my whole life out of myself, that it was in jeopardy, might fall into the sea and be lost.' But there was no slaughter. An absurdity made them both laugh, and immediately they were in love again. Sylvia was relieved to have unburdened herself, but at their parting was even further convinced that she could not love him any less, 'even to preserve our delight'.

The *redintegratio amoris* was, predictably, short-lived. By March Sylvia was again perturbed by Buck's behaviour. He had started to take her out – to the buffet at Paddington station, to a board-school concert, anywhere but to the flat. 'I find it hard to accept that he should prefer this as an evening's entertainment to coming here,' Sylvia wrote in her diary, 'but every day defeats me a little more, and though I am bewildered, I feel there is nothing to be done, and take it for granted, let go, be silent over the loss of it, since I am too sad and middle-aged for whistling.' She faced the new decade feeling weepy, sleepless and suffering from migraine. To her horror, she heard herself singing to herself out of tune, and two odd throwbacks to her Harrow days disturbed her disproportionately. One was meeting a friend of Victor Butler, a balding business-like man in whom she could just recognise a Harrow schoolboy of twenty years before. The other was a friend of her father's from Cambridge who came to talk for a while and on leaving said, '"It is strange to see you. You are extraordinarily like your father." And a feeling of ghostliness came over me, I the ghost straying in this old man's mind, touching, calling up I know not what there.'[101]

In this emotional period she wrote the rhapsody to spring in 'Opus 7', saying afterwards 'I am still so moved I dare not think how bad it may be' and, on re-reading *Mr Fortune's Maggot*, was swept away by the sequel she had always wanted to write, the coda to guiltless Timothy's story: 'after tea I sat down and wrote about 2,000 words – all most injudiciously, everything that David [Garnett] says is, and himself proves to be, so fatal, for I have no notion what will happen.' A dream that night sorted out the whole plot of 'The Salutation', a filip after the struggles she had been going through for months with 'Early One Morning'.

Not being in a very decisive or practical frame of mind, her friends' problems loomed large and oppressive to Sylvia. She felt helpless when Dorothy Warner was ill in the winter and was deeply affected by news that Francis Powys, Theodore's younger son, might have consumption. Dickie, the elder son, 'steadfast and sensible', saw the family through that crisis, but trouble brewed up again when Francis came to live at home and Theo began to feel threatened, almost bullied, by what he likened to a young bull coming into an old bull's field. Theodore was in an unusually confiding mood with Sylvia in December, one day putting up an umbrella in order to kiss her, the next telling her of his secret contingency plan to go away and live by himself, in defence of, as he said, 'that curious part of a man he calls his soul. I will guard that. I will fight for it if need be.'

Unknown to Sylvia, she was the subject of not exclusively admiring and charitable conversation at Beth Car. But Theo was fonder of her than ever; the fact that she seemed to have dropped 'Eikon Animae', and his perception of her private unhappiness made him tender and supportive. Sylvia had been especially preoccupied on a visit to Chaldon with Charles Prentice in February 1930, only a fortnight after the attempted show-down with Buck. Looking at a mist hanging on High Chaldon, the grassy hill near Theo's house, she thought 'at first it seemed to me that the mist was my sorrow, and I stared, feeling that this would explain everything if only I could attend. Then the mist was me, transiently obscuring the outline of a lasting grief. I had just settled this when Theo put his arm around me, and carried me back against the wind, still talking to Charles about Lucretius.'

Mutual concern for Francis's health had led to Sylvia meeting up with Valentine Ackland in London on several occasions that winter, to exchange news. Talking of Francis's poetry (he had written a book's-worth, and wanted advice from Sylvia on how to get them published), Sylvia asked to see Valentine's, the poems she spent all her creative energy on, and much of her time. Sylvia read them the same evening. 'Some were bad. None were sham. Of the comparisons which occurred to me, I went back to pebbles, poems sleeked and shaped by the workings of a restless mind. I could see they were immature; but it was as written poems they were immature: there was no immaturity in the intention.'[102] Valentine did not tell Sylvia all the news from Chaldon, nor that the offer of her cottage to Sylvia had become known in the village, and that the farmer who owned it had taken umbrage at apparent sub-letting and had thrown Valentine out. Since then, she had been staying in lodgings at Florrie Legg's, as Sylvia discovered from Violet Powys later.

Sylvia was in Chaldon again on Easter Monday, after a weekend which had seen Violet's birthday and silver wedding anniversary. When Sylvia, Theo, Violet and Valentine went for a walk up the Drove, the road leading northward out of the village towards the Five Marys, Violet pointed out a cottage for sale along the way and suggested that Sylvia might like to buy it. It had been the home of the late Miss Green. Fetching the key from The Sailors Return just opposite, they let themselves into the dusky, neglected living-room of one of East Chaldon's least picturesque buildings. But it was solid, it was freehold, and might do as temporary accommodation for Valentine, whose cottage hung on Sylvia's conscience. There and then Sylvia asked if, pending redecorations, Valentine would be the late Miss Green's steward. With admirable lack of fluster, she accepted, and Sylvia left for London the next day full of plans and philanthropy.

The sale of the cottage went through on 19 June and cost Sylvia £90. The surveyor's report began: 'This is a small undesirable property situated in an out of the way place and with no attractions whatever',[103] but went on to admit that the cottage was structurally sound and dry under its sloping slate roof. While Sylvia was collecting household gear in London and sending Ronald Eiloart over to plan a new hearth and a back door (essential for escaping from visitors), Valentine was digging over the wilderness of garden and fitting out the shed. But thinking ahead to the autumn, when the work was due to be finished, Valentine began to wonder whether or not she would want much of Sylvia's patronage. She found Sylvia rather unsettling, and her manner abrasive. Sylvia seemed 'intolerably nervous'[104] that summer, and it was painful to Valentine, not least because Sylvia and Charles Prentice had become subjects for humour among the Powyses. 'They must jeer at me too,'[105] she concluded gloomily. Francis had been to stay with the Tomlins at Swallowcliffe and reported Tommy as saying that Sylvia's friends 'are now only to be found among those fools who will encourage her empty-headed wit'.[106] Understandably, Valentine did not want to get involved in this slanging match, 'But I wish I did not *want* to live with Sylvia. I do,' she wrote in her diary. 'But while I can easily bear and must often enjoy her love of power, and the consequent dominion over my liberty – I cannot and will not endure a demand for forced tact and diplomacy and, above all, that social submission which anyway I cannot give.'[107] Privily, she had been observing Sylvia, her clothes, her hands, and had taken a photograph of her in a deckchair at Beth Car. She began to dream of her too, dreams of beautiful houses, declarations of love – sad on waking to have lost the dream-Sylvia's 'eager and loving look'[108] which she was sure she would never see on the real woman.

On 23 September, the fourteenth anniversary of her father's death, Sylvia left Inverness Terrace for Chaldon. Valentine came with her mother's car and Willie, the chauffeur, to pick her up, standing over an undiagnosable piece of furniture saying sternly, 'Is this wooden thing to go?' while Sylvia tried to comfort Dorothy, who was in tears. It was not intended as a permanent removal. Sylvia's flat at the Warnerium remained her home, and Miss Green was to be second fiddle to it. The general idea was that Sylvia would go to Dorset for a month or so at a time and that it would provide a quiet working-place. Her visits and Valentine's would not coincide much, for Valentine had a flat and commitments in London too. It would be a convenience.

The next eight days were spent putting the finishing touches to Miss Green. When Sylvia arrived, the cottage had been whitewashed inside and its woodwork painted pink, the flower beds were dug and raked, a potted geranium stood by the front door and Mr Miller, the carpenter, was putting up shelves. There were two adjoining bedrooms up the narrow stairway, both facing westwards with views of High Chaldon. Valentine took the inner bedroom, with her satinwood bureau in one corner, a washstand in another, a rag rug, a yellow rug, blue curtains and a madapollam cover of Sylvia's making on the bed against the dividing wall. Sylvia's room contained a larger bed, a dressing-table, a Japanese rug and was predominantly red. In the large living-room, they strove to eschew the quaint and cottage-like, and a sort of *urbs in rure* effect was gained from the Regency gilt mirror with its candle-sconces (there was, of course, no electricity or running water at Miss Green's) in which were reflected the writing-table, two papier mâché chairs, a Persian rug, a horsehair sofa and a chest upon which lay a 1646 Bible and a Prayer Book. Beyond this room was a kitchen of the same width as the living-room, but only a few feet deep. Here was an old copper and a new oil-cooker, lamps, a meat safe and three pails; one for water, one for milk and a third full of sand as a fire precaution. Ronald's new back door opened out onto a good-sized back garden, the water pump and privy.

Sylvia was staying at Mrs Way's and Valentine at Florrie's for the week, but having been bitten in the wrist by a Great Dane from the vicarage on her first day, Sylvia had to leave the greater part of the unpacking to Valentine, whom she thought 'like a nice son', bandaging the dog-bite, moving furniture, lighting Sylvia's cigarettes. 'I lean more and more on her trousers,'[109] Sylvia wrote. They sat in the pub together, Sylvia hoping to cultivate just the right balance between intimacy and sophisticated detachment. They would be, she said – more than a little ambiguously – like the Ladies of Llangollen.

Sylvia had decided that the position of steward might be an invidious one for Valentine, and so was preparing to tell her that the cottage was an outright gift. In the event, she chose the wrong moment for the discussion and Valentine went back to London for the weekend thinking of Miss Green as indisputably 'Sylvia's cottage', as indeed it remained. Sylvia had moved in by the time Valentine returned to Chaldon and greeted her with a half-cooked duck and one enormous and alarming mushroom from the Five Marys. The next morning Valentine came down, dressed in a silk dressing gown and emerald slippers, to lay and light the fire and breakfast, much to Sylvia's irritation, off a cup of cold water only. What Sylvia did not know then, nor for many years, was that Valentine was a secret and guilty drinker. What had started as an aid to sociability and relief from menstrual pain had taken on a great significance in Valentine's life. By some standards she may not have drunk much, but she believed herself to be enslaved to the bottle, and therefore disgusting to herself. The headaches, swoonings, migraines, collapses and 'heart-attacks' which soon became a cause of acute concern to Sylvia were all to some extent drink-related. Hence, when Tommy Tomlin turned up at Miss Green's during that first week in October, 1930, it was not the tensions between Sylvia and her former love that Valentine noticed, nor Tommy's quick and sardonic wit, but the fact that he was 'going along my path' and was 'half-destroyed by drink'.[110]

On 11 October, their second Saturday together in Chaldon, Sylvia and Valentine were at tea at Beth Car when they heard that the oppressed servant-girl at the vicarage, sent thither from a lunatic asylum, had tried twice that day to escape. It was not the first time, and the matter was notorious in the village, but this new development incensed the two women and they went immediately to call on the tenant of the house, a Miss Stevenson, only to be told that she was not in. They went home to eat a hurried supper, then back, wrathful and united in their determination to have the matter out. An acrimonious interview followed, with Miss Stevenson trying to exonerate herself, Sylvia loosing off threats in a dove-like tone and Valentine sitting 'white and motionless like Justice'. 'As we walked from the door, speechless, Valentine shook her stick in the air [...] Righteous indignation is a beautiful thing and lying exhausted on the rug I watched it flame in her with severe geometrical flames.'[111]

That night, as they lay on either side of the partition wall, the wind rose and a screech-owl went down the valley. Sylvia, who was already half-asleep, heard Valentine say that she hoped it would frighten the woman at the vicarage. Thus a slow, intermittent conversation began, against their custom, between the rooms. Sylvia was still slightly inattentive when she heard Valentine say solemnly, 'I sometimes think I am utterly unloved.' 'The forsaken grave wail of her voice smote me, and had me up, and through the door, and at her bedside,'[112] begging Valentine not to believe such a thing. In a moment, Valentine had gathered her up into bed, and they were lovers.

The cool autumn morning into which Sylvia woke was unlike any other. Everything had changed, unsurmisably and for the good. She was joyful, and she was secure in her joy. The difference in their ages – Valentine was twenty-four, Sylvia thirty-six – and the sameness of their sex, things which in cold blood might have presented themselves as impediments to a lasting love, were simply part of the new landscape in which Sylvia moved. She was excited as never before, released and unconstrained. She was also due back in London the following day, which in the circumstances seemed intolerable. They parted the next afternoon with the intense pain of the newly-in-love.

[13. 10.30] [London] seemed full of simulacra, and Teague took me out to dinner, and I was torn between [113] where I was, and the cottage, where my ghost walked. Yet I cannot forever besiege the past, there is a treachery to the future too, and perhaps the deadlier, and life rising up again in me cajoles with unscrupulous power, and I will yield to it gladly, if it leads me away from this death I have sat so snugly in for so long, sheltering myself against joy, respectable in my mourning, harrowed and dulled and insincere to myself in a pretext of troth.

3

1930–1937

I

Mary Kathleen Macrory Ackland was born on 20 May 1906, the daughter of Robert Craig Ackland, a West End dentist, and Ruth Macrory, the youngest daughter of a wealthy barrister. As a child, she lived at 54 Brook Street, Mayfair, a tall house which contained her father's surgery on the ground floor. 'Molly' was a serious, earnest and attractive child, with grey eyes and long, nut-brown hair, and was considered to be her parents' favourite. Her sister Joan, who was eight years her senior, was a devoted bully, painfully jealous of Molly. She watched over her younger sister's every move and induced in the girl an abnormal degree of self-consciousness. Valentine's youth, according to her confessional memoir, *For Sylvia*, was made up of a series of misfiring efforts to do right, to please her parents and be loved by her sister. She grew up with a completely unanswered need for reassurance, affection and guidance, things her parents omitted to notice in their concern to give her a decent upper-middle-class upbringing. In the process they passed on to Molly a fear of money which never left her, for though they were well-off, lived luxuriously and spent a great deal, the Acklands worried about money constantly and often spoke to the children as though they were on the edges of poverty.

Molly loved her mother deeply, but found her manner embarrassing, not to say intolerable sometimes. Ruth was a pious Anglo-Catholic, a pillar of the Church, a member of the Mothers' Union at the executive level, committee woman, tea-organiser and non-stop talker. She was active rather than effective in her doings, kindly, vague and sentimental. She spent a great deal of time trying to be a friend to her daughters, but was incapable of showing them an example of maturity and left all exercise of parental authority to her husband. An incident which took place when Molly was eleven or twelve indicates some of Ruth's inadequacies as a parent. Ruth was going away, leaving Molly in the care of Joan and the maid, Blossom, both of whom secretly persecuted the younger girl. Molly dreaded her mother's departure so much that she became ill and Ruth, with a car at the door waiting, said she would stay if Molly's temperature was up. Panic-stricken, the child held the thermometer against her hot-water bottle – too long. It read 110 degrees:

> It was obvious that I had somehow caused it to go up, but I denied that stoutly. My sister then demanded that I should swear on the Bible that I hadn't made it go up. I quailed, but swore. However, my mother simply looked uncomfortable and said she expected that I would be all right. And went away.[1]

'As a child I was stranded,' Valentine wrote later. 'I was without any real or solid person to hold on to. My mother was always as she is now, although when she was young it looked like vivacity, charm, recklessness, kindness of heart, and so on. But it was – *she* was – always totally unreal.'[2]

She was a lonely little girl, who at a very young age yearned to be a poet. In the attic at Brook Street, she had two games; one was 'Men of Harlech', the other 'Land of my Fathers' – the first martial, the second 'a song of spiritual matters [...] by which I worked myself into a curious state of exalted melancholy' because of the line 'the land in which heroes AND POETS rejoice'. She was tormented by having to choose between these songs, wanting the '*careless, debonaire*, light and easy and famous and brave and swaggering' Men of Harlech – '*but I always felt guilty when I chose that game.*' When she chose to be the poet rather than the hero she became 'at ease in sadness, and felt myself to be in harmony, set rightly in the pattern.'[3]

Robert Ackland was a melancholic man, unhappy in his family life and convinced that he had not achieved his full potential. He had wanted to be a doctor but had not, he said, been able to afford the training. He was senior dental surgeon at St Bartholemew's Hospital for many years and was awarded the C.B.E. for his work during the war on pioneer plastic surgery. He had organised and run two special Red Cross hospitals for the treatment of facial injuries, where with painstaking skill he rebuilt the faces of the wounded, impressing his daughter very strongly with the idea of miraculous repair, an important concept throughout her life. Ackland was dedicated to this work and was remembered for his 'never-ending sympathy, kindness and care for all who were suffering or in distress', but it was also very tiring; 'he never really recovered from the strain.'[4] His manner with his children could be gruff and distant, but he was never indifferent to them. As Valentine wrote later, 'My father did love me, and sometimes I knew it.'[5]

In August 1923, when Molly was seventeen and had just 'come out' in the grand manner of the London debutante, Robert Ackland died suddenly of cancer. Molly was stunned, but her mother decided to ignore the usual period of mourning and 'forced upon us [...] a strange desperation of enjoyment – as though I owed it to her as a duty to be as reckless and assertive as I could manage.'[6] The year leading up to Robert's death had been overshadowed by the Acklands' discovery, in the summer of 1922, that Molly was in love with a young woman she had met at finishing school in Paris. It had been a very innocent affair, but the horrified parents were convinced otherwise and punished their daughter by sending her to a domestic science college in Eastbourne, an establishment which Molly hated and which, unknown to them, was given over to the very vice from which they were trying to separate her. Robert died never having forgiven Molly for her 'unnaturalness'. He had told her, in abusive rantings following the discovery of her 'lesbianism', that she would go blind, and possibly mad; that no man would want to marry her, that she would be a spinster, a social outcast. Believing all this, and at the same time knowing that there had been nothing wrong in her love for the other girl, Molly practised typing and playing the piano with her eyes shut, and encouraged herself to become engaged, which she did twice in one year, with a sense of relief from doing the right thing at last.

During the first of these engagements (to a planter in Java she had not seen for six or seven years who proposed to her by cable), a cheerful twenty-eight-year-old woman, Bo Foster, fell in love with Molly, and they had a long-lasting affair. Molly did not by that time see anything incompatible between having a woman lover and preparing her trousseau. Love was one thing and marriage another. Molly had been part-way converted to Roman Catholicism under the influence of Bo when she met a young man at a dinner party, and so enthused him with a fervour for religion that he proposed to her the next day. She accepted, excited by the detachment and speed of the 'romance'. 'I have thought of no one else since last night,'[7] said the young man, whose name was Richard Turpin. This was the high point of the relationship. He kissed her and she was shocked and revolted by how violent it was and immediately began to have second thoughts, but Ruth, like a character in a farce, entered the room at that very moment and went into hysterics, protesting that Molly was already spoken for; the presents; the tickets – 'but in her groan I detected the same enjoyment that I was feeling.'[8]

The marriage took place at Westminster Registrar's Office on 9 July 1925. In a fit of impatience, Molly had given her fiancé a day's notice, despite his protestations that they had not yet been received into the Church and that his parents had not met her. Molly pointed out that a civil marriage would force the Church to hurry up, which it did. They were received, baptised and confirmed within a week and had their wedding at Westminster Cathedral on 17 July.

Bo Foster did not attend the wedding, but a young friend of hers, Rachel Braden, did. Turning aside from her wedding procession, Molly said to her in controlled tones, 'I'm fainting for a sausage.' Molly, who at five foot eleven and a half was the same height as her husband, wore as a head-dress a white medieval-style nun's coif, framing her pale face and completely concealing her hair, which during the morning she had had Eton-cropped secretly. In 1925 this was still novel enough to be shocking, and coming downstairs in her going-away clothes she was 'gratified by the sensation I caused'.[9] She liked the very boyish look it gave her as well as the sensation, and never grew her hair long again.

The honeymoon was postponed because Richard had to have an unspecified operation, but to dissemble this, Ruth insisted they drive off from the reception as if to the station. Once round the Park and they were back at the Acklands' service flat in St James's Court. The honeymoon, when it happened, confirmed their incompatibility. Molly did not like to be near Richard and 'his hands seemed too large and curiously insensitive. I was thinking about [Bo] all the time.' Richard himself had distracted thoughts: his relationships before marriage had been exclusively homosexual. After repeated attempts to feel desire for each other and consummate the marriage, it was decided that Molly should have an operation to remove her hymen, and she went into a nursing home. During her stay there, with constant loving messages from Bo and angry scenes from Richard, she received an invitation from Rachel Braden to convalesce in Dorset, in the small village some of Rachel's artist friends knew of, East Chaldon. Molly bought some men's flannel trousers, and went.

Thus her marriage ended. Though Richard came down to Chaldon to try to reclaim her, Molly was increasingly determined never to live with him again. She loved the liberty offered by Chaldon, the reviving company of Rachel and of the Powyses, whom she quickly came to 'revere'. She had changed her appearance dramatically – now she changed her name, and though Ruth, Joan and Richard all imagined that these were temporary aberrations, that 'Molly' would soon be back in Mayfair, settling down to married life, Valentine had other ideas.

While Sylvia was enjoying fame as the authoress of *Lolly Willowes* and writing *Mr Fortune*, Valentine was living between the cottage at Chaldon and a small flat she had taken in Bloomsbury and mixing with an artistic set to which Rachel had introduced her. She sat to several artists for the figure, among them Eric Gill, Betty Muntz and Oliver Lodge, son of Sir Oliver

Lodge the spiritualist and a friend of Tommy Tomlin. Towards the end of 1926, when she was still officially married to Richard and still attached to Bo, Valentine became pregnant as a result of a brief affair, with whom is unknown. She was very pleased at the turn of events and became preoccupied with the idea of having a daughter, who would be called Tamar, and whom she must have intended to raise alone, or perhaps with Bo's help, for though Richard was prepared to acknowledge the child, Valentine spurned him again and they agreed to divorce on the grounds of nullity. The proceedings took place early in 1927 and Valentine, pregnant and promiscuous, swore before a series of secular and ecclesiastical courts that she was *virgo intacta*.

At Chaldon in the spring she fell down a bank and miscarried, at somewhere between sixteen and twenty weeks of the pregnancy. It was a great blow to her from which she attempted to distract herself by drink and an increasingly hectic sexual life. All the time she was writing poems with certainty and fervour. 'They were always very bad,' she wrote, 'but I was confident that I was a poet.'[10] Valentine had a real, undeniable and delicate gift but was never a 'professional' and wasted years of her life trying to be one. The craving for fame as a young woman and too much leisure in which to feel guilty for not being able to write, or not write well enough, set patterns of disappointment and guilt which seriously impoverished her creative life. Her sensibility, poised so precariously between the despair with which she perceived her work as failed and the ecstacy which occasioned that work, was a fine one, completely attuned to poetry. She lived for it.

In the summer of 1928 Valentine began an affair with Dorothy Warren, owner of the Warren Galleries in Maddox Street, the niece of Lady Ottoline Morrell and a god-daughter of Henry James. She was handsome, rich and sophisticated and was immediately attracted to Valentine's apparently haughty, silent presence. The extent to which Valentine allowed herself to be carried along by events at this time shows a detachment from her fate which was both reckless and desperate. Dorothy was a sadist and Valentine emerged from her first 'attack' – it was literally that – bleeding profusely from her wrists and ankles, sick and swooning under the laudanum Dorothy had administered. Within ten days Valentine was half-demented and nursing 'a hope that I may kill myself',[11] for she was at once revolted and fascinated. Fortunately, though the liaison with Dorothy Warren lasted on and off for two years, they slept together infrequently. Dorothy became engaged at the end of 1928, writing to Valentine, 'We have the same religion, Philip and I.' Her fiancé was a dealer in jade and Dorothy intended to turn the Warren Galleries over to it after she had completed her current series of exhibitions. The last of these was the notorious show of D.H. Lawrence's pictures which took place in June 1929 and which, coming on the heels of *Lady Chatterley's Lover*, provoked a police raid and the confiscation of thirteen paintings.

Valentine's other affairs were of a less alarming nature. She had several male lovers, but as she said herself, 'I was naturally more inclined to love women than men'[12] and her women lovers, especially in quiet Chaldon, were legion. Bo Foster was the only enduring relationship she had and Valentine always returned to her – until she fell in love with Sylvia.

Lying awake after she had sent Sylvia back to bed that first night, Valentine listened to the inn sign creaking and realised that the six-year affair with Bo had been dealt its death-blow. She longed for the new love to be a lasting one, but from the start doubted her worthiness of it. She decided not to tell Sylvia of her drinking: if the relationship were to be short-lived there was no point; if not, as she hoped, the problem might disappear of its own. Sylvia had also been entertaining thoughts of unworthiness. She felt ugly, old and soiled by the compromises of the last ten years. Her doubts were the reflexes of a cautious mind, unwilling to put itself into a vulnerable position, but they evaporated under the realisation that caution, too, was one of the dingy habits she wanted to throw off. Valentine assured her that to protest unworthiness would be a denial of Valentine's own fastidiousness, upon which she prided herself. And that settled it.

> I, so wary of traps,
> So skilful to outwit
> Springes and pitfalls set
> Am caught now, perhaps.

Though capture, while I am laid
So still in hold, is but
The limb's long sigh to admit
How heavy freedom weighed.[13]

II

Having fallen in love, Sylvia rapidly changed her plan of spending the winter in London. She was to come back to Chaldon in November, having dispensed with all her other commitments during October. Hours later, this plan too was abandoned and they were counting the minutes to a meeting in London. In this separation, which lasted four days, their extraordinary correspondence began. On the train from Wool to Waterloo Sylvia wrote the first of hundreds of love-letters. Valentine despatched hers, with a mourning-ring as love-token, as soon as she got back to the empty cottage.

Once Valentine was in London, Sylvia spent as much of her time as possible at 2 Queensborough Studios, Valentine's dusty, usually untidy attic room. There they made love at leisure: 'I had not believed it possible to give such pleasure, to satisfy such a variety of moods, to feel so demanded and so secure, to be loved by anyone so beautiful and to see that beauty enhanced by loving me. The nights were so ample that there was even time to fall briefly asleep in them.'[14] Valentine's room was covered in drafts of poems, books, expensive accessories and beautifully tailored clothes. There was also a Siamese cat called Haru and Valentine's collection of tiny objects, one of which was a working silver revolver. Sylvia marvelled at how precariously she had come by her happiness, ease and delight having been markedly absent from her earlier loves: 'What ecstacy to sit up in bed looking out on that Gothic prospect of chimney-tops, drinking tea and eating a ham sandwich, and watching her detached collected movements about the large and lofty room, Haru's shadow prancing upon the ceiling.'[15] She watched Valentine's face too; 'the stillest face I have ever known. Amusement sharpens it slightly into that fox's smile, but it disdains to smile for pleasure, or turn aside from its melancholy beauty.'[16]

At the end of the month, Valentine took Sylvia for the first time to Winterton in Norfolk, which she considered her home, although 'The Hill' had only been a holiday house for the Acklands. 'The Hill House' itself was a fairly unexceptional Victorian villa but its outbuildings, greenhouses and trees all held cherished associations for Valentine, whose happiest moments as a child were spent alone, reading poetry, writing, walking over the dunes which were all that stood between the garden and the cold eastern sea. The house had been kept up since Robert's death, but not adequately, and Valentine, who revelled in the villagers' exclamation of how like Mr Ackland 'Miss Maaalie' looked in her trousers, dreamed of inheriting the place and restoring something of the old order and old happiness. Sylvia noticed how in Winterton Valentine behaved with an almost swaggering confidence, and was accepted by everyone. A former family servant, Caterina, showed Sylvia all her mementoes and photographs – 'the Mollie-museum' – the pretty child astride a rocking-horse, the debutante, the bride.

The lovers lounged in the inn and on the quay, played childish games on the beach, writing their initials on the sand, and Sylvia saw with the delight 'the secret of [Valentine's] lovely gait: the footsteps were exactly aligned on a narrow track, regular as machine-stitching.'[17] Going back to London in the Ackland family car, mesmerised by Valentine's suave driving, Sylvia made her mind up to tell Buck how things stood. It was a calm, kind meeting. 'My poor Teague, I can scarcely believe it is done; nothing more became it than its ending [...] There was no dazzle of love in my eyes, no nursed delusion, or self-conning. Yet I have never liked him so well, seeing him thus clearly.'

Sylvia went back to Chaldon in November in trousers and a fisherman's jersey, having bought a tennis racket, driven the car (which she found easier to do in the dark, when there was less visible danger) and played more chess than in the whole of her life. In Chaldon, Sylvia and Valentine behaved so shamelessly that the village became rather prim and unnoticing and Katie Powys, who had been in love with Valentine, became fiercely jealous. Mrs Way, who came in to clean, found Sylvia and Valentine sitting up in bed together and cried out cheerfully, 'Twins!' The oil man came upon them embracing in a doorway and averted his gaze. Two women passed within feet of them rolling about on one of the Five Marys, all much to Sylvia's delight. Valentine supposed that the old debate on her sex would break out again in the village, for it had never been satisfactorily resolved and Mr Child knew for certain that she was a man.

There is nothing in Sylvia's diary to suggest that she did not feel Valentine to be sharing her extreme happiness, but Valentine always slightly mistrusted good fortune. For her, moments of joy, whether caused by love, poetry or any other thing, had always to be set in the context of their own transience. She was much more attentive to Sylvia's words than was Sylvia herself and would be plunged into private despair – and private drinking – by implications which Sylvia certainly never intended. When Charles Prentice arrived at Miss Green for Sylvia's birthday on 6 December 1930, Valentine began to wonder whether or not her own position was in jeopardy – an idea which would have shocked Sylvia had Valentine put it into words instead of into her diary. Sylvia's ease with her many friends, her sharp, often cutting wit, made Valentine uneasy. It was the private and not the public Sylvia she had fallen in love with, and when they settled into a way of life together, Valentine deliberately chose not to accompany Sylvia to parties, dinners and friends' houses except when attendance was absolutely unavoidable.

On the day following Charles Prentice's visit, Sylvia heard a thud upstairs and rushing up, found Valentine collapsed on the floor of her bedroom, icy-cold and insensible. When she came round, Valentine explained that it was 'heart – a collapse' and Sylvia spent an agonised, sleepless night at her bedside, thinking her near death. Valentine was ill for two days, and on the third day had 'another heart-attack', but ordered Sylvia to leave her alone. Four days later, in London, there was another collapse, this time at the wheel of the car. Coming out from the doctor's, Valentine told Sylvia that it was migraine, 'and potentially fatal'. The effect of all this on Sylvia's nerves was, of course, considerable.

It is odd that Sylvia did not, apparently, connect these collapses with drink, or smell, with her fine nose, the whisky which Valentine could not always – certainly not while collapsing – have concealed. 'I thought sometimes that she *must* know,'[18] wrote Valentine, who was increasingly ashamed of herself and felt trapped by her debilitating dependence. The problem complicated itself as time went on because whereas at first Valentine had lied to protect Sylvia, later she lied because she feared Sylvia's reaction to having been deceived.

On 12 January 1931, they drove from Lavenham to spend the night in London, where Sylvia had tickets for a Schnabel concert at the Queen's Hall. On their way to 113, Sylvia said very simply and decisively that she wanted no one but Valentine. It was a statement of complete trust, and their subsequent love-making was exceptionally happy. The next morning Valentine said that it had been a marriage-night. 'For my part, why not?' wrote Sylvia, many years later. 'I loved, I increasingly honoured, and if being bewitched into compliance is obedience, I obeyed. As for fidelity, it seemed as natural as the circulation of my blood, and no more meritorious.'[19] From then on they were committed to each other, and kept 12 January as a wedding anniversary, the most solemn of the many festive days of their private year; Valentine's Day, birthdays, the anniversary of seeing Miss Green's cottage, moving in, becoming lovers – all marked by delightful small gifts, for they were both remarkably talented at choosing presents.

Sylvia was neither writing nor attempting to write much. In 1930 the limited edition of *Elinor Barley* had been published by the Cresset Press and Sylvia had finished her long narrative poem Opus 7, begun in 1929. 'Early One Morning' had languished and been put by. Later she re-made part of it into a short story. When *Opus 7* and *A Moral Ending* – three stories in a limited edition with an introduction by Theodore Powys – were published early in 1931, Sylvia had no major project in hand. For the first time in months she was doing a little of the music editing she was obliged to finish for the Oxford University Press, but besides that, and a little 'vile' poetry, there was nothing.

Because of the smallness of Miss Green's cottage, Sylvia and Valentine would retire severally to Florrie Legg's to work, later renting the tiny dissenting chapel from Mr Goult, the carrier, for the same purpose. He used it to store parcels in. Valentine was very concerned by her own lack of output in the months since she had moved in with Sylvia. She couldn't understand why being happy seemed to inhibit her from writing poetry when her uncomfortable affair with Dorothy Warren had had the opposite effect. Gloomily she concluded, in the manner of much of the bargaining that went on in her childhood, that she might be driven to leave Sylvia, her only happiness, if she were to write 'properly', and her reverence for poetry was such that this became a real dilemma. Sylvia was in a difficult position as regards Valentine's poems. She had been polite and encouraging rather than enthusiastic when she had read Valentine's poems in 1929, calling them 'pleasing minor verse'.[20] Of course, once she was in love with Valentine and knew more about her poetry, and how important it was to her happiness, enthusiasm was the least she felt or showed. The poems meant infinitely much more to her, especially since all the newer ones were about their love. She began to perceive Valentine's way of writing – lyrical, short and loose-formed – as superior to her own, purer and more difficult. She also saw that it would not, as it stood, make Valentine into what she wanted to be, a published, widely-read poet. In her diary Sylvia wrote, 'if I can teach her the necessity for being a charlatan, that conjuror's trick which Housman has so perfectly, I shall have done something. It is, perhaps, the peck of dust we must all eat before we die, but eat it we must to show we are alive.'

As the months went by at Chaldon, Sylvia and Valentine's lives 'joined up imperceptibly, all along their lengths',[21] although adjustments could sometimes be difficult. Their first and possibly worst row had at its root the absolute difference which existed between them over matters of domestic economy. Sylvia was used to efficiency in housekeeping and would not throw away half a tomato, enjoying thrift as it should be enjoyed – as a vice. Valentine, on the other hand, had been conditioned to despise such behaviour as indicative of poverty, and thought that Sylvia demeaned herself with housewifely fidgetings, when in fact she was exercising her ingenuity. Sylvia made efforts to suppress her worst excesses, but the habit was so ingrained and so sensible that she could not lose it altogether and she resigned herself to cultivating extravagance alongside it, which she mastered very quickly and well. Valentine's insistence on 'the best' or nothing at all intrigued her as part of a discriminating character: even before they were lovers and Sylvia had suggested that they could buy certain tools for Miss Green's from Woolworth's, she noticed a shudder of disapproval pass across Valentine's face. There were differences, too, over music; differences in response. 'I became rather tiresome and absorbed,' Sylvia wrote apologetically, noting how, when listening to Beethoven's Seventh Symphony on the radio, Valentine had left the room abruptly. A few weeks after this, when the Matthew Passion was being broadcast, 'I sat listening and she sat staring.' There were a number of concerts in London Valentine had to stare through that first winter, as Sylvia had bought her usual season tickets, but it was the last time she bought them. Concerts and operas, so much a part of her former life, became rare occurrences, for she could not enjoy going often without Valentine, and Valentine preferred not to go. Also, as their life together was centred in Chaldon, it was impractical to think of regular excursions to the capital. This was not because Valentine did not appreciate music, but because she could not appreciate it, in her 'layman's' way, in front of Sylvia, just as she never played the piano or violin in front of Sylvia, though she had learned both those instruments. So, though their lives may have joined up along their lengths, and remained so joined, their breadths remained oddly differing and unknown and, like all wise lovers, they left a little strangeness between them, a little privacy. Sylvia felt a responsibility not to spoil what she had found in Valentine, 'to house, and yet not to tame, this wild solitary heart, so fierce even in its diffidence. And I, lumbering, so I seem to myself, after, clogged with all this cargo of years and tolerance and mind's dust.'

At that period the phenomenon of two women living together or sharing a hotel bedroom was assumed to be innocuous and respectable, even when one of the women was dressed like a man. The war had left many spinsters little choice in that matter, and to find ladies living as companions was a commonplace. Ostensibly, Sylvia and Valentine were such a pair, for though the oil man had caught them embracing, they did not make a habit of behaving like lovers in front of other people; on the contrary, they maintained very proper married manners in public. Those who knew Valentine, however, were perfectly able to guess what their relations were, and one by one the penny dropped among Sylvia's friends too. Many, while not disapproving of lesbianism as such, found it hard to continue the same sort of friendship as before because Sylvia-in-love was such a distant, preoccupied figure compared with the Universal Aunt of former years. Oliver Warner did not grudge Sylvia her happiness, but took a strong dislike to Valentine and referred to her (not in Sylvia's presence) as 'the white slug'.[22] Buck, a worldly and unshockable man, had given them his blessing. So too had Theodore Powys, not in words but in his unbroken friendship – unlike Violet, who went through a period of snubbing Miss Green's once she was satisfied what was going on there. Charles Prentice did not, apparently, realise anything for some time. Purefoy and Arthur Machen thought no ill of them for several years, only opining that Valentine might be improved by a little make-up, but were deeply shocked when they found out that Sylvia and Valentine were lovers. Purefoy could not have 'cut' Sylvia for the world, but they were never so close again. On the other hand, it is said[23] that Vera Raymond, also shocked, tried to intervene and wrote Sylvia a letter pointing out what a terrible mistake it was and why couldn't she see sense, and so forth. Sylvia, incensed with Vera for doing this, and with Harold too for condoning it, wrote back in an equally forthright way and her seven-year friendship with Vera ended abruptly in acrimony.

Nora Eiloart had met Valentine during the summer of 1930, when Ronald was in Chaldon helping with the cottage. With her quick and critical eye she immediately formed an unfavourable impression of the masculine young woman, who for her part thought Nora 'a rather lovely woman'.[24] Sylvia was not in love then, but later it must have been fairly clear to Nora, even at a distance, that there was more to all this gadding up and down to Norfolk and inseparability than a convenient house-sharing scheme. Sylvia knew that she would have to go to Little Zeal in the summer for a month or so as usual, and intended to tell Nora and Ronald outright how things stood, but events overtook her when, on 23 March, a week before the Easter of 1931, she received a telegram in Chaldon – 'Ronald dead'.

When Sylvia arrived at Little Zeal the next afternoon, she heard how it happened. Ronald had complained of a dull ache under his collar bone in the morning, but went out to continue work on a small garden studio he was making for Nora. At tea-time she went out to find him and saw his feet sticking out from round the corner of the building. He was dead, of angina, aged forty-two. Already there was talk of an inquest (though it was deemed unnecessary in the end) and arrangements for the funeral were under way, and in the long day which had elapsed since finding Ronald dead, Nora had become ominously brisk and self-controlled. After an initial collapse onto Sylvia there were no more tears.

Sylvia was taken upstairs to see Ronald's body. His hands were folded idly and to Sylvia he looked very beautiful, sharing the 'secret' look she had seen on her father's face. There was plenty to remind her of that other death, from Nora's assumption that she would sleep with her to Sylvia's inhibiting conviction that she was no comfort to her mother. Sylvia began to feel her own loss, too, for she had been very fond of Ronald, and esteemed his qualities as having earned her father's admiration. She also began to see how completely he had been responsible for the good relations between her mother and herself since the marriage and how, now he was dead, things were falling back quickly into the old antagonisms. Nora, then aged sixty-four, had determined to stay on at Little Zeal with the dogs and the garden, and though she did not like Sylvia any better than before, would now require longer and more frequent filial attentions from her. After all, Sylvia had no ties – it would be no skin off her nose.

Sylvia's half-formed plan of telling her mother about her marriage was put by, as Nora was in no state to attend to such news, but the strain of being separated from Valentine so abruptly and for such a long time – it was expected that Sylvia would be in Devon for two weeks – seemed unbearable. As it turned out, they were apart only eight days, but between them wrote thirty long and impassioned love-letters. Flowers and telegrams, schemings for clandestine meetings, visits to the post office in South Brent, all this must have produced an unseemly excitability in Sylvia.

With arrangements for the funeral still going on and the vicar and Nora somewhat at cross purposes, Sylvia could not restrain herself from trying to bring the conversation round to Chaldon and the possibility of Nora visiting – perhaps that very weekend? – suggesting that Miss Ackland might be able to teach the gardener to drive, as Nora would be stuck with a driver-less car, and other wildly impractical suggestions, all turning on the presence of Valentine, her virtues and capabilities. Even through the fog of bereavement, Nora was onto this in a flash and when one of Sylvia's schemes bore fruit and Ruth Ackland, on a pretext of condolence, came to tea at Little Zeal – driven there, of course, by Valentine – Nora wasted no time in sounding out her opinion of their daughters' 'sudden and intense friendship'.[25] Ruth thought she fended this off cleverly by being bland and unforthcoming on the subject, saying only how 'nice' – a favourite word – it was for the two young women. But Nora need only have looked at Sylvia when she came back into the room, her face dishevelled from a snatched embrace in the kitchen, to have her question answered much more comprehensively. Nora, putting the situation together for herself, stole a march on Sylvia, who was never able to make the proud announcement she had planned. Ruth, whom she disliked on sight, and Valentine, whom she now despised, became prime targets for Nora's scorn and sarcasm.

Valentine drove Sylvia back to Chaldon on Good Friday, a day earlier than expected because Uncle Bertie had arrived providentially at Little Zeal. Miss Green's cottage was filled with flowers, but Valentine seemed exhausted and distraught: 'it almost broke my heart to think how lonely she had been, and tormented with every fear,' Sylvia wrote in her diary. One thing was clear – they would avoid another such separation at all costs.

In May, they went to Winterton for Valentine's birthday, when a shower of presents one to the other cheered Ruth out of a money gloom. On the same occasion, Sylvia was taken to meet John Craske, a man of pure Norfolk fishing stock who had been forced to leave the sea due to lingering ill health and an abcess on the brain, which had left him subject to comas and stupefaction. In his long invalidism he had begun to paint, and when Valentine first visited him in 1927 – hearing that he made model boats – she found his cottage full of remarkable seascapes painted on any and every surface. The watercolour of *The James Edward* she bought that day for thirty shillings, 'the utmost money I dared spend',[26] was Craske's first sale. Dorothy Warren saw the picture in London and wanted to know more about the artist, suggesting that if Valentine could go on her behalf with a blank cheque and buy as many pictures as possible, they could stage a Craske show at the Warren Galleries. Valentine, whose sense of a fair price put her at an instant disadvantage in all business transactions, cashed the cheque for twenty or twenty-five pounds and gave the money to the Craskes in return for a great many pictures. When she told Dorothy Warren what she had paid for them, 'for one moment I saw a look of incredulity on her face'[27] – hardly surprising, since Dorothy had previously offered ten pounds for a single picture and sold several subsequently at a comfortable profit. The pictures were shown in 1929 and attracted good notices. Craske was hailed as a Primitive, though Sylvia was to write later that 'if Craske is to be put into a category, he must be placed with the Intuitives – a companion to John Clare.'[28] By 1931, Dorothy Warren was planning a further exhibition to include some of the needlework pictures Craske had begun to make in the late twenties, pictures which particularly appealed to Sylvia on her first visit to the red-brick cottage in East Dereham: 'The room was filled with Craske's work, pictures in wool, silk, paint, – even the ornaments painted with ships and lighthouses,'[29] and she bought several works.

Sylvia and Valentine spent a couple of weeks in London on their way back to Chaldon, and Dorothy Warren made the Craske business an excuse to see Valentine alone. On one of these evenings, Sylvia dined with Bea, who was as delightful as ever, though carried further and further into her husband Mark's career at the BBC, where he was soon to become Principal Conductor. Two nights later, Valentine was again with Dorothy and Sylvia had Percy Buck to dine at the neglected Warnerium flat. At lunch Buck had met Einstein, who said of his own theories, 'When it has been discovered if they are correct – for myself I do not know – one of two things will happen. If I am right, the Germans will say I was a German, the French, that I was a Jew. If I am wrong, the

Germans will say I was a Jew, and the French, he was a German.'[30] Teague played the piano for her – something he always avoided doing before – and they had an argument about Isaiah, 'and it was all very peaceful and pleasant'. When he had gone, she went up to talk to the Warners and was not too concerned where Valentine had got to until the phone rang at two in the morning and Valentine, in a weak voice, asked her to come round to Queensborough Studios. 'The room was all upheaved, rugs scratched up, scars on the wooden floor, ink spilt, furniture awry. Valentine herself very flushed and breathless and black-eyed, walking up and down and staring from the window.' Dorothy (and her dog) had attacked Valentine when she came back to see the Craskes, knocked her down, tried to strangle her with a tie, threatened to knock her face in with a kettle, hit her on the face with her fist and knocked her head against the floor repeatedly. Valentine escaped by going limp, only to have Dorothy try to throw her out of the window. All this was followed by abuse, recriminations, threats of suicide, an attempt to tear up Valentine's poems and tears. Dorothy had stormed out, only to come back a little later with a calm sweet smile to say, 'You see, when I am angry I am always violent.'[31] Sylvia was furious when she heard all this and swore vengeance on 'that woman', but Valentine would not have it, for the same reason she refused to hit back at Dorothy – it wasn't honourable.

They went back to Chaldon relieved to be alone together for a while, but fending off visitors proved difficult since Gamel Woolsey and Gerald Brenan, two young writers who irritated Sylvia, were in the village, Alyse Gregory was unhappy, Betty Muntz was in love with Valentine and Katie Powys had developed an obsessive passion for Sylvia. One visitor they always welcomed was Granny Moxon, an ageing countrywoman who lived in the thatched cottage next to The Sailors Return, and as such was their nearest neighbour. She had cropped white hair under her battered hat, a gypsyish, weather-browned skin, a laugh 'exactly like a woodpecker's cry' and the endearing habit, in times of great stress, of dropping on her knees and praying to herself. 'Granny' had befriended Valentine when she first came to Chaldon, recognising in the young woman not only a true love of the country and the skill to learn its ways, but a lonely, proud nature like her own. Valentine came to think of her as the mother she would like to have had, almost literally an 'earth-mother'. It was Granny who taught Valentine to dig, lit the first fire at Miss Green's and constantly reassured Valentine 'Thee'm be all right'.

Valentine needed such reassurance. The summer of 1931 ran her into gloom again, for no obvious reason: 'We walked up the hill and along the violet path looking for snakes. I was still a little touchy, still under my cloud. What *are* these clouds? I believe drink – or else no poetry for some time, or else a deep inferiority-complex. All three, I expect. A bad, devilish trinity.'[32] Sylvia was writing poems, correcting the proofs of Theodore's novel, *Unclay*, cooking, sewing, gardening, loving. Valentine saw herself sinking further and further into a disadvantage, not only as a writer, but financially, for she disliked her dependence on Ruth's allowance of £300 per annum and Sylvia's patronage. An evening spent at her accounts showed her to be six pounds in debt, but as usual this only depressed her and egged her on to spend more. The day after the account-book, when Sylvia had left for a weekend in Devon, Valentine bought herself a pair of crocodile shoes in Weymouth and the following for Sylvia:

a) a very lovely mourning clasp, to wear as a bracelet – sewn on wide black velvet. Date: George II (£6.16.6 & cheap)

b) a picture of Queen Vicky's wedding (sic) (2s)

c) a picture of St Matthew, looking very evil (7.6d)

d) a little French contraption, for cutting flowers and such-like – rough, but quite pleasing (9d)

e) a bead purse – to be put away, for when she needs a present! (£1.10.0)[33]

The day's shopping cost her about two weeks' allowance.

A week later Sylvia herself indulged an extravagance so enormous that she surprised and rather unsettled herself. Valentine had been longing to buy a car, and after test-driving a disappointing Alvis early in July (asking price ten pounds), they had asked the Dorchester car-salesman to keep his eye open. His eye picked out a second-hand two-seater sports Triumph in red and cream, with red seats and a dickey at the back, which so excited Valentine and was such a complement to her driving skills that Sylvia could not refuse it: 'looking out cautiously I saw her gazing into the engine with a look which, combined with the pleased pink she had hoisted driving back, assured me it was a car to get. So I bought it then and there, trembling faintly: £110' – twenty pounds more than the price of the cottage. But if it is more blessed to give than to receive, it is also easier, and Valentine had plenty of time before the delivery day in which her happiness could be nibbled at by melancholy second thoughts. When the car arrived, however, there was unalloyed excitement and a succession of small pleasure jaunts, one of them to Droop, north-west of Dorchester, a place Theo had long wanted to see on account of its name. And when the inevitable letter came from the bank telling Sylvia she was £38 overdrawn, she announced there was nothing for it but work and immediately began some magazine pot-boilers.

A decade later Sylvia made this distinction between Valentine's sensitivity and her own: '[Valentine] has more heart. My heart is passionate, but it has a rind on it, a pomegranate heart. Hers has a fine skin, a fig heart.'[34] In 1931, she did not seem to appreciate quite how fine a skin it was, and by trying to help Valentine's career as a poet, probably hindered it. When Charles Prentice came to stay in Chaldon in July, Sylvia made use of the visit to solicit Charles's opinion of Valentine's poems. Sylvia had taken the matter entirely into her own hands, selecting from a large bundle those she thought would most interest Charles. Had Valentine been left to approach him herself, or to send the poems in to the Chatto & Windus office, they would both have been spared the uncomfortable situation Sylvia's solicitude landed them in. Valentine, sitting opposite Charles in the living room at Miss Green's, watched him reading and re-reading with a puzzled expression, pulling at his side-hair nervously, and her heart fell. The answer he gave Sylvia in the end was such a classically non-committal publisher's answer that it is a wonder she accepted it: 'We [Sylvia and Charles] talked about publishing. I think he would have made a proposal for Ch & W, were things not in such a bad way now. As it was, he counselled that she should write more, and more let-out-ly.' Sylvia could not have made matters better by apologising to Charles for the inconvenience and dullness. He protested his excitement, but as Sylvia noted in her diary: 'It was a well-controlled excitement, certainly.'

Things were noticeably different the next day when Charles sat down to read Sylvia's latest poems. He was engaged by them, and at ease. Sylvia was sitting in the same room, writing, and Valentine, who had noticed him admiring her, wondered what Sylvia would do if Charles proposed marriage, they seemed so easy sitting in perfect silence together. And would the poems that Charles was then reading, love poems coincident with the poems he had read the previous day, leave him with any doubt in his mind as to the situation? Poems such as Sylvia's 'Since the first toss of gale':

> ... For long meeting of our lips
> Shall be breaking of ships,
> For breath drawn quicker men drowned
> And trees downed.
> Throe shall fell roof-tree, pulse's knock
> Undermine rock,
> A cry hurl seas against the land,
> A raiding hand,
> Scattering lightning along thighs
> Lightning from skies
> Wrench, and fierce sudden snows clamp deep
> On earth our sleep.
> Yet who would guess our coming together
> Should breed wild weather
> Who saw us now? – with looks as sure
> As the demure
> Flame of our candle, no more plied
> By tempest outside
> Than those deep ocean weeds unrecking
> What winds, what wrecking,
> What wrath of wild our dangerous peace
> Waits to release.[35]

Valentine, though she retained a jealousy of Percy Buck and this niggling fear that Charles Prentice might at any moment drop on one knee in front of Sylvia, did not doubt Sylvia's love so much as her constancy, simply because that was what she doubted in herself. Valentine had little idea of what a deeply romantic figure she was to Sylvia; reading *The Arabian Nights* aloud by candlelight, wearing her inscrutable 'Chinese' face, tossing Sylvia into bed at a moment's notice, exhaling perfumes and cool elegance. Asked once why she was never unfaithful to Valentine, Sylvia said, 'Because she was the best lover I ever had.'[36] For her own part, Valentine's fears were inseparable from a love which occupied her whole heart:

> Sylvia is writing a poem, I think – judging by the sharply-indrawn breath, and her endless cigarettes. She is curled up on the chair by her writing table, elbows on the table and one leg curled under her small buttocks. Her hair looks very black against her pretty pink coat. How narrow her hands are – How deeply I love her. My eyes constantly stray from this page, across to her. How much, and how completely I love her.[37]

III

Visits and visitors seemed to take up more and more of Sylvia's and Valentine's time. 'If they are unpleasant, they need not be asked again,' Valentine decided, jealous of her privacy with Sylvia and never pleased to be billeted out at Mrs Way's, but few of their guests fitted the category. The Machens – Arthur, Purefoy and the twelve-year-old Janet – came in July, drank a great deal and played cricket at Beth Car, where Theo fielded holding a kitten. After them came Mrs Keates, who still 'did' for Sylvia at Inverness Terrace, with her two young daughters. It was Mrs Keates who showed them how it was possible to bathe in the copper – if you drew your knees up to your chin and clasped your shins, in the manner, Sylvia noted, of ancient British burials. Nora would not come to Chaldon, so Sylvia was duty-bound to spend at least a fortnight that summer at Little Zeal, while Valentine took Ruth to Paris for a holiday. Both lovers pined terribly during this time.

In October they took a houseboat at Thurne in Norfolk and while they were there they heard that Ruth was intending to draw her horns in by letting the London flat and moving to The Hill House permanently. Valentine felt that it would help her mother if someone was with her for the first few months at The Hill, so reluctantly she and Sylvia locked up Miss Green's cottage and moved into the flat above the Acklands' garage at Winterton, sharing meals and outings with Ruth, but retaining a degree of privacy. Ruth's implication that she was giving rather than receiving favours was irksome, as was her habit of coming in on their private anniversaries and making much of them – a dinner-party and presents for Valentine's Day and nosegays on their beds for 12 January. It was during this winter that Sylvia's deep dislike of Ruth took root, for what she had not thought about before, or attributed to kindliness and tolerance, was shown up by living at close quarters to be desperate attempts by Ruth at complicity, for she would do anything to hold on to Valentine's love and respect.

Valentine's worries about money reached a peak at Winterton that autumn, and she became suicidally despairing at the thought that even were she to 'climb down' – as her mother put it – over poetry, there was no job she could do to earn money on a satisfactory scale: another oversight of her education, along with accounting. Her overdraft terrified Valentine so much that Sylvia gave her a cheque to 'tide her over', although when Nora, in a similar gesture of spontaneous generosity, had offered *her* £50 in the summer, Sylvia had refused it, 'feeling proud and scrupulous'. Towards the end of their stay in Norfolk, Sylvia finished a lengthened and revised version of 'The House of the Salutation', the story she had started in 1930 as a sequel to *Mr Fortune's Maggot*. The new story formed the basis of a collection which was published late in 1932 under the title *The Salutation*. The book included 'Elinor Barley', 'The Maze' and the three stories from *A Moral Ending*, all previously published in limited editions, and nine other stories, some of which had appeared in periodicals.

'Early One Morning' was included too; nine pages was all she salvaged from the novel which had taken so much of her time.

The title story, 'The Salutation', set in Chile in the 1920s, is a haunting, melancholy piece in which Sylvia's powers of evoking place, mood and the complex forces which govern ordinary human behaviour found their perfect expression. 'I wrote it out of my heart as an *amende* to my poor Timothy [Mr Fortune]. Not that I could make him happier, but to show that I did not forget him.'[38] The sorrowing traveller in the story is never named as Mr Fortune, and the references back to the earlier novel are few: Sylvia did not want to flaunt her pursuit of this character into another book. She could not make him happier, a ruined man, dragging his sorrow across the South American pampas, and her apparent reticence to interfere with the man or the story is what gives 'The Salutation' its truth to life. The protagonist has, at one point, been watching a large clumsy rhea and identifying himself with the bird when it is shot, before his eyes:

> With a confused impulse of compassion he rushed towards it, but even as he reached it it lay dying. The shot had entered its neck; a ruffle of loosed plumage showed where the spine was broken. Now that it lay on the ground its bulk seemed enormous, a death as portentous as a man's. And he turned to look for the murderer.
>
> There was no need to look for the motive. Opposite slays opposite, as fire and water writhe in their combat, as lion and lamb wage their implacable enmity. Slender, fiercely erect, racked with youth and pride, the boy with the gun stood in a trance of hatred, defying a world of rheas, a world of harmlessness, dowdiness, ungainliness. There could be no mistaking his intent. Apollo could not have bent his bow with a more divine single-mindedness to destroy; and seeing him, the impulse of blame was quenched in the man's heart. One might as well have blamed a flash of lightning.[39]

Sylvia felt that 'The Salutation' was 'the purest, the least time-serving story I ever wrote, and [...] one of my best',[40] but being in a collection of stories it did not attract the sales or amount of attention accorded to her other books. The reviews it did get were appreciative, and one or two were perceptive as well. R.H. Mottram in *The Bookman* wrote of the element of 'possession' in the story, 'nearly always a benign spiritual seizure which [...] drives these perfectly credible, if never commonplace, men, men and beasts just over the border of their ordinary existence into a dimension or plane of being which is not ordinary'. This quality of credible extra-ordinariness is present in all Sylvia's best work. As for the emotional and imaginative engagement which can be called 'possession', sometimes it is a moot point who 'possessed' whom more: Sylvia the book or the book Sylvia.

Sylvia and Valentine left Winterton in March 1932, and in the following May took a short holiday in Paris. They were delighted to be there together for the first time and, in that worldly city, to find their relationship so readily accepted. Sylvia noticed the looks Valentine attracted and the following glances of congratulation to herself. Outside a grocer's shop in the Rue Mouffetard, Sylvia was suddenly aware that she wanted to write a novel about the 1848 revolutions. She had had the two main characters in her head for some time and now they 'started up and rushed into it [the book]'.[41] Braced by Paris and Valentine, Sylvia was again engaged on a novel, though not, as it turned out, along any former lines.

On their last day in Paris, Sylvia consulted a fortune-telling machine on an arcade, asking if her lover would be faithful. 'Oui, malgré les folies' was the remarkably accurate answer. 'Les folies' were part of Valentine's life. Whether she had new lovers during the first few years of their marriage or was simply maintaining the prior commitments of old ones is not clear, but certainly Sylvia was neither surprised nor upset by Valentine's behaviour and was proud of the attraction Valentine held for many women. 'She was so skilled in love that I never expected her to forego love-adventures. Each while it lasted (they were brief) was vehement and sincere. They left me unharmed and her unembarrassed.'[42] At Miss Green's, Sylvia used to delight in the stories of Valentine's past conquests and even made a little chart, filled in with coloured inks, to show the number, gender and duration of Valentine's affairs since 1924, which in 1932 numbered twenty-seven, at least five of which were with men.

Valentine was feeling less gloomy about her writing and had had several poems published in magazines – including one, the American *Saturday Review*, which rejected a poem by Sylvia at about the same time. But there was no prospect of Valentine having a book published yet, though Charles Prentice assumed that Sylvia's poems would follow their usual course into print. Realising the hurt this would cause Valentine, Sylvia struck upon an ingenious plan while they were staying in the small village of Tinhead in Wiltshire in October 1932; they would send out their poems together for publication in a single volume, anonymous but for the initials 'T.W & V.A' on the title page, 'because of her fame and known name', Valentine wrote in her diary. Sylvia's motives were nicely mixed; part blackmail of her publisher, part a pure desire to make poems she believed good available to readers, part the personal motive of making readers available to Valentine. But even in the first excitement of making lists, Valentine had her doubts, or qualms of conscience. Sylvia was very pleased with her plan, and was already busy putting it into practice. 'She has concocted a most suavely blackmailing letter to "*Dear* Charles",' wrote Valentine. 'Poor devil. But his bald head is smooth enough to slide out of her small, slim fingers – I think.'[43] Charles replied asking to see the collection, and a month later he provisionally accepted it, causing Valentine elation, and more doubts: 'I am two thirds in favour and one third not. I have still a lingering desire to be only myself – but I suppose it is foolish to wish so – At least: to wish to *appear* so publicly.'[44]

Sylvia's idea to publish the poems unattributed, as well as being suitable to the 'purity' of Valentine's poems, was also an acknowledgement – instinctive or deliberate – of their discrete nature. Valentine's poems express a sensibility, not a personality and were in that respect not only unlike Sylvia's own poems but impervious to the charlatanism Sylvia had thought to teach. Poetry was not a career to Valentine, but a frame of mind. Her ambition was, in Bea Howe's words, 'to capture and transfix the true character of the elusive, fleeting moment'.[45] Her poems were often written quickly and did not necessarily benefit from revision. Her few long poems are not particularly satisfying, for length was in Valentine's case at odds with her natural manner: sensual and essentially 'slight'. They are the sort of poems which may well lose by being read *en masse*, for each poem is a 'made thing'. Possibly the best way to have published Valentine's poems would not have been in a collection at all, but separately, like broadsheets, to be tasted one at a time. A poem such as 'Summer Storm', for instance, displaying what is both good and bad about Valentine's poetry, might seem, in a book sixty pages long, merely tiresome:

> 'I will not!' I say, 'I will not!' – Saying
> I will not, while all through the air around me
> Resounds, 'I will – I will!' Swallows playing,
> Birdsong, leaved trees, all confound me –
> Confuting truth with truth, hope against hope, despair
> Bundled between them, by one side or the other
> Used as a bludgeon – 'I will not care –'
> ('I care – I care – I care –')[46]

'Birdsong, leaved trees', now almost taboo words among poets, were already suspect in the Thirties and Valentine's liberal use of them automatically disqualified her from being considered serious or modern. The fact that birdsong and leaved trees is what she saw was beside the point, for her more forward contemporaries eschewed such subject matter as leading on inevitably to the sentimental. Valentine was aware of this problem, but believed of her poems that '*inside* the mood is the true mood of this time [1933] – Flinching, apprehensive, intent, fearful, and yet intent and intending – But, here is the fear – my poems may not manage to reflect that; I can only say that, for myself, I am aware of it – It is there, in me – But if it doesn't come out, I'm no good.'[47]

Sylvia and Valentine seemed very settled at Miss Green's cottage, as Alyse Gregory, their friend and neighbour from across the downs, noted in her journal: 'Sylvia and Valentine had built their life much as married people build theirs, only it is more sensitively poised – their little love birds, their canary, their vases of spring flowers, V's daggers and pistols, the sentiment they attach to the objects about them.'[48] But the winter of 1932 proved to be the last they spent at Miss Green's. On Valentine's twenty-seventh birthday, 20 May 1933, they were out on a drive from Winterton when Sylvia's whim led them up an unmarked turning near Sloley, along which Valentine caught sight of a beautiful small manor house. Backing up to take another look, they saw that it was empty and to let. They talked it over, and decided to try to take the house for a year; it was large, lovely, in Valentine's beloved Norfolk and at £50 annual rent, reasonably affordable. Miss Green's cottage had never been intended to house two people permanently and it was proving too small. Though they would regret leaving it for sentimental reasons, leaving Chaldon village would not be too great a wrench, for it had changed for them in the last year; Granny Moxon had died of cancer, Shepherd Dove, her devoted admirer, had also died, and a distance had grown between Sylvia and Valentine and Beth Car, due not only to the death of the Powyses' elder son Dickie in 1932 but to Theodore's and Violet's guardedness surrounding their adoption of a baby girl early in 1933. Sylvia thought that 'they will both be rather glad than sorry when our eyes remove their gaze to Frankfort Manor.'[49]

Sylvia arranged, with Oliver Warner, to sell the remainder of the lease on 113 Inverness Terrace, for she neither needed nor could afford the flat now. At last they would have a house large enough to hold all their belongings, a stately and beautiful house, fit for Valentine. Early in July, all the negotiations done with, Sylvia and Valentine, in the Triumph's successor, a green MG Midget, drove up Frankfort Manor's sweeping approach.

IV

Frankfort Manor was a seventeenth-century house with a Dutch gable and a Norfolk reed thatch. It had been partly remodelled in the early nineteenth century, and retained a Georgian elegance inside, with some confusing later additions, including 'an intact Edwardian long hall, complete with carved oak staircase and c.1900 beams'.[50] The house was composed of two long, low storeys and was made of brick, coated with worn yellow limewash: 'the colour of the brick showed dimly through, so the general tint of the house was that of a ripening pear with streaks of vague rose and pale madder flushing its sallow skin.'[51] Dozens of trees stood around the three-acre garden; beech, oak, Spanish chestnut, elm and ash, providing a barrier around the house while not overshadowing it, and beyond the trees were cornfields and farm land. The outbuildings were numerous and fascinating: a large stable, 'rustling with rats', harness room, coach-house, wash-house, vinery, pigsty and privy, In one of the loose-boxes they found a rusty bayonet, in the vinery a curled and faded notebook recording the weather of 1887. There was a nuttery, two asparagus beds and a kitchen garden an acre in size, divided into four plots and surrounded by flower borders and a fruit wall. Beyond that was an orchard and a paddock. An ancient pear tree stood propped on a crutch in the orchard; there was an apricot trained against the stable wall, soft fruit, shrubs and, inside the house, the delicious scent of Gloire de Dijon roses which put their heads in at the upstairs windows. Quite by chance, Sylvia and Valentine had found themselves a 'kind paradise'.

Valentine was completely at home in the 'landed' atmosphere of Frankfort. She stalked the grounds with her rifle, shooting at rats; she chopped wood, perused the outbuildings by lantern-light at dusk, dug the garden. Every day brought her a new delight exactly tailored to her tastes; a greenfinch's nest, a white-currant bush, a family of stoats playing on the lawn, which she could observe with the small pocket telescope Sylvia had given her. 'Another day, [...] we met a hedgehog walking up the drive,' Valentine wrote in her autobiography, 'another day, in full sun, I was picking green peas into a colander and saw the earth near my feet heaving, and a mole emerged, and I caught it instantly, in the colander, and carried it in to Sylvia, who was writing in her room, and set it down beside the typewriter on her table.'[52] They had a writing-room apiece, an airy sitting-room made larger by an enormous speckled mirror, and four large bedrooms, of which they chose the grandest, the one with the powder closet. The kitchen was large, with an uneven brick floor and old-fashioned range. There was no electricity at Frankfort Manor: the county gentleman who was landlord to most of the village and had his own private generator, refused to have electricity cables strung across his land.

Almost as soon as they had moved in, William the chow began

to sicken and fail, and on 31 July he had to be put down. Sylvia grieved profoundly for him: 'one of my roots has been cut through, and for a while I thought I could not endure this place, which had promised such kindness and struck with such slyness and flattered with the bland mockery of turtle-doves.' As a result of William's death, the 'rough' cats began to show themselves – a family of thick-furred scavengers who lived in the grounds and outbuildings and did much to keep down the corresponding families of rats. Soon they were coming to the back door for food, though they did not mix with the three house cats Valentine had acquired – a tabby called Meep and two grey kittens called Caspar and Boots, the first cats Sylvia had lived with since her Mister Dive. There was a goat, too, named Victoria Ambrosia.

There was a great deal to be done at Frankfort. Their lease specified that Sylvia and Valentine should keep the garden up and cut the deep, mossy lawn at the front of the house only by scythe. When they arrived, the kitchen garden was given over to potatoes and bindweed. They lifted the potatoes and sold them to the local fish-and-chip shop, then began the long work of digging over and planting winter vegetables. They worked hard, and as long as the daylight allowed, leaving writing until the evenings, and when Sylvia was not in the garden or her writing-room, she was in the kitchen, making jams, jellies and pickles of every conceivable kind. As the autumn advanced, the extent of the damp in the house declared itself: some floorboards needed replacing, doors were warped off their level. There was a rat-hole in the bathroom window-sill. They soon realised that they could not attend properly to both house and garden and employed a local girl called Irene to live in and housekeep. They also had to employ a man to do the heavier outdoor jobs, such as the required scything. All this required money.

Sylvia was working sporadically at her novel about 1848, 'Summer Will Show', but had to give most of her time to writing stories, poems, articles and reviews which could be sold to some of the many periodicals of the day. Sylvia's income from royalties on her Chatto & Windus publications amounted to only £74 in 1932 and £127 in 1933, compared with the record year, 1927, when she earned over £1,200, and her father's royalty payments were falling year by year as well. An indication of how concerned she was about making an adequate income from writing at this time is the painstaking listing in her diary of finished pieces, where they had been sent, how much they fetched and who owed her the odd guinea. On 25 August 1933 she wrote, 'Try as I will, and live as we do on vegetables, I can't keep within my estimate; and today there was nothing for poor yowling Meep and if Irene hadn't wisely breakfasted off Meep's liver, there would have been little for Irene.' When the apples were ready, they sold apples and when the cats kittened, kittens, and by the end of the year Sylvia was drafting the following notice for the local post office window, a mile away from Sloley, as there was no village shop:

> Christmas 1933 is imminent
> Send your friends a carton of
> home-made CHESTNUT JAM. An epicurean jam.
> Tastes like marrons glacés, makes a delicious
> winter desert. 2/6 a carton
> or Rhubarb chutney   2/
>   Apple chutney   2/
>   pickled nasturtium seeds   1/6
>   lemon-scented verbena sachets   1/

Trade was not brisk, and the friends who were sent chestnut jam as a Christmas present were mostly Sylvia's and Valentine's.

In November 1933 their joint collection of poems was published in the United States by Viking Press – the title, *Whether a Dove or Seagull*, derived from a poem of Valentine. Chatto & Windus bought in printed sheets from America for their own edition of only 622 copies, which came out in March 1934. The names of both women appeared in full on the title-page and the following rather stern 'Note to the Reader' served as a sort of manifesto, a subtle modulation on their original idea:

> Of the poems in this book, fifty-four are by one writer, fifty-five by the other. No single poem is the result of a collaboration nor, beyond the fact that it contains the work of two writers, is the book collaborative. The authors believe

that by issuing their work under one cover the element of contrast thus obtained will add to the pleasure of the reader; by witholding individual attributions on the page they hope that some of the freshness of anonymity may be preserved. The book, therefore, is both an experiment in the presentation of poetry and a protest against the frame of mind which judges a poem by looking to see who wrote it.

As soon as the American edition was in her hands, Valentine began to have serious doubts about the efficacy of the method. American reviewers seemed to concentrate solely on comparisons between the two poets – inevitably, as their attention had been tweaked thither and Sylvia's comment, printed on the dust-jacket, that Valentine was 'a more promising poet than ever I was, am or shall be' seemed tantamount to a challenge. One reviewer said of Valentine's style (having used up twenty column inches guessing which were her poems) that it 'moves [...] sweetly'. This irritated Valentine intensely. 'What I have *got* to say is *not* sweet,' she protested, 'and what I *want* to say is not sweet either.'[53] On 9 November, Sylvia wrote to Charles Prentice, asking him to include a key at the back of the English edition, indicating who wrote which poems. Valentine, she said, did not mind about the American edition, but felt that anonymity 'would exasperate our island critics. She also smarts under the fact that when we gave the book to Llewelyn Powys and told him to mark what, in his opinion, was who's, he gave all her best poems to me.'[54]

The key to the poems in the English edition undermined the stated aims of the book as set out in the 'Note to the Reader' and, if anything, puzzled reviewers more. Austin Clarke, writing in the *New Statesman and Nation*, said the authors failed to see 'the mundane flaws in their syllogism', and added 'the reader will be tempted to test his own powers of literary detection until, darting backwards and forwards from one end of the book to the other, he develops a crick in the neck.'[55] It was generally assumed that Valentine was a man, and two papers went as far as suggesting that Sylvia had invented 'him' as a pseudonymous decoy. Few of the reviewers got past the novelty of the presentation to discuss the poems themselves, though those who did were praising, on the whole. Humbert Wolfe, a keen admirer of Sylvia's poetry, was unusual in supposing Valentine to be a woman and finding in the book 'a growing together – accidental perhaps in fact but not in essence – which gives a strange unity to the whole.'[56]

Whether a Dove or Seagull was dedicated to Robert Frost, a poet whom Valentine revered. Frost was sent a copy of the book by Louis Untermeyer, who had championed Sylvia's early poetry, but it was more than a month before Sylvia and Valentine received his polite letter of thanks. Frost had found the book disturbing, writing to Untermeyer, 'I hardly know what to write either to you or to them. If *you* could have got along without two or three of the more physical poems in the book, you can imagine how much more philosophically I could with my less cultivated taste [...] It is possible to make too much of the episode – whether joke or clinical experiment. I am well past the age of shock fixation. But if I promise not to make too much of it, will you promise too? You won't take it as an infringement of the liberty of the press if I ask you not to connect me with the book any more than you have to in your reviewing and lecturing. Don't you find the contemplation of their kind of collusion emasculating? I am chilled to the marrow, as in the actual presence of some foul form of death where none of me can function, not even my habitual interest in versification. This to you. But what can I say to them?'[57] Three weeks later he was writing again to Untermeyer: 'For goodness sake be quick and write me out or print me plainly the address of that couplet in England. I can't seem to read the writing of the only letter of theirs I can lay my hand on. And I must say something polite to them soon or the silence will get too hard to break [...] The book has beauties, of course, and they should be acknowledged.'[58] So the 'couplet' never suspected that by dedicating their book to Frost, they had earned his disapprobation, nor how many other people, including Untermeyer, found it disturbing.

Untermeyer's wife, Jean Starr, had no reservations in her admiration of Sylvia and Valentine, and included some interesting observations of them made in the summer of 1934 in her book, *Private Collection*. Of Sylvia she wrote: 'she is so *alive* that her vital awareness is translated into everything she thinks and does. She can make an event of the fact that the carrots have come up large and healthy in her garden; a casual stroll on the lookout for mushrooms becomes a kind of picnic; a passing remark on one's appearance is, by an affectionate inflection, almost a caress. [...] [Sylvia] is all in one piece. Everything has been assimilated – music and learning and country lore and wit. And her letters flow spontaneously into form like her conversation.'[59] Of Valentine she wrote, 'she was like a very handsome boy, with her high-bred and somewhat haughty features, her close-cropped nut-brown hair, and the look of a real dandy [...] her trim shirts and sports jackets, even in the country, were *comme il faut*.'[60] Jean was living by herself at Miss Green's cottage during that summer and found it disappointingly plain – 'there was no thatch, there were no climbing roses, no leaded casements'[61] – and excessively small, a fact impressed upon her by her large black wardrobe trunk, which refused to go up the stairs and had to darken the living room. The discomforts of the place were, to her, obvious, and she set about to cheer it up, much to the horror of Valentine and Sylvia who, on a visit to Chaldon during Jean's stay at the cottage, hardly recognised Miss Green under her rustic make-up.

At the time of the publication of *Whether a Dove or Seagull* in America, Valentine was writing a great deal and, it seems, contemplating setting up a magazine of some sort, for a letter from Llewelyn Powys endorses such an idea enthusiastically. Llewelyn had already shaped the project to his own philosophy and preoccupations: 'a revival of the Religion of Aknaton and the removal of all restraints that interfere with man's natural happiness'.[62] 'This very exciting idea of yours' was already far from what Valentine had envisaged, and, unsurprisingly, the magazine never came to birth. Valentine's correspondence with Llewelyn was bearing fruit in other ways though. In the winter of 1933 Valentine was beginning to read political tracts and pamphlets, about the Nazi regime in Germany, atrocities in Africa, colonial misdemeanors, drawn on from one to another with increasing horror and concern. Sylvia was not conscientious in following up the lists of leaflets Valentine recommended her to read, but Llewelyn was, and soon he and Valentine were swopping outrages by every post. Sylvia did not share Valentine's deep sense of responsibility towards the world nor see the necessity to spring-clean her own assumptions and attitudes so thoroughly. She rather preferred a set opinion to an open one, while genuinely admiring the opposite trait in Valentine, seeing it as a mark of Valentine's integrity that she wished to question and investigate so much. Valentine's glory as well as her bane was that she had no capacity whatever for indifference.

The deaths of Granny Moxon and Shepherd Dove – ill-handled by the panel doctor – and the generally bad conditions of agricultural labourers in Chaldon and Sloley were not academic matters to Valentine, but of the first importance. Being counted as gentry, she felt a further responsibility to her oppressed fellow-creatures, and the ways in which she helped them (often by driving them to and fro or writing to officials) were never patronising, nor mistaken as such. More so than Sylvia, she had an unobtrusive way of going about these things, and was quieter. Her reading of political tracts had set off a chain of thought about social problems, but though Fascism, growing stronger by the day in Europe, revolted her completely, she still questioned the left-wing views which stood opposite it:

> I think it well to develop the conscious part of our minds *individually*. *Individually* we can do anything.
>
> It is collective action that I fear.
>
> I think we shall find ourselves reduced to being like the ants that walked in an unbroken circle around the rim of the basin, or we should be like them, if ever the *genuine* Bolshevik regime got us. Because we should have agreed to follow each other always, to behave always each one like the next one.[63]

Valentine had been reading the *New Country* poets – Auden, Day Lewis, Michael Roberts and Stephen Spender – and their technique as well as their left-wing views caused her to reassess her own position as a poet. Having always thought of the poet's role as an exalted one, that of a prophet, it was an easy transition to begin to think of the poet as a spokesman. She began to test out different forms and deliberately manipulate her style, trying to follow, as she felt her challenging contemporaries were, a 'time-instinct', 'the only true guide an artist has'.[64] Painters and sculptors, she observed, were much more at liberty to do so, but the poet had to risk appearing incomprehensible at first, before his readers had acquired a 'trained eye and ear'. Valentine, essentially a lyric poet, showed no subsequent incomprehensibility in her work, for it was beyond her to be wilfully difficult, but had, in all the important ways, taken on board the contemporary developments in her art.

Between the American and English editions of *Whether a Dove or Seagull*, Sylvia had been working at a satirical *roman-à-clef*, intended to be a much-needed money-spinner. 'Some of it strikes me as very funny', she wrote to Oliver Warner, and related how Valentine had been alarmed and 'slightly reproachful'[65] to find Sylvia laughing hysterically at her own jokes. She wrote it under the name Franklin Gore-Booth, and intended to preserve strict anonymity over its authorship, as it contained portraits of Theodore and Llewelyn 'to the life'.[66] Such scruples proved unnecessary when the novel was rejected by Chatto & Windus in the spring, the first such blow Sylvia had ever received, and one which she took with remarkable grace, writing to Harold Raymond, 'don't let us be hurt, either of us, over what is only a traffic. I have the greatest esteem for my butcher, whose fillet steak is all I could desire; but when I thought there were too many lights [...] in the cats-meat, I told him so without flinching. Nor did he, from what I saw, flinch much either. I should hate to think I had less philosophy than my butcher has ...'[67]

A week later a much worse blow fell at Frankfort Manor in the shape of a sudden, inexplicable and deathly plague among the cats. It affected cats, dogs and squirrels first, and the local people feared it might spread to the cattle, as had a plague sixty years before. Meep, who was in kit, was removed to Winterton, but the two grey cats died, as did at least two of the rough cats, and the rats, who were unaffected by the disease, began to take over the outbuildings. The plague struck quickly and was as quickly gone. Meep's grey kittens returned to Frankfort Manor and helped alleviate the gloomy atmosphere which had prevailed during that unhappy week in March. Sylvia, working in the rich soil of the lovely garden, listening to Valentine whistling contentedly nearby and hanging the grey kittens in trellised pink roses to be out of the way, felt it 'impossible to know greater happiness.'

In April, though, Llewelyn wrote from Chydyok that another mentally deficient servant girl had run away from the vicarage. This, the same issue that had brought them together in 1930, immediately touched Sylvia and Valentine and they wrote to endorse the petition Llewelyn had got up among the villagers of Chaldon, demanding of the landlord (the vicar) that the matter should be investigated by the Council, under whose licence Miss Stevenson operated. Llewelyn had consulted a J.P. friend of his before drawing up the petition, which contained the signatures of forty local people, including Alyse Gregory, Llewelyn, Theodore, Katie, Gertrude and William Powys and James Cobb, the West Chaldon farmer, and he was confident that they were proceeding quite legally. When the document was sent up before the County Council, however, it was found not to bear the necessary riders of confidentiality which would have protected the signatories from what happened next – a libel claim.

At first, Sylvia and Valentine were only mildly perturbed by this development. The solicitor they consulted pointed out that Miss Stevenson would be out for damages, and the best – and cheapest – course would be to apologise. This they were prepared to do until they were faced with a continuing liability for damages, regardless of any apology. At this point they chose to persist with the allegations, which were well-founded and undramatically worded. When the writ of libel was served it cited only four of the signatories of the petition, those from whom money was deemed extractable; Sylvia, Valentine, Llewelyn and James Cobb.

They were persuaded to appoint a K.C. to conduct the defence, who in turn needed a junior. As the date of the trial neared, it became obvious that the expenses were going to be high and, whatever the outcome of the case, they would be unable to afford to go on living at Frankfort Manor. They had taken the house in the hope that they might be given the opportunity to buy it, but the hope had proved groundless. They would be ousted sooner or later by the young owner and, with this new oppression over money, they decided to minimise the wrench by leaving sooner. On a visit to Chaldon in August 1934 to discuss the case with Llewelyn,

Valentine noticed that the barn-like house standing alone in a field on the road to West Chaldon was empty. This, they decided, would be easier to live in than Miss Green, which after Frankfort would seem ridiculously small, so they arranged to rent the barn, 24 West Chaldon, and let Miss Green to Jimmy Pitman, a young labourer whose thatched home had been bought from the Weld Estate by Betty Muntz to form part of her studio.

They left Frankfort Manor in November, deeply regretful. Their sixteen months there remained for both women the embodiment of all that was good and happy in their relationship. 'Goodness is like a flower of the locality,' Sylvia wrote. 'We were never again so unimpededly good as we were at Frankfort Manor.'[68]

> Lovely the house is, sheltering and kind,
> Warm and faithful against besieging winter,
> But we shut the door, and nothing remains behind.[69]

V

24, West Chaldon stood in the middle of a field under High Chaldon hill, about fifty yards in from the road which runs between East and West Chaldon. It was rented from a farmer who was in turn a tenant of the Weld estate, the major local landowner. The house had no electricity, no mains water, sanitation or damp course and though distempered thoroughly and decorated by Sylvia and Valentine before they moved in, always ran with condensation at the least excuse. There was no bathroom; they had a chemical toilet and bathed in a galvanised tub in front of the fire, using water hand-pumped outside and heated in a copper. It was obviously not a house where either Sylvia or Valentine felt they would stay long, though the two and a half years they spent at West Chaldon were happy ones: 'we loved and we loved and we loved,'[70] as Sylvia wrote it, remembering '24' many years later.

Valentine had private reasons for approving of the new house: 'It will be solitary and sombre and stern and perhaps I shall be able to take myself in hand,'[71] she wrote, thinking of her continued dependence on drink, which was making her feel trapped and desperate. In 1935, she made a concerted effort to give up drink altogether, marking her diary in her accustomed way with 'D.D.' – Devoid of Drink – on each successful day.

The libel case opened at the Dorchester Assizes on 18 January 1935, heard by Mr Justice Findlay. Llewelyn, a chronic consumptive, was very ill at the time but determined to attend the trial in person. He was taken across the downs in his sister Katie's dog-cart, and from Chaldon to Dorchester in Mrs Thomas Hardy's car. His entrance into the courtroom on a stretcher, defiantly clutching a daffodil, prompted the headline in the *News of the World* on 20 January: 'Dying Man in Dorset Assize Drama'. At the trial, it was claimed that the occasion of publishing the petition, i.e. it being sent to the Dorset County Council, was not 'privileged' because the words 'Private and Confidential' did not appear on it. Having ascertained this, it was the jury's job to decide whether or not the defendants had acted maliciously in publishing it. After the summing-up, which took place on 21 January, the jury was absent for an hour and a half. The verdict went against the defendants; Llewelyn Powys and James Cobb were fined £100 each, Valentine and Sylvia £50 each in damages. The costs, which they were presented with two months later, were an altogether more serious matter. Llewelyn's costs amounted to £573 8s 3d, Sylvia's and Valentine's a staggering £733 15s 3d. Valentine wrote in her diary, 'I've had to raise a loan – I can NEVER pay it off now',[72] and indeed she owed her mother money for over twenty-five years because of it. Sylvia set about selling some of her shares – a last-ditch measure, for her generation was extremely reluctant to touch capital, and Sylvia had kept hers intact all through previous financial crises. Small donations towards the costs came in from sympathisers, but even so, Sylvia and Valentine were left very badly off by the case, eating rabbits shot by Valentine with her .22 rifle, and sometimes little else.

Valentine's concern about the spread of Fascism in Europe and the popularity of the Fascist party in Britain had already directed her towards taking politics more seriously, and in a more practical spirit. She had had reservations about Communism as recently as 1933, when she and Sylvia met a Communist in London who said he would die to protect his portrait of Lenin. His piety and the fact that he was 'possessed by the [...] spirit of self-justification through violence' had deeply offended her. 'But Communism is all mixed up with religion now', she wrote in her diary. 'It is the new religion – As bad as the others have been.'[73] By 1934, however, her attention to the Nazi atrocities had changed her mind. The trial in Germany of the Bulgarian Communist Dimitrov, accused of organising the Reichstag fire of 1933, also helped convince Valentine, and Sylvia, of the rightness of the Communist cause. Sylvia particularly admired Dimitrov's 'extraordinary courage and enterprise and *poise*',[74] reading in *The Times* each day of the proceedings, how Dimitrov defended himself brilliantly by turning the tables on his Nazi accusers. While Sylvia was reading *The Times*, Valentine was reading the *Daily Worker*, to which she began to subscribe in December 1934. Valentine also subscribed to *Left Review*, the magazine set up by Edgell Rickword in 1933, and she began to write a series of articles for it, called 'Country Dealings', exposing the bad conditions of the poor in the country, citing real cases and plenty of facts, gathered first-hand in Chaldon and Winterton. Sylvia, impressed by the intensity of Valentine's convictions, began to consider her own. She found that they were dislikes rather than beliefs: 'Priests in their gowns, anti-semitism, the white man who is the black man's burden, warmongers – I had long been sure of them but, beyond a refusal to give money to people who came collecting for missionary societies, my convictions remained unacted desires. Perhaps this was not enough.'[75] A mordant poem of Sylvia's, 'In this Midwinter', which appeared in the January 1935 issue of *Left Review*, shows how quickly and completely Sylvia followed Valentine's lead:

> In this midnight, shepherds, not a saviour possibly.
> No godling, God not even in turncoat mufti of doubt.
> Man having rationalised destruction inalienably
> Needs God no further. See, not a King is out.
> War, famine, pestilence, not a saviour now, shepherds.
> Light not lantern on such an idle errand.

In the spring of 1935, after the usual formalities of application, they were both admitted as members of the Communist Party of Great Britain.

There were no half-measures about this step. They threw themselves into Party business with all the energy of the newly-converted disposal. In February they attended a United Front demonstration in Hyde Park and met Tom Wintringham, the socialist M.P. and writer, with whom they had many dealings over the subsequent months and years. He was one of a number of new friends Sylvia and Valentine made through political activism, many of whom they had nothing in common with but Party loyalty. After a May Day rally in London, Sylvia wrote to Julius Lipton, a young poet: 'I appreciate how lucky we are, coming newly into the Party, and from such a dubious quarter, middle-class homes and genteel upholstery, to have met you so early and to have had your greeting and welcome'[76] – the tone of which is almost apologetic. Later she was to write that in the early thirties, the Communist Party of Great Britain 'was accepting new adherents from what it thought of as the Bourgeoisie and called the Intellectuals'.[77] If at first Sylvia felt conspicuous in the Communist Party, she did not let it trouble her and indeed tried to turn her apparent inappropriateness to advantage, more than pleased to exploit gentility to further the cause. In *Summer Will Show*, the book Sylvia was working at seriously all through 1935, the heroine, Sophia Willoughby, has a similar experience of finding her class and background difficult for the revolutionaries of 1848 to overlook. The Communist Ingelbrecht, approving a comment, remarks: 'I wish more republicans thought like this aristocrat. But your brains are in the wrong place. They should be under a red cap instead of a fashionable bonnet. Why were you not born one of your own poachers, Mrs Willoughby?'[78]

Asked, in an interview forty years later, about her politics, Sylvia said, 'I became a Communist because I was agin the Government but that of course is not a suitable frame of mind for a Communist for very long. [...] I was a Communist, but I always find anarchists very easy to get on with. I think that's because if the English turn to the left at all, they are natural anarchists.'[79] A great part of her attraction to Communism was its anti-authoritarian stance. In extremist politics she found a satisfactory way of expressing her personal revulsion from all the corruptions, large and petty, done in the name of democracy and tolerated for the sake of peace and quiet. In this sense, her politics were idealistic. The letter to Julius Lipton goes on to make a criticism which only a recent convert, mindful of the rubric, could make. She is writing of a concert at the Aeolian Hall on the evening of the May Day rally:

> Music is important enough, but not concerts adjusted to the usual convention; and though this one was well enough, and one quartet by Starokadomsky really admirable, it was a little tainted with snobbishness and pretence, a Party snobbishness of people going there and applauding the music, not because they like music in general or this music in particular but because they had been told it was Soviet music and therefore to be applauded of course. But they gave themselves away, as shams must; for the pieces that had the greatest applause were those which had the least to distinguish them from any other capitalist luxury music.

Music, about which she was so sure-footed, showed her that, (though her observation is not free of a snobbishness of her own) but as time went on such discriminations became rarer as Sylvia's, prejudices in favour of all things Soviet developed and hardened. Having espoused the cause, she stood by it and brought to bear on adherence to matters of Party faith all her strength of character.

Another element in Sylvia's wholehearted enthusiasm for Communism was the way in which it underlined the sense of ostracism she and Valentine had been made to feel because they were lesbians. Rather than being slightly outcast, they could move themselves beyond the conventional altogether. Thus Communism conferred a blessing on their marriage and, because it was so closely tied up with their love for each other, became sacrosanct.

The first of Valentine's articles on 'Country Dealings' appeared in *Left Review* in March 1935, and criticised the scarcity of good, state-run hospitals 'OPEN TO ALL – ALWAYS', illustrating her argument by relating the events leading up to Granny Moxon's death. It ends rather clumsily with Valentine saying 'Communism would be a good thing for us, comrades' (not a necessary reminder to *Left Review* subscribers), but the two following articles, published in May and September, showed her more at home with her material and arguments. Her subjects – the actual conditions hidden under a picturesque thatch, the poor pay and precarious status of the farm labourer, the cheap-skating of landowners – were all very close to her heart. Behind every political point was a personal observation. Her third article contains a description of the 'Intellectuals' of her home village – Chaldon – amongst whom, interestingly, she no longer numbered herself or Sylvia:

> Down here [...] we do not suffer from the County much. Our gentry are the Intellectuals. They are nicer, on the whole. They shut the gates and do no damage to the crops (such crops as there are) and sometimes they will take up a case of injustice and support the exploited and reason with the farmer, occasionally with good results. But they are not really profitable, except that they tip well. They have an idea that the land-worker is ideally situated, that he has unmatched opportunities for studying Nature, that he has, because of this constant contact with the mother, sublimated his needs and desires, and that they themselves can achieve content-ment and all-wisdom by copying the labourer's way of life.
>
> So they take the best houses and spend their days in the open air. Some of the more devout do their own housework and cooking. Further than that, wisely, they do not go. The only solid consolation is that none of them do their household washing, and this brings in a few shillings to the publican's wife. But beyond that there is nothing much to be said for them, from the worker's point of view.[80]

In the spring, Valentine bought a duplicating machine of the drum-and-stencil variety and used it to produce news bulletins, letters and agitprop leaflets for local Party sympathisers. She was also putting her articles and thoughts together for a book about conditions in the country, her first separate publication. Sylvia had no involvement in this, preferring to exercise her ingenuity in composing satirical sketches and biting book reviews for *Left Review* and tuning her intellect to the needs of the Party. In a letter to Julius Lipton of 13 April 1935, she argued how important form was to 'our party's poems', being easier to learn and easier 'for the worker to carry round in his memory'. Even in the context of the idealism of the times, this is slightly absurd, and ironically close to the 'Intellectual' attitude which Valentine had satirised in her article. But partisanship was now the principle by which Sylvia lived.

Rallies and marches, a sortie into South Wales to demonstrate at a pit-head, political meetings, committees; these activities dominated both women's lives in 1935. On 6 May, they organised a bonfire on top of the Five Marys in opposition to the King's Jubilee junketings in the village, and were pleased that the dancing at their party lasted much longer and was more exuberant. And when Sylvia decided that she would like to visit Tushielaw again, twenty years after her last holiday there, they drove to it via Burnley and enjoyed – for the first time – a 'magnificent view of industrial towns'.[81]

Their visitors that summer were mostly Party-related friends: Tom Wintringham and his wife Kitty, a couple called Bob and Isa from Bournemouth, two young communists, Kit and Pat Dooley, and Edgell Rickword's wife Johnnie. Janet Machen, then eighteen years old, was able to come and visit without her parents, and was treated by both Sylvia and Valentine with great fondness, more like a younger sister than a cousin. Elizabeth Wade White, the rich young American Sylvia had befriended in New York in 1929, came to stay too. Sylvia was very pleased at what she thought was a degree of political zealotry emerging in the impressionable Elizabeth during her visit, not perceiving the real object of the young woman's enthusiasm: Valentine. To Sylvia she was just someone – with money – who might prove helpful to the Party.

Sylvia and Valentine had bought a small second-hand caravan in which to sleep in the garden; 'and if it weren't for the fact that second-hand air-mattresses leak, and have to be reblown up at intervals of every two hours or so, I could describe it as very restful and refreshing,'[82] Sylvia wrote to Julius Lipton. It was a handy place to be out of guests' way, for some guests, like Jean Untermeyer, could be wearing, and Sylvia and Valentine still longed more than anything else for each other's company. Little worker to carry round in his memory'. Even in the context of the

Miss Green's together, Jean had been so impressed by Sylvia's and Valentine's attentions: 'I was always being urged to rest, and one would come to my bedside with the indispensable hot-water bottle against the damp, the other with a steaming cup of Sedebrol to make sure that sleep should come and relax me. Happy memories!'[83]

During her stay at '24' in 1935, Jean Untermeyer did Sylvia an unimaginably good turn. In the course of conversation Sylvia described 'some absurd thing which had happened in the village and she [Jean] said, "You really ought to write that for the *New Yorker*."'[84] The idea of the *New Yorker* taking any such thing, written by her, seemed to Sylvia so unlikely that she made a bet with Jean that the magazine would reject her. Later in the year, she submitted 'My Mother Won the War' and the *New Yorker* accepted it, publishing the story on 30 May 1936, the first of over a hundred and fifty stories to appear in its pages over the next forty years. Apart from the distinction of being admitted to the *New Yorker* 'club', the subsequent widening of her following in America and the fact that, by having a market, she had a motive to develop her talent as a short-story writer, Sylvia's association with the magazine made her financially secure (once the effect had taken hold) for the rest of her life. She used to refer to the *New Yorker* as 'my gentleman friend' and, remembering the bet with Jean Untermeyer, once said, 'I had to forfeit the five pounds. But on the whole, it was a good bargain.'[85]

Unfortunately, Valentine never found herself such a golden goose and remained a very low earner from her writing. The disparity in their incomes, which grew yearly, was not of any importance to Sylvia, though it troubled Valentine deeply. Her instinct was to provide for and cherish Sylvia, and her conscience and pride were against being constantly supported, being a 'parasite'. Sylvia disclaiming this made no difference to her feelings.

1935 was, on the whole, a good year for Valentine. Party business kept her occupied and she seemed at last to be getting the better of her drink problem, marking 'D.D.' against 126 days. She was working hard and seriously at her book, called 'Country Conditions', taking herself and it off for days at a time to Rats

Barn, over the downs from '24'. Her method in 'Country Conditions' was expository rather than discursive, and akin to the method of her poems, expressive, lyrical. Her political commitment and the example of like-minded contemporary poets (Auden, most inevitably and strongly) was such, though, that she felt it desirable to adjust the method of her poems to serve better the purpose of the time. The issues were what mattered, not some increment in a personal poetic development. The urge to justify her politics, convert and answer her own class was strong and resulted in poems such as 'Communist Poem, 1935'. It is interesting to note how the explanatory style of this poem was adopted by, rather than assimilated into, the 'core' of her own voice, just as literary influences in her earlier days – of Dickinson, Thomas, Lawrence, Hopkins – had been taken up, and as easily put by.

"What must we do, in a country lost already,
Where already the mills stop, already the factories
Wither inside themselves, kernels smalling in shells,
('Fewer hands – fewer hands') and all the ploughed lands
Put down to grass, to bungalows, to graveyards already.

What's in a word? *Comrade*, while still our country
Seems solid around us, rotting – but still our country.
Comrade is rude, uncouth; bandied among youths
Idle and sick perhaps, wandering with other chaps,
Standing around in what is still our country."

Answer them: Over the low hills and the pastures
Come no more cattle, over the land no more herdsmen;
Nothing against the sky now, no stains show
Of smoke. We're done. Only a few work on,
Against time now working to end your time.

Answer: Because the end is coming sooner
Than you allowed for, hail the end as salvation.
Watch how the plough wounds, hear the unlovely sounds
Of syrens wring the air; how everything
Labours again, cries out, and again breeds life.

Here is our life, say: Where the dismembered country
Lies, a dead foeman rises a living comrade.
Here where our day begins and your day dims
We part – announce it. And then with lightened heart
Watch life swing round, complete the revolution.[86]

There is very little special pleading in this poem. The doom-laden view of England was not peculiar to Communists, nor to Valentine in particular, but a widely-held recognition of the crisis which the whole capitalist world was experiencing. Everyone was affected by the decayed state of the economy. In the political polarisation which followed, Valentine – the ex-Young Conservative – went far to the left, with many of the intellectuals of the day. It was a natural step, presenting itself, in the words of the title of a book which had influenced her, as The Only Way Out. Sylvia's standpoint was not quite the same: it was not so purely humanitarian, further to the Left, ideologically severer and, on account of her greater age, she had a different historical perspective. Sylvia's long poem 'Red Front', read as a declamation in Battersea late in 1935 and again in Whitechapel in 1936 (Sylvia was not able to attend), with its worker-memorable chorus in common time, harks back to the Great War, the war promoted as the one to end wars, and takes an overview of the whole period, using the image of 'the saddest wine that ever was pressed in France' for the war's legacy:

Who would have thought the blood of our friends would
    taste so thin?
Would so soon lose body, would even before them greyed –
Had time kept troth – discolour, dwindle and pine
Into a shallow cider tanged with tin?
Who could forecast this malady of the vine,
Or guess that a draught so heady in its beginning
Should peter out into verjuice, and a bouquet
Of metal and decay? –
And that we who toasted them then should sit here dumb,
Unjoyed and yet athirst, and yet dreading the jolted cask,
    dismayed

To stir in the stumbling echo the rolling of tumbrils, the
sullen footfall of a drum?[87]

To the cynic, this might present itself as Sylvia's attempt to co-opt
the war-dead into the Party rank and file, but she was not
time-serving here. The alarming passage about the war which
appears in the middle of her otherwise 'light' narrative poem,
Opus 7, is just as bitter, if not more so. She did not suddenly pick
up these observations with her Party card, but they fell into place
in the context of her politics, and if she had been flippant before
about the antics of politicians of all parties (and she had), it was
due to a residual faith in The System, that old vintage: 'but it was
madness we quaffed'.

The practical application of Sylvia's and Valentine's politics to
life in Chaldon sometimes proved difficult. They had hoped to
organise a Chaldon Women's March on the Weld estate office in
April to complain about the condition of houses in the village, but
the West Chaldon women were in no state to be organised, since
they were all at each other's throats over the goings-on of a local
seductress (called, implausibly, Blanche Rocket). Sylvia, who had
found eight dead rats in the well, went alone to challenge the
Welds with a glass of their contaminated water, though the upshot
of this protest is unknown. The general election of 14 November
1935 provided better opportunities for Sylvia and Valentine to
raise the political awareness of the village: they canvassed support
for the Labour candidate, organised Labour meetings in the village
hall (the former Sunday School) which were chaired by a labourer,
and drove to electoral meetings all over the area. Sylvia discovered
in herself a talent for heckling: 'I found that of all things I loved
making rude remarks at the top of my voice and that the top of my
voice was gratifyingly loud and nasty.'[88] When Sylvia was not
heckling, Valentine was tooting a hand-horn at appropriate
moments. On polling day itself, which was wet and blustery, the
MG came into its own and Valentine clocked up 102 miles taking
villagers, one at a time, to the polling station where Sylvia waited
from ten in the morning till the polls closed at nine, 'entertaining
them or being entertained'.[89] The Conservative got in, of course,
but Sylvia and Valentine felt the moral victory was theirs.

In January 1936, Sylvia finished the novel she had been writing since 1932, *Summer Will Show*. It was a much longer book than any of her previous novels and completely different in tone, pace and purpose. The story, set in 1848, is that of a young English landowning gentlewoman, Sophia Willoughby, who, having lost her two children by smallpox, decides to seek out her estranged husband Frederick, a sentimental, malleable man living extravagantly in Paris. It is her husband's mistress, though, with whom Sophia throws in her lot, an ageing Jewish *demi-mondaine* called Minna Lemuel, whose dramatic character dominates the book. The events of the two revolutions of 1848 in Paris unfold around the growing intimacy between these two women; and Sophia, at first completely removed from the revolutionary cause, gradually perceives its importance and gives herself over to it. The biographical parallels are obvious: Minna and Sophia are to a great extent Sylvia and Valentine; Sophia's modulation from aristocrat to revolutionary Communist both a depiction of Valentine's own conversion and a parable for the Thirties. But the book is not properly a propaganda effort. It was started long before Sylvia espoused Communism. Because she did not discard the early part, the political message of the book is not completely integrated in the way one would expect of a novel written primarily to promote the Party. Though Sylvia hoped it to be a salvo, it was not widely recognised as such when the book was published late in 1936. It is the narrative, taut and ruthless, which arrests one's attention.

The relationship between Sophia and Minna Lemuel is the backbone of the narrative, and Minna's influence all-pervading. Minna is one of Sylvia's most charming creations, observed at length and with remarkable attention to gesture and tone of voice, the actress tricks that make her at once 'the world's wiliest baggage' and a genuine innocent, 'completely humble and sincere'. Part II of the novel plunges straight into Minna's dramatic narrative of her escape from the pogrom in Lithuania, and here Sylvia achieves an important coup; having said that Minna is a spell-binder, she makes her one. The narrative, with its complete change of pace and tone, pushes the reader into the Parisian drawing-room along with Sophia. One is, for its duration, more of a listener than a reader.

Summer Will Show is an unillusioned book, a quality remarkable in a political novel. Idealists and exploiters of ideals are viewed in the same clear light. There is no sentimentalising or romanticising of the cause Sophia espouses, indeed she never does anything so definite as espouse it, and is not ever completely accepted by the people she chooses to help. There is no revolutionary halo around the part she has to play, nor round her – the reader is not spared her slightly acid feelings of having been snubbed by the real revolutionaries. This is part of what makes *Summer Will Show* a really remarkable historical novel. The ordinariness of historical events, even revolutions, is conveyed intact; there is not a breath of quaintness or 'period feel' to the writing. As in her later novels, there is a complete identification with the period chosen, a contemporary feel which goes far beyond the scope of historical accuracy to a sense of historical actuality.

At the same time that Sylvia was finishing her novel, Valentine was completing *Country Conditions*. She was writing poems as frequently as ever, and in addition sending in 'reportage' to the *Daily Worker* and *New Masses* on a regular basis. She was a fervent writer to the papers at this date and would send off letters of protest or warning sometimes to as many as eight newspapers simultaneously. In one short article for the *Daily Worker*, she reminded readers of a book published in 1934, *Germany Unmasked* by Robert Dell, and pointed out how Dell's predictions of inevitable European war seemed to be coming true, and in a note in a separate edition of the *Worker* she advised comrades to tune to Athlone 531m. after the BBC news and compare the broadcasts. No Mosleyite meeting or unseemly state fraternisations went unprotested by her, and often the letters to the local papers carried the signatures of the Chaldon Powyses as well, and, of course, Sylvia's. All was vigilance and urgency. Valentine felt it was her duty as one who saw what was happening to alert those who, as yet, had not seen.

It was in the *News of the World* in March 1936 that Valentine read how a Lancashire cotton worker, George Brennand, had walked the 300 miles from Blackburn to Dorset in search of a job and, having collapsed outside Dorchester, had been taken to the County Infirmary. She was so moved by this story that she went to visit Brennand in hospital and there heard that he was about to be discharged. He had nowhere to go, so, on an impulse of pity, Valentine offered to put him up at 24 West Chaldon. This turned out to be one of her less satisfying acts of comradeship. Brennand was at the house for a week, during which time Sylvia thought she would certainly lose her temper, for he was a boastful, over-talkative man, given to singing 'Abide With Me' in a loud voice for no particular reason. In an article in the *News of the World* that week, under the heading 'Poetess's Kindly Act', 'Miss K. Ackland, the poetess' told the paper 'We are trying to find him work',[90] which she did conscientiously, writing letters of introduction for him and driving about after jobs. These efforts did not bear fruit, though, and Brennand cheerfully went back to his sister's house in Lancashire.

East Chaldon received further coverage in the press when the *News Chronicle* – presumably prompted by someone in the village – published a short article called 'Seven Authors in Search of Peace', lamenting the plight of those who 'strove to write their perfect book' while 'thousands of trippers' jostled past their front doors on the way to Lulworth Cove, a beauty spot about four miles from Chaldon. The seven 'Chaldon' authors were Theodore, Llewelyn, John Cowper and Katie Powys, Alyse Gregory, Valentine and Sylvia and, as in a fairy tale, their years of peace and inspiration also numbered seven. 'Then came the Tourist, and for two years T.F. Powys has not written a line.' Author-spotters had, apparently, parked outside Beth Car to catch a glimpse of Theo and, in Violet's words to the reporter, 'thrown their banana-skins into our garden. It is terrible, and it is getting worse.' Theodore took a more metaphysical view: 'I have a queer dislike of humanity [...] My brothers are like that too. We have a love for the individual, but a dislike of humanity. I don't suppose it is fair of me to object to visitors. To the village woman every strange face provides a new interest, every car distracts attention from the monotony of home routine.'[91] In another paper, covering the same story under the title 'Powysland', Theo added, 'When we see a motorist we hope, in our queer way, that he might be a burglar, but he is usually nothing more interesting than an honest gentleman.'[92] Sylvia's only contribution to the article was to appeal to the reporter not to reveal the whereabouts of her cottage.

What was much more on the minds of Sylvia and Valentine that summer was the situation in Spain, the growing urgency of which acted as a catalyst on so many people's politics, propelling significant numbers of Sylvia's and Valentine's contemporaries into the Communist Party and the International Brigades. At last, there was an issue so clear and so fundamental to democracy and human rights – the defence of a legally elected government against a rebellious right-wing military – that no right-minded person could ignore it. The support it engendered in this country for socialist ideals and the subsequent swelling of Party ranks must have been very satisfying to the two women, justifying their own efforts over the preceding year to awaken the populace to the dangers of Fascism, and raising them from crank status to the status of prophetesses. The Party was more acceptable than ever before in 1936, financially strong and almost popular, and Sylvia's and Valentine's positions in it were strong too, for they had proved amply their loyalty and readiness to take on inglorious, necessary jobs. Within eighteen months of joining the Party, they had become its leading local members. Sylvia was sent to Brussels for three days in September 1936 as a member of the British delegation to an International Peace Congress, organised by the Party, and was to be sent out again, this time to Paris, on unspecified 'Party business' the following year. In June 1936 she was elected secretary of the Dorset Peace Council, a job involving an enormous amount of paper work, which she undertook efficiently and willingly. They were also founder members of the local Readers' and Writers' Group affiliated to the Left Book Club and were doggedly committed money-raisers for the Party, Valentine especially taking pride in each small contribution and noting them all down. They began soliciting money for Harry Pollitt's Spanish Fund very soon after the attempted coup in July which triggered off the Spanish Civil War.

At the beginning of the war, Valentine longed to join the *miliciana*, the women combatants on the Government side, and some cryptic entries in her diary in August – 'called to London', 'saw Harry', 'waiting', 'hopeful' – suggest she came near to realising some such ambition. Beth Valentine and Sylvia were willing and free to go to Spain at a moment's notice, but the Party did not take them up on their offer to be first-aid volunteers. On 16 September, though, they had a telegram from Tom Wintringham in Barcelona, calling them up, as it were, to work with a Red Cross unit there. Wintringham had joined the International Brigade at the start of the war and his wife Kitty had gone with him to Spain to work with the first-aid groups. Wintringham was later the commander of the British Battalion in Spain, fell foul of the Communist Party and was expelled for the sort of independent action of which his contacting Sylvia and Valentine is a minor example.

Sylvia and Valentine set sail from Southampton on 18 September and arrived in Barcelona eight days later, having been turned back twice at Port Bou before they succeeded in crossing into Spain, an effect of the British Government's policy of non-intervention. They were met by Wintringham, who took them round the hospital where their unit was based. The work was clerical as much as medical, and lasted only three weeks, but in that time Sylvia developed a passion for Spain to match her passion for politics, seeing embodied in the spirit of Republican Spain the principles she held most dear:

> I don't think I have ever met so many congenial people in the whole of my life, liking overleapt any little bounds of language. My substantives were Spanish, my verbs, being picked up locally, were Catalan. I got on beautifully. Barcelona, by the time we saw it, was I suppose the nearest thing I shall ever see to the early days of U.S.S.R. ... the very first days, when everything was proceeding on the impulse of that first leap into life. After the military rising, combatted in its first showing by an almost unbelievable mixture, police and middle-class (it happened all of a sudden when the workers were boxed in the factories) after a couple of days fighting, Barcelona was taken over by committees of trades union men, and the workers' militia; in other words, it is a Soviet town. [...] And you cannot imagine, after this mealy-mouthed country, the pleasure of seeing an office with

a large painted sign, Organisation for the Persecution of Fascists.[93]

Sylvia was very much impressed with the tranquillity of Barcelona only two months after the 'July days', when soldiers from the nearby barracks of Montjuich opened fire in the Plaza de Catalonia, triggering days of fierce and bloody fighting. Evidence of the battle was in the state of the churches, all gutted and boarded up, and in the wreath of flowers, replaced every day, which hung on one particular tram, used by the citizens to storm the military barricaded in the baroque church on the Ramblas. Sylvia and Valentine looked approvingly on the graffiti and posters asserting No Pasarán and the little stalls around the Plaza: 'Mixed with the old wares, the flowers, the shaving brushes, the canaries and lovebirds, the watermelons, are new wares: militia caps, pistols (toy-pistols to our shame be it spoken), rings and badges and brooches carrying the initials of the anarchist F.A.I. and C.N.T., the Trotskyist P.O.U.M., the Communist P.S.U.C. and U.G.T.'[94] They bought a selection of these things and some less politically pertinent objects such as handkerchiefs and ties and, on their return to England, donated them to the Daily Worker to auction for the Spanish Fund.

Sylvia admired the people of Barcelona, their sober determination and spirit as they drilled with broomsticks, having sent most of their weapons to threatened Madrid. The Spaniard Sylvia got to know best on this visit, and the one she admired most, was a large, generous woman called Asunción at whose house on the Calle Joaquin Costa Sylvia and Valentine were lodged and who personified for Sylvia the common sense and right-thinking of the ordinary people, 'a people naturally intellectual, and with a long standard of culture'.[95] 'People like Asunción have not any nationality at all, I feel. They just belong to the good, with a few local traits and a language.'[96] Also billeted at Asunción's house was a young Englishman called Steven Clark who was in Barcelona to make a report for a group sending medical aid to Spain. Valentine had first seen him through the window of a hotel in the city and had been impressed by his carriage and handsome head. When Steven came down with influenza during their stay, and Sylvia and Valentine helped to nurse him, a long friendship began.

One of the jaunts for foreign visitors was an inspection tour of the *torres*, the large villas on the hills overlooking the city where the rich had so recently lived. The houses had been preserved, their art works and heavy taste in sideboards all in place. Only the valuables which were meltable and considered by the *Comité* as being of no artistic interest had been removed. All this was in keeping with the Government's policy of protecting Spanish art from the civil war, but it was not this moral contrast with the destructive behaviour of Franco's men which interested Sylvia most. In an article for *Left Review*, published in December 1936, she noted something else about the phenomenon:

> The works of ecclesiastical art are in the museums, the churches are bare and barred. Apologists in this country have tended to stress the first statement, but the second is the more significant. Those systematically gutted interiors are the more impressive when one contrasts them with the preservation of the villas. In the villas was as great, or greater, a demonstration of luxury, idleness and superbity. In the villas were objects infinitely more desirable as loot than anything the churches could offer. Had the churches been sacked, as some say they were, by a greedy and envious mob, that mob would have sacked the villas with more greed and better satisfaction. But the villas are untouched, and the churches are gutted. They have been cleaned out exactly as sick-rooms are cleaned out after a pestilence. Everything that could preserve the contagion has been destroyed.[97]

And, as Sylvia pointed out in the same article, what went on in Barcelona was not, as assumed by many at home, a Marxist-inspired plot, though she might have wished it to be. Barcelona was an anarchist town and 'it was the people themselves who, deliberately and systematically, put the churches out of action.' Sylvia nursed a soft spot for anarchists all her life. In a letter written soon after her return from Barcelona, she said of anarchism, 'the world is not yet worthy of it, but it ought to be the political theory of heaven.'[98]

Sylvia and Valentine left Port Bou on 14 October and arrived back in Chaldon on the 22nd. Valentine immediately set about writing articles and reports based on what she had seen in Spain. One letter to the *News Chronicle* appealed for food ships to be sent out to counter the acute shortages occasioned by floods of refugees into the cities. It was a humanitarian appeal, not a political one, and stressed that groceries 'cannot possibly be considered as dangerous weapons'. This was published on 7 November, the day on which the rebels reached the suburbs of Madrid and the Republican Government left the city – all except the leader, Largo Caballero. The next day, the first International Brigade was on the streets of Madrid, driving Franco's rebels back, the first of many such tentative holdings-on. The fall of the capital seemed so imminent that Germany and Italy recognised Franco's 'Government' on 18 November, though in fact the general did not take Madrid for another two and a half years.

On 24 November, Valentine was called to London by Party officials. She was needed to drive one of two lorries going out to Valencia, just the sort of job she had longed to do. Back at '24', Sylvia waited in agonies, contemplating the risks Valentine was taking: 'I sat alone in the house, frozen with cold and despair, rigid with courage and party loyalty.'[99] But when Valentine reached London, she found she had a temperature of 103 degrees and a pain she attributed to colitis which got progressively worse, and on 26 November she was waving the lorries off, rather than driving one away. Sylvia came to fetch her home, where she remained ill for about a week, and the Party, unsurprisingly, never made Valentine another like offer.

VI

Summer Will Show was published while Sylvia and Valentine were in Spain and *Country Conditions* soon after their return. The political significance of Sylvia's novel was lost on the reviewers, most of whom were struck rather by the difference between this book and her novels of the 1920s. 'The small but devoted public of her past,' wrote the *Chicago Tribune*, 'may regret her abandonment of a genre distinctly her own, but "Summer Will Show" will bring her a wider public', while another paper put it more crudely by referring to Sylvia as 'the woman who wrote *Mr Fortune's Maggot* nine years ago'. During those nine years, Sylvia had gradually fallen out of the public view, and she was never fashionable again, though she always had appreciative readers and sold reasonably well. In America, where her initial impact had been greater, her memory stayed greener, and the appearance of her distinctive stories in the *New Yorker* ensured her a small but devoted following. In England, her new political commitment did nothing to enhance her popularity with reviewers, nor did authorship of *Lolly Willowes* cut much ice with Communists. Fortunately for Sylvia, the dynamic behind both her inconsistency and her unshakeable opinions was a complete indifference to the opinions of people outside her sphere of affection. According to Valentine, Sylvia never read reviews of her own books, though she valued the comments of friends and fellow-writers very much. The pecking-order of writers did not interest her. 'People always want to fix a standard for everything,' she once said. 'I do wish they would just let something happen and watch it without thinking they must look it up in Crockford's or somewhere.'[100]

Country Conditions, which was published by Lawrence & Wishart at two shillings, was reviewed well, but not much outside 'the Party parish'. The book's political argument was very clear and expressed without melodrama in Valentine's portrait of a depressed agricultural village, a thinly veiled East Chaldon, and a put-upon family, the Dorys, based on Jimmy and May Pitman, who were still Sylvia's and Valentine's tenants at Miss Green's cottage. Valentine included in the appendices figures comparing farm wages across Britain to prove that her depiction of life in Wessex was not untypical of conditions throughout the country. Finally she set out comparisons of the hours and wages of workers in the USSR with those in Germany and Italy, to widen the field of her argument. It was this that riled the reviewer in the *Times Literary Supplement*, who dismissed the whole book as distorted propaganda, 'resolutely arguing from the particular to the general. The particular hamlet set before us by the author may exist precisely as she describes it: to hold it up as an example of the English village is quite unfair.'[101] This was the only really unfavourable review; many were enthusiastic, and what was constantly noticed was the effectiveness of Valentine's method: 'eloquent in its restrained indignation'.[102] As for the sales (it was a very short book, almost a tract), the publisher reported that they were 'keeping up quite well' and that he had sold 402 copies in the first month. Her first royalty cheque was for £4 0s 4d – hardly a fortune, but a distinct improvement on her dealings with Viking Press, where her account never broke even due to the quantities of copies of *Whether a Dove or Seagull* she ordered for her family and friends.

1937 began bleakly with the news first of the death of Ralph Fox, an English novelist fighting in Spain, and then the deaths, printed in the same newspaper column, of Stephen Tomlin and Dorothy Warner. Tommy's marriage to Julia Strachey had broken up finally in 1934 and his life had been increasingly miserable and uncreative since then. 'For the past 3 or 4 years we had scarcely seen him,' wrote Virginia Woolf in her diary on 19 January 1937, 'when we did he seemed ravaged by his own misery; couldn't work, had been a failure; tore everyone & everything to bits in a kind of egotistical rage. Rosamund L. said he would sit on the lawn there by the hour denouncing women, complaining of his own lot. And he had grown immensely fat, white unwholesome looking, & was said to drink.' Tommy had been taken into hospital just before Christmas suffering from blood-poisoning after what had seemed a routine tooth-extraction under gas. He became very ill with pneumonia on top of the septicaemia, seemed to be improving, but died suddenly on 5 January, aged thirty-five. 'A tragic, wasted life;' wrote Mrs Woolf, 'something wrong in it, & wrong that we shouldn't feel it more. Yet one does, by fits & starts, this very fine spring morning.' Whatever Sylvia's feelings were, she did not share them unless with her diary of that period which no longer exists, and there was no question of her wishing to attend the funeral at Ash in Kent.

Dorothy Warner's death was just as unexpected. The history of the Warnerium since Sylvia's departure in 1930 had not been happy: Dorothy had had recurrent bouts of mental illness, Oliver had attempted suicide. By 1936 the couple had separated and were considering a divorce, but Dorothy contracted pneumonia following a blood-transfusion, and died the day after Tommy, aged thirty-seven.

On January 17th, Sylvia and Valentine received more alarming news in a report that Tom Wintringham had been killed in the particularly fierce fighting in and around Madrid during those weeks. He was not dead, as it turned out, though he was wounded soon after. The intensification of the war and the death of acquaintances such as Fox and another Communist, Jerry Birch, gave a sense of urgency to Sylvia's and Valentine's political activities at home. They attended Peace Council meetings in Bridport, Labour Party meetings in Weymouth, a Peace Rally in Yeovil. They were esteemed sufficiently – either for their mild publicity value or for their sheer reliability – to be put on the platform at a Labour meeting alongside the local Parliamentary candidate and Sir Stafford Cripps. And all the time, Valentine was writing articles and reviews, sending out pamphlets, answering correspondences with earnest readers of her book and writing a great many poems. It was at this time too that she and Sylvia used to drive round nearby Bovingdon Camp, placing small anti-war leaflets on the Army's tanks.

Late in June, 1937, Sylvia and Valentine were invited to attend the 2nd International Congress of Writers in Defence of Culture, which had been organised before the outbreak of the Spanish Civil War and was to take place in three centres, Barcelona, Valencia and Madrid at the beginning of July. Sylvia and Valentine were to be part of what Sylvia described as 'a depressingly puny and undistinguished British delegation'[103] which also included Edgell Rickword, Ralph Bates, Frank Pitcairn (Claud Cockburn), John Strachey and the twenty-eight-year old, newly converted Comrade Stephen Spender. Despite the Foreign Office's refusal to validate any of the delegates' passports for Spain, on the grounds that 'cultural reasons' were not sufficient, the party set off, late, for Paris – Sylvia's first, and not pleasurable, experience of air travel. They crossed the Spanish border at Port Bou on 3 July, using false passports arranged for them by André Malraux. Malraux then accompanied them in the fleet of luxury cars which bore the defenders of culture along the mountainous coastal road to Barcelona.

The Congress itself, made up of one hundred and ten delegates from twenty-seven countries, many of them experienced congress-goers, had already moved on to Valencia, the capital of Republican Spain, for the official opening on 4 July by Juan Negrine, the President of the Spanish Government. The Writers' Congress was the most prestigious of no fewer than five congresses going on in Valencia during the first two weeks of July, all supported by the Government as part of a propaganda push. When the British party arrived in Valencia on the evening of 4 July, they were taken immediately to the Consistorial Hall where the second session of the Congress was about to begin, and were greeted enthusiastically. The hall, though gashed and pitted by bombs, had been decorated for the congress with two enormous panels hung behind the platform on which the names of defenders and martyrs of the Republican cause had been inscribed. Between these panels hung the five-pointed red star, symbol of the Popular Front and of the International Brigades. On the platform were several members of the Government and the chairman of the Congress, Alexei Tolstoi.

Sylvia was the fourteenth of the delegates to speak at that session; they included Julien Benda, José Bergamin, Alexei Tolstoi, Tristan Tzara, Anna Seghers and Ralph Bates, leader of the British section. She made a short speech in French which was then translated into Catalan, saluting the Spanish people and reminding the Congress that culture only belongs to the people if it is defended. Not all the contributions were as concise as hers, and after a banquet – all laid on by the Government – she and Valentine fell into bed at their hotel in a state of exhaustion.

The next day the whole Congress moved on to Madrid, one of the front lines of the war, where the main business was to be done, or at least where the ten set themes were to be discussed: The Role of the Writer in Society, Dignity of Thought, The Individual, Humanism, Nation and Culture, The Problems of Spanish Culture, Cultural Inheritance, Literary Creation, Reinforcing Cultural Ties, Aid to the Spanish Writers. On the way from

Valencia to Madrid, the convoy stopped at a village called Minglanilla where the mayor immediately offered to provide an impromptu lunch. As the delegates waited in an inn, drinking lemonade, some of the village children crept in under the tables to have a closer look at *los intelectuales*. 'An Englishwoman'[104] gave them mint pastilles from her pocket; another delegate did tricks for them. The extravagantly hospitable meal which the mayor provided was interrupted by the sound of singing outside, and when the delegates went over to the window and onto the balcony they saw the village children gathered to sing 'The Internationale' and the Republican song known as 'Riego's Hymn'. The delegates applauded and called down greetings; the children, who had probably never themselves eaten a meal like the one cooling indoors, shouted back, 'Viva la republica!' 'Viva los intellectuales!' – 'that extraordinary, unbelievable greeting'[105] as Valentine later described it.

The stop at Minglanilla made a vivid impression on many of the writers present. The enthusiasm with which they were greeted and the hopeful confidence of the village women (there were no healthy young men left there) in the power of the literate brought many of the delegates up sharp. Some, like Valentine, found it very moving and saw in the spirit of the village 'the real future of culture'[106] – a culture in which the word intellectual was never used ironically. Others, like Stephen Spender (in his 1951 account, it must be said, not in the article he wrote in 1937) saw little but irony in the whole episode: 'Speeches, champagne, food, receptions, hotel rooms were a thick hedge dividing us from reality.'[107] The women who, in tears, urged delegates to make known their private and collective tragedies, or who pressed on the foreigners their last scraps of food had, in Spender's eyes, pathetically misplaced their hopes. 'Somehow the villagers of Minglanilla thought that the Congress of Intellectuals was a visitation which would save them' and there was 'something grotesque about it'.[108]

This difference in perception illustrates some of the causes of the pronounced antipathy which grew between Stephen Spender and Sylvia on the trip to Spain in 1937. What she resented in him was the apparent shallowness of his Communism, his almost perverse individualism, his youthful conceit and a tendency to hog publicity. She would have taken his unease at Minglanilla as proof that he was politically compromised and socially embarrassed. For his part, Spender was obviously irritated by Sylvia's voice, manner and apparently blind Party faith, and he caricatured her fairly mercilessly in his memoir *World Within World* as the 'Communist lady writer' who 'looked like, and behaved like, a vicar's wife presiding over a tea party given on a vicarage lawn as large as the whole of Republican Spain. Her extensory smiling mouth and her secretly superior eyes under her shovel hat made her graciously forbidding. She insisted – rather cruelly, I thought – on calling everyone "comrade", and to me her sentences usually began, "Wouldn't it be less selfish, comrade", which she followed by recommending some course of action highly convenient from her point of view'.[109] 'An irritating idealist, always hatching a wounded feeling'[110] is what Sylvia wrote of Spender in a letter to Steven Clark. During her visit to Spain, Sylvia was not in the least interested in the phenomenon of herself abroad; what passionately engaged her were the Spanish people themselves and the practical application of the abstractions of the Congress. Anyone floating around being disruptively cynical or simply furthering their own ends she treated with contempt.

Sylvia loved Spaniards and especially admired Spanish women. When they were in Madrid and the civilian centre of the town was under bombardment by Franco's forces, Sylvia noted that 'the women, on whom these persuasions of shell and bomb are lavished, wear, one and all, whether they are old or young, stupid or intelligent, whether they look well or tired – and most of them look deadly tired – the same expression of indomitable concentrated rage. If you talk to them they are as friendly, as kind, as you please. But the moment they leave off talking this look of whitehot bad temper comes back. It was the most impressive thing I saw in Spain.'[111] There was no sentimentality in her feeling for these people, but a great deal of emotion. Bearing this in mind, and Sylvia's physical responsiveness to anyone in distress, there seems little doubt of the identity of the English writer whom a Spanish journalist and writer, Corpus Barga, observed with admiration at Minglanilla as the delegates were preparing to move on after their lunch:

A Spanish woman all in black from head-scarf to shoes [...] was in the embrace of an English woman writer [...] Her husband executed, her brothers dead in battle. Behind the woman in mourning a child hid in the folds of her skirt. The English writer, knowing no Spanish, understood and comforted her, drawing her ever more closely into her embrace. In the end the two women walked back and forth in each other's arms, weeping without tears [...] The child followed behind, not letting go his mother's skirts, while neighbours looked on passing comments:

"She's not really from here, she's a refugee," they said of the woman clad in mourning, and about the English writer: "No doubt she has found someone from her own country who is comforting her."

It was true what the women of Minglanilla said, and the governments of Europe lie. The illiterate Spanish woman had found someone from her village in the English writer, who had to get into the car and, extending the top half of her body through the window kept hugging her, reluctant to separate herself from her *paisana*.[112]

The Hotel Victoria, where the delegates were staying in Madrid, had already been hit by shells and there was a real danger of it being hit again, though the fighting seemed oddly remote as the guests sat down to another sumptuous banquet on their first evening. Valentine took comfort in the fact that the waiters were calm and that, after a while, one scarcely noticed the sound of distant gun fire. The dinner over, the guests began to sing and converse; some soldiers came in and sang too, but later, 'just as everything was going on well and many of us had got down to talking about literature, which we liked doing, the waiters, with suddenly serious faces, began closing the shutters and putting out some of the lights. Then people began walking out of the room, into the passage, down the stairs. And suddenly the only noise in the world was the noise of gun-fire.'[113]

There was always an air raid at five o'clock, so everyone set their alarms for that time and went down into the hotel foyer for safety. In a letter to Alyse Gregory several years later Valentine recalled 'the strange amorousness' which overcame the sleepy guests that first night in Madrid:

> Sitting on the marble floor of the hall, in close groups of ten and twenty, almost everyone turned to love-making. I went upstairs to fetch my cigarettes [...] and as I left my room, in the flashing darkness of three stories up, I was seized by someone who had come up after me. I found that it was the red-haired Dutch delegate, no word of whose language I knew and who could only speak French with the utmost difficulty, and not at all when he was excited. We had a very sharp struggle (for I was extremely startled, having my mind set on shells and war!) and ran downstairs with the utmost speed – into that odd confusion of amorous bodies ... a kind of lunatic Babel. I remember detaching Sylvia from a West Indian negro who was weeping on her breast but who seemed perfectly contented to be moved gently onto a next-door French woman who herself had been making very sophisticated love to a tall, large Swedish woman next to her. And then, to make all things totally mad, two English journalists burst in through the front door shouting, "The Hospital is on fire – who wants to come and see –"
>
> That was my first night there and I *loathed* it. Loathed it. But I know much more than I would have ever known if I hadn't seen it and been in it.[114]

Valentine loathed it, and was drinking fairly heavily to hide her fears from others, but Sylvia seemed almost to relish the situation and was partisan enough to enjoy watching an aerial battle over the city on the second night: 'our fighters went up straight into the formation of fifteen Caproni bombers and scattered them. I have never seen such flying, such speed and precision.'[115] Sylvia's enthusiasm was such that she could at times be almost frivolous: on an official tour of the front line at the Guadarramas, conducted at *siesta* time for the safety of the delegates, Sylvia made a flippant remark about the propaganda value of her attracting an enemy pot-shot. With a certain degree of self-control, Valentine pointed out that it would be merely wasteful, as the papers would probably overlook the incident. Valentine herself was in no mood to make jokes – 'in Madrid, while I was new to it, the sight of one house broken and destroyed made my heart beat so that I could not breathe' – and on her return to England she wrote to Alyse Gregory, 'War is INFINITELY worse than we imagine it will be.'[116]

The delegates were driven to the Congress Hall in Madrid through shelled and bombed streets, the Catalan driver stopping before various heaps of stones and announcing how many had been killed there. The hall was a new brick building on the outskirts of the city with guards outside to salute the delegates and a military band inside to greet them with Riego's Hymn. The first session was interrupted by the announcement that the town of Brunete had fallen to the Government. There was applause, singing, tears, the clenching of fists and later the militia arrived, waving flags and a grim trophy, the tunic of a Moorish captain. Everyone knew that the victory would spark off reprisals, and that night at the hotel was again noisy and disturbed.

In Madrid, Sylvia and Valentine had the opportunity of making the acquaintance of several of the distinguished delegates: Ilya Ehrenburg, Pablo Neruda and Ludwig Renn, the German Communist novelist who had escaped from a concentration camp and joined the International Brigade. Renn was staying with the other delegates at the Hotel Victoria and going off to the front each morning. To Sylvia the 'affinity of mind' many of the delegates shared was an affirmation of the benefits of internationalism. Despite the language barriers, the delegates did not 'stiffen into cliques', with the exception of the neat and self-contained Soviet group who, in Sylvia's opinion, 'were ludicrously like the traditional British Raj'.[117]

Sylvia's attitude was, in general, enthusiastic and uncritical. There was no word from her on the great controversy over André Gide's book, *Retour de l'URSS*, which had so precipitately lost him his position as a contemporary Party saint, nor did she seem aware of the violent factions between Trotskyists and Stalinists within the ranks of the Republican army, nor of the arrival of a British and French Trades Union deputation the day after their own arrival in Valencia to investigate the murder by Stalinists of the labour leader, Andres Nin. One of Sylvia's most persistent theories about Spanish republicans, developed among the ruined churches of Barcelona the previous year, was that they did no gratuitous acts of violence or damage. When Stephen Spender tried to disabuse her of this notion by re-telling the voluntary confessions of a Catalan taxi driver, Sylvia and Valentine, in Spender's words, 'turned from me in a pained way. Then the lady novelist remarked to the poetess: "Isn't it strange that now, for the first time after all these long, long days, I feel just a little bit tired?"'[118]

This incident took place at Port Bou on the return journey from the Congress. The delegates reached Paris on 14 July, in time to join a Bastille Day march and conclude their business. Sylvia and Valentine got home to Chaldon on 16 July, full of plans for articles and propaganda, and Sylvia consumed by a 'raging passion for gossip', wanting to know everyone's responses to the Congress.

It was the last time they were to come home to Chaldon. Very soon after their return they saw advertised in the local paper a house to rent on the outskirts of Maiden Newton, a village eight miles to the north-west of Dorchester. Tired of fighting the damp and discomfort of 24 West Chaldon, and pleased with what they saw at the viewing, Sylvia and Valentine took up the tenancy and on 23 August 1937 moved into Mrs West's house by the River Frome.

4

1937–1947

I

This place is most beautiful. We love it far more than we thought we should. The river is an incessant pleasure, and is always handing us small nosegays of beauty or entertainment. The latest nosegay is a posy of three fat young water-rats who have just learned to swim. They cross the river swimming with every limb, their tails lashing about, their eyes beady with purpose; and swarm up the bank and sit in a clutch, pressed close together, chewing the same iris stalk. Now the nightingales have just arrived. They came on a night of sharp frost, it was curious to hear their passionate excited voices singing of summer on that rigid silence of frost.[1]

Sylvia wrote this to Steven Clark nine months after moving to the new house. It stood on the Maiden Newton side of the river, but was considered part of Frome Vauchurch, the hamlet across the bridge. One of the chief attractions of the house for Sylvia and Valentine was that it had no immediate neighbours, but the village was not far, only a hundred yards up the lane, and contained a number of shops, a number of pubs and a railway station. 'Ugly, but practical' was Sylvia's verdict, and though she and Valentine missed the noble contours of Chaldon, and lamented their ascent into the bourgeoisie, Maiden Newton's ugly comforts were sufficient to console them.

From across the river, the house looked very much like a cumbersome beached boat, being built right at the water's edge with a balustraded deck protruding over the river and running the whole length of the house. It was a plain-headed building which had survived its low Victorian birth more by luck than design. Its whitewashed stone had been covered over in many places by corrugated metal sheets, supposedly a protection against damp, which gave the house a distinctly jerry-built look, but as Sylvia and Valentine never removed them one must assume they didn't mind. Inside, the rooms were not many, but ample: on the ground floor was a long dark passage-way leading to the kitchen at the further end of the house. Off the passage-way to the left were a dining room and Sylvia's sitting-room, both overlooking the river. Upstairs were three bedrooms, a boxroom, bathroom and Valentine's sitting-room, immediately above Sylvia's and with views in two directions. There was a little room for fishing-tackle, which Valentine also used as a work-room, and a larder which answered to all Sylvia's desires. For the first time they were living together in a house with electricity and hot water.

Outside, and mainly to the front of the house, was a garden about a third of an acre in size. One of the first things Valentine did was to plant willow-slips all along the river border, for though there were several mature trees they wanted a more effective screen for the house. No enormous feats of gardening were undertaken that year, though. They were busy with other matters and gave the third of an acre only a tenant's care, for they did not expect to stay very long at Frome Vauchurch.

Tom, the surviving Frankfort grey, was the only pet to make the move. Sylvia and Valentine had given away their spaniel Towser, acquired at '24', to Jimmy Pitman. Victoria the goat had either perished or, more likely, been given away too, and a kitten with distemper called Endymion, whom they had nursed, had died. The river, though, held many pleasant surprises; there were otters, swans, moorhens, a heron occasionally on the opposite bank and an embarrassment of trout. Valentine began fishing for them as soon as the move was over, and acquired a little cosh 'called demurely "a priest"[2] with which to kill a landed fish quickly. In her diary she began to tot up her total catch as systematically as she had formerly done with Chaldon rabbits.

The return from Spain had fired both women with added energy for campaigning and their political activities took on a less parochial nature, partly due to the fact that Maiden Newton was less permeable to Communism than East Chaldon had been. At the end of September, Sylvia was in London to meet with a group of left-minded writers who formed the executive of the Association of Writers for Intellectual Liberty. Called to set up the committee, of which Sylvia became Secretary, were Cecil Day Lewis, Montagu Slater, Rose Macaulay, Mulk Raj Anand, Amabel Williams-Ellis and Goronwy Rees and, as before, Sylvia was unsparing of those whose commitment seemed questionable – in this case, Rose Macaulay. Macaulay had protested that the committee was being too political and should concentrate more on what was being done for culture by the two sides in Spain than on their ideological differences. To this Sylvia retorted that the only cultural development reported of the Spanish Fascists was their recent burning of the works of Dickens. Rose Macaulay, not to be done down, lamented the ignorance shown by one country of another's culture. Sylvia agreed, adding how few people in England would have the first idea which Spanish books to burn or not.

About a week later, Valentine went as a voluntary worker to Tythrop House, near Thame, which was about to be opened by the Basque Children's Committee as a home for refugee children from Bilbao. It was a frustrating job, beset with administrative teething troubles, and Sylvia, unable to bear the prolonged absence of Valentine, and concerned that she was being overworked and ill-fed, went up to Thame for a couple of days to help with the cooking and the intimidation of the woman in charge. By the end of October, Sylvia was in London again, seeing her committee, attending a P.E.N. meeting, calling in at Party headquarters and the *Left Review* office, where she reduced Edgell Rickword to silence and his wife Johnnie to helpless laughter by pointing out that *Left Review* should really not expect its contributors to write for no pay – was that not, after all, a form of black-legging? Sylvia also saw Oliver Warner and his new wife, Elizabeth, at a dinner at the National Liberal Club where Arthur Machen was giving a speech, 'an account of how he once went down a rope-ladder'.[3] Purefoy did not at first seem very pleased to see Sylvia but warmed up on a little gin. It was as busy and sociable as Sylvia's former life in London had been, except that being anywhere without Valentine was intolerable – almost a physical pain.

One reason for the exaggerated activity of that month was that Valentine was romantically in love with a young woman and Sylvia wanted to leave them alone together, first at Frome Vauchurch, then at Thame, where Valentine had taken the 'young white goose'. This was a magnanimity which Sylvia felt easily able to afford. She was very fond of the girl in question; had, indeed, encouraged Valentine to act on her first impulse of desire, for Sylvia, then aged almost forty-four, was above all unwilling to have Valentine's sexual desire for herself tainted with longings and regrets for others. Valentine was as easily smitten with lust as ever, and her handsome masculine appearance led inevitably to excitements among both the worldly and the simply curious of their female acquaintances. Sylvia always knew this and knew, too, that their love for each other was rock-solid, the immovable centre of their lives. Sylvia was not jealous of this latest love because it was doing Valentine nothing but good, and she told her so. She also made it clear to Valentine that, as circumstances alter cases, she might not always be able to encourage every affair; that if Valentine ever fell in love with someone who did her damage, Sylvia's feelings about that person would be very different. It was a ghastly anticipation of what was to happen later.

Sylvia, being the more willing and able public speaker of the two, was rapidly becoming a more prominent Party activist than Valentine. Soon after their return from Spain, Sylvia was on a platform in Dorchester's Labour Hall with John Cowper Powys, making a speech about Spanish culture and literature and begging a collection, not this time for the Communist Party's Spanish Fund, but for a fund she and Valentine had set up to alleviate the soap shortage they had witnessed in Spain. Ludwig Renn had pointed out to them how demoralising it was for the militia to remain entirely soapless and how nothing was being done to help. In Paris, on their way home, Sylvia and Valentine had arranged for £25-worth of soap to be sent from Marseilles to Madrid and, as soon as they got to England, began asking round for contributions. 'We set about it without much spirit. At least *I* did. Sylvia had more vigour and more hope, as usual,' wrote Valentine to Alyse Gregory, and recorded some of the responses to their appeal: the Dorchester meeting raised £4 5s, May Pitman gave 2s, the fishing-women at Winterton 25s, four waiters in a train dining-car 5s, four shop-girls in London 10s, Joan Woollcombe, Valentine's sister, gave nothing, Joan's servant 5s, Rosamund Lehmann £5 and Vita Sackville-West £1, with the following note attached: 'I hope you will forgive me when I say that your letter was one of the funniest appeals I've ever had! I thought the Spanish need for soap was chronic, and not just due to the war!' to which Valentine responded in her letter to Alyse, 'if she can find it just stolidly funny, then how funny the less civilised beings to whom we've written must think it! But it hasn't worked out like that – and I am thankful. I think perhaps I haven't a very strong sense of humour at any time, and at present it seems to be completely dormant!'[4]

In October, Sylvia was on a platform again, displaying her oratorical skills. She was opening the Dorchester Labour Party Fayre:

> I made a beautiful little speech. Beginning with what pleasure one can get out of a Fayre, and how socialism stood for more pleasure in the world. I mention this sentiment only because at this juncture an enormous and very common old woman who was in charge of the jumble stall said Hear Hear in a voice like thunder, and applauded most passionately. Then I went on to say that it was a privilege too, that without the struggles and sacrifices – all the stallholders began to simper – of those who worked now and worked in the past there would be no Labour Party in Dorchester; and then, with my eye fixed on the co-operative stall covered with little packets of groats and soap, I said that we must remember (implying in our prayers) that in some countries in Europe it would be

impossible for people like us to meet together openly in order to raise money for our cause. [...] Minna herself could not have bettered the melancholy candour and simplicity of my tone. In fact it was perfect except that overcome by my own effect I sat down having forgotten to say the Fayre was open.[5]

It is clear that Sylvia relished the opportunity to educate the people of Dorset, however mild the occasion. Given a more obviously political occasion, such as a Labour Party meeting, she could be astute and prophetic, as her notes for a speech show. It was not enough to be organised, she told the Trades Unionists; Germany had Workers' Unions which had been made a mockery of under Fascism. She called for commitment to the unions and argued that a union card should be the worker's dearest possession. In Spain such a card was 'dyed red with the heart's blood of those who carried them':

This war in Spain is not a Spanish Civil War (what the Govt and BBC have taught us to call it). It is an international war, and it is a class war. It is a conflict between a ruling caste, and the people.[6]

In Britain, she said, the seeds of the struggle which had subdued Germany and Italy and which threatened Spain had already been sown. Fascism was an international pest: 'Guernica was a town very much like Sherborne and Hitler's bombers would be as ready to destroy the one as the other. They would come as fast at Mosley's bidding as they did at Franco's bidding.' Her subject, ostensibly Spain, was widening out. Spain was a vital issue, she said, because it had a vital lesson to teach: 'On whether we learn that lesson or not depends whether this crusade will be a step towards victory or merely a period in which some of us make speeches and some of us make good resolutions.'

It was a period in which Sylvia was preoccupied with strategy, for which she had a natural predisposition. She was frequently in contact with Edgell Rickword and full of suggestions on which she hoped he might act. One was that there should be an inquiry into elementary school history books, another, more extreme and urgent, was that the Party should expel Stephen Spender before he decided to leave of his own account, as seemed likely. Sylvia felt that Spender had 'gone off' as a poet since joining the Party and that the Party may have been, directly or indirectly, the cause: 'This is the most serious aspect of the whole situation to my mind,' Sylvia wrote to Rickword, 'SS may not matter very much; but it does matter if our methods are such as to damage imaginative workers, because in that case, whether they leave us or stay with us, we lose them for the best they were worth.' Behind this problem can be discerned the antipathy between Sylvia and Stephen Spender, a continuation of the old quarrel between Bolshevik and Menshevik. Her solution to it was entirely in keeping with the hardest Party line, and a solution of which 'Uncle Joe' – a character she esteemed highly – would have been proud: 'Having brandished him [Spender] so much in the beginning it will be a great mistake not to brandish quite as much the fact that he has not proved up to our standards. In fact, let us be sure that it looks like a purge, and not a miraculous escape of Jonah the prophet.'[7]

A note in Sylvia's diary shows that as early as December 1937 Valentine was herself feeling uncomfortable with the Communist Party, though of course there was no question of Sylvia applying the same rigorous treatment she prescribed for Comrade Spender. 'I suppose,' Sylvia wrote, 'that CP is at once too tight a pot and too draughty for her roots to settle in to their own comfort. She feels at once unused and misused.'[8] It could also be the case that Valentine wanted to indicate she could not follow Sylvia at the same pace down the fellow-travellers' road, being the less intensely involved of the two. Certainly, Sylvia had become prey to some absurdities of ideology, such as her observation of drivers in the New Forest, along a tricky part of the road in bad weather: 'All along this stretch we noticed that lorries were polite and friendly, whereas not a single gentry-driven car showed the slightest movement towards courtesy.'[9]

At the end of 1937, Sylvia was finishing another novel, her fifth. *After the Death of Don Juan* is Sylvia's least known novel, published in a modest edition in the autumn of 1938 and 'swamped', as Sylvia once said, 'by 1938–39 events'.[10] The story, set in late eighteenth-century Spain, begins where Da Ponte's libretto for *Don Giovanni* leaves off: the report of the libertine Don Juan's descent into hell fire, his reward for a life of wickedness. As the novel unfolds, Sylvia makes three-dimensional the two-dimensional characters of the opera, a subversive process, for the extra element is the workings of human nature and it undermines completely what the reader thinks he knows at the beginning of the book. Even the dire climax of the opera (and of Molière's play) is overturned, for this is a worldly and cynical book and Sylvia grasps the essence of the character of Don Juan by showing him as a survivor.

In Sylvia's story, three of the characters from the opera, Dona Ana, Don Ottavio and Leporello, journey into the provinces to break the news of Don Juan's death to his father, Don Saturno, a philanthropic landowner, whose backward village, Tenorio Viejo, is too small even to appear on the map:

> The castle stood on a small hill, the original square stone keep rambling off into lower levels of russet-tiled barns and storehouses. On a further hillock stood a church. It had been built with more pretensions to architecture than the castle, but less solidly, and its cupola had slipped awry, like an old woman's head-dress. Between the church and the castle straggled the village, an array of lime-washed hovels. The olive trees in their cultivated earth looked like the spots on a leopard's skin, the vineyards were few and poor. There were no meadows. All around were the mountains. Some cultivation had struggled up them, forcing its way between the shaggy oak-woods. On the higher slopes the colour of the earth, fading from the valley leopard-colour to an ashen whiteness, showed that cultivation need strive no further.[11]

What would transform the bleached valley is, of course, water, but Don Saturno's plans for an irrigation system have been inhibited by his son's profligacy at the gaming tables and in the bedchambers of Seville. One of the book's ironies is that at the end, it would appear that the estate will get its water, but for all the wrong reasons, and only if Don Juan – not dead at all – can reclaim his tenants' land. As a political novel, it is entirely different in kind from *Summer Will Show* and shows a shift in interest from the ideology of Communism to its practical applications. It is a very neat, very literary book, employing a sort of Marxism even in its method, for there is no protagonist; each layer of Spanish society as seen in the microcosm of Tenorio Viejo is examined in turn, each with equal weight. Don Saturno the enlightened gentleman, Don Francisco the disaffected school-master, Don Gil the sacristan, Don Tomas the priest, the miller, his avaricious daughter and the peasants fit effortlessly into the scheme of the book, 'a parable', as Sylvia described it, 'or an allegory, or what you will, of the political chemistry of the Spanish War, with the Don Juan – more of Molière than of Mozart – developing as the Fascist of the piece'.[12] Among the peasants a multiplicity of views is represented: there is Ramon, the man of moderation, Andres the strategist, Jesus the atheist, Dionio the god-fearing innkeeper, hot-blooded Diego and an equally differentiated group of women, very limited in their sphere of action but by no means without opinions. Creating and keeping alive such a mass of characters is an achievement in itself, but the way in which Sylvia accumulates their small motives towards a catastrophe is both technically brilliant and deeply entertaining. What is somewhat surprising is that such a devout Communist as Sylvia was in 1937 could have produced such a detached, politically objective novel – a mark, if one were needed, of her imaginative integrity.

It also seemed that Sylvia was incapable of producing any two books the same. There is remarkably little consistency – except in a prevailing intelligence – between one of her novels and the next, a fact which partly explains why she has escaped the close attention of literary critics. She was not interested in developing a 'presence' as a novelist; the individual book was what absorbed her, and when she was writing she was as much as ever bound up in the fictional world she was creating. This emotional engagement ensured her work its immediacy. She was clear about her priorities, as she explained in an interview late in her life: 'Really I believe that the thing that forms the structure of any narrative and holds it together is the importance of the narrative, the interest one has in the narrative. That's why Defoe is such a master because he's *really* interested in the story.' As for the inconsistency (it was to become more marked as the years went by), she said in the same interview, 'I remember a passage in Walt Whitman where someone or other is accusing him of being inconsistent and he says "Am I inconsistent? Well, I *am* inconsistent. Within me I contain millions!"'[13]

Sylvia was least inconsistent in her work for the *New Yorker*, which was taking several stories a year. Writing for a specific market certainly did not inhibit her imagination, but it did unobtrusively single out a certain tone in her writing, a tone which she was able to refine and, by constant usage, perfect. This is not to say that her *New Yorker* stories are unvarious, but that the mild discipline of a limited consistency enabled her to produce, over the years, a handful of masterpieces.

In 1937 Harold Raymond suggested that Chatto & Windus should publish some of the *New Yorker* stories in book form (Charles Prentice had retired – early – in the mid-Thirties), but Sylvia was uncertain how they would transplant into native soil, if at all. This was enough to slow down plans for a book, further slowed down by the outbreak of the war, and *A Garland of Straw* was not published until 1943. Meanwhile Valentine had been sending pieces to the *New Yorker* too, and though they took a couple of poems, her short stories and articles were rejected, which was becoming the usual story. Valentine earned next to nothing from writing during these years. The sort of magazine she contributed to regularly – *Country Standard*, *Left Review*, *The Countryman* – paid poorly, if at all. Sylvia, on the other hand, had earned an average of £250 a year as an author in the period 1933–7. Her 'gentleman friend' was a man of means.

II

At the end of 1937, Sylvia and Valentine received a letter from Elizabeth Wade White, the young American woman who had stayed at '24' in the early days of their political fervour. She had raised $1,180 for Spanish Medical Aid, run by the Quakers, in her

Connecticut home town and had received invitations to meet both Mrs Franklin D. Roosevelt and a naturist colony. 'Such a pity they could not be combined,' Sylvia wrote in her diary. 'That was a good day's work when we fired her.' Elizabeth was so 'fired' that the Quakers asked her to go to Spain to do some publicity work for them. She stopped at Frome Vauchurch for a few days on her way over.

1938 was a bad year for the Republican side in the Spanish War: Franco was receiving even more German and Italian support, and his offensive was redoubled all across Spain. In August, his forces began to break down the hold of the Republican lines and penetrated the Catalan Front by the year's end, with disastrous consequences for the Government side. When Elizabeth Wade White got as far as Paris on her way to Spain in the autumn of 1938, she heard such alarming news about the progress of the war that she wrote to Sylvia and Valentine that she was returning home. They replied with an invitation for her to come to Dorset for an indefinite stay. Soon after her arrival Valentine fell in love with Elizabeth, and by November they were lovers.

At first this new affair did not alarm Sylvia, except in that Valentine was so quiet about it. The constant presence of Elizabeth in the house became a strain, though, and Sylvia moved from her shared bedroom with Valentine to the spare room. 'According to the lights of the day,' she wrote later, 'I was behaving correctly in a quite usual situation. The only item by which I could have bettered my conduct would have been to take a lover. But I desired Valentine as sensually as ever, which saved me from that complication, as it saved me from any deviation into maternal kindness.'[14] By Christmas, however, the situation had crisped up considerably; Elizabeth had begun to show moods, and Sylvia, released by these from the grip of her good intentions, allowed herself to be unhappy — for herself and for Valentine. The festive season passed by grimly and 12 January arrived, the eighth anniversary of their marriage, with a love poem from Valentine pinned on the pillow of Sylvia's single bed, but no Valentine.

At the end of January, Barcelona fell to General Franco and it became clear that the Republican cause in Spain was in imminent danger of complete collapse. The turn of events bitterly discouraged Sylvia, but was hardly unexpected after the 'Munich betrayal' of September 1938, an event which had roused Sylvia's deepest anger. Early in 1939, though, the wind had gone out of her sails, for all her energy was sapped by personal unhappiness. In February she came to the conclusion that she would have to leave the house at Frome Vauchurch, as the situation was becoming intolerable to her, but Valentine begged her to stay, and she did. Elizabeth had been with them for almost four months and her parents, concerned at how she was, sent a suitor of hers from New England to investigate. His report back could not have been very reassuring to the Whites, for both Sylvia and Valentine took a violent dislike to him and though he was able to get Elizabeth as far as London for a while, he was not able to persuade her to come home. Elizabeth came back to Frome Vauchurch, but a few weeks later, possibly because she felt a change of address might allay her parents' fears, she moved into part of the Dairy House in East Chaldon, where she could entertain Valentine alone.

On 28 March 1939, Madrid and Valencia surrendered. The Spanish war was over, and the European war came a step nearer. Soon after, Sylvia and Valentine received a request from Louis Aragon to house temporarily Ludwig Renn, who had been interned by the French Government on crossing into France after the fall of Barcelona. Sylvia found his presence at Frome Vauchurch immensely salutary; here was a man whose character she esteemed, who had endured real hardships and had kept his integrity and manners intact. She saw how, in her anxiety not to show hurt feelings, she had got herself into a false position with Valentine and had been cast adrift from her own resources in the process. By trying to act well, she had limited her ability to act at all.

Elizabeth was thirty-two, Valentine's junior by a few weeks, and naturally did not choose to 'share' her with anyone else. This was her first profound experience of falling in love, and seemed to call for a special degree of commitment. Unfortunately, it was the latter of which she reminded Valentine most frequently, and Valentine's love and lust for Elizabeth became inextricably mingled with a sense of guilty responsibility which prevented any member of the triangle from being satisfied with the situation, let alone happy.

Sylvia and Valentine had been invited to another Writers' Congress, this time in New York. In ordinary circumstances, they would not have attended, but the trip offered such a good opportunity for Elizabeth to go home and yet not be parted from Valentine that at the end of May they all sailed for America, including Renn, whose passage was paid by Elizabeth.

Elizabeth went to her parents' house in New England while the Congress was in progress, but Valentine joined her there soon after and Sylvia stayed alone in New York, meeting old acquaintances such as Anne Parrish and new ones, notably a young composer, Paul Nordoff, who had written an opera around the story of *Mr Fortune's Maggot*. Nordoff sent Sylvia the score, which she returned with a warm and praising letter: 'There are innumerable things I could specially praise: the economy, the absence of fuss, the power of inventing the right device [...]; but I would rather praise the *unanimity* of the work; for plenty of music has good qualities, fine details of invention, and yet is not good and fine music; but yours both has, and is.'[15] They met soon after and took an instant liking to each other. Nordoff was a bright-eyed, energetic and eccentric young man, and completely devoted to his art, a breath of fresh air in the New York heat-wave and a release for Sylvia from her equally stifling personal preoccupations. 'It is so gratifying of you to say in your letter that you like me,' she wrote to him in July. 'Things of that kind, which can be very important, people usually omit to mention. Personally, I have no use for unspoken affections, and so I will most readily reply that I like you a great deal, and look on my meeting with you as one of the best things I have found in this country.'[16]

They had been in America for over a month and Sylvia was expecting a date to be settled for going home – without Elizabeth – when a plan first mooted in Dorset was brought up again and Elizabeth found them a house to rent, all three together, for the rest of the summer. It was in Warren County, Connecticut, a farm-house belonging to a family called Kibbe. Sylvia fell in with this obviously unsatisfactory arrangement because she was desperate to be with Valentine again and sensed that Valentine, too, wanted her nearby. In her autobiography, Valentine wrote of that trip to America that 'Over there everything became chaotic and, for my part, disgraceful. If Sylvia had not stayed by me then I should have been damned out and out. I was lecherous and greedy and drunken there, and yet I had two very serious loves in my heart, even then – and poems, too, in my head.'[17] Falling in love with Elizabeth had brought Valentine out of a period of lassitude in her creative life, and this was very important to her, for she had an almost superstitious fear of not being able to write. This and the renewal of lust and a genuine love for Elizabeth made the affair seem worth pursuing, despite the unpleasantness of the situation at Warren and Elizabeth's increasing possessiveness. Of her own part, Sylvia commented later, 'Mere fidelity could have become a bore and a reproach; it was my dependence on her which called back her sense of responsibility and steadied her footing.'[18]

A prior engagement of Elizabeth's gave Sylvia and Valentine two days alone at the Kibbe farm house, 'two long days of childish happiness', in which Sylvia felt restored and hopeful. With Elizabeth's return, however, things fell back into their former pattern; Valentine and Elizabeth sharing the front room, Sylvia down the passage by herself. During the day, they went for endless motor tours of Connecticut, seeing the 'sights' in the methodical way Sylvia and Valentine both disliked. At night, in thundery heat, Sylvia lay awake listening to Elizabeth's voice complaining to Valentine, for by this time Elizabeth had become determined that Valentine should make a choice, commit herself, begin to treat her – Elizabeth – with some respect, with some gratitude, with some consideration. The weather got hotter and hotter and the news on the radio, crackling with static, was of war brewing up in Europe.

Two visitors helped to relieve Sylvia's unhappiness at Warren; Paul Nordoff was one, coming over from a cottage he had rented to work in and bringing with him a great deal of carefree conversation and a stranger's prerogative to be irresponsibly amiable. Elizabeth didn't like him, and saw Sylvia's immediate revitalisation in his company as a form of indirect criticism, an impression which Sylvia made no attempt to correct. Elizabeth was, in Sylvia's opinion, in a monomaniac state, and impermeable to the obvious. They maintained a rigid politeness, but did not converse. The other welcome visitor was Janet Machen, in the

States on what turned out to be a very long stay, twenty-two and full of youthful candour about Sylvia's situation as she saw it. The family tone and a release into light-heartedness and familiarity were tonic to Sylvia, but the visit did not last long.

On their last day at the Kibbe house, in early September 1939, news reached them that Britain was at war with Germany. They were all ready for the journey to their next destination, Celo, in North Carolina, where they had been offered the use of a cabin half-way up Mount Mitchell, and they went ahead with the trip, passing through New York, animated with war news, on the way. While Sylvia and Valentine were at Celo, without Elizabeth, it became clear to them both that they would have to return home, though Valentine was still in the grip of her affair, and was confused and exhausted. Nothing had been resolved and a large gulf of unshared experience was growing between Sylvia and Valentine which made their stay at Celo a constrained one. Valentine was ill for part of the time, and troubled for the rest of it. Sylvia was in an agony of solicitude for her, and at the same time waited to see what her own fate was to be. On one of her solitary walks, Sylvia was attacked by a swarm of wild bees; on another, she was confronted by the sight of a black snake devouring another snake: 'The swallower was firmly coiled, to get a good stance, and the top third of it was erect. The swallowed was about half-way down, and protesting with wavings and wrigglings. I hoped to watch this to the end, but the swallower saw me and flounced away, still with raised head.'[19]

Elizabeth was in New York when they returned to the city at the end of September to try to book a passage home. New York was extremely humid and uncomfortable, the war news – of the *Courageous* sunk with five hundred lives lost – was bad, and Sylvia felt that there was a certain hostility towards the English in America: 'We carried the infection of war, we were lepers.'[20] Sylvia became more and more dejected waiting about in the hotel where Valentine and Elizabeth shared a room and where she again was in a room by herself. Despite her unhappiness, Sylvia maintained her excellent manners and her charm, though sub-dued, was as potent as ever. On a visit to the offices of the *New Yorker*, she met her young editor, William Maxwell, who was to become a dear and valued friend. Many years later, she wrote to him: 'It is strange to think that during that summer when I was feeling as hollow as a hemlock stalk you were there all the time; and that when I came to *The N.Y.* office I was so accomplished in dissimulation that you thought I was the person who wrote so airily and securely.'[21] Maxwell was immensely impressed by her: 'her voice had a slightly husky, intimate quality. Her conversation was so enchanting it made my head swim. I did not want to let her out of my sight.'[22] Maxwell tried to persuade Sylvia to stay in the United States, 'where bombs were less likely to fall on her', but she declined, writing in a letter to him soon after, 'I have the profoundest doubts about this war. I don't feel that it is being fought against Nazidom, and while Chamberlain is around I doubt if it will be. And I can't suppose that going back will better it or me. But for all that, I feel that my responsibilities are there, not here.'[23]

Sylvia did not, however, want to leave America alone. Elizabeth, who had been calm and cheerful on their return to New York, tried to pin Valentine down: she should make a choice, and, because of the war, why not stay in America? Several hot evenings passed in the statement and reiteration of this theme until one when Valentine fell exhausted into Sylvia's room and, eventually, explained how Elizabeth had driven her past all patience with the suggestion that Valentine should become an American citizen – for safety's sake. Valentine had damned such an idea outright – it was indeed a major miscalculation of what she could or could not bear – and immediately she and Sylvia began packing for another hotel.

Their only subsequent meeting with Elizabeth on that trip was a formal farewell at Elizabeth's club before boarding the SS *Manhattan*, bound for Southampton. In their cabin, Valentine collapsed onto Sylvia, reassured her that they would recover their love, and in an instant the old intimacy seemed to be restored.

In mid-Atlantic foundered the island of Atlantis.
There toll the bronze bells of the city of Ys.
There driftingly dance upon the unvexed tides

1. Sylvia, her father and his spaniel Friday in the mid-1890s.

2. 'Tib' in her sailor's hat.

3. Sylvia and her father skating in Switzerland, c. 1909.

4. George Townsend Warner in a form room at Harrow.

5. Percy Buck in 1904.

6. Nora in the 1920s, after her marriage to Ronald Eiloart.

7. Charles Prentice, Sylvia and T. F. Powys outside Beth Car in the 1920s.

8. Molly (Valentine) Ackland in December 1914.

9. Sylvia in her flat at 113 Inverness Terrace.

10. Miss Green's cottage.

11. Valentine's wedding to Richard Turpin, July 1925.

12. Valentine at Winterton in 1928.

13. Bea Howe and Sylvia at Frankfort Manor.

15. 24, West Chaldon.

14. Valentine feeding the cats at Frankfort Manor.

16. Valentine and Sylvia at West Chaldon with Kit and Pat Dooley, Victoria the goat, Towser and Tom.

17. Sylvia, Valentine and Asunción in Barcelona, 1936.

18. Frome Vauchurch.

19. Sylvia in the garden at Frome Vauchurch, 1948.

20. Sylvia and the cats in Valentine's sitting-room, 1960s.

21. Joy Finzi's drawing of Valentine dead, November 1969.

22. Sylvia at her desk overlooking the river, 1977.

Drowned sailors with their Atlantidean brides
(But the head being heaviest they dance heels uppermost).
And there, mid-way between one coast and another coast,
Dimming, merging, falling from the light of day,
Past colour sombred and past texture sodden,
Wallowing downward towards the lost, the foundered, the
  forgotten
Down, down to the innocence of legend it recedes –
My sorrow, embossed with mountains, darkened with
  forests, laced
With summer lightning, quilted with rivers and dirt roads
My sorrow, stately as a cope, vast as a basilica –
My sorrow, embroidered all over with America,
That at a word from you in mid-Atlantic I threw away.[24]

III

The *Manhattan* docked at Southampton on 11 October 1939, after a crossing made worse by the fact that its proper ballast of pig-iron had been requisitioned for munitions. As the passengers were waiting to disembark, a lone voice launched into 'Land of Hope and Glory': 'For a moment it was remarkably like being torpedoed. And people who had looked perfectly brave and sedate during the voyage suddenly turned pale, and looked round for escape. There was of course no escape. The singing came from a large fur-coated white-haired lady surrounded (rather like Britannia) with a quantity of parcels. And she sang all through that embarrassing stanza. Then she paused, and looked round challengingly. We all pretended we had heard nothing unusual, nothing, in fact, at all. After a while she sang the doxology. After that she sang no more.'[25] There really was nothing to sing about yet. Sylvia and Valentine returned to Frome Vauchurch with their newly issued gas-masks, to the black-outs, evacuees and air-raid shelters of the Phoney War.

On the boat, Sylvia and Valentine seemed to have been restored to each other, but the protracted unhappiness of their stay in America had left them both very vulnerable to doubt. Rather than a true *reintegratio amoris*, what Sylvia later called a 'long iron frost'[26] set in. Neither wanted to offend the other; both had lost confidence in their power to love, and so things went on, very cautiously, each waiting for signs that their marriage had survived intact.

The signs which Sylvia saw appeared to prove that there was little hope. She was not naturally cautious or passive, but America had worn her down, and Valentine was still in part committed to Elizabeth. On 25 October, as a lone diary entry for 1939 records, Sylvia was alone in the house when the phone rang:

> It was a cable from Elizabeth, I can remember this much: Yes to all your questions. I guessed the sort of questions. Embarrassed and sick at heart I went into the bathroom, and looked out of the window. There, between the dip of the two green hillsides and a level storm-cloud, was a new sea. The pale, early morning sky, but it had a quality of the water element, seemed at once thicker and more lustrous than air. It was a heavy, milk pale, faintly sparkling sea, pushing and brimming in to this new bay between our two hillsides. And beyond this pale sea was the heavy purple cloud, heavy with rain and dark in the morning.
>
> I could not doubt but that it was the sea, though no one but I would ever know of it. All day I saw it, new, cold, pale, a heavy and absolving weight of water. And could not but think it a sign to my uneasy unhappiness that is now almost inattentive, so natural does it seem to me to get such cuffs as this morning's, so rare is it now, to be surprised by any moment of illumination. And this seemed as though it were the last, and with the validity of a last thing.

Another cable accident occurred a few months later, as Sylvia was preparing to leave for Rat's Barn where she was going to finish her collection of stories, 'The Cat's Cradle Book'. The telephone operator called with a query about a cable, and read back to Sylvia the words Valentine had intended for Elizabeth. This incident so impressed on Valentine the falsity of her position that she wrote to Elizabeth to say things could not go on; but the wariness between

Sylvia and Valentine still continued: certain actions, certain words had become invalid because of their associations.

Valentine had been drinking heavily all through the American trip and did not stop when she returned to England at the beginning of the war, when, she once said, she was drinking a bottle of spirits a day (though wartime shortages may soon have regulated this). Worried by her dependence on drink, she consulted her doctor in Weymouth, who told her that the only way out was through an exercise of will-power, that very few people were successful and that the prognosis was bad. This made Valentine depressed, and her dependence if anything greater, and so her drinking went on – Sylvia, apparently, never aware of it as a problem.

The naval war of the winter of 1939 may not have seemed too threatening to the population of West Dorset, but the events of early 1940 did. Hitler overran Denmark and Norway in April with alarming ease, and the Royal Navy had difficulty holding the position won at Narvik. By the summer, the governments of Poland and Belgium, the King and Queen of Norway and the Queen of the Netherlands were all in exile in London; the British Expeditionary Force, once so sure of hanging out its washing on the Siegfried Line, had been caught in a pincer movement, and was trapped at Dunkirk. France was within weeks of capitulation to Germany. Early measures taken at home to provide some protection for civilians now lost their air of pointless routine and were undertaken in earnest, and in the wake of earnestness came a deal of inefficiency. Sylvia wrote wearily of an ARP air-raid rehearsal in Maiden Newton: 'It is like a knock-about farce film done in slow motion, and at intervals some member of the local gentry pipes up to say, "Well, let's hope it will never be needed", or "We can't really get on with it without Mr Thompson", or "Has it started yet, do you know?" The most melancholy thought is, that if there is a real raid they will all dauntlessly turn up to mismanage it, for their courage is as unquestionable as their artlessness.'[27]

Sylvia had joined the local branch of the WVS at the beginning of the war, and was appointed Secretary, working two days a week at the headquarters in Colliton House, Dorchester. The section was led by an admiral's wife, Mrs Anita Egerton, and had a pyramidal structure, flattening down through layers of county womanhood to the village representative and her team of workers. All the women were local, all were volunteers, most of them were middle-aged and many had other wartime jobs. The WVS performed a number of dogsbody services for Civil Defence and the ARP: mending servicemen's clothing, organising first-aid groups and blood donating sessions, knitting by the acre. Sylvia's section had one main responsibility, to organise rest centres for evacuees from the cities. She and Mrs Egerton had to make routine inspections of these centres, dusty halls often full of Home Guard equipment or moth-eaten blankets left by the Rural District Council. There were rehearsals for emergencies, there were checkings of supplies, but most of the time rest centres were far from being in a state of readiness.

On 14 June 1940, Paris fell to the German Army. It was for Sylvia one of the most sombre days of the war. 'Paris has fallen – has been abandoned,' she wrote in her diary. The occupation of Paris, cultural pivot of Europe, and the fall of France which followed two days later, was 'a flaring, presaging comet in all men's eyes'.[28] People had to admit now that the war was going very badly indeed and that a German invasion of Britain was the inevitable next move. For Sylvia, it revived all the vehemence of her feelings about Fascism:

> Fascism is the revolution of the bourgeoisie [...] We should attack [...] via their children, as the church does.
>
> There is a great deal to attack.
>
> I think I envy the French. Hearing Churchill in a very bad paragraph announce we would fight on, etc, I found in myself a sense not only of exasperation at the numbers more who must be killed and maimed in a war that never reached its purpose but also the frustrated impatience of an experimental scientist. For war – this sort of war – is no way to attack fascism. And I am fretted to think how every day my chances of seeing other methods tried out are diminished. I feel like a scientist who has to wait in a queue to get to the laboratory – while both the laboratory and he are under bombardment.[29]

Two nights after this, a lovely summer night, Sylvia was lying in bed when she heard a new aeroplane noise – a German plane. Her immediate reaction was to sit up, to protect herself. A British bomber was another matter: Sylvia took a grim satisfaction in hearing them go over towards France, for she was a pragmatist. If the war had to be fought, it had to be fought effectively, though she had almost as little faith in Churchill's effectiveness as she had had in Chamberlain's. She looked to the Soviet Union for an example of unambiguous opposition to Fascism, overlooking as she did so the implications of the pre-war Nazi–Soviet pact and the likelihood of Stalin's motivations being as much territorial as ideological. She felt the lassitude of one who has at last been proved 'right all along'; for indeed, if the British Government had intervened in the Spanish Civil War, things might have turned out very differently. And she began to think of how vainly she had worked for the Spanish cause, and how she wished she could have done more: 'Strange how there was room for one in that war: and in this – none. This war has not issued a single call for the help of intellectuals. It is just your money and/or your life.'[30]

Later in the year, when large formations of bombers became a frequent sight in the sky above Frome Vauchurch, Valentine noted how, as in Madrid, her own reaction was very different from Sylvia's. She wrote to Alyse Gregory that she felt 'a curious kind of sad, diminished pleasure that they were "Ours" and not "Theirs". But the main thought, at first, was a trembling fear because of the people who, while I was looking at those planes, were still walking and talking, shopping, kissing, thinking, feeling – and who, because of those planes, would be dead, very soon.'[31] She had nothing to temper the workings of a sympathetic imagination, and in any tale of atrocity felt a painful identification with both the victim and the perpetrator, a sense of shared guilt. The inhumanity of the war doubly shocked Valentine because she felt culpable. Sylvia did not feel culpable, but righteously indignant.

No will of mine, groaned metal
Wrenched me out of the pit where I lay sleeping
Fired me and quenched me

Drove me out, a shadow sweeping
Over where men and wholesome fields lie sleeping.

No will of mine, spat the petrol
Raised me from that still depth where I unquickened
Slept, and betrayed me
Drop by drop into a reckoned
Into a dying quickened and darkened.

No will of mine, shrieked metal,
But insatiable destiny of solid fettered
To gravitation
Ache of homesickness implacable,
Hurls me down to shatter and be shattered.

No will of mine, the pilot
Whispered, from my young wife and from my sleeping
Children to this work
Sent me out, a sower reaping
The curses of women who clutch their babes unsleeping.[32]

In July 1940 there were fears that the east coast might be invaded, so Sylvia and Valentine moved to Winterton for a few months to be with Ruth. A few weeks later, The Hill House was requisitioned by the Army as an anti-aircraft battery, and Mrs Ackland was obliged to store most of her furniture and effects and take a small house in the village. Thirty years of clutter had to be sorted through, a task made more difficult by Ruth being in charge of it. As Sylvia wrote to Paul Nordoff:

> Ruth has no more sense of order than a magpie, and goes trotting and breathing heavily from her bedroom to the potting-shed in order, say, to restore a gimlet she's found in an old right-foot boot ('How did it get there? I must have been hanging up a picture') and leaving a long trail of little booklets on spiritual healing, litanies for the Mothers' Union, nut-crackers, balls of string, all the God knows whatses which she carries around in a sheaf, and lets fall like

affrighted Proserpina, on the smallest movement – and she's always on the move.[33]

They vacated The Hill House in the middle of August, expecting to see Ruth back in it after a couple of years. But the house was less of an immediate loss than the landscape, for the dunes which Valentine loved were heavily mined and no one could walk on them, or get down to the sea. Hearing an explosion one day, they looked out and saw a soldier running, holding in his hands the booted end of another soldier's blown-off leg.

Sylvia and Valentine returned to Frome Vauchurch in November, where in their absence an incendiary bomb had fallen through the spare-room roof. That winter saw the worst period of the blitz, though the immediate threat of invasion had been lifted by the defeat of the German airforce in the Battle of Britain. Mr Weston, the Maiden Newton grocer, began to tire of being harangued for incompetence by his customers and tried to impress on them the difficulty in getting certain supplies from bombed Bristol and Southampton, but, as Sylvia noted, was 'working in the stiffest clay'. She and Valentine also felt unpopular in the village: 'I say to Valentine that the billeting officer has probably been assured that we are dangerous fifth columnists. What more likely? We were anti-fascists long before the war. And our neighbours, receiving a strong impression that our views were uncongenial and reprehensible, will now remember their impression rather than our views. Accordingly, they will feel convinced we are, and always have been, black-shirts.'

The war had begun to get its teeth into civilian life. Purchase tax was rising steadily; like many people Sylvia and Valentine had been forced to sell their car – a Vauxhall 6 – because of the prohibitive price of petrol. They began keeping 'table rabbits' to counter the food shortages: a male called Joseph and a doe called Mary (later supplanted by a better breeder called Beyond Rubies); but they found it difficult to kill and eat them, and sold off those which didn't become pets.

One of the Führer's bombs fell that winter on the London home of Percy Buck (who had been knighted in 1936), destroying all his notes, papers and music and his entire library. It also destroyed the typescript of *Psychology for Musicians*, a book he had completed at the outset of the war and put aside for later publication. Undaunted by this personal disaster the resourceful Teague, then in his early seventies, set about rewriting the whole book from memory. It is unlikely that Sylvia ever heard of this feat, or the bombing of Buck's house, until much later, if at all. She had lost touch with him, as with Charles Prentice, who, after leaving Chatto & Windus, had become involved in a debilitating and destructive liaison with his sister-in-law. During the war, Prentice went to Africa to travel, pursued by 'his gad-fly'[34] and was to spend the rest of his life abroad, a tormented and broken man.

One other ghost from her youth had been in Sylvia's mind, though, and that was Tommy. Sylvia was writing for the *New Yorker* all through the war; the money was welcome (when it arrived – Sylvia suspected the government of diverting dollar cheques into armaments funds) and she had got into her stride with the form. Occasionally, she turned to autobiographical subject matter for her stories, as with her stories about Tommy, who appears under the name Billy Williams, disburdened of his neuroses and with all his charm about him. For Sylvia this editing of painful episodes 'Out of my Happy Past' was a healing process, and one she was to apply liberally to her memories of her mother later on.

Valentine had done some WVS work with Sylvia, driving a mobile canteen round to outlying groups of soldiers, and they also did fire-watching duty together, but new wartime labour laws soon required single women to do more than that, and Valentine, being within the age range obliged to sign on for fulltime work, began an unhappy career as clerk in the offices of the Territorial Army in Dorchester. Although she was a good typist and a meticulous worker, Valentine did not fit in there at all and wilted under the lack of privacy and quiet, the obtrusive pettiness and inefficiency of the office. 'I've been *too long free*, that's the truth!' she wrote in her day-book. 'I am assured by those who know that it will be much worse before it gets better, and in myself I feel a desperate dread because those words seem to imply that it won't "get better" until I myself have been purged of the remembrance of what it is like to be free.'[35] The only comfort for Valentine was the thought that she had pulled no strings to secure herself more congenial work, as her sister Joan, a successful career woman in London, had suggested. The office provided certain diversions: Valentine liked to watch and listen to the other clerks (and became excited by hearing one say she had just seen a beautiful 'Bewick' — in fact the girl had said 'Buick'); she had plenty of time in which to write letters and read books, but for the most part it was unremittingly dull to have so little to do:

> I have never known one could be so spendthrift of time! It goes by like a morning slug over a cabbage leaf ... and when it's gone one realises that it could have been like a dragon-fly on a water-lily leaf: and then, from past experience and future hopes, believes that it COULD have been — perhaps WAS, the dragon-fly. But it is gone and gone forever, and wasted and spent. [...] on Dorchester station, one evening, I saw a crate — no, three crates heaped one on another — each one full of carrier-pigeons in little separate compartments. They were all quite still. I saw their bright eyes and thought how, inside every one of their narrow heads and within the minute wicker-work frame of their bones, the most violent compulsion in the world was beating and beating: how their passionate urge to fly, to go to the one place noted and marked in their desires, was throbbing inside them as they stayed there, each separate and each still as leaden birds. Children poked them and people spoke to them but they did not stir. My heart almost broke with desire to open up those boxes and see the cloud that would surge out of them and the lovely rush of their escape.[36]

Sylvia abhorred the effect which the office day worked on Valentine, but was powerless to change any part of it. There was little chance of Valentine moving to another job, because as an 'unattached' woman she could be moved anywhere in the country for factory or munitions work, and neither of them could have borne the separation. So Valentine continued six days a week at the Territorial Army while Sylvia worked two days a week at the WVS and was still able to do some writing in her spare time. In

1940 she had published a collection of stories in America, *The Cat's Cradle Book*. The whimsical-sounding title and framework of the book (stories told by mother cats to their kittens) ill-prepare the reader for fifteen remarkable short satires, told in the ruthless pure narrative style of the best fairy stories. The 'cat's view' of human morality was the means by which Sylvia was able to carry on her old joke of defamiliarising the familiar, reversing expectations – a favourite technique in many of her early poems and a technique she returned to, with variations, all her life. It served her well as an ironist and as a moralist. 'I sometimes think that I am alone in recognising what a moral writer I am,' she once wrote. 'I don't myself, while I am writing, but when I read myself afterwards I see my moral purpose shining out like a bad fish in a dark larder.'[37]

Two of the stories from *The Cat's Cradle Book* appeared in the *New Yorker* the same year, but apart from stories, Sylvia had begun some larger projects; one novel (which never got off the ground) about what happened to Hamlet when he was in England, and another about a community of nuns in fourteenth-century East Anglia. This story, written and rewritten slowly and with long interruptions, became her novel *The Corner That Held Them* and took over six years to finish.

Sylvia followed the events of the war with a keen and knowledgeable eye, but in 1941 she had – and took – the opportunity to be more than simply an armchair strategist, and began an extraordinary career as a lecturer, first for the Workers' Educational Association, then for the Labour Party and eventually for the forces. The range of subjects she covered was quite phenomenal. To the RASC (the Royal Army Service Corps) she spoke on architecture from neolithic man to Wren, to the 'Weymouth women' of the Labour Party she spoke on matriarchy and the role of women from the Renaissance to the nineteenth century. To a group of non-commissioned officers she gave a series of talks on the history of the United States, to another army audience she discoursed on the history of Modern Germany and Russia since 1905, subjects obviously pertinent to the war. She spoke about Pepys and Evelyn, about Lenin, about the Crash of 1929, about the Pilgrim Fathers, about the dangers of being bored in wartime; as she wrote to Harold Raymond, 'you would never believe what a lot of subjects I can talk about [...] I haven't repeated myself yet, though we are getting wilder and wilder. Next time I discourse to them [the RASC] it will be on How Bugles Blow; and I still have theology up my sleeve.'[38] Just as her father had used historical precedents to illuminate events of the Great War, Sylvia sought to clarify the issues of the Second War through the teaching of history. 'I myself think I teach history very well', she wrote to Elling Aanestad, 'going on the principle that one can't make it too much like the Chamber of Horrors and the Musée Grevin.'[39] By 1943, when she was giving as many as two lectures a week, she was drawing up a scheme for a book on domestic history, encouraged by her father's publisher, Blackie's. The book came to nothing, but it is interesting to see how far she followed in George's footsteps and to what extent they shared a vocation for prophecy.

In the spring of 1942, when invasion was again thought likely, Sylvia and Valentine were told in confidence that in the event of the Germans landing, their house had been selected as a machine-gun post. Subsequently, they removed their favourite possessions and books and put them into storage. The leader of the Home Guard in Maiden Newton took it upon himself to organise Ladies' Classes in rifle-shooting and hand-grenade throwing, thinking to prepare a resistance force among the women. Sylvia and Valentine attended these classes regularly; Valentine to help with the instruction, Sylvia to learn. It was a sombre form of education.

It seemed that the longer the war went on, the more hysterical and inefficient the average village became. 'It is becoming my belief,' Sylvia wrote to Paul Nordoff, 'that if our local villages were invaded, nobody would have time to notice the enemy, they would all be too busy taking sides over Mrs Tomkins and Mrs Bumkin.' Ruth Ackland was a prime example of Mrs Tomkins:

> In her ardour for service she has undertaken the charge of so many things that as far as I can reckon she will be essential in five different places at once; and as she attains terrific velocity, fells whatever stands in her path, and is permanently

fitted with a screaming device like a German bomb, she will create incalculable havoc amid both defenders and attackers, besides spraining her ankle and getting very much out of breath. I often think that Mrs Ackland is the real reason why Hitler has not yet tried a landing on the East Coast. She thinks so, too.

It is very odd to look at all these poor consequential idiots and remember that war might at any moment make real mincemeat of them. Even under the shadow of death man walketh in a vain shadow.[40]

By January 1943, Valentine was finding the TA office beyond her powers of endurance and applied to be transferred somewhere quieter. She would have met with little success had not Sylvia manoeuvred at the Civil Defence Unit, with which the WVS shared a building, to get Valentine a job as secretary to the Controller. Valentine was relieved at the change, but felt ashamed of the method which had effected it. Sylvia on the other hand was very pleased with herself; the Civil Defence office was not as chaotic as TA, and of course being in the same building meant that she and Valentine could see each other more regularly.

On the ground floor was the National Salvage depot where clothes, bones (for soil fertiliser) and books were collected, salvage being increasingly important due to the blockade power of Germany's submarines. Sylvia knew from her lecture circuit that there was a high demand for books among the men based at the local anti-aircraft sites and that the Army Welfare library was ridiculously limited. One soldier had resorted to reading its selection of sentimental Victorian children's stories. Soon Sylvia and Valentine were sending a steady supply of salvage books to Army Welfare, particularly technical books, which were in high demand. The process of sorting through became quite specialised, a consignment of books in Italian, for example, being sent to an Italian Prisoners' Camp.

The two women were admirably suited to spotting rare, valuable and interesting books among the piles of volumes condemned to be pulped. In 'perhaps the only significant result of our war-working careers'[41] they built up a stock of books for the

Blitzed Libraries scheme, thirteen crates of which went to Exeter after the war, and they bought in a dozen or so rare books, valued independently, giving the proceeds to National Salvage. One rarity which turned up at the depot while Sylvia was there, a portfolio of contemporary drawings of the Indian Mutiny, was sent to the Government of India's department of archives.

In the winter of 1942–3, the war news became 'bloodier and bloodier'; Singapore had fallen, the Japanese were in Burma, the British had retreated to India, the Germans were holding on in the six-month battle for Stalingrad and in North Africa the victory at El Alamein had not been followed up by an overall victory. 'The air is darkened with sins coming home to roost,' Sylvia wrote of the situation in India and Hong Kong. Her admiration and support (she collected very small amounts locally for Soviet Aid) were still mainly with the USSR: 'Amid our ignominious news I remember last autumn and how I knew that the defence of USSR was the defence of my deepest concerns: and I know it still: though I would like to think we would be advancing too. Instead of which that damned clever general, Rommel, has retaken Jebadiah.'[42]

It was a bitterly cold winter. On a morning of twenty degrees of frost Valentine went out to pickaxe artichokes from the vegetable garden, there being nothing else to cook. Paraffin was hard to get, and hard to keep, as pilfering was on the increase, and Sylvia and Valentine began to direct their Sunday leisure towards cone-gathering for fuel. They still celebrated birthdays and anniversaries with pleasure, but the gifts were necessarily less grand and numerous than before. On 14 February 1943, Valentine gave Sylvia 'a canton enamel box, and snowdrops and daffodils. I gave her a very industrious exceedingly handmade and regrettably tubular Fair Isle scarf.'

In March, Valentine had to move to a new office on the first floor, which had the advantage of being remote and unvisited. Here she got on with what work there was and, as secretary to the Civil Defence controller, led what she considered an oddly domestic life, waking the colonel from his afternoon nap, attending to his opinions, never answering back. Compared with this, WVS was positively vibrant. Sylvia had installed a photograph of Stalin above her desk to counter Mrs Egerton's Churchill and had developed various ways of defusing women of the Tomkins and Bumkin sort – one was by refusing to answer them until she had lit up a cigarette exaggeratedly slowly. Sylvia had a growing liking for Mrs Egerton, a genteel and unassuming woman. As the two most senior representatives of the WVS, they had to attend a wide variety of events together. One morning in March they were observers at a Civil Defence invasion exercise, which had been organised with a noisy insistence on secrecy:

> We hung about after lunch, waiting for zero-hour. The dive-bombers turned out to be low-flying spitfires fitted with screamers. They flew very beautifully, but the screamers seemed a mistake to me. Why advertise? It is the *Silent* plane which would frighten me. Guns went off: dogs barked. We drove home, visiting Charminster on the way. Java is falling. And so from hour to hour we rot and rot.[43]

On just another such manoeuvre a month later, the Spitfire fired to the right instead of to the left and killed a group of observing intelligence officers, including a brigadier and the local education officer, whom Valentine knew and admired.

When the WVS were asked to form part of a parade around Dorchester to mark Warship Week in March, Sylvia joined in, much to Valentine's disapproval. The group was assembled at its starting-point when the members all succumbed to doubt as to the proper fashion in which to carry a ceremonial gas-mask. Should it be to the right or to the left? Over the shoulder or under the arm? Sylvia suggested that they should be worn like swords, 'but unheard, for they were all undressing'. The parade set off in pouring rain, past an admiral drenched from head to foot, taking the salute from a platform in the High Street.

Perhaps Sylvia's greatest war effort was in the field of self-control, for she showed remarkable endurance in the face of the 'consequential idiots' who would ordinarily have been flayed by her tongue. After one WVS-run blood-donating session, she collapsed into bed 'singularly tired by smiling so much: sensation enforced by Miss Cl[apcott] saying "Miss Warner is so wonderful.

She seems to have a smile for everyone."' The novel which Sylvia was writing at the time – *The Corner That Held Them* – deals almost exclusively with the behaviour of an enclosed community of women and it seems likely that she used some of her observations of the predominantly female population of wartime Dorchester for her book.

As the war threw Sylvia and Valentine more and more among company not of their choosing it made them both yearn for the leisure in which to cultivate friendships in a civilised way again. One day, when Sylvia was standing in the High Street, waiting to go home after WVS, she saw 'with unmitigated astonishment, a distinguished woman in Dorchester'. When she looked again, it was Valentine, who had stopped the car when she too caught sight of a distinguished woman and realised it was Sylvia. Later in the year they were both pleasantly surprised by the appearance in the lounge of the King's Arms, Dorchester, of a tall thin woman of great elegance, who walked in, holding a large onion. Sylvia was in no doubt but that it was Nancy Cunard, with whom she had corresponded over the Spanish War, and introduced herself. They talked about Spain, France and the onion – a valuable possession at that date – and that same evening Miss Cunard and her companion Morris Gilbert were guests for dinner at Frome Vauchurch.

'Our friendship was instantaneous, secure and detached; we exchanged opinions, never confidences,'[44] Sylvia wrote. Nancy Cunard was forty-seven when she met Sylvia and Valentine, and had led a colourful, joyless life. She had been notorious in the Twenties for her anti-conventionality, but personal publicity was nothing to her. Her eccentricity, elegance and breeding tended to draw attention away from what was really unusual in her – a capacity for hard work and a predilection for acting on her principles which many fellow-idealists did not share. It was this very practical side of her character which particularly appealed to Sylvia, and her seriousness in the face of a cause. She was devoted to Spain and to France, admired the Soviet Union and had many Communist friends and connections, though she herself had never joined the Party. For Sylvia and Valentine, she brought a breath of Europe with her, and they snuffed it like exiles.

IV

Black Out! Shut out the dusk
The dying looks of day,
The sunset like a husk
Whose fruit is shrivelled away

Shut out the breath of clay
That clouds the window-pane,
Murmuring, Look now well upon this light you may
Or may not see again.

Black Out! Shut in the glow,
The fireside looks that dwell
On books in peaceful row
And children peaceable.

Oh hide it, hide it well!
Lest men should see your light
And from the darkness march, and from their ranks rebel,
And end the war tonight.[45]

There was no end to the war in sight in the winter of 1943–4, although the Russians had forced the German army back as far as their own border with Poland. The British bombing raids on German cities, begun in the spring of 1943, were destructive rather than effective, but Sylvia welcomed them as a necessary evil. The day on which the first thousand bombers went over to Cologne, she wrote in her diary: 'God knows I was almost on my knees in thankfulness for the news we had done something. But O the poor bloody army, which is assuming a female role of sheltered domesticity and retirement, broken by bouts of such frightful activity as only women are expected to undertake.'

Early in 1944, Sylvia was expected to undertake work of 'national importance – which means they will try to put me into a laundry'[46] when the latest set of labour laws extended its reach in her direction. She was given a part-time job as secretary-dispenser to a local doctor, Dr Lander of Evershot, though this gave her less time with the WVS, where she had made herself indispensable. Sylvia resented the system of values behind the new laws, as she wrote in a letter to Nancy Cunard: 'Being kept by a husband is of national importance enough. But to be femme sole, and self-supporting, that hands you over, no more claim to consideration than a biscuit.'[47] Her resentment was greatest, as usual, in the defence of Valentine. In a letter, again to Nancy Cunard, she described Valentine's situation at work in dramatic terms: 'What is wrong with Valentine? It is called pyrexia, a state of private fever. What it is really is just what one might expect if you put a poet in an office for three years on end, and ask it to travel in the same train daily, and give it too much to do, and surround it with ugly faces and loud voices and hearts like linoleum.'[48] Poets have been known to survive office life, and worse. Sylvia's anger had fallen on the nearest target, but there were other reasons for Valentine's almost suicidal depression during the spring of 1944. It was not simply that Valentine had not the leisure in which to write, but that she felt she could not write; subsequently her experiences remained oddly unrealised. For Valentine, seeing something and expressing what she saw were mutually dependent parts of a process of celebration, or more properly, *assent* – an important word in her vocabulary. Without that, things happened – a hare might pause on the field opposite, a kingfisher open its wings in sunlight – but the moment passed and she did not participate in it.

In addition to this, Valentine had a number of other worries: her habitual worries about money and health, her concern that she 'encumbered' Sylvia in some way and that their love had never completely recovered itself since their unhappy trip to America. Valentine considered her own age to be advanced (in 1944 she was about to be thirty-seven, the age at which Sylvia had fallen in love) and bearing this in mind, it is possible that she found Sylvia's fifty years quite alarming. In some ways Sylvia was still very young-looking: her hair was predominantly black, and the war had kept her thin. She was as hardy and healthy as ever, but she was fifty. And as a bass note to all the things that troubled Valentine was an awareness of the relative pettiness of them. She was 'overcome and overwhelmed by shame'[49] that in the midst of the war she could be overset by purely personal worries.

In the late spring, the South Coast area was given over to preparations for the invasion of France. A ban on movements in and out of the area was imposed and non-residents had to leave. The roads were full of lorries and soldiers, the sky full of planes, and Maiden Newton full of the U.S. army. 'In this accumulation of metal, soldiers seemed intensely fragile, *objets de luxe*,' Sylvia wrote. 'One stared at the craftsmanship of their eyelashes and fingernails, their eyelids like flower-petals.'[50] Valentine had a bag packed, ready for emergency evacuation. In it was a complete change of clothes, two pairs of socks, sand-shoes, nails, screws, a composite tool, soap, some food, the means with which to make a fire, tobacco, a pipe, a money-belt including some small bits of gold, four miniatures of Shakespeare's plays and poems, a pocket chess set, torch, paper, pencils and a small manuscript volume of Sylvia's poems. What Sylvia packed, if anything, was never recorded, but a local widow revealed to Valentine the contents of her emergency bag: a tin of dog food, a clean handkerchief and the deeds to her house.

Late in May, a marauding Messerschmidt was being chased towards the coast by a Spitfire and, as was the custom with bombers, jettisoned its remaining load as it fled. As it went over East Chaldon, it dropped a bomb which fell in the garden of Miss Green's cottage, completely destroying the house. Jimmy and May Pitman got out in time to be injured rather than killed: May had heard the all-clear sound from Dorchester and drummed her family out of their beds on an instinct of danger. Nothing else in the village was damaged, though the remaining bombs fell on Chaldon Down, where the marks can still be seen today.

Sylvia and Valentine digested the news in sombre silence. The little 'freehold salt-box' was inseparably associated with their falling in love, and its destruction seemed portentous as well as shocking. They did not speak about the bombing, nor did they attempt to go and see the damage, purposely avoiding the village for more than five years afterwards. To Theodore Powys the destruction of Miss Green must have seemed the perfect justification for his move inland to Mappowder in 1940. At the very beginning of the war, though, he had felt sufficiently fearless to joke about such an eventuality, saying that any German pilot who dropped a bomb on Chaldon would be dismissed for incompetence.[51]

Events in the war were moving fast and on 6 June the Allies landed on the Normandy coast. By 24 August Paris had been liberated and the German army was in retreat. The Russians were pushing across Europe from the east and Sylvia rejoiced to think that her cousin Hilary Machen, then a prisoner of war in southern Germany, might almost be within earshot of the Red Army's advance. At home, the 'doodlebugs', German V1 bombs, and V2s were being lavished on British towns and cities, especially London, and this renewed aggression, combined with a lifting of the residence ban, brought a flood of evacuees into the West Country. The dusty rest centre system, Sylvia's particular responsibility at the WVS, had to adjust rapidly from being hardly needed at all to being overstretched. They were given twenty-four hours' notice in which to clean the centres, make up beds and prepare hot meals for the first consignment from the capital, a party of fifty-four women and children.

Rest centres were intended for housing refugees temporarily, until they could be found places with local families, but in the event, the process of absorption simply did not take place. According to a report Sylvia made for the WVS records, the Londoners arrived 'not knowing what they would find, and when they found it, they mistrusted it. They were geared to the terror and excitement of London, and country peace and quiet nauseated them. And they had nothing to do; and so they expected everything to be done for them. The Rest Centre workers found them incomprehensible, uncontrollable, mannerless, dirty and ungrateful.'[52] Attitudes hardened quickly on both sides, and there was more antagonism than rest in most of the centres. New parties arrived, and the villages dreaded getting them, with the result that many evacuees had to stay weeks in makeshift accommodation which was all the centres could provide. Sylvia took in two women from the first lot: 'a big melancholy woman, a little like the searching Demeter, and her eighteen-year-old daughter who has asthma, not improved by stifling in an Anderson. It is so shameful, so disgraceful, that one is expected to *choose* them, to pick as in a slave-market. I don't feel as if they could ever forgive me for having chosen.'[53] Valentine and Sylvia had rearranged the house for their earlier evacuees, bringing bedroom furniture downstairs to convert the dining-room and thereby retaining some privacy upstairs. Neither of them, naturally enough, relished playing hostess to strangers. Sylvia wrote to Nancy Cunard: 'I expect it will be hell. The two previous lots, full of virtues, irreproachable, were hell. The first set made the house stink of breast of mutton, [...] I've forgotten what was wrong with the second lot, nothing I think except that they were here.'[54]

Sylvia had been relieved of one duty, and that the most congenial – her dispensing job at Dr Lander's. This happened after Valentine's depression, persisting all summer, bore fruit in the form of an acute stomach pain. Sylvia called Dr Lander to the house, where he pronounced her unfit to work and issued a series of weekly certificates to corroborate his diagnosis. He agreed with Sylvia's opinion that Civil Defence was damaging Valentine's health and that she should be moved – preferably to his dispensary, where she could work longer hours than Sylvia and act as chauffeur when necessary. After a few weeks, the Controller of Civil Defence became irritated by his secretary's prolonged sick-leave, fired her, and Valentine took over an elaborated version of Sylvia's former job in the late summer.

The job suited Valentine very well. She loved the delicacy and orderliness which dispensing required and she had medicine in her blood, or at the very least, her teeth. All the same, she was slightly wary about taking it on; she was unsure whether or not Sylvia really minded being deposed (Sylvia really did not mind) and being 'unqualified' made her feel incapable, and she wrote to Alyse Gregory:

> Sylvia is wonderful at the job; she has some knowledge of plants and drugs and knows their latin names & she has a character that does not doubt itself: when she makes a mistake she does not doubt for a moment but that it is *not* a mistake, and when she discovers beyond doubt that it *is* one,

she feels no despair. I wish I had that kind of courage but as I have not I must study to endure instead.[55]

By the end of 1944 it was clear that the Allies had the upper hand in the war. The Russians were in East Prussia and the Third Army had crossed the German border to the west. By February 1945 the fate of Germany had been planned out by the Allied leaders at Yalta, British and Canadian troops had reached the Rhine and the RAF had carried out its last – and heaviest – raid, this time on Dresden. With an end to the war in sight, reports were only just coming to light of what had been going on for the past six years in the concentration camps in Germany and Poland. Six days after the taking of Belsen and Buchenwald by the British army, Valentine made the following entry in her day-book:

> I was fishing. The river went along very smoothly and the fish sprang and splashed; the evening air was full of birds and about to change into being full of bats. It was exceedingly lovely, still and gentle and everywhere pale, blossoming trees, very tall and creamy in the half-light.
>
> There is no escape from the people dying in the Nazi concentration camps. War Reports, on the BBC, bring stories and accounts which are obviously authentic. And these dead people, these dying people, wander everywhere. Their misery, condemnation, fatal agony spreads over the whole width and length of the stream of life.
>
> I thought 'I would gladly lay down my life to help clear this load and scum of suffering away –' and instantly realised that to *lay down a life* is the sickness itself. [...]
>
> When I was going to work this fine and lovely April morning I heard the garden thrush singing and I thought immediately: 'They must have heard thrushes in Buchenwald – how they must have lusted to catch them for food.'[56]

The shock of revelations from the camps subdued any spirit of celebration which Sylvia and Valentine might have expected to feel at the news, on 30 April, that Hitler had committed suicide in Berlin. It was clear that this meant, in effect, the end of the war in

Europe, although V.E. Day was not proclaimed until 8 May. 'I was sure we would all collapse, perhaps die of joy,' Valentine wrote. 'Instead it feels as if we had all died of fatigue and impacted rage before the joy came ... Probably there'll be photographs of drunken crowds in Piccadilly and reverent crowds in village churches – They won't be true – they won't be representative!'[57] When peace was finally declared, Valentine wrote, 'we both felt peculiarly tired and perhaps we were rather particularly polite to each other. I had to work, which was ordinary, but I felt odd and unreal [...] And most profoundly, indistinctly gloomy.'[58] Violent hostilities continued in the Pacific between the Americans and Japanese and wartime conditions at home persisted unchanged. It was hard to see what had really altered.

Much was to alter. The atomic clouds over Hiroshima and Nagasaki dispersed to reveal a new world, profoundly affected by the human and material losses and the scientific advances of the war. There seemed little room for Sylvia and Valentine in it, who felt, quite rightly, that the system of values in which they had grown up and flourished was being rapidly eroded. It seemed that what the war had crystallised in the British character was its bourgeoisness; even the socialist post-war governments and the Welfare State they introduced seemed petty by comparison with the Communist dream. The war lay like a deep trench between Sylvia and Valentine and their salad days, and was unbreachable. Sylvia wrote to Paul Nordoff, early in 1946: 'No one in wartime can quite escape the illusion that when the war ends things will snap back to where they were and that one will be the same age one was when it began, and able to go on from where one left off. But the temple of Janus has two doors, and the door for war and door for peace are equally marked in plain lettering, No Way Back. And the dead are not more irrevocably dead than the living are irrevocably alive.'[59]

V

On their first visit to London after the end of the war, Valentine and Sylvia were struck by how few elegant people were to be seen and how few hats. London was overflowing with high quality food and they ate the most extravagant meal they had had since 1939, though it lay rather heavily on their consciences, food shortages still being acute in Europe. The two women rejoiced in the sight of St Paul's still standing, but it was a great shock to see so many familiar places ruined. Inverness Terrace was heavily damaged, later demolished, and a whole side of Mecklenburgh Square, one of Valentine's old haunts, had been destroyed, 'completely flattened', Valentine wrote to Alyse Gregory, 'smell of smoke and fire still hanging over the streets and pieces of the fixtures of the houses still littering the basements and gutters. Front doors ajar, and stately rooms beyond, with pit-holes down to the earth instead of floors, and small trees and jungles of dying loosestrife grown up almost to the front windows.'[60]

Sylvia and Valentine were looking round for a possible new home because their landlady, Mrs West, had begun to talk of re-occupying Frome Vauchurch. Although they did not think it would come to an eviction, because of their rights as tenants, Sylvia and Valentine made contingency plans and got as far as inspecting a house for sale in Edinburgh, an elegant Georgian town-house with a garden sloping down to the water of Leith. But despite its elegance and low price, and Sylvia's love of Scotland and longing for city life again, they decided against it and soon afterwards began negotiations with Mrs West through the Ackland family lawyer to buy Frome Vauchurch. In 1946 the deal was completed, and it was Valentine, not Sylvia, who was the purchaser, using a loan from Ruth of £2,200, repayable at 4½% interest.

Their joint finances were fairly weak at the time. Valentine had kept on her job as dispenser to Dr Lander's successor, Edmund Gaster, because she needed the money and Sylvia was not earning very much from the New Yorker because her time was increasingly tied up in writing her long novel about convent life. When rumours reached them that Sylvia was being considered as a possible member of the BBC's 'Brains Trust' panel, 'Sylvia was at first very grand about it but said, when I said twenty-five pounds! that she would do almost anything for that.'[61] Their attitudes to money still differed widely, as a small incident over a bill shows. Valentine had notice from a magazine that they were going to pay her £15 for a short story she had submitted, an enormous stroke of luck in her eyes and a boost to her spirits. At the same time, however, a bill arrived for £31 for repairs to the second-hand car they had bought in 1945, and Valentine was immediately dismal and deflated, her earnings vanished before she had even received them. Sylvia, on the other hand, supposed Valentine would be pleased because her new £15 covered almost half the bill.

Valentine's fortieth birthday in May 1946 set her thinking about mortality – or rather immortality, as death was an almost constant preoccupation of hers, but now she began to think about the soul. 'It became of first importance to me,' she wrote a year later, 'not so much to hoard up virtue and find a creed or a faith, for those things did not seem to have anything to do with the matter, but I felt a compelling desire to find out about the nature of the soul and if, as I suspected, it proved to be necessary to cultivate and care for it, to make it strong and put it in the way of freeing itself easily from the body, then I felt it was now my main concern to do that.'[62] The books she was reading at this time indicate the sort of journey she had set out on: Plato's Last Days of Socrates, Kabir, Vaughan, Traherne, St Augustine, Yeats, Epictetus, Seneca, Montaigne. These were 'like matches struck in darkness. They have each flared up very strongly and vividly in my night and in that moment of brightness I have seen the outline of my soul.'[63] She began to think of her spirit as something which had been neglected in favour of her body and mind, something which she might still be able to revive, if she were to make an enormous effort to nurture and tend it. The idea of her spirit having gradually wasted away connected very clearly in Valentine's mind with the lessening of her conviction that she was a poet. She began to hope and trust that if she could revive her spirit, the conflicts and frustrations she encountered in her creative life might be resolved too.

Her addiction to drink was, she felt, a symptom of the same spiritual debilitation. She had sought medical advice on a number of occasions and in 1940 had undergone an expensive commercial 'cure', to no lasting avail. In the summer of 1947 she sustained a whole month 'D.D.', but then fell back more violently than ever. She began to despair of ever gaining control over herself.

This state of things changed dramatically soon after Sylvia's and Valentine's return from a holiday in Ireland in the autumn of 1947. On the night of 8 October, Valentine staggered to bed, drunk and despairing; she felt 'as if eternity were opening all around me; and it was as black as hell.' Then, as she recounted in her autobiography, 'for no reason that I can give, instead of climbing into bed and putting out the light [...] I knelt down and – with this vertiginous black Eternity surrounding me – addressed Emptiness like this: "Is God there?" There was no reply. Everything was completely dead. I had no sense except of emptiness and the rushing swirling dark.'[64] Into this emptiness, and 'without faith or hope', she vowed never to drink again, got into bed and fell asleep. The next day was blighted by a powerful hangover, but by evening she became aware that she was 'walking in tranquillity and with perfect confidence'; she had turned herself around.

Her reading continued and acquired a focus, Nicolas Herman and St Augustine taking precedence over Greek philosophers and oriental mystics. 'And where have I come to?' she asked in her diary of 11 October. 'I do not know yet. I may know soon. I wish I may. Words are troublesome because of what they "mean" above, below and behind their first-apparent meaning; *faith*, for instance; and *belief*.' The process of 'rebirth' intrigued her. She knew it did not intrigue Sylvia at all. Sylvia did not accept, consciously or otherwise, the Christian mystics' idea that the present world is a 'vale of soul-making'; nor did she feel any impulse to develop her personality or question it. There is no sign of her being in the least critical of Valentine's spiritual 'quest', though; indeed, she may not have even noticed the crisis taking place. She would have noticed (and for the most part approved) Valentine's reading, the more frequent presence of God in Valentine's talk, the improvement in Valentine's spirits and health, the philosophical turn of her poems of 1948, without concluding that there had been some radical change. But Valentine felt changed – or changing: 'It is a curious sensation to think of oneself as a work in progress: after so long being accustomed to think of oneself as a creator.'[65] Everything had become new, had to be relearnt, in the context of having a soul. Valentine was not just 'translating' her old life, but beginning again:

> You can live on the country, they say, and do better so
> than to carry provisions which, under that sky, will rot.
> You can travel fast or slow; there is nothing to tell you
> how much further you have to journey until you arrive,
> how much further before you reach –
>
> Reach what? I do not know.
> All I know is the blight of the North wind, the carrion
> patience of winter hanging up there in the sky,
> and the blow that is aimed from the Pole, that is aimed to
>   destroy us.
> These things, and the date of starting, are all I know.[66]

5

1947–1950

I

Sylvia dreamed last night that she was staying in an hotel (I think in London) and it was depressing and she was impatient to get out into the streets. As she went across the hall to the front door the manager of the hotel, a soapy, unpleasant man, intercepted her and told her she must be *very* careful whenever she went out, because – 'Look!' he said, and showed her – Directly in front of the door-step [...] there was a very deep pit [...] At the bottom of this shaft there was a pale pinkish light, moving always slightly or looking as though water lay there, lighted somehow, or catching from somewhere this pinkish light.

She was very frightened, and the more so when she heard a voice from this deep shaft, desperately reiterating 'Remember the Pit! Remember the Pit!'

In her dream she felt an extremity of fear at this, and then with a great effort of will, out of a determination not to be compelled by any terror but to continue doing what she had intended to do, she ordered the hotel manager to make it possible for her to go out. Which he did, by placing planks over the opening to the pit – but, he unctuously explained, it was necessary to leave a gap, a dangerous gap, and she would have to cross carefully. And it was a wide space that he left,

> down which she could have fallen, but she did not; she
> crossed in safety and came out onto the street.[1]

Valentine recorded this dream of Sylvia in March 1948, because
she felt the behaviour in it to be characteristic and admirable.
Sylvia was a vivid dreamer and at times of stress her dreams
seemed to her especially significant. This dream of the pit, which
struck Valentine as showing bravery, seemed to Sylvia more an
expression of fearfulness.

The fears which preyed most on Sylvia's mind were to do with
her mother, Nora, who had rapidly become senile. As late as 1946,
Nora had been merely eccentric, and still lived at Little Zeal, alone
except for her two remaining dogs, a chow and a pomeranian,
both old and musty. Nora, then aged eighty, had been cantanker-
ous towards Sylvia for many years, but her sourness was gradually
extending to everyone except Evans the gardener, Mr Boucher, a
neighbour whom she considered to be an admirer, and herself. As
a result she had become very isolated. Sylvia made light of her
mother to other people – it was one way of keeping some control
of the situation. When she was visiting her aunt and uncle in
Amersham in 1940, Arthur Machen had noted that Sylvia 'told a
stream of stories about her mother, the point of them being mostly
against her mother; but all very amusing.'[2] By the late 1940s,
when Sylvia went on her regular but short visits of filial duty, she
found Nora's endless talk and its aimless, repetitive nature,
exhausting and depressing. Nora was so deaf that the radio had to
be turned up painfully high, and that set the dogs off barking.
During one particularly fierce Dartmoor gale, Nora was unaware
that anything untoward was going on outside until she noticed
boughs of trees passing across her window. Sylvia made Valentine
promise that if ever she went the same way, Valentine was to shoot
her.

The following year, Nora's condition worsened considerably
and when Sylvia visited her, at first Nora didn't know her
daughter, then ignored her. The old resentments, angers and
jealousies began to work themselves out – delusions, too, for every
time Nora had some message for Sylvia to take to a dressmaker, or
a packet of lace for some long-dead acquaintance. 'She was like a

mad infant, pitiable and terrifying,'[3] and Sylvia was frightened again, for the first time since her youth. Nora was in generally good health, and not insane, but she was incontinent and needed constant attention. The district nurse came once a day, but that was not enough, and the doctor believed that Nora could last in the same or worse condition for years. Sylvia went to Devon in December 1947 and thought she might get through the visit 'by shutting both eyes', but things did not improve, and she began to search for a suitable nurse-companion. Unable to find one, Sylvia considered for the first time the possibility of putting Nora into a home, despite the promise she had made some years before that her mother would never be made to leave Little Zeal. It was either a home, or Sylvia herself becoming the nurse-companion. This she refused to do: as she wrote to Steven Clark, 'if this course leaves any specks on my conscience, as I daresay it may, I will rub them off at my leisure. But go down quick into the pit I will not ...'[4]

Valentine had come down to support Sylvia after a few days, distressed at the tone of her letters. Sylvia was afraid that Nora might attack Valentine, for she made no bones now about her violent dislike for the younger woman, but in the event, Nora didn't seem to recognise her properly, or chose not to, and Valentine avoided Nora's room carefully, not least because she couldn't bear the stink of it.

Valentine had never stayed at Little Zeal before, and having the leisure to look round it found it full of exquisite furniture and antique objects, 'like a museum, or a curiosity-shop'. She also had the opportunity to observe Nora's behaviour, which horrified her: '[Nora] has been, all her life, a vain, domineering and self-gratifying woman and now she lies in her bed living over and over the situations in her life when either she was arousing envy or desire or was herself experiencing one or the other. [...] she tells over and over the triumphs she has had – social triumphs, triumphs of despotism, triumphs of wit or domination. And then she chatters, in her loud, crazy voice, about the men who have admired and desired her and what she said and did and wore and the way she managed them.'[5] Nora had sharp dips down into idiocy and upward into something like normality, when she would show a sudden flash of affection or gratitude towards Sylvia.

Sylvia did not respond to these, though; it was too painful, and Valentine dared not speak to her of her feelings, knowing as she did that 'all Sylvia's experience of her mother had been miserably unhappy and full of torment. Nora has hated and thwarted her and done, as it were by instinct, everything she could, at all times, to suppress and injure her. Although I do think she has felt pride, at times, and sometimes pleasure too, in having Sylvia as her child. But it is probably true, as Sylvia says, that Nora's only appreciation of anything or anyone has been founded upon the glory they gave her or the regard they brought her.'[6]

On Christmas Eve 1947 Sylvia took her mother to the Windermere Nursing Home in Paignton, stayed long enough to see Nora settling in to domineer a young nurse, then went back to Dorset exhausted. But going to the home seemed to worsen Nora's behaviour and on the first night she was found getting into the bed of a ninety-three-year-old male resident, and told the nurse who came to his rescue, 'I was just going to kill him.' Every day she tried to get to the front door by stealth, only to find she had forgotten for what reason. She became absorbedly vain about small luxury items, spending a fortune on silk stockings and kid gloves, sent for from London stores, and wrecked her room several times, apparently trying to find exotic clothes from her past she felt were hidden there.

When Sylvia went to visit, she was surprised that the matron insisted on going in with her as a sort of bodyguard, for Nora had been telling everyone that when her daughter came, she was going to knock her head off. Valentine felt that this ferocity of Nora was mostly a sham, an exercise of power, and that the crazy voice and bullying expression were to some extent assumed. But sham or no, Nora was at this time almost constantly aggressive. On one visit, she told Sylvia to open the wardrobe, saying she had four pairs of boots in there 'for kicking people with'. The only thing in the wardrobe was a pair of bedroom slippers, which Sylvia brought. Nora became very cross and said, '*Those* wouldn't hurt anyone.'[7]

The nursing-home was expensive, and Little Zeal had to be maintained, Evans paid, the dogs looked after. Worst of all, as Sylvia found out, Nora had 'spent the last few months of her wits in becoming overdrawn'[8] and there were debts to be covered. Nora had assured Sylvia years before that she had been cut out of her will, so there was no question of post-obiting to cover these expenses. Sylvia's usual expedient of pot-boiling was neither sufficient, nor, at the time, very effective. She had only just finished *The Corner That Held Them*, a very preoccupying book to write. In its shadow had withered a novel about family life, begun in 1946, and 'Amy', a novel begun in 1947 and abandoned four years later. In 1948 Sylvia began another story, set in contemporary England, about a Swedish *au-pair* girl arriving at the country home of her new employer to find that the lady is dying. The first, completed, part of 'Song Without Words' is among the best things that Sylvia wrote, psychologically compelling and remarkably evocative of an English winter landscape, but the second part of the story ran dry, and was shelved.

Sylvia had published two books since the end of the war, *The Portrait of a Tortoise*, which was a selection from the writings of Gilbert White, tracing the story of his tortoise, Timothy, and *The Museum of Cheats*, a collection of twenty-two short stories. *The Museum of Cheats* is almost entirely about the war at home and the types of behaviour – new and old – engendered by it. Many of the people and situations, according to notes Sylvia once wrote, were 'studied' from life, including the most improbable, such as 'Rosie Flounders'. When Sylvia was compiling the book, she became dissatisfied with some of the material and wrote the title story as a substitute. 'A general survey of bunkums',[9] it is much longer than anything else in the book and was presumably intended to make the collection cohere, but its jauntiness prevents this, being out of key with the other stories. Among these are several excellent stories – perhaps more accurately described as sketches or studies, for they rely only slightly on plot – which convey the tone of provincial life in wartime – 'Poor Mary', 'English Climate', 'The Cold', 'Waiting for Harvest'. Satire, so imperative in the Spanish campaign, and irony, so unavoidable in the run-up to the war, have given way to an overpowering sense of melancholy disillusionment, not so much in the author (there are the subtlest sideswipes in all these stories) but in the texture of the writing, which had to form a suitable vessel for the sad, shabby, petty and pitiable characters Sylvia was observing. As the curator of the Museum of Cheats realises on his return from fighting with the Maquis to dealing with the petty intrigues of Tipton Bacchus, 'he was handling a much smaller gun; but the target was equally the same.'[10]

'Boors Carousing' in The Museum of Cheats is about a writer, 'studied from myself' according to Sylvia, who, distracted by visitors, has been unable to work on his novel and instead wrote short stories, 'a prey to human nature – which is poison and dram-drinking to the serious artist'.[11] The story goes on to have him interrupted again by an eccentric and reclusive neighbour whose house down-river is troubled by flood. Going into the old lady's house after grudgingly helping her, the writer realises that she is a genteel alcoholic and on returning home begins to make a story out of her. He is drawn to her because they are two of a kind – both 'dram-drinkers'. Sylvia had used this image for the obsessive nature of the act of writing before, in Opus 7, speaking of Rebecca Random, her gin-soaked heroine, and her own progress through the poem as its author:

> Each day declares
> yesterday's currency a few dead leaves;
> and through all the sly nets poor technique weaves
> the wind blows on, whilst I – new nets design,
> a sister-soul to my slut heroine,
> she to her dram enslaved, and I to mine.[12]

Almost half the stories in The Museum of Cheats had been published first in the New Yorker, where Sylvia's work had become well-established. In 1945 she had been honoured by the magazine with a First Reading Agreement, in effect a higher rate of payment and a contract granting the New Yorker first refusal on new stories. Though this should have given Sylvia a degree of stability, by 1947 she was finding it frustrating to have to wait months sometimes for a decision before she could try to market a story elsewhere. She felt, as she complained to William Maxwell, 'as though I had plighted my vows to a refrigerator'.[13] In the longeurs between dollar cheques she turned to other sources of income, modest though they were by comparison: adapting a novel by her American friend Anne Parrish for a radio play, contributing articles and stories to magazines, notably *Our Time*, the successor to *Left Review*, the *New Statesman* and *The Countryman*, and accepting a commission to write a book about Somerset, which she did in the summer of 1948, going out for long car rides and walks with Valentine to study the county in detail.

Somerset, which was published in 1949 in a series edited by Clough and Amabel Williams-Ellis, Communist friends of Sylvia's, is a book which would seem to justify Sylvia's stated wish to be a landscape painter in another incarnation. Her sensitivity to colour, texture and quality of light was never given greater scope than in this 'err-and-stray' view of the county – 'I am constitutionally incapable of resembling a guide'[14] – full of the most stimulating descriptive prose, such as this paragraph about Ham Hill stone, the most distinctive local building material:

> One of the charms of this tawny south Somerset stone is its great variability. Not only does it weather from its first butter-colour through every shade of golden tabby down to a greenish tint which is almost as dark as pond-water, but these hues respond like a chameleon to changes of light and humidity. I had never thought Crewkerne a town of much distinction (though it has a handsome large church with an acrostical epitaph in it, and a fair in late summer: it was at this fair in the innocent nineteen-twenties that I saw on a placard outside a booth the boastful claim: 'All Our French Artist's Models are Alive'); but one evening when the sun came suddenly out after a day of rain I saw Crewkerne light up with an intensity of colour I have never forgotten: topaz and beer-bottle brown, and tawny yellows beyond comparison.[15]

The book is also full of recondite information and surprising digressions from the usual guide-path – notably a description of the seasonal modulations in the smell of apple. It is a sensualist's book, written in a style which conveys the intimate quality of conversation.

The Corner That Held Them was published while Sylvia was finishing work on *Somerset*. It is her most ambitious novel, one in which she abandoned many conventional elements of novel-writing, such as the use of a protagonist or a plot, and set out instead a long, well-paced and consistently well-imagined chronicle of life in a Fenlands convent, Oby, between the years 1345 and 1382. It was the period of the Peasant Revolt and the Black Death, 'one of the salient events of economic history, one of the few that possesses a date,' as George Townsend Warner had written in *Trade, Tillage and Invention*. Economics dominate the book, as they dominated the lives of the nuns; Sylvia was to say much later that she began the story, 'on the purest Marxian principles, because I was convinced that if you were going to give an accurate picture of the monastic life, you'd have to put in all their finances.'[16]

It is, indeed, a very worldly book; not a historical novel, but a piece of highly artificial 'realism'. It is full of suppressed ironies, but deliberately empty of significance; idiosyncratic, absorbing and entertaining. Detail (often the smaller the better) is of great importance to the author in describing lives – and deaths – which were 'essentially trivial', and there is no overall pattern to the book, except that of time passing:

> The weather was intensely sultry. Thunderstorms rattled overhead but did not break the drought. The little rain they wrenched out of the clouds had scarcely touched the earth before it rose up in a steaming mist. The nuns, exhausted by kneeling round Dame Isabel and repeating the prayers for the dying on behalf of a woman who seemingly could not die, found it hard to conceal their weariness and disillusionment (for it is disillusioning to discover that compassion, stretched out too long, materialises into nothing more than a feat of endurance). [...] there lay Dame Isabel, mute as a candle, visibly consuming away and still not extinguished. Every time she opened her eyes they were more appallingly brilliant. It was an exemplary end, but not a consolatory one. Even her patience seemed to take on a quality of deceit and abstraction, it was as though she were calculating the hours that

must pass before they would leave her alone. When at length she was dead the reflection that they had done everything they could for her was confused by a feeling that they and not she had stayed too long.[17]

Freed from the pressure of plot and the pressure to be consecutive and significant, Sylvia was able to examine, slowly and carefully, how society functions, illustrating through the lives of the Oby nuns the delicate interdependence between one person's behaviour and another's. She could not have done this by writing a conventional novel, nor by filling up her book with facts and a bogus sense of history. It was her genius to be able to imagine a time, place or person so fully as to be as good as real – or better – and she always seemed to find exactly the right and revealing detail to convey her meaning with astonishing freshness and force. 'Just a shift in a cloud will transform a landscape however well you know it,' she once said. 'There are details about it you never noticed before, and I think it's so with ordinary daily life. There's a shift of lighting and you see everything quite differently, and if you can catch that moment before the effect has gone then you can hope to write something that is convincing.'[18]

The Corner That Held Them remained Sylvia's own favourite among her novels. She had had to struggle to write it during the war and it was in many ways a book purely for herself, using a technique which exactly suited her. She had used the trick of not having a protagonist before, in *After the Death of Don Juan*, and had found that it afforded her a new freedom to introduce a large number of characters and attend to a multiplicity of 'points of view'. *The Corner That Held Them* has many more characters, covers a much longer period of time, and is more slowly paced than the earlier novel, and the effect of universal sympathy is so pronounced that one no longer sees the author's controlling hand in it. Little wonder that Sylvia felt the book had taken on a life of its own, and that she could not 'finish' the novel in any other way than simply stopping it. She tampered more with this book at the proof stage than with any other, and even when it was printed and bound – 'in its coffin' – could hardly let it go, and began to write a sequel.

The reviews were good, but on the whole rather short, and, as usual, seemed to view Sylvia's work as tame and comfortable, just the effect she never intended. Late in her life, she wrote to Norah Smallwood, her editor at Chatto & Windus from 1939, that 'if I ever hear the word style about myself again I shall burst and die.'[19] But it was her fate to be thought of as a stylist. The expression of her ideas was so unusual and stimulating that it often proved more memorable than the ideas themselves. In the early novels, the ideas were not so directed or so important as in the novels from *Summer Will Show* onwards, but the stylistic effects were very marked, and perhaps this disparity is what gives those earlier books their sense of adding up to less than the sum of their parts. In the later novels, where her purpose was more serious and her fanciful side subdued, Sylvia was still thwarted by her own manner of writing, which was essentially surprising and diverting.

Much of the 'charge' of Sylvia's books comes from the fact that they are highly emotional and yet highly controlled by the intellect. The surprise and freshness of her style, though, is very largely due to the construction of her similes. In them she chooses apparent incongruities to illuminate a real relation, often juxtaposing two or more totally different sense impressions to discover possibilities in description quite outside the expected. Consider her description of Nissen huts – 'as melancholy as yaks'. The phrase perfectly and succinctly conveys a number of impressions; the curving downward shape of both objects, their droopiness and slight absurdity, shagginess and solitariness. These effects are very glancing, for the pace of Sylvia's prose is fast. Often an image suggests itself as she is writing, as in this description of holding a dead poodle, written in a letter to George Plank, 'so limp, George, and so touchingly rounded and curly: like a sleeping puppy, like a cluster of grapes'. This is both tender and striking. The visual image is perfect, and the choice of the word 'cluster' infinitely more expressive than any 'bunch' could have been. A single word could often carry a whole extra level of meaning in Sylvia's similes, as in the flavour of the tart in this description of 'the Sunday burst of hymnody ... from church or chapel', 'so much like the gush of juice when one cuts open a rhubarb tart'.[20]

In the years after the war Sylvia was writing some of her best poems, poems with a strong interest in narrative and character, such as 'Seven Conjectural Readings' and 'Gloriana Dying'. These were quite different in kind from the intensely personal love poems she wrote occasionally for Valentine; they were technically and intellectually tight and the sort of work which would have made into a satisfying and successful book. Twenty years had passed since the publication of *The Espalier* and *Time Importuned*, but Sylvia had never ceased to compose poetry. It was in many ways the medium most natural to her, giving expression to her musicality and her essentially verbal intelligence at one and the same time. Her manner as a poet had changed: she no longer imitated other poets for ironic effect or relied so heavily on pastoral and allegorical subjects. Her subjects were still consciously unfashionable though, and increasingly drawn from myth and history. She continued to use archaisms, inversions, the transposition of parts of speech, and occasionally coinage, to stretch the language over her meaning. This penchant for old words, or the second meaning of words, makes her poems appear quaint at first glance, but they are not quaint. As Donald Davie has written, she was the 'most English of poets',[21] whose register was deliberately chosen.

Although she wrote in 'professional' quantity, Sylvia no longer put her poems forward for publication, except occasionally in magazines. Possibly she had ceased to think of herself as a poet in that way, though it seems more likely that she had Valentine's feelings at heart, having, albeit with the best intentions, made such a mistake with *Whether a Dove or Seagull*. Valentine could barely look at the book any more, and had crossed out the half-title in her own copy, writing 'Almost Opposite' instead. On the fly-leaf she had copied out part of a poem by Robert Graves: 'Who rhyming here have had/Marvellous hope of achievement/And deeds of ample scope,/Then deceiving and bereavement/Of this same hope.' Valentine's poems were as commercially unsuccessful as ever, and she as disheartened over them: 'I have come to thinking that I shall not try any more at all,' she wrote to Alyse Gregory, 'except to make money by the little articles I can sometimes turn out; for that I badly need to do. I *cannot* write with my tongue in my cheek, and I cannot make a thing look palatable when I feel myself that it is poisonous. This is as much lack of technical skill as possession of integrity, I think; but in any case, it means nothing like a steady income.'[22]

Valentine's and Sylvia's lives had diverged considerably since the war, a fact that was to have serious consequences. There was the business of Valentine's new spirituality, an essentially private matter, but also one she felt instinctively she could not share with Sylvia. In addition, the differences in their ages was more marked than at any previous time: at the end of 1948 Sylvia was fifty-five, greying and the possessor of a dental upper plate. Her interests were increasingly centred around her writing, the house and the garden, in which she had begun to take a passionate pride since the purchase of the house in 1946. Valentine was forty-two and still handsome and lithe. Through her work at Dr Gaster's she made several close friends among local people, most of whom admired Valentine without, at first, knowing her as a writer at all. Many of her general acquaintances never knew her as a poet, and many bored Sylvia to tears, a fact of which Valentine was painfully aware. Sylvia's own friends usually came from further afield and corroborated her identity as an intellectual and a writer. Sylvia's persistent success meant that it was no longer possible, in this matter of writing, for them to treat each other as equals, an admission which cost them both dear.

The surprised pleasure with which Valentine had found herself on a spiritual 'journey' in 1947 had dissipated by the end of 1948, for the process of starting life again in the awareness of having a soul brought with it other, painful awarenesses. Viewed in the new light, Valentine's past was an unadorned wasteland of selfishness, destruction and insensitivity. She became filled with a sense of her own worthlessness and wastefulness; a list of past loves became the occasion for violent self-reproach and remorse for the 'damage' she had done them; thinking of herself as a child only led her to thinking she had betrayed that child, wasted the talent which should have increased. She began to believe that there was no good in her, not because of inherent badness, but because she had wilfully driven out the good:

> And all those years, those lovely years and months and weeks and days and hours – all beautiful with an eternal beauty, I

wasted and fouled – debauching them with such grossness of behaviour, such horrible profusion of badness, that by now, at this age, I am more than half an idiot – [...] idiotic almost to despair.[23]

Valentine showed Sylvia this and a number of other entries in her diary to do with the ideas she was developing about her soul and about God, a gentle way of indicating which way her journey was taking her. Sylvia saw all too clearly, and abhorred the change which was robbing Valentine of her self-esteem. She answered several points raised in Valentine's diary in as detached a way as possible, but without masking her criticism. It was the last time she felt confident enough to speak directly and with control on this subject. To Valentine's assertion in her diary that 'Only the eternal Creator could conceivably forgive what I have done,' Sylvia replied:

You are aligning yourself with the great majority of Xian thinkers in thus expressing a latent dislike of God; for to draw this rigid line between what you can do and what God can do is, in effect, to assert that you and God have nothing in common, that though you may love him (odi et amo) you do not think that humankind can accept him as a fellow-citizen of the universe. This arbitrary quarantining of the creator is the odder in the sentence quoted because it is so plainly unjustified. It is ridiculous to assert that forgiveness is only possible to God. To err is human, and to forgive is human, too [...]

If you want to have a personalised God then I think you must admit that he is made in your image (you cannot make him otherwise), that he is the sum of what you consider humanly good and admirable, and that though he may be different in essence he is similar in nature. In fact, if you have a personalised God then I think you should recognise him as so much a human conception that belief in him involves you in the obligation of not considering him as alien to you ... the only forgiver, the only creator, the only this and that. [...]

> Though if you do not have a personalised God, none of these troubles need arise.[24]

But this did not change Valentine's position, which was already very firm, nor did it, apparently, alert her to the vehemence of Sylvia's feelings. The entries in Valentine's diary became longer and more Christian by the day, until a few months later, in April 1949, when her preoccupation with God was swept aside: Elizabeth Wade White, against Valentine's wishes, was coming to visit.

II

Between February, when she and Valentine had been on holiday together to Italy, and April, when Elizabeth came to Dorset, Sylvia had been entirely given over to writing a libretto for Paul Nordoff, who had a commission from Columbia University to write an opera. Italy had given her the theme – the last days of Shelley – and the theme had fired her with enthusiasm. Her libretto, 'The Sea-Change', was a work she fell upon with complete enjoyment. It was a form new to her, and invigoratingly liberating: 'I wish I could write librettos for the rest of my life. It is the purest of human pleasures, a heavenly hermaphroditism of being both writer and musician. No wonder that selfish beast Wagner kept it all to himself.'[25] Sylvia was still glowing with excitement from this when the day came on which Valentine was to meet Elizabeth in Yeovil, and by the end of that day, Valentine was in love again, very strongly, and with very strong reservations:

> Elizabeth has been here. Towards her I feel a violent desire to possess, a profound obligation to love, a feeling of assertiveness and a dangerous excitement because of this. I can look at her with dislike, and feel bored by her; I can find time drag when I am with her and feel perfectly alien to her – and then at a touch all that is blown away and all I need in the world is

> to *know* that she is mine. I could readily kill her, obviously;
> but not kill myself because of her – and I would die, I think,
> without Sylvia.[26]

I think. Valentine's torment was that she did not know, and was in a 'doubled' state of mind, being differently and sincerely in love with two people at once. But this uncertainty could not last long and when Elizabeth came back in May to spend three nights in Dorchester at a hotel with Valentine, Valentine felt the time had come to commit herself. She promised to take Elizabeth to live with her, 'not any longer as mistress, not any longer with reservations':[27] it was a promise of marriage.

Seeing Valentine come home from her days in Dorchester, made suave and handsome by love, Sylvia realised that her hope that Elizabeth might blow over was a misplaced one. Valentine told her how things stood: Elizabeth's mother was ill, dying of cancer, but when Elizabeth was free to come to England, she would, and from then on they would live together. An even greater shock came later when Sylvia understood that Valentine meant for them to live together *all three*: Valentine and Elizabeth as lovers, Sylvia as companion. This plan, with its ghostly repetition of the arrangement under which they lived at Warren in 1939, was instantly and vehemently rejected by Sylvia. Her realisation of how degraded she would be by such a way of life released her from the first stupor of grief, and she began to think of the practical implications of leaving the house, the cat, the dog (a Pekinese called Shan), the river, for leave she felt she must: 'I would rather have the sting of going than the muffle of remaining. Practically, too, it is much easier to find a roof for one than for two.'[28]

She and Valentine went on as before, but very subduedly, waiting for news of Mrs White's health that might trigger off the mechanism of separation. They went for drives to the places they had always meant to visit together, entertained Ruth on her birthday and went for other sorts of drive, to places where Sylvia might find a suitable new home. They both conducted themselves very calmly. For Sylvia, there was an air of unreality about it which was impossible to overcome. As she wrote to Alyse Gregory, the only person in whom she confided what was going to happen, 'the new solitary life I shall lead has come suddenly nearer, like the leap the moon makes from a sky of wind and vapour. And that, too, I cannot really believe in. I can visualise everything about it except myself in it. It is like looking into a mirror that reflects everything but one's face. For all that, I believe I welcome this sudden gesture of time. Yes, certainly, I do. The attrition of waiting is as dangerous as a wound that may turn to gangrene.'[29]

Unknown to Sylvia when she wrote this letter, Valentine had been told by Dr Gaster that a swelling she had felt in her right breast on and off for about four years might be cancerous and that she should visit a consultant. Valentine was deeply frightened, but decided not to burden Sylvia with her fears until they were confirmed. The diagnosis was of mastitis, and Valentine was prescribed hormone treatment and a fitting to wear. Outside the surgery she told Sylvia the good news, but Sylvia's relief was mixed with shock at the fact that she had been kept in ignorance: 'it was as though we were already apart.'[30]

During those days when her health was seriously in question, Valentine had been in what she described as 'a state of contained panic', desperate and dreamlike. She realised with absolute clarity for the first time that she could not live without being in close daily contact with Sylvia, and wrote to tell Elizabeth this. In her diary she wrote:

> I feel completely astray at times: Sylvia is so deeply dear to me, so completely integrated that we are practically incapable of sense or sense of life when we are apart. Although I am far *less* than she in all capacities, yet her capacities and mine agree together, so that we have become almost wordless, from living so closely together, and in most cases we have no need of speech [...] and the thought of being about to live a day-to-day life away from her is completely staggering: it makes me dizzy – I cannot comprehend it. And the sight, and knowledge in my heart and mind and *bones*, of her desolation and woe and shock appals me so that I am really stricken in my heart, and cannot endure it without going almost mad.[31]

But still she made ready for the separation; even justified it to herself in terms of the spirit. God had ratified the pledge between Elizabeth and herself; now she must 'try the spirits, if they be of God'.[32]

Meanwhile three flesh-and-blood women were in deep confusion and unhappiness. Mrs White died in the summer and Elizabeth was, in theory, free to come over, but perhaps because Valentine's insistence on keeping in close touch with Sylvia looked like a dilution of the original plan, Elizabeth began to make all sorts of emendations and adjustments which diluted it further. She could not come over immediately, and when she did, it would be for a month only, a trial month at Frome Vauchurch, during which time Sylvia could stay at a hotel instead of moving out entirely. Sylvia received this news aghast: 'It was a come-down, and an affront – such an affront that I could hardly look Valentine in the face.'[33]

While they waited again for Elizabeth to specify the month and confirm her air passage, Sylvia began her preparations for leaving. She cleaned out cupboards and drawers, sorted linen, did everything possible to tidy herself out of sight, even to unpicking her initials from the pillowslips and towels. Valentine made over Sylvia's sitting-room on the ground floor for her own use, and her own sitting-room for Elizabeth's. They put away objects and china special to them, put away love-gifts. 'I contrive to take care of [Elizabeth's] feelings,' Sylvia wrote in her diary, '– it is the extreme of moral affectation.' But much more than Elizabeth's, it was her own feelings she was trying to protect.

In the same spirit of cleaning and clearing, Valentine decided that she could not part from Sylvia without telling her at last of the drink problem which had dogged her for so many years. Sylvia received the news with surprise, but no horror. She looked on Valentine's deception as 'heroic' and marvelled at the self-control and good manners involved in keeping such a secret, for Sylvia swore she had never seen Valentine drunk. How Valentine managed to hide the evidence of an addiction from Sylvia over a period of seventeen years is puzzling. It would appear that Sylvia had no idea of a problem existing at all, believing the story only because Valentine told it her. When Valentine tried to implicate the hand of God in the matter, however, Sylvia was privately dismissive, sure in her own heart of where all credit lay: 'to me, she was the miracle.'[34]

Valentine made her deliverance from drink the starting-point of an autobiography she had been finishing during the summer of 1949 and which she presented to Sylvia as a record and explanation of her life up to that date. Addressed to an impersonal Reader and insisting, in the text, on the anonymity of the author, it would appear to have been written with publication in mind, if only as a means of imposing form on what is otherwise a painfully personal account. The unremittingly remorseful tone of the book (which was not published until 1985) and its joylessness are indicators of Valentine's state of mind during that turbulent summer, a time when she was 'sold into multiplicity':

> Whether I have been set askew in my judgement by those long years of drunkenness and waging useless warfare, I do not know; or whether I am as I feel myself to be: so made that I really can, in truth, be in love with two separate and most alien people. But I know beyond any doubt that my whole being is rooted in Sylvia – that out of my being, however base and bad it seems to be, this matchless love and faith has grown, which is the love she has for me and I have for her. As I write this she is downstairs, listening to some poems of Ronsard being sung on the Third Programme: the sounds come up to me very clearly, and the July evening is slowly darkening. It is just ten o'clock. I know that I shall remember this evening always, and that it may be the most searing torment to my soul, or it may be an almost sweet, light pain only – remembered when there is no more threat of pain to come.[35]

In an oddly intimate and colluding way Sylvia and Valentine went on together towards their separation. They chose a dove-coloured, overcast morning in July to visit Chaldon and see, for the first time, the ruins of Miss Green's cottage, bombed five years earlier. The steps into the garden remained intact, but there was barbed wire around the rubble of the house. Valentine climbed over it and wandered in the garden, calling out to Sylvia when she found familiar plants among the tall grass. Sylvia stood and looked at the crumpled water-butt, the young buddleias growing in what used to be her kitchen and, on one of the two remaining pieces of wall, Ronald Eiloart's well-made hearth. They said little to each other and drove away up towards the Five Marys, passing as they turned the corner the thorn tree under which Sylvia had plighted her troth in 1930. Sylvia cried only rarely, but she cried then.

Back at Frome Vauchurch, Sylvia continued to sort and clean, and to tidy the garden. She was unable to write, except for a few letters. The lovely summer evenings were spent sewing – always by hand – 'for my trousseau as divorcée'. With characteristic ingenuity, though possibly to peculiar effect, she concocted a blouse for Valentine out of a 1938 green silk dressing-gown, but seeing her love wearing it was struck down by a sensual melancholy:

> [...] under it her arms were milk-white, slender, timelessly young. I kissed the hollow of her elbow – gentle now under my lips, and no stir beneath the skin. She looks as beautiful now as when she was beautiful with love for me.
>
> The torment of the flesh is so much purer, so much nobler, than the torment of the mind. It keeps an unbruised innocence.[36]

Sylvia never grudged Valentine pleasure, so it was a particularly piquant grief to her that the agent of all this regenerated loveliness was someone for whom she had no liking and little respect. Earlier in the summer, Sylvia had managed to vent some of her spleen by being sardonic and quoting favourite French epigrams in the cooing and dovelike tone she reserved for her most barbed utterances. As Elizabeth's arrival drew nearer, Sylvia began to lose fight, and if she wanted to comment on the latest dreadful 'carping' letter from America or on the contents of a piece of luggage in advance, did so only to Thomas the cat.

By the beginning of August, Elizabeth's arrival date had been set for 2 September and Valentine went about finding Sylvia a suitable hotel to live in for the month. Posing as Sylvia's secretary, she drove round the countryside in the new Vauxhall car which was also part of the preparations for September and at length chose the Pen Mill Hotel on the outskirts of Yeovil, a sober sandstone building near to the station, reasonably priced and with a view across the road to a small stand of trees. Yeovil, a town without romance, seemed a good choice for a month in the wilderness. It was businesslike, had as yet no pathos of association for Sylvia or Valentine, and later, when it would have, could easily be avoided.

Practical considerations filled up the remaining days together: the laundry, the larder, the box-room, the garden – everything was unnaturally clean and tidy, a fortress against the stranger. But despite her best efforts, Sylvia was tormented by the anticipation of Elizabeth's physical presence in the house: 'In three weeks she will be here. Her foot trailing on the stairs, her glance dawdling over our possessions, her voice and smell filling the house.' She began to have bad dreams about Elizabeth, one where she was being squashed, and other, more worrying dreams, full of images of desolation. In the last week of waiting, she found herself almost wishing the days away, 'and yet I know that they may be the last days I shall live with her.' For the first time in her life, Sylvia experienced boredom in Valentine's company when she had to listen to a series of lengthy discussions about Elizabeth's situation and future. They even had something like a row, stemming from a repeated comment of Valentine's that Sylvia was making a bogey out of Elizabeth. In her own defence, Sylvia produced a letter, found that morning on one of her clean-outs, from Valentine in 1941, reassuring Sylvia that they were securely together again. This made Valentine angry, and she produced another letter, one that she had never yet shown Sylvia, which she felt justified her position. A sleepless night followed, and some difficult days, but Sylvia did not regret having spoken, for she felt that Valentine was not crediting her with any ordinarily base feelings. If Sylvia made a bogey of Elizabeth, Valentine was certainly making something of a martyr out of Sylvia. 'She ought to understand,' Sylvia wrote in her diary, 'that I am not a complete idiot before I go to Pen Mill.'

On 31 August, the last preparations were done, the bags were packed, the bed for Valentine and Elizabeth was made up by

Valentine and Sylvia. After the first night in Yeovil, the plan went, Sylvia would come back to look after the animals while Valentine was on her way to fetch her visitor from the airport in London. At six o'clock, Valentine drove Sylvia to the Pen Mill Hotel. By nine o'clock, Sylvia was already feeling desperate:

My room looks out on the main road, with buses – behind is the station. I have a view of the laundry, some public trees, and a poor, almost real wood. I have a choice of a bent-wood chair, an easy one that is not easy, and the window-sill, which is best. It is really a nice room, plain, and clean, no pictures; and at dinner there was a good deal of that pathetic English food, so well-meaning, and so dreary. There is a nice waitress, foreign I think. All the other guests are men. Valentine rang me, and there has been a Mozart qu[arte]t, and presently there will be the Winterreise. And I feel idiotic with grief, with care, with bewilderment, with exhaustion of spirit. This is where I have travelled since May. Yet my love left me swearing I was her love. [...] For one moment, in the dining-room, I staggered to life, feeling myself returned to that melancholy, saturnine young animal wandering about for Tudor Church Music – at Wimborne, at Norwich, and in Oxford.
And so I think of refugees.

III

The days passed incredibly slowly. By the time Sylvia set off to spend the night at Frome Vauchurch on 1 September, she felt as though she had already expended all the ingenuity and strength stored up to last out the month. At the house she found loving messages, a tray of delicacies and a letter full of love, praise and dependence. She slept with Thomas in her arms and felt hopeful, almost happy. Elizabeth's plane had not yet landed. Back at Pen Mill the next day, her optimism soon drained away: 'now I am in my severe little isolation-cell, and how soon, how tragically soon the feeling of home establishes itself – looking round on it ownerly.' But the letter Valentine had left her in the typewriter at Frome Vauchurch allowed Sylvia a window in her isolation cell. It allowed her to break the agreement they had made not to write to each other during the month apart – an absurd plan, as even one day had proved.

The written word is a much safer vessel for love than the spoken word. It is chosen with deliberation and set down carefully. And a love letter, netting something of the lover's physical presence in its very ink and paper, is always a love token, whatever else it may or may not be, a material thing, with a permanence and validity beyond the words it is made up of. The letters Sylvia and Valentine wrote to each other that September, the most moving of their correspondence, formed the place to which their exiled love retreated, and grew. Sylvia's letters began as rather repining but cheerful descriptions of her exploits in Somerset: the walks she took on Sedgemoor, the churches she visited, cats she met – all in a tone geared to reassure Valentine, a tone significantly at variance with that of her diary entries. And it seems that Valentine was reassured by it, almost to the extent of feeling jealous of Sylvia, for Valentine herself was finding life at Frome Vauchurch extremely exhausting, not least because of the constant talk and lack of the solitariness she both loved and needed. But as Sylvia squeezed herself towards the end of the first week, her letters became much more frank. She had read Valentine's autobiography and was clearly appalled by its unremitting self-reproachfulness, what Sylvia saw as a Ruth-begotten insistence on guilt and blame. Because she saw a mortal danger to her love, and perhaps because she felt she herself had little left to lose, Sylvia wrote a letter of extreme clarity and urgency, a deeply emotional letter but without a trace of sentimentality or mystification. Telling an exact truth is expensive to the spirit, and Valentine's incomplete response (Valentine found criticism of her mother increasingly hard to take) left Sylvia feeling dull and deflated. Words had failed her. Packing to go to Alyse Gregory's house at Chydyok for the weekend, Sylvia felt 'as derelict as an old bus-ticket'.

It was a comfort to Sylvia to walk across Chaldon Down, massive and familiar. Alyse was waiting for her, as she recounted in her own journal: 'I walked along the cliff path to meet her

[Sylvia] in the soft wind with the cattle lying in heavy serenity. I waited in the shade of a clump of elder trees. Then I saw her figure coming along, very smart, with a too heavy bag, so charmingly responsive, so easy to entertain, her mind ready to turn in any direction, so cultured, a woman of rare distinction.'[37] Both women were slightly constrained to begin with and Sylvia felt that Alyse was almost too discerning a companion for comfort. This uneasiness disappeared in the evening, however, when they listened to a broadcast of Beethoven's violin concerto together: 'at the two pizzicato notes in the third movement I heard Alyse chuckle with delight, and from that moment we became freed and intimate and talked for a long while [...] I admitted to her, as openly as to a midwife, the curious sense of security and riches it had given me to discover what frankly base and hateful feelings I had experienced about E. "I can contain this also, and still be myself."'[38]

Alyse Gregory was Sylvia's only confidante. She was a stern listener with a wise heart, well able to understand something of Sylvia's difficulty, for Alyse had been part of a similar triangular relationship between herself, her husband Llewelyn (who had died in 1939) and the American poetess Gamel Woolsey, at the time when Sylvia and Valentine were first living in Chaldon. The friendship between Sylvia and Alyse was more intellectual than emotional: 'we share so many thoughts in common,'[39] Alyse wrote, and they shared many tastes too, especially for French literature and music. Alyse's combination of formality and openness was tonic to Sylvia, as was the beauty of the downs and the sea after so many dark nights of the soul in Yeovil, and when she had to go back to Pen Mill, it was with a heavy heart: 'For three days I have had support from someone who has been, is, for all I can be sure, as unhappy as I. The visit was all I hoped it might be – and now it is over, and I stare myself in the face again. And Chaldon was so beautiful, and its ghosts so living, so much more living than I.'[40]

Valentine's letters to Pen Mill were loving and solicitous, but Sylvia was unhappy at the new insistence on gratitude which was creeping into them: Valentine's gratitude for her present happiness. Having behaved well, Sylvia now had to pay for it and be thanked, and feel dowdy. On the evening of 12 September, an evening when she seems to have returned to her diary time and again, Sylvia wrote, '*Den allen schuld recht sich auf erden.* I understood that, this evening, lying in deep misery, thinking of a passage in Valentine's letter about how she in her love with Eliz. can live innocently – and that is because I am steadfast "and completely without guile or reservation". *Recht sich auf erden.* She lives and loves innocently with Eliz. because I am shaken with fear and doubts, ravaged with physical and mental jealousy, and steadily murder myself in concealing it.' When she saw Valentine the next day, Sylvia found it impossible to shift from under this cloud and felt herself to be dull company, even a burden. Valentine was looking well and lovely, 'and it is this Eliz. whom I hate and strive against who renews her beauty.' She came with the news that Elizabeth's passage had been put back a day, a great blow for Sylvia who was literally counting the hours until she could go home. Valentine was also having trouble finding someone to look after the house and the animals for two weeks in October, when she and Sylvia had provisionally planned to go away together to Norfolk to recuperate. These set backs seemed part of a generally melancholy outlook: everything was shifting and formless, all plans were provisional. Sylvia went back to her room and worked on doggedly at the translation of *La Légende de la Mort*, a collection of peasant stories from Brittany. It was a task she had set herself, an intellectual diversion, a link with her put-aside writing self. And when *La Légende* failed her, she fell to darning stockings.

But if that week saw Sylvia's side of the scales weighed down, by the middle of the following, penultimate week they were moving upwards to something like a balance. On a day when Elizabeth was in London seeing Ruth, Sylvia went to Frome Vauchurch and spent the morning with Valentine, walking in the garden, talking, and in the afternoon, while Valentine was at work, cast herself into acts of domesticity, cleaning, making soup and apple jelly. With the end of her stay in view, Elizabeth had begun to press for firm plans and decisions, when really Valentine was no nearer knowing what to do than before. Day-to-day life with Elizabeth was more stressful and less comfortable than with Sylvia, and Elizabeth herself had a partner in America to be considered, or abandoned. Valentine still loved Elizabeth, though she no longer wanted to live with her, or felt it right. She began to speak of applying for a three-year visa for the United States, or of having Elizabeth to live nearby. Listening to all this in the excitement of a day at home with Valentine made Sylvia feel hopeful once more, and she went back to Yeovil with 'fuel for my HMS Implacable, and steadied on My Love's love'. Considering the alternatives, Sylvia was in no doubt that Elizabeth in Dorset 'and myself always with one hand on the back-door knob' was infinitely preferable to Valentine moving to the USA, so much so 'that I can't allow myself to think of it. Better a running fight than to sit besieged by fears ...'41

The last week rounded into view, and Sylvia moved, for variety's sake, to Hillside Hotel, half a mile further into Yeovil. At Frome Vauchurch, planning had turned into nagging and evenings of monologue – 'what Eliz: so rightly calls getting down to fundamentals' – such as Sylvia had overheard at Warren in 1939. Letters from Elizabeth's lover in America, which Elizabeth produced probably to impress on Valentine her need for protection, only convinced Valentine that they should each return to their former partners. The harangues went on, and Valentine was exhausted and saddened by them, but there was something else too, as Sylvia noticed when Valentine came to take the books and typewriter home in the car: she was grieving for Elizabeth's imminent departure.

During that week, Sylvia spent a day in Paignton with Nora, who had fallen out of bed and bumped her head and seemed 'in brilliant health, glittering' as a result. She told Sylvia that she was going to have a baby and that her old aunts had been to see her. She asked Sylvia where her mother was and, looking at her own reflection in the wardrobe mirror, wondered who was that old woman. 'Her wheel turned – odd words get into it. "No wolves" she said "No value in life. Like Swift." This pierced my heart.'

Valentine's mother was piercing too, in a different way. She and Elizabeth liked each other very well, even looked like each other, in Valentine's opinion. Ruth's long and fussy letters to Valentine at this time prompted Sylvia to remark in her diary, 'How she [Ruth] will make God bite his lip that he ever thought of harps –

or indeed, heaven.' The evening before Sylvia went to Paignton, Ruth had phoned her to say 'she was glad that I at any rate was having *such* a splendid time – declining into *quite*, quite splendid, like a collapsing top. I suppose she is angry because I am not at home to support Valentine. Very proper too.' What Ruth did or didn't know about the situation is unclear. Apart from her conversations with Alyse, Sylvia had kept her own counsel. Even to an old friend such as Bea Howe she said little, and what she did say was deliberately misleading. A letter to Bea, explaining why she was not at home, said 'I have at this moment basely deserted her [Valentine], though it is by mutual agreement. She has an American friend staying with her, not an infliction, for Valentine likes her; but so do not I, said the cookmaid, and so I am staying at a funny hotel in Yeovil, and wallowing in walks on Sedgemoor.'[42]

On 29 September Sylvia was driven home by Mrs King, the local garage-keeper's wife. Valentine was taking Elizabeth to the airport and was due back the next day. The house was autumn-smelling and melancholy and Sylvia wandered about in it like a stranger. The next morning she still felt unelated as she walked up to meet Valentine's train. Valentine looked exhausted and said little. Her arm was aching and her spirits were low. That night, Sylvia was woken by Valentine calling out in her sleep in a despairing voice, 'I am so cold!': '[She] cast herself against me, still in her sleep. I lay with her head on my shoulder, and I tried to warm her; and as she warmed the smell of love came from her, that smell of corn and milk that I shall never smell from her again except love for another causes it.'[43]

By the time they went to Norfolk on 4 October, it was clear that there was to be no miraculous restitution of love. Valentine was completely preoccupied with thoughts of Elizabeth and could not be happy. The house at Horsey they had rented was austerely comfortable, isolated and very near the sea, but its likeness to Lavenham and Winterton brought sad comparisons of then and now to Sylvia's mind. Then she was Valentine's pride and delight; now she was unavailing, almost a nuisance: 'Sorrow comes over me like a mist, and I feel myself lost and fading, and at a touch or a word, the mist thins; but then it comes on again.'[44] Valentine was now rising early in order to write to Elizabeth, just as, in

September, she had for Sylvia. Drives out were drives to cable or post. While Valentine was sending a cable from Yarmouth one day, Sylvia saw in the harbour an old battered boat called *Trustful*. In her diary she remarked, 'I wish I were painted *Trustful* – or that I were not haunted with this feeling that something is going to fall on me. I wish I were not such an abject coward.' For they said very little about Elizabeth – much less than in September – and what Valentine did say made it clear she was looking forward to a 'next time', implying, by her reticence to speak yet, some news she was withholding. The 'disease of Elizabeth', Sylvia felt, had got hold of Valentine more strongly than ever before, and would consume her. As for herself, Sylvia believed that 'soon [...] I shall lose my last power to hold out, it will become such an obsession of helpless anxiety, of impotence, of insignificance.' She began to have disturbing dreams again, all in brown, 'the madman's colour', and hoped she was not going insane. Almost automatically, she started to make contingency plans, and force herself to write again.

They went on from Horsey to Winterton, and from there home to Dorset, with Valentine gradually becoming more forthcoming about Elizabeth's plans, and showing Sylvia copied-out parts of the letters which contained them. Sylvia was appalled more at the 'cold and cruel' style of these letters, 'hideously eloquent', than at Elizabeth's proposal to come over for two long visits to England in the new year. Dreadful too was the discovery that when Valentine wrote back to Elizabeth 'she *writes like* Elizabeth, with the same superfoetation of provisoes, qualifications, sub-clauses.' Towards the end of October an all-or-nothing demand arrived, so potentially damaging to Valentine that Sylvia suggested that she herself should leave home to minimise the hurt. The first part of Sylvia's diary entry that day is reminiscent of what she decided in 1929 when Percy Buck's love for her was failing: 'For now it seems to me that the only way in which I can save her anguish is to love her less: that she can only reach a peace of mind, and a wholesomeness of mind, and retrieve some sort of good out of this calamity, by ceasing to know that she is my only love and my only life.' Then, in a slightly changed hand, as if added later, 'And yet I will not accept this, for it is of an unclean spirit. I love.'[45]

Valentine wrote to Elizabeth the same day, saying there must be a trial year together. It was a clear offer, and sternly worded. She and Sylvia waited with growing impatience almost a fortnight for an answer, which, when it came, was so indecisive that Sylvia could contain her wrath no longer:

> I felt myself shaking, everything grew brilliantly light, I knew I was going into action, and at last would use all my guns. I spoke – I heard my voice harsh and loud – and said exactly what I thought of such a letter, and of the heart that could write it.[46]

What she thought was increasingly vituperative over the following weeks and months, for Sylvia no longer felt any obligation to protect Valentine from her opinions. After this flagrant proof, in Sylvia's eyes, that Elizabeth was 'a fool, a bore, selfish and faithless', it could only be wrong to remain silent. Valentine herself had been deeply offended by Elizabeth's response and wrote back that she could never again consider living with her. She needed no prompting: her judgement was confirmed, not swayed, by seeing Sylvia 'going into action'. Valentine was one of the very few people, possibly the only one, who could have witnessed such a sight and not been intimidated.

There was a lull in letter-writing following this, and things seemed to settle for a while. Sylvia celebrated her fifty-sixth birthday quietly, surprised that she was able to: 'While one goes on living all the time, and *because* one goes on living, one does not realise the extremity which one has lived through.' Forcing herself to write had produced one story, 'The Sea is Always the Same', based on a visit to Cromer with Valentine during their stay in Norfolk. Sylvia had been very pleased to finish it, the first real creative work she had completed since 'The Sea Change' the previous spring, and in her diary wrote 'one is not grateful enough to the poorer gods, the demi-urges, who run out with their vulgar little cups of gin and peppermint when the real gods turn away the cup of nectar.' But gin and peppermint – if such it was – was not good enough for the *New Yorker*, who turned it down.

Ruth came to oversee the turn of the year, insisting on every conceivable traditional accompaniment. She stood at the open doorway to dismiss the old year, saying 'Get out, you horrible old thing!'[47] then made everyone stand in the garden to hear the bells. Valentine had to do the first-footing, and coming in clasped Sylvia and kissed her 'a year-full'. Life seemed to be returning to normal and Sylvia woke one morning feeling relaxed – the first time since the previous May. Valentine was not feeling well, though. Back pain and the discomfort in her right breast continued and though in November the consultant had again discounted cancer, she felt unhappy about it and the hormone treatment she was still receiving. In her spiritual life she was also uneasy, for her chain of thought about the soul and God had snapped during the Elizabeth upheaval, and she was left saddened and intellectually bereaved. 'Very little shines to me now', she wrote in her diary. 'It is as though I were growing old; my spirit growing slow to notice, hard of hearing, stiff-jointed and reluctant to move from its chair or its bed – or its grave.'[48]

Early in the new year the whole Elizabeth business blew up again, when they heard she was coming back to England. By the end of January letters between Valentine and Elizabeth were as frequent as ever. Elizabeth had a date in March for her arrival and was seeing a psychiatrist in preparation. She also had a literary research project in hand, in case Valentine had assumed that love was the sole purpose of the visit. 'The year turns towards Elizabeth's determined new assault', Sylvia wrote. 'It will be hard to keep myself unspotted again. If need be I must go. Rather than live falsely with my love, I must go and live truly by myself, not linger out a purposed overthrow.'[49]

On 12 February, Sylvia was distracted from her sorrow by a call from the nursing home to say that Nora, who had been comatose for several months, was getting weaker. Sylvia and Valentine set off by car early the next morning, but when they arrived in Paignton they heard that Nora had died in her sleep. Sylvia sat alone by the body for a while, looking at her mother calmly for the first time in years: 'Her face was composed, stern, not sad; her little nose soared out of it like the dome of St Paul's. It was not like my father's death-mask – being so much older she seemed infinitely more dead, and abstract like a work of art. Only her hair when I caressed it was light and living.'

Sylvia could not grieve that the ghastly period of Nora's senility was over, though she sympathised deeply with those who mourned for Nora; one of the nurses at the home, Evans the faithful gardener and Mr Boucher, whom Sylvia found wandering among the graves at the crematorium when the funeral took place three days later. The little purple coffin, chosen by Sylvia, and its one bright bunch of tulips and iris, were soon despatched to the furnace. 'Out of such bare material, out of mere birth and death, we spin the intricate web of love, we distil it from these poor bones and ashes, and with it conceive the tale that is told and ended when we die.'[50]

Nora's will, which Sylvia had been told excluded her, named Sylvia as residuary legatee. The estate included Little Zeal, which had been let to a young naval officer and his wife, David and Marion Deuchar, in order to pay Nora's expenses. Although Sylvia never thought of evicting her tenants, she now had the security of owning a house, somewhere to go one day, if the worst came to the worst. She was also now the sole beneficiary under the terms of her father's estate, receiving £420 in royalties from Blackie's within the month, for George's excellent history and English textbooks were still in common use in schools.

Sylvia stayed in Little Zeal with the Deuchars until after her mother's burial. On the morning after the cremation, she received a parcel addressed 'Mrs Warner' – it was the casket with her mother's ashes, 'a curious sensation to get one's mother by post; and rather hastily I took her upstairs and unpacked a small violet cloth-covered casket, with a shiny name-plate.' The ashes were to be buried in the garden, on whose instructions is not clear. Thirty-four years after George's death, perhaps Nora had finally lost her desire to lie in the double plot at Harrow. She was buried under a cherry tree. Evans dug the hole and Sylvia put her in it, with some moss and snowdrop bulbs.

Sylvia's new 'moderate competency' gave her a little more room for action. When Valentine had another bad letter from Connecticut and began to dread Elizabeth's return, Sylvia was able to suggest that they go away together to Paris, run away together, in effect. Valentine refused. Sylvia reflected that had she had money instead of debts a year before, the whole Elizabeth episode might have been avoided, and her own life's 'real meaning' retained. 'Poor Nora, she would not have wished me this.'

Over the next month, Sylvia sank further and further into a profound melancholy. Her bad dreams continued: Valentine faceless and wrapped in a brown shawl, Elizabeth arriving with a furniture van. One evening she had an 'overwhelming impression' of Charles Prentice, who had died in Africa the previous summer, in the room, about to take her out for the evening and treat her kindly. She was feeling ghostly herself, and extremely lonely – the sound of her own voice talking to the ailing Thomas or to the cows in the next-door field frightened her. The week before Elizabeth's arrival, Sylvia felt helpless: 'I am as much outside the action as the chinese stagemanager who trots through the players in a black suit and ridiculous bowler hat, laying down cushions for the suicides and removing the swords he previously handed to the aggressors. I dug in the garden, and sat with my back to the window, and did all I could to hide my fallen face.'[51] Valentine, seeing that Sylvia was distressed, told her sadly that she could give no more reassurances, no more promises, having broken so many. She then kissed Sylvia violently – 'It was like blows on my face, saying "I *will* kiss you if I want to". I have never been an obstacle, God wot! I am too much of an animal to keep even a self-defensive lent.' How Valentine had come to the conclusion that Sylvia no longer wanted or needed passionate love puzzled her a good deal, but there was no changing it. Valentine interpreted all Sylvia's remarks in that light, and Sylvia herself had lost her spontaneity over such matters. 'She deceives herself about me far more than I deceive her,' Sylvia wrote. It seemed now too late for the holidays Valentine wanted to plan for 'after Elizabeth', too late for hope, which had brought Sylvia nothing but shame and self-contempt over the past year, and she stopped writing her diary: 'It is all written and re-written.'

But, like a miracle, Valentine came back from London saying it was all over, which, bar a few extra flourishes, it was. Valentine had known, before she went, where her real commitment lay, and it was with Sylvia. In her diary she had written of the difference she perceived in her two loves – not only a difference in nature but also in quality. The greatest unhappiness was her failure to show her love to Sylvia, and to her prayer, made three years before, 'that I may be as Thou wouldst have me', she added 'But next, oh very close on that, "that I may be restored to Sylvia as she would have me".'[52]

She went to London, not in a cynical state of mind, but longing to enjoy herself. She was not in the least ashamed of this, only regretful that she did not enjoy herself more often. The three days with Elizabeth, however, were an unmitigated disaster, and Valentine saw that Elizabeth's moods were so unpredictable and so often draped in black, that there was no point in deluding herself any longer: 'It is not love of her. I loved, I still love, my fancy, nothing else.'[53] Elizabeth came down to Dorset, lingering out the last few bars of the piece, but the affair, that had been so much more than an 'affair', was over. Sylvia was at home when she heard the Dorchester to London train going by that was bearing Elizabeth away. On a sudden impulse, she threw open the window of Valentine's room, 'feeling that something was being borne out of the house ... and at the same time I think I counted every second of that pause in M[aiden] N[ewton] station, as consciously in pain for Eliz: as she could be.'

The same afternoon, Sylvia noticed that Thomas was dragging his back legs. He was ill and in pain. They nursed and soothed him overnight, and early the next morning Valentine took him out into the garden and shot him. He was the Frankfort kitten, survivor of the murrain, and Sylvia's best companion in her loneliness. 'It will always seem to me,' she wrote, 'that he did, in his faithfulness, stay by me till she came back.'[54]

6

1950–1969

I

The early 1950s were full of threats of war, unstable and uncomfortable years in which Britain's dependence on the United States weighed heavily on the nation's self-esteem. The atomic and hydrogen bombs, and a manifest readiness to use them, had given the United States world military dominance, unchallenged until 1953 when Russia developed its own bomb. The cold war polarised nations into two crudely-delineated factions: the Communist bloc, dominated by the Soviet Union, and the capitalist West, increasingly under the influence of America. Sylvia deplored this influence, in both its cultural and political aspects, and felt it was eating away at Europe. After the invasion of South Korea by North Korea in 1950, it seemed to her that America was bent on war, and would certainly drag her dependent allies into it: 'I realised with horrible clearness what Europe would be like when there is no more Europe,' she wrote in her diary. 'The Vatican, the industrialists, Monte Carlo and Spitzbuhel – and the Americans, remaking everything so as to have more of what they want.'[1]

Sylvia was still a loyal Communist, though not a very active one. 'My mood is *centrifugal*,' she wrote to Nancy Cunard in 1949, apropos an invitation to attend another congress, this time in France. 'I can't at this moment of history warm to the thought of a congress about anything. Why, indeed? There is so much to be anxious about: but somehow I can't believe that anything will come of congressing and gathering just now. A sitting on already boiled eggs, a clucking of past hatchings.'[2] In the elections of February 1950 and October 1951, she and Valentine voted for the Liberal, 'dubiously, since it is only a negative vote.' They still took the *Daily Worker* along with *The Times*, and Sylvia continued to support Stalin, though what she knew of him is impossible to ascertain. Stalin was not yet a *mauvais sujet*, nor the Communists of the Thirties red-faced apologists. The trouble with British Communists in the early Fifties was just that; they *were* 'of the Thirties', rather thin on the ground and somewhat dated. As Sylvia had written to Nancy Cunard in the late Forties, 'far too many of the up and growing intellectuals are now POUM [Trotskyists], or going in that direction. And one has to face it, the communist intellectuals are mostly on the wrong side of forty, look old-fashioned, etc.'[3] Sylvia despised the 'careerists' who had left the Party for this reason. When the King died in February 1952 and Sylvia and Valentine went into Dorchester for the Proclamation, she noticed how 'only a very few old-fashioned people like ourselves (all communists, I presume) had attempted to be subfusc.'

For many years after the war rationing was still in operation, petrol scarce and cigarettes – Sylvia's and Valentine's lifeline – sometimes scarcer. There was not a great deal to buy, but Sylvia found herself suddenly well-off again with the money from Nora's estate and the *New Yorker*. Following the dry years of 1949 and 1950, Sylvia was writing well; ideas for stories seemed to present themselves at every turn, and she had so many acceptances from her 'gentleman friend', that she began to qualify for bonus payments, in addition to the basic fee and the retainer she received under her First Reading Agreement. All this – and in dollars – made it possible for them to think of moving from Frome Vauchurch to something grander, to buy another new car and begin to travel abroad regularly, to France mostly, and Italy. It also made it possible for Valentine to think of giving up her work at Dr Gaster's, a drain on her energies for its £150 per annum.

Leaving the job at Gaster's was only a wrench for Valentine in so far as she liked to feel she was paying her way. She hoped, though, that by having the time and peace of mind in which to write, she might again be able to earn something as a writer. It did not help her fragile self-esteem in the least to hear Sylvia, in one of her flashes of insensitivity, describe 'what Valentine does' to Marchette and Joy Chute, two American writers paying their first visit to Frome Vauchurch: 'Valentine works for a local doctor.' The incident prompted the following entry in Valentine's diary:

> I do not *dare* announce to myself that I am only a writer as earlier generations of women were tatters and cross-stitchers or blanketted the poor ... nor, knowing now that a demon of vanity and self-deception has occupied me, can I without hypocrisy make a gesture of giving it up – this business of writing and filling in forms, at 'occupation' as 'writer' – Nor do I dare give up trying to write. But I can't reconcile myself, yet, to accepting it as a hobby.
>
> [...] So I am trying to accustom myself, in my head, to seeing myself as others see me: as the younger and duller of a pair: as one who is part-friend, part-secretary: as Dr Gaster's woman who comes in for part-time and does the cards: as 'I believe she writes too, but I don't know what – little bits here and there, I think –' (which is *perfectly true*): as the person no one can understand what Sylvia sees in her – and so on.[4]

What Sylvia saw in Valentine was the person she admired above all others, whom she loved with her whole heart and who had been restored to her, seemingly against the odds. Watching Valentine in a crowd of people at London Zoo, Sylvia thought her 'as elegant and aloof as an unicorn'; among the swans at Abbotsbury she was 'like a goddess borne on a cloud'. But Sylvia's degree of love and admiration was so unusual, so strong and strongly-willed, that it is hardly surprising Valentine could sometimes not believe it possible, or believe that it applied to herself, feeling, as she did, guilty and debased by the events of 1949. She still loved and was fascinated by her own 'vision' of Elizabeth, though the real woman irritated her now, and she still loved Sylvia, although a sort of physical embarrassment had grown up between them. 'So often lately I have felt longings towards her,' Valentine wrote in her diary, 'and every time they have been quenched by self-mistrust. Maybe it is better so, after so long – I am getting old. It is a pity I do not always remember it.'[5] In the light of this, it seems there was a sombre truth as well as a simple one in what Sylvia wrote to a friend at about the same time, imploring him not to be tormented by fantasies of losing his lover: 'think of me,' she said. 'Here I am, grey as [a] badger, wrinkled as a walnut, and never a beauty at my best; but here I sit, and yonder sits the other one, who had all the cards in her hand – except one. That I was better at loving and being loved.'[6]

That letter was unusual in referring to the rift between Valentine and herself. Sylvia's correspondences, which were increasingly important to her during the Fifties, were primarily conducted for pleasure. The posthumous selection of her *Letters*, published in 1982, is an indication of her genius as a letter-writer; her powers of observation and description and her humane, sardonic wit are evident on every page. The letters are a gauge of her intense interest in life and the value she placed on friendship. Those she wrote to most frequently were all practitioners of one or another kind of art; Paul Nordoff the musician, George Plank, the American artist and illustrator, the poet Leonard Bacon, the novelists Anne Parrish and William Maxwell, Nancy Cunard and Alyse Gregory. She wrote very quickly in her elegant, elongated hand, and her letters, like her diary, convey the same sense of speed and mental agility, as if her ideas were occurring to her at that very minute, as they probably were. And, remarkable in someone who habitually covered the same day's events in several totally dissimilar letters and a diary entry, Sylvia hardly ever felt the temptation to repeat even her best jokes.

In the summer of 1950, Sylvia had been asked to write an essay for the British Council's 'Writers and Their Work' series on Jane Austen. She enjoyed writing it so much that she longed to do 'a longer book on J.A. called the *Six-fold Screen*, a book on the novels, really applying criticism to them.' She had often been compared with Miss Austen herself, by reviewers who mistook both writers as essentially genteel, but there was more to the comparison than they may have intended. As her title suggests, Sylvia's view of Miss Austen was of a worldly writer with a subversively satiric purpose. She was pleased with her essay, 'a neat piece of work, but nothing to what the Sixfold Screen will be, if I get round to it.' Unfortunately, she didn't.

In August 1950 Sylvia flew to Ireland alone to inspect a large property in County Clare, which she and Valentine hoped might be 'the new Frankfort', but wasn't. They were both keen to move at the time; it seemed the most clear-cut way of making a new start and shaking off the melancholy hangover of Elizabeth. Later in the year the Deuchars announced that they had been posted to Hong Kong and would be leaving Little Zeal. Sylvia and Valentine debated the advantages of moving there, but found more in the disadvantages to deter them. And though they had once thought of possibly rebuilding on the site of Miss Green's cottage in Chaldon, they dismissed that too and when a man from Winfrith offered to buy the plot in the summer of 1950, Sylvia and Valentine did not hesitate to accept his £50.

Valentine was more enthusiastic than Sylvia to leave Maiden Newton. One reason, and a factor in rejecting Ireland and Devon, was that Ruth was getting old and Valentine wanted to be nearer Winterton and in a house large enough to accommodate her mother if need be. Valentine had been told in confidence by the doctor that Ruth's heart could carry her off at any moment, and this news made her extremely anxious. Sylvia also expected the worst, for in her opinion, '[Ruth] will probably go on like this for a long while yet; for she is set in her ways, and one can stay almost indefinitely at Death's door if one has planted one's camp-stool in a sunny corner of it.'[7]

On one of their increasingly frequent visits to Winterton, Sylvia and Valentine found a house near Salthouse on the north Norfolk coast to rent for the winter. It strongly appealed to both of them and they immediately arranged to let their own house and take it. Great Eye Folly was a former coastguard station which had been fortified during the war and stood four-square and castellated on the edge of a noisy pebble beach, 'like a hooded hawk on a clenched fist – like my family's crest, indeed',[8] wrote Valentine. The beach and the sea stretched endlessly to either side of the house, which was really a tower, and in a high wind sea spray tossed up against the living-room windows. Behind it lay the marshes and sea-water lakes which separated Great Eye from the main road and across which a narrow causeway ran. In the distance Salthouse church rose up very large in the flat landscape and on Sunday nights, with all its lights on, looked like an ocean liner.

Sylvia and Valentine stayed at Great Eye Folly for five months, writing, walking and battling against the weather. At high sea, the car had to be parked right against the front door and in a high wind Sylvia was forced to crawl on all fours from the door to the rubbish pit. There were no mod. cons at all: no electricity, no drinking water and the bathwater was hot sea-water, pumped up by means of a small petrol engine. When the weather turned really cold in December and January, the Folly was islanded in ice, the road to Holt became impassable and the waves froze on the shore. 'The east wind sobs and whimpers like a Brontë in the kitchen,' Sylvia wrote in her diary. She loved the place, and Valentine talked of trying to buy it.

But they did not buy Great Eye Folly, nor any other of the expensive, impractical houses they viewed while in Norfolk. Seeing so much of Ruth made Sylvia realise the depths of her dislike for the woman, and the extent to which Ruth and Joan manipulated Valentine. And Ruth's lot, which Valentine had been made to feel was verging on the tragic, was not so bad as to merit a hasty removal to Norfolk. Coming back to Winterton from another viewing, Sylvia noted 'the fire was glowing, [Ruth's] slippers were warming, Alice had made a laid tea, and Mr Pye was in attendance. For utter discomfort, neglect and misery, it looked pretty comfortable.' Sylvia lost interest in house-hunting and began to want to go home. 'I want to go to something I am sure of, whose ways I know, whose demands I know are not beyond my strength. Oh Sylvia, can it be that you want to *Retire*?'

They went back to Frome Vauchurch in March 1951. While Sylvia was in Norfolk, she had sold Little Zeal for £3,000, but the job of emptying the house lay ahead of her. Much of the furniture and fittings she gave away or sold in Devon, bringing back only a few favourite or useful things to Dorset. In the privacy of home, she began to go through Nora's papers, destroying many old photographs and most of the contents of Nora's deed-box, which contained 'some distressing revelations' about the management of her father's estate, 'but all done and destroyed now, and so much and no more for them: except to beware of heredity.'

In many ways, Sylvia did want to 'retire'. She wanted peace in which to garden, write and enjoy the company of Valentine and of Niou, the Siamese kitten they had bought in the summer of 1950. Niou was named after the Perfumed Captain in *The Tale of Genji*, and they loved him intensely from the first, so much so that their Pekinese dog, Shan, was given away to some people in Swanage because he seemed jealous. Also, Sylvia had begun another novel and longed to concentrate on it. It was about an early-Victorian family in Norfolk and she began it at great speed, writing twelve thousand words in the first week. At the sixty-third page she felt her impetus wavering and the next day, when she introduced a Mr Theophilus Templeman into the narrative, 'everything curdled [...] and I went to bed in despair.' From then on it was work, as usual.

It was a relief to Sylvia to find another novel in herself, for she had begun to doubt she could write any more. She had also begun to doubt the worth of her short stories, feeling that she was becoming too slick with them. A comment by Chekhov which she had found in a book struck Sylvia as applying so nearly to herself that she copied it out in her diary: 'You have grown heavy, or, to put it vulgarly, you have grown stale and you already belong to the category of stale authors. Your style is precious, like the style of very old authors.' After rereading a story which she had written in 1927, Sylvia discerned 'a shocking weakness about the amiable characters, which I suspect still persists'. It persisted to some degree in her humorous stories, which could sometimes, as she admitted herself, sail near to archness; but the facility which she considered potentially dangerous was more a mark of having strengthened her style rather than having weakened it, and the period following these proddings of self-doubt was the beginning of her most assured and mature years as a short-story writer. The first book to come out of it, *Winter in the Air* in 1955, was the first of her collections to seem all-of-a-piece – not unvarious, but more controlled. She did not include in it any of the comical stories she wrote for the *New Yorker* during the same period dealing with her family and childhood, which were collected after her death in *Scenes Of Childhood*, nor her series about Mr Edom, the antiques dealer. As she had written to Harold Raymond in 1937 when he first suggested publishing her *New Yorker* stories in England, they could be seen as 'too English for the English'. *Scenes of Childhood*, an anecdotalised autobiography of Sylvia's youth, certainly seems stranger than fiction, and rather funnier. 'I can always appease my craving for the improbable', she wrote to William Maxwell, 'by recording with perfect truth my own childhood.'

The *New Yorker* did not always accept Sylvia's stories at their first submission, and they were not in the habit of paying for stories they would not use. Often pieces were sent back with suggestions for revision, carefully considered by her editor and devoted admirer, William Maxwell. 'Farewell My Love' (retitled 'Winter in the Air' for the later collection), a moving story based loosely on Sylvia's situation in September 1949, was one such, and a story, being close to her heart and written very flowingly and fast, which Sylvia was unwilling to tamper with. But although she did not agree with Maxwell's suggestion to change the ending, she accepted it, for, she had to admit, other stories she had been unwilling to change really were better afterwards.

Valentine's anxieties were of a more serious nature. She was so oppressed by failure that she feared to realise fully the extent of her shortcomings and the waste of her life, for then, she felt, she could only kill herself. She strove – successfully – to hide from Sylvia the pure desperation she was feeling, though she could not help appearing very subdued and often ill at this time. Sylvia accounted for Valentine's depression by the fact that she had to keep on writing without any recognition or encouragement. 'Perhaps if I were a christian,' Sylvia wrote to Alyse Gregory, 'I could be heartless enough to admire how her character is tested by tribulation; but I am not: it is a sight that is an agony to witness at times, and at other times a dull drag on my heart. Besides, I don't believe for an instant that characters are improved by misfortune, unless they are of the grossest and most suety kind. Hers survives: but by virtue of an original grace.'[9]

Sylvia told Valentine once that she had almost been a Christian for a week in her youth, but that was all. Valentine was unsure herself whether to place Sylvia with the atheists or the agnostics. In a letter to a friend, which she copied into her diary at Sylvia's request, Valentine gave a very interesting analysis of Sylvia's attitude to religion:

> [...] she is to a great extent 'allergic' to each & every form of religion, including its manifestations even in apparently unreligious individuals. [...] She has a positive horror of any form of religion, which she believes to be immeasurably dangerous and destructive. [...] She bears most patiently with my excursions into various Faiths, and is interested in many of them, and sometimes charmed by the outward trappings: but *always* because of their association with Man as a creative artist ... the imagination that conceived the idea, the fancy that contrived the ritual, the social forces of the time, which conditioned this or that form of Faith or worship.
>
> I do not know anyone who more consistently follows what I should privately call the dictates of the Spirit. She invariably acts on instant impulse, without taking thought, in matters of emotion or urgency, and invariably acts with a dazzling brightness. I have seen her in situations which really have been as bad as any that – say – Mauriac has imagined, and she has emerged without a stain. Her character is very complex, and of course I do not even think that I understand it as a whole, but the parts I am capable of assessing or observing are (it seems to me quite obviously) formed and conditioned by the action of the Spirit ... But she is serenely determined to declare that there IS no Spirit ... And what does that matter? Not a whit, thank God![10]

At the time when Valentine wrote this, she was feeling restless at home and was even wishing her old job back, if only to give her a sense of being useful and to assuage slightly the embarrassment of living off Sylvia. When the possibility of another job came up, that of secretary to a rich young widow, Sylvia opposed the plan strongly, on the grounds that it would waste Valentine's time and strength. She suggested that Valentine should work for *her* instead, doing secretarial chores and housework which would free

Sylvia, the earner, to write, and still leave Valentine, the writer, some time for poetry. Though kindly meant, there was much in this to upset and offend Valentine, but she swallowed the pill to her pride as if it were a familiar dose and continued to 'work' at home, doing little and feeling lonely, for Sylvia often shut herself away for the whole day when she was writing. 'Busy and idle' is how Valentine saw her life; 'I am almost quite sure that I am *done for*.'[11]

Valentine's health was not good, pestered with numerous small complaints she felt were all part of a general malaise stemming from the emotional turmoil over Elizabeth. One of these complaints was arthritis, which prevented Valentine from doing any heavy gardening. Ruth's suggested remedy was that Valentine should become a Roman Catholic, and thereby be able to go to Lourdes and be cured. Sylvia thought she should go to Manchester and see a specialist. Though fatalistic about her health, Valentine was too well-informed to be a hypochondriac, and was generally better at diagnosing conditions than the doctor. When Sylvia came down with a mysterious spotty illness in April 1952, Gaster and his assistant at first thought it was gallstones, then a chill, then chicken-pox, then possibly small-pox, and a man from Dorchester was sent in to scratch her feet. Valentine said from the start that it was shingles, as it was. Her own chronic swelling and ache in the breast, for which she had undergone a series of painful injections in 1950, was always called mastitis by the doctors. Valentine, however, was doubtful, and could only write the word in her diary using inverted commas.

There seemed to be nothing to do to combat her depression but practise fortitude, though she was often tempted to find some easier way out, tempted especially to drink again, for she had been able to overcome fearfulness when drunk and, importantly, felt it had freed her to write: 'when I was thoroughly sodden I wrote with a kind of stumbling blind felicity – didn't I? And now I am merely good – and DUMB.'[12] It was hard to refuse drink, when Ruth was always rattling bottles at her and when guests drank with Sylvia, or, like Nancy Cunard, got drunk with Sylvia. And Valentine was, as ever, worried about money. Ruth had alarmed her with the news that she was mortgaging off parts of the family estate in Northern Ireland, the property on which Valentine's future income depended. Her annual allowance had not changed since her majority, when she had felt it only just adequate. Unknown to her, Sylvia, also alarmed by Ruth, was putting away vast sums of money in an account in Valentine's name, against her 'widowhood': £1,000 in March 1953 and all her subsequent First Reading money £4,000 invested in shares. Valentine, thinking herself on the brink of insolvency, concentrated hard on making economies, often in ridiculously small matters. An enormous expense did not frighten her half so much as the price of a new pair of stockings, though enormous expense could always awe Sylvia, as when she had to write the cheque for their latest car, '£1121 10. 0. Purchase tax £401 10. My God.'[13] Sylvia's answer to this was her usual one. The afternoon the car was delivered, she was busy planning a new story for the *New Yorker*.

When a family friend sent Valentine £30 out of the blue for a holiday in Cornwall, Sylvia was pleased until Valentine remarked that it was clearly the answer to a prayer she had made three nights before, when in a money panic. Sylvia found this irritatingly superstitious, and unnecessary: 'It is as if she prayed for cabbage when the garden is full of it.' At the same time, Valentine was observing a private Lenten fast, giving up sweets and cakes to combat both greed and overweight at one blow. She had also given up 'talking about Elizabeth'.

In 1952 Valentine earned nothing whatever from her writing, the first completely barren year since she began to write in 1926. But she had another idea for money-making taking shape. Sylvia and Valentine had become very friendly with the Siamese cat breeders from whom they had bought Niou, Vera and Arthur Hickson, and Vera, a keen auction-goer, had taken Valentine with her to sale rooms on several occasions. Valentine loved the excitement of getting a bargain and discovered in herself a remarkable talent for spotting unusual and valuable items among the mixed lots. When the house began to fill with these objects, Valentine thought of a way to continue the pleasure of buying without having to face the inconvenience of possessing, and suggested to Sylvia that they could turn the long sun-parlour – the larger of their two glass-built lean-tos – into a 'semi-shop'. Sylvia had a few minor misgivings, but soon they were clearing out the room and arranging what seemed at first rather too few wares on Sylvia's piano, which she rarely played any more, and on the bookshelf which contained their left-wing and Communist books, demurely hidden from the eyes of the county by means of a curtain.

Their first customers were Dr Gaster's new assistant and her companion, one of the very few lesbian couples they knew, with whom they had become friends during the previous year. Valentine was enjoying the shop, ('we cannot call it a shop'), which as well as providing a healthy £41 profit in its first month, brought her many new acquaintances, predominantly female and leisured, some of whom Sylvia found less congenial than others. To warn Sylvia that she wanted to be rescued from an over-talkative or unpleasant customer, Valentine would lean casually against a set of bells and Sylvia, emerging from her sitting-room, where she usually spent the working day, would see them off.

Some of the new acquaintances Sylvia loved without reserve, the Hicksons especially. Their home, Cauldron Barn Farm, near Swanage, seemed to her an earthly paradise of cats, flowers, peaceable animals and graceful people. However, even an earthly paradise was no substitute for being with Valentine, as Sylvia found when she volunteered to look after the farm while the Hicksons were on holiday, and she pined for Valentine as much then as in any of their separations. During that fortnight, she finished the first draft of her Norfolk novel, now called 'The Flint Anchor': 'I waded about the house among cats and old Ben [the dog], and felt as though I were in Hades among the shades. I longed for my love to revive me.'[14]

One morning in March 1953, Valentine, who always rose early and made breakfast, woke Sylvia with the news that Stalin had had a stroke and was dying. 'It was "Uncle Joe" she said, turning back to the former affection and loyalty.' Sylvia was profoundly sad: 'I have grieved and trembled. After him, there is only Churchill of the Europeans who feel Europe; and he cannot be relied on against the USA,' but her eulogy of Stalin the man was embarrassingly concentrated on his physical attributes: a certain likeness to Thomas the cat and the memory of his voice heard once on the radio in 1943, 'a voice so living, so warm, so sturdy, that I would like to remember it on my deathbed as an assurance of the spirit of man.' Valentine's diary entry was similarly swooning: 'no one could see that grand brow and those eyebrows, and that strong, lively hair springing from the brow'[15] – and so forth. Valentine disliked the way in which Stalin was being reviled already at home and in America. At the same time she had written to Harry Pollitt resigning formally from the Communist Party, a move to quell Ruth's persistent anxieties. 'This was a most difficult thing to do,' she wrote in her diary, 'for it was embarrassing, and seemed so absurd when I had been "lapsed" for so long and was at no time a member they would have noticed. [...] Finland shook me first, and even before that, the attitude of Party members to Tom Wintringham [who had been expelled] shocked me, and I would not conform, even at that date, [...] I was always a heretic – but in those halcyon days they tacitly allowed heretics to live: and seeing that made me think that they would come to find it possible to share the world with them in amity!'[16]

Sylvia did not resign, formally or informally, though it seems she had not been a paid-up member of the Party for some years – probably not since the beginning of the war. She did not feel Valentine's desire to 'clear-up' the matter, although the urgency of her politics had been replaced by a sort of weary pragmatism to the extent that she was able to vote, in a 1955 election, for whom she thought the best candidate, even though he was a Conservative.

Sylvia was feeling increasingly isolated. Many of her friends were dead or dying: Geoffrey Sturt, Mrs Keates, Gertrude Powys and Edmund Fellowes all died within a year or two of each other. Percy Buck had died in 1947, the same year as Purefoy and Arthur Machen. Sylvia took a touching pleasure in the company of Janet Machen, her last remnant of close family (Janet's brother Hilary had been out of touch for years). Janet had married soon after the war and was living in Bristol with her husband and two children, Catherine and Matthew. 'Janet's voice, and Janet's familiarity of blood, are extraordinarily pleasant to have beside me. I have, with her, the rare sense that I can trust her not to dislike or misunderstand or try to re-shape me. It is restful.'

Sylvia's friend, the novelist Anne Parrish, was almost blind and could no longer write frequent letters, though she strained her clouded vision through a magnifying glass in order to read the typescript of 'The Flint Anchor', which was dedicated to her. And the death of another American correspondent, the poet Leonard Bacon, left a space which Sylvia knew would never be filled again. 'I have lost a *confidant*, a person to whom I could write quite freely, without reservations, without considerations, without any dross of personal circumstances. [...] he found me charming, and delightful, and was content only with that. No-one to call me Charlie, Lamb lamented. I have plenty to call me Sylvia, but no-one to call me Dear Miss Warner [...] And I miss his masculinity, deeply. My intellect was man-made, is still preponderantly masculine – and that part of me has lost a comrade.'[17]

Another great loss came with the death of Theodore Powys. All through the summer of 1953 he was ailing. When Sylvia and Valentine visited him at Mappowder in July, he looked 'down and marked for death' and, propped against the door-frame, waved them off with both hands – 'a sick man's exaggeration of a healthy man's gesture.' Violet was distraught and Theo, terrified of being taken to hospital and handed over to 'those *photographers*' was often harsh with her, alternately sullen or bristling with black humour. Early in August he had to go to Sherborne Hospital – he paused at the door to inspect the sign 'To the Chapel' – to have a growth removed which the doctors feared might be cancerous. In the event, he was allowed home after a biopsy and told that he would have to return the next month for his operation. When the results of the tests showed that Theodore did have a cancer, he was told it was only an 'ulcer', but he refused to have any operation and thereby regained a little peace of mind. Next time Sylvia saw him he looked 'physically quite different, and he was affectionate and as nearly demonstrative as he could ever be, yet I felt much amiss; [...] Poor darling Theo: as I write this, the word is written on my brain, *Ennui*: the ennui of a violent character constrained to a doctrine of non-offensiveness.'[18]

Theodore died on 27 November and was buried four days later at Mappowder. '[T]he coffin came out upright, as though it were walking out on its own volition, or rather, as though he were walking it out to its burial. It was a mild grey-skied day, the doors of the village church were open during the service, and while the parson was reading the lesson from St Paul a flock of starlings descended on the churchyard and brabbled with their watery voices, almost drowning the solitary cawing rook inside the building.'[19] Many familiar Chaldon people were at the funeral and Harold Raymond was there too, representing Chatto & Windus. It was the first time he had seen Sylvia in over twenty years; they had corresponded over business matters, but kept out of each other's way. Valentine wrote in her diary that night: 'So Theodore lies in the earth, and more we do not know. But if the earth is ever a home to a man, it is a home to him – I almost feel as though it were his by right, as if it were his inheritance, as if he had come into his own by this day's work.'[20]

II

On 6 December 1953, Sylvia surveyed her sixty-year-old self: 'Fatter, alas! – and heavier, and growing stiff in the knees and in the eyelids, and not so supple either in my wits. But cheerful in my spirits and in my guts still, my grey hairs strong-growing. My hearing, thank heaven, as good as ever.' She was happier, she felt, than ten years before, when Elizabeth Wade White was still a threat; she had the cats – two, since the purchase of another Siamese kitten, Kaoru – and the garden, and her writing was going well. *The Flint Anchor* was published in July 1954, in a decent edition of five thousand which almost sold out within the year (though the book was not reprinted). It tells the story of John Barnard, a conscience-stricken Norfolk merchant, upholder of the right and unwilling agent of endless wrongs. The characterisations of Barnard, his spoilt daughter Mary and sardonic, alcoholic wife Julia are extremely well-done and the evocation of early nineteenth-century Norfolk deft and thoroughly convincing. It was a story Sylvia was almost literally at home in, for the spark from which the narrative kindled was an event in her own family history, the departure in disgrace of her great-great-grandfather, John Warner, from the pious East Anglian family he had married into, the Townsends. It was in the next generation that 'Townsend' was incorporated into the surname, probably to act as chaperon to 'Warner', a bad influence, the first male Townsend Warner being George, that anxious and religious man who ran Highstead School. There were other links with Sylvia's family in the book, notably an accretion of familiar attributes and incidents concerning her father, mother and grandmother which built up round the characters of John and Julia Barnard. But *The Flint Anchor* is a book primarily devoted to its own story, and what family myths and memories Sylvia used are made over, like Sylvia's most ingenious needleworks, into something of quite different shape and purpose. Skating, for example, was inextricably linked in Sylvia's mind with her father, yet when she writes of John Barnard skating on the frozen lake at Rougham Hall, the points of similarity never stray beyond the circumstantial:

> John Barnard swept by unheeding, with his arms folded across his chest and his gaze fixed on the araucaria that grew at one end of the lake – a fine specimen, and the first to be planted in Suffolk. He approached it, he passed it, and with an energetic stroke of his right foot he set off away from it on a fresh journey towards it. He did not even use it to count by, now. It recurred like a Sabbath. With every circle of the lake he travelled a stage deeper into a region that was partly the kingdom of heaven and partly Cambridge. Not since Cambridge had he felt so inoffensive. Not till the kingdom of heaven could he feel so detached. In heaven it would be possible to see one's wife, and the children whose passport thither had been the dearest concern of one's life, with the calmness of mind that belongs to the place where there is no marrying or giving in marriage. One would see them, and sweep by them. And there would be no speech or language, any more than there is among the heavenly bodies, but a voice would be heard among them, a solemn jubilee, as of wings, or as of the ice resounding underfoot.[21]

The book was well reviewed, and Sylvia's versatility rightly praised, though she was no longer 'news' to the literary press. One reviewer went so far as to say 'A carping contemporary may wonder why, in 1954, such a book should have been written at all; but since it has been, it is easy to enjoy it.'[22] In this light, Chatto & Windus's fears that the book might be too controversial hardly seem justified, but after submission of the typescript Sylvia had been told that the passage in which the fisherman Crusoe declares his love for Thomas Kettle would not do. Sylvia was scornful when she heard this, and scornful of the firm's prim delay in telling her, and she refused to withdraw the passage. She did, however, agree to perform 'a little castration', and sent the script back with a new paragraph to make the matter plainer.

In November of 1954 Sylvia was in London, alone, for a weekend of cultural debauch which included the British Museum, Sadlers Wells, the Diaghilev exhibition, Picasso and Courbet, the theatre, Bea, Victor Butler and her publishers, Ian Parsons and Norah Smallwood, a woman Sylvia esteemed highly. It was at Norah's flat that she was made a tantalising offer: to translate *Contre Sainte-Beuve*, Proust's evolution of his own aesthetic through the examination of that of the critic Sainte-Beuve. The book had been published for the first time in Paris that year, and Chatto & Windus wanted to publish an English translation as soon as possible. Sylvia was delighted and intrigued and began to experiment with the text as soon as she got home, to see if she could do it. Immediately, the book caught her up in its arms, and she sat at it, 'spellbound, tongue-between-teeth', and accepted the project.

'I live in a queer duality,' Sylvia wrote a fortnight later, 'half of my mind busy with his Countesses, half slutting about in the kitchen.'[23] Translating Proust was an absorbing occupation, but Sylvia had not anticipated how restful it would be too, freeing her from the fear of 'going dry', which was always a possibility in her own writing, and being much more resistant to interruptions, the bane of her creative life: 'One of the reasons why I so much enjoy this translating is that it compels me to use my intellect hard – and without the agonising jolts of having to back out of my own work to answer door-bells and cook meals.'

In those days, when the door bell of the shop wasn't ringing, or the phone going, it was very likely that the dog would be barking –

Candace, a black miniature poodle Valentine bought at the end of 1954. Sylvia had greeted the news that Valentine wanted a poodle with dismay, sure that the cats, whom she adored, would suffer and the peace of the household be shattered. But Valentine was longing for a new small creature to love and be loved by and thought Sylvia's antipathy unreasonable. She had little idea, though, how theatrically 'Candy' could behave, left at home with Sylvia. The dog set up such a baleful howling that Sylvia began to dread Valentine's absences. After a while, they devised a way of quietening the dog by squirting water from a water-pistol into its mouth, but the method was not always foolproof. On one occasion, Sylvia was crawling about on her hands and knees after Candy, water-pistol poised, when the vicar came to the door on one of his very infrequent visits. Sylvia was on the brink of explaining herself when she remembered her father's advice never to apologise in such situations, and merely wished him a good morning. Mrs Finch, a character in Sylvia's story, 'A View of Exmoor', refuses in a similar way to explain to a rambler why, in the middle of Exmoor, her daughters are dressed to impersonate a painting by Gainsborough, her son is wearing a blood-stained shawl over an Eton suit and she is holding a birdcage: 'He [the rambler] looked so hot and careworn, and I expect he only gets a fortnight's holiday year through. Why should I spoil it for him? Why shouldn't he have something to look back on in his old age?'[24]

Sylvia realised that Candace was, for Valentine, 'a new medicine against her melancholy [...] And alas, her woe, her void, can't be stuffed up with a poodle.' When Valentine had a story read on the radio or an article published in a magazine, she would sometimes now not tell Sylvia, for fear of being an embarrassment and being disappointed herself. Though they still loved each other deeply, their former joy seemed blunted, an aspect, they both supposed privately, of growing old. Sometimes a sense of times past would sweep over them, as when, in the spring of 1954, they stopped the car in a lane to pick primroses together: 'It was such innocence, such happiness,' wrote Sylvia, 'that I felt as though it were Chaldon twenty-five years ago. But I also know that Chaldon twenty-five years ago was not in the least like that. The sun's levelling rays stripe longer shadows, and light, but do not set on fire. And since last autumn I have come to feel ineluctably old.'

Through the shop and its reverberations Sylvia and Valentine came to make several pleasurable and long-lasting friendships; one with Reynolds Stone, the artist and engraver, and his wife Janet, who lived at Litton Cheney, not far from Maiden Newton, another with the Pinney family at Bettescombe Manor, near Bridport. Janet Stone had a wide circle of literary, musical and artistic friends, whom she was dedicated to entertaining, and through her Sylvia met Gerald Finzi, the composer, and his wife Joy. To dine at Litton Cheney, or at the Finzis' house at Ashmansworth, and meet such people as Edmund Blunden, Frances Cornford, Benjamin Britten, Peter Pears, L.P. Hartley (George Warner's admiring pupil), John Piper and John Nash was a pleasure Sylvia had almost begun to think impossible in the provinces. And though Valentine did not often share it with her, being painfully shy of 'parties', it was stimulating to Sylvia to be in intelligent company, like taking a vitamin she had long done without.

Valentine was not sure what was lacking in her own life, but as her fiftieth birthday approached she felt a desperate need to set herself on a right course and be freed from the uncertainties which had dogged her for years. Sylvia was preoccupied by the long and intricate job of translating Contre Sainte-Beuve, leaving Valentine feeling isolated. Towards the end of 1955 she found herself, much to her own surprise and against her better judgement, considering returning to the Roman Catholic Church. She wanted to be able to worship and join in the rites, but there were seemingly insuperable obstacles to that; her own inability to do so 'in simplicity, without cerebration',[25] her distaste for English Catholicism and its 'minority-movement' politics and the likelihood of being dragged into the 'buns-and-coffee aspect of their society [...] the little jokes about Father-This and Mother-That; It seems to RUSH me away from God.'[26] If she could just slip back into the church quietly though, thought Valentine, she would do so without hesitation.

On 12 January 1956 Sylvia and Valentine celebrated the twenty-fifth anniversary of their marriage – or almost did. They could not agree on whether the night in question had been that of the 11th or the 12th, so Valentine gave her present on the 11th and Sylvia hers on the 12th – a sad portent.

In her diary Valentine continued to fill page after page with the disincentives to rejoining the Church – a sure sign that she was preparing to overcome them. She had been taking advice from Father Weekes, the Dorchester priest, and also Bo Foster, Valentine's long-ago lover who was now living in Dorchester, an active member of the Conservative Party and a devout Catholic still. The biggest disincentive by far was the effect Valentine knew her re-conversion would have on Sylvia and the threat it would pose to their life together, which she anticipated with remarkable clarity:

> So many things are involved here: her contempt for anyone who 'submits' intellectually (which I share): her feeling of loyalty – but I do not know the exactly right word to describe it – for the Church of England as by Law established (which I share) and her affectionate familiar knowledge of the Prayer Book and King James Bible (which I feel: for no prayers anywhere can match the beauty and perfection of the Collects nor any text match that Bible – and the Church of England is magnificent, like St Paul's ... so here is another agonising thread attached to me!) and her enjoyment (which I share, heaven knows) of the Voltaire, Anatole France school ... the shrewd, pertinent, disillusioned wise ones who write like angels and who have been our masters and guides all our lives ... And, of course, much more than just these things: I know that her respect for me (what she has, and I think she has some, though I do not know what it is based upon) will be knocked away for good and all: and for me that is the most appalling prospect: a real maiming of myself, and even worse it *could* be: a maiming of her, coming on top of so much else she has borne, and somehow weathered.[27]

Four days later she spoke to Sylvia, in a rather casual way, about becoming a Catholic again, but the conversation so quickly waltzed off onto the question of whether or no she *could* rejoin without a new hat (in which to go to London, to confession) that

Sylvia did not allow herself to become alarmed. 'I hope it may rest there', she wrote in her diary. 'I think it may, as in fact she has one very suitable hat.'

Valentine had been sent a novena by Father Weekes to apply a little grease to the slow machinery of decision, and Valentine performed it, though it caused her private embarrassment: 'the awkwardness of the language & the downright silliness of the "hymns" & some of the remarks I am to make to Our Lady put me into a state of definite UN-grace!'[28] When Sylvia went into Valentine's room about a week after this, her eye fell immediately on a new object there, 'a small rosary by her bed, curled up neat as a snake. The comparison was instant, it must have shown in my look, or in my prim removal of the gaze; for afterwards in my sitting-room she began to talk more of going back to that bosom; and her objections were the kind of objection that, I thought, she had already discounted or slighted, and she talked without the smallest accent of dubiety or effort in her voice: she talked as though she had "gone and done it".'[29] Sylvia still tried to maintain a calm face towards all this, thinking both that it might blow over and that she should not interfere in Valentine's private affairs. Valentine, misled by Sylvia's reaction into believing she approved the idea, went to bed with a lightened heart.

The next day Valentine showed Sylvia pages of her diary relating to her movement back towards Catholicism, to explain herself. It was a mistake. To Sylvia, they were simply horrifying and corroborated all her fears about what was happening to Valentine; worse, what had already happened. It was as if Valentine had been stolen away from under her nose. Valentine saw with desolation that Sylvia was suffering from 'severe shock': 'she looked frighteningly like she had looked about Elizabeth – shaken and on the edge of sudden tears.'[30]

It became difficult, almost impossible, to talk about the matter after this. On 11 March, Sylvia noted in her diary, 'This morning Valentine drove to the Cat. church at Weymouth. A difficult matter to enquire into. I heard it was very full. I presume it may shortly be fuller.' Valentine was very keen to remain 'anonymous' for as long as possible, hence her choice of Weymouth for the Mass, but as soon as she told the three or four people she felt 'had to know', the news began to spread and became what Valentine had dreaded, an item of small gossip. Valentine could attend Mass, but not communicate yet, for there were business matters to clear up. It was discovered that for some reason the decree of nullity which had terminated Valentine's marriage was void in the eyes of the Church. Until she could trace the documents and the husband to prove otherwise, she was still Mrs Richard Turpin. Sylvia, knowing that on the heels of documents and husbands would come penance and contrition, began to fear that if the Church kept her to the letter of the law, Valentine might be forced to leave her and that certainly their long and happy years together would now have to be reviewed in the light of sin.

There was only one mitigating factor in all this for Sylvia and that was that Valentine had said of Mass that it gave her pleasure: 'So *pleasant*, she said; and the old spell snapped back and worked again, and I knew I could accept it, if it is pleasant to her.'[31] Sylvia decided to stand firm and try to weather it as best she could. She understood matters of faith, for she had one of her own, Valentine, to whom she had promised to be true twenty-five years before. '[Valentine] swears it will make no difference to our relation – and a minute later I was saying that I should undoubtedly settle down and get used to it. These two statements are incompatible, and both are sincere, and what happens with a sincere incompatibility I shall have to find out.'[32]

Six weeks later, when Valentine was still pursuing proof of the nullity of her marriage ('the last hurdle in the Grand Ecclesiastical', as Sylvia called it), Sylvia wondered, after a happy day together, whether she was really beginning to get over the shock, 'or whether I am acclimatising, with my usual despicable hold on life, to a pis-aller.' Valentine was happier by the day, though it troubled her to be in 'a tract of country we cannot walk about in together'. 'For my part, I think it would be better to walk about in it freely, even if we disagree about whether it is pleasant or not: but I think it exasperates her unbearably, and I think she cannot overcome her sense of *wariness* with me, when we are on that ground.'[33] Wariness was inevitable when Sylvia was forever biting back remarks, and there was much to remark: Valentine's growing collection of statuettes by her bedside table, the recital of prayers before bedtime ('like taking up a drawbridge'), the candles lit to Blessed Martin Porres when Kaoru stayed out for the night, the keeping of such anniversaries as Valentine's shot-gun reception into the Church back in 1925. 'Flippancy is the only answer, the only remedy,' Sylvia decided, though again this was unshared country, for Sylvia could not refer to the church in Weymouth as Our Lady Queen of Winkles nor to her devotional candles as 'blue nightlights' in front of Valentine. Looking at a pious prayer leaflet one day in Valentine's absence, Sylvia laughed so incontinently that Mrs Chubb, the charwoman, put her head round the door to see if Miss Warner was all right. But 'Holy Crumbs' was what Valentine read every morning and night with a straight, indeed sombre, face.

Valentine had rejoined the Church intending to keep as low a profile as possible, but she could not help attracting other people's curiosity and attention; her very modesty conspired against her, drawing her further into the Catholic social life she had wished to avoid. Her capacity as chauffeuse was often in demand, and her sense of duty prompted her to take up the tiresome jobs no one else wanted to do. Sylvia began to resent the side effects of religious observance, the lack of leisure it left Valentine, and the headaches, caused, so Sylvia believed, by early Mass on an empty stomach, followed by 'church-porch button-holings'.

There was no doubt that Valentine was a valuable new member of the flock. She was unostentatiously devout and always sincere. Though she had hoped to be at best a 'bad Catholic', she was in fact a very good one, certainly in matters of observance. And the fascination which she had always held over certain types of women continued to work in or out of a church, leaving her with an impressive list of converts to her credit, among whom was her own sister Joan. The relationship between the sisters had improved rapidly since Valentine was made to feel that Joan relied on her. Valentine had such a compassionate and protective nature that she found it almost impossible to refuse any appeal to it. She pitied Joan and, just as she had done as a tormented small child, longed to gain her love and trust. They began to see much more of each other and share holidays in Norfolk on a motor launch, where Candy was a welcome guest, and Sylvia not. Joan even went so far as suggesting she and Valentine should live together in

Norfolk, and have a jointly-owned antiques shop. As ever, she was desperate to emulate her younger sister.

Ruth, who was eighty in 1957, also wanted to live with or near Valentine, and Valentine kept her eye on estate agents' windows in Dorchester for her. Sylvia was very displeased with the way Valentine was mauled by her 'vampire-bat' relations, and often incurred Valentine's wrath saying so. Valentine was constantly alarmed by reports of disaster and near-death in Winterton, but Sylvia took the news of the latest 'heart-attack' calmly enough: 'One day the Wolf will really get her [Ruth], poor wretch – but till then she will go on like this, spending and causing others to be spent.' In 1959 Ruth went to live, temporarily, she thought, with some nieces in East Sussex, Valentine's plans for Dorchester having come to nothing. Ruth found the change of scene and company invigorating, as always. When Sylvia and Valentine took her out for the day to Worthing, Ruth was frisky as a kitten and 'in raptures telling everyone how ill she is'.

Catholicism led to a number of serious arguments at home about politics, which Sylvia and Valentine both used to show up the underlying hypocrisies in each other's behaviour – Sylvia for being unchanging in her views, Valentine for having altered hers. Sylvia maintained a very unchippable admiration for Stalin all through the 1956 Politburo renunciations and revelations of Stalin's purges. The one matter in which she had to admit herself disillusioned was Stalin's exclusion of the French at Yalta, but for the rest, the blacker he was painted, the more firmly she stood by him and scorned his detractors. There was not a glimmer of disapproval from her at the Russian invasion of Hungary in 1956, though it horrified Valentine, who thought it as provocative and unjustifiable as Hitler's incursion into Czechoslovakia in 1938. They also disagreed profoundly on the Russians' treatment of Pasternak. Sylvia felt her old enemy Stephen Spender was right in saying (in a letter to the papers) that anything that happened to Pasternak in Russia would be the fault of those exploiting him in the West. Valentine was furious, incredulous, and told Sylvia that she was *mad* to 'white the Russians by blackening someone else'. When Sylvia cited Franco's treatment of writers and journalists in Catholic Spain as being much worse, Valentine agreed, but added that Franco had never had any pretensions to respecting intellectuals, whereas the Russians 'have played that old gramophone record (which once sounded charmingly true) for so long now that it is full of cracks and pits and blanks ... and still they play it. (I suppose it has become like the *Blue Danube* to our mothers! Most of us – the aging soi-disant Intellectuals – soften and twitter and break into happy tears when we hear it – remembering the heavenly waltzes of our gaudy youth, clasped in the Bear's arms ...)'[34]

One of the last issues over which they were to feel politically unanimous was the proposed building of an atomic reactor on Winfrith Heath, which first came to their attention early in 1956. There was great opposition to the plan, naturally, from the local people; fear of explosion and contamination, the certainty of the landscape of the Heath unalterably changed for the worse; the influx of workers, lorries, noise and mess into the area. Sylvia and Valentine immediately set about writing to the papers and making their objections known. Sylvia also had the active support of Reynolds Stone, and together they wrote to *The Times* about the reactor. The next January, when the public inquiry was being held, Sylvia was asked to speak in opposition to the choice of location. The scientists at the inquiry appeared to her 'a shabby, scurvy-looking lot', a far cry from the scientists she had known in her youth. Her turn came on the third day: 'I spoke briefly on the letters after our *Times* letter, and came home on a cold frosty night. It is all no use. The heath is doomed.'[35] The speakers for the project were all men of substance, those against an inept woman and a cranky common-land expert. Construction of the plant began the same year.

A little while after the inquiry, Sylvia and Valentine were discussing the matter with Katie Powys and Alyse Gregory, who was desperately unhappy about it (the reactor is visible from every hill-top on Chaldon Down). Alyse asked to what purpose does one strive 'against mobs, officials, atom bombs' and how, she asked Sylvia, should she feel about such wasted efforts at the end of her life? 'I said, "When I die, I hope to think I have annoyed a great many people." And Katie, suddenly breaking back into the old Katie, rubbed her hands on her knees and shouted out, "That's it. That's it. I *like* to hear that."'[36]

The 'chasm' opening between Sylvia and Valentine disturbed Sylvia mentally as well as emotionally and she began to have not only the brown dreams which intimated to her coming madness, but a recurring 'vision' of a brown, slug-like creature she referred to as 'the horror in the hood' and which, not surprisingly, frightened her a good deal. On bad days, she felt herself more and more like the senile Nora; on good days she was simply 'ripe for otium cum dignitate'. Though flippancy was one sort of medicine against her unhappiness, it could not be used too often, nor against Valentine. In the spring of 1957 Sylvia put off Paul Nordoff from visiting because she felt it might make Valentine feel isolated, even 'ganged-up-against': 'this Roman Catholic business is like a third person in the house (as you said) and a third person bent on mischief-making. If you came now, and we absorbed ourselves in the opera [Nordoff was working again on his opera of *Mr Fortune's Maggot*] it would expose her – in the state she is now in – to feeling out of it and unwanted, and that would drive her further into this damnable R.C. persuasion that mortifications are sent from God, Crosses to be embraced, sufferings offered up. [...] *you are the only person to whom I speak of these things at all*. I try to think of them as little as possible. For while she still loves me – and she does, however far away all this has dragged her from my side – I don't want to alarm her by looking careworn or horrified, or plain dumbfounded. And besides, Paul, I must face it, though it destroy me. Part of it must be my fault. She would not, she could not, have turned back into that church if loneliness, unhappiness, sense of frustration, disappointment, disillusionment, had not driven her.'[37]

The sincere incompatibility could not have existed if they had not remained the centre of each other's life, remained, from two different perspectives, true to the same love. Unlike in 1949, when she was worn down by hoping, Sylvia did not hope for anything, and Valentine did not pray behind Sylvia's back for a conversion or change of mind. They had learned to 'accommodate' each other fairly quickly: what took some getting used to was that many things had not changed. When Valentine was talking, in October 1958, of what would give her most pleasure, it was 'lying in a meadow beside a river looking at swallows with Tibbie beside [me]' and a conversation about the Mass that looked as though it might turn nasty was saved by an image Valentine employed, as Sylvia recorded in her diary: '[the sacrament] is everywhere, but only complete in the mass itself, which is the rainbow, though rainbow elements exist in every drop of dew, every splash of water. Such a poet!'

It was to remind Valentine of herself that Sylvia prepared a small collection of Valentine's poems for private printing, *Twenty-Eight Poems*, in the autumn of 1957, but Valentine was not excited by it and hardly looked at the proofs. She was not writing much, for she had little confidence or creative energy left, and no illusions. She had passed from being 'Dr Gaster's woman' to being the lady who ran the little antiques shop, one of the Catholic women who breakfasted together at the King's Arms on a Sunday morning, the tall lady in gent's suiting who walked around Dorchester with a black poodle in attendance. To the gypsies who called every Michaelmas, she was Sylvia's 'lovely daughter'. It was only Sylvia's eyes that saw Valentine the poet.

Sylvia herself had a book of poems published in 1957, *Boxwood*, a collection with an odd genesis. Reynolds Stone had been commissioned by Ruari Maclean of the Monotype Corporation to make sixteen engravings and find suitable quotations to match them for a book which was primarily designed as a specimen for a newly-cut type, Dante Roman and Italic. Reynolds was having difficulty finding any appropriate quotations for his lovely engravings of trees, lanes, streams and hillsides and Sylvia offered to help him out by writing some short verses herself to 'illustrate' the illustrations. When Norah Smallwood saw *Boxwood* after it was printed, she wanted Sylvia and Reynolds to enlarge it for publication by Chatto & Windus. Sylvia at first 'gently blew on the project, which I feel is rather to[o] Georgian and precious to do any of us any good', but later relented, to please the Stones, and Chatto's slightly longer version of the book appeared in 1960.

To Alyse Gregory, at a time when Alyse was desperate and defeated, Sylvia had written the following advice:

I think as one grows older one is appallingly exposed to *wearing life* instead of living. Habit, physical deterioration and a slower digestion of one's experiences, all tend to make one look on one's dear life as garment, a dressing-gown, a raincoat, a uniform, buttoned on with recurrent daily breakfasts, and washings-up, the postman, the baker, the one o'clock and the six and the nine o'clock wireless bulletins. I know I am exposed to this vile temptation myself, however much I abhor it; but for myself I found one remedy, and that is to undertake something difficult, something new, to reroot myself in my own faculties. But even to make a kettle-holder is better than nothing – and indeed, if one is unaccustomed to making kettle-holders, it can be a most reviving experience. For in such moments, life is not just a thing one wears, it is a thing one does and is. [...] [Do] something you wouldn't do normally, which will tax your wits without involving your heart, which will benefit nobody but yourself and therefore contain no original sin of disillusion, which will be both abstract and self-regarding. Probatum est. I would often have been lost without such little tricks. We are never too old for technical exercises, my dear; and a woman who can whistle Justus ut palma while she paints the portrait of a thistle has already put up a new defence between herself and dying – because while she does so, *she is living.*[38]

Levity, fortitude and cunning: the older Sylvia got, the better she knew how to use them and the more her 'despicable' grasp on life strengthened. She had Valentine's company, the river, the garden – in which she worked extremely hard and happily – the cats, both loved and admired, and Niou the favourite, the confidant. She had numerous domestic and artistic skills – it was another of her dicta that one should never give up anything one does well – sewing, painting, making collages and découpages, being thrifty – her old self-indulgence – cooking idiosyncratic, extraordinary meals, making dolls, which she did occasionally for her closest friends ('When I am making them they mean Everything'). Above all, she had an enormous capacity for enjoying herself, and a capacity for joy: 'In the evening the Amadeus played opus 132; and I danced to the last movement, I rose up and danced, among the cats, and their saucers and only when I was too far carried away to stop did I realise that I was behaving very oddly for my age – and that perhaps it was the last time I should dance for joy.'[39]

III

Sylvia's friendship with Joy Finzi had deepened since Gerald Finzi's death in 1956, and through Joy Sylvia met again her protégée from Harrow, Ruth Moorsom, who was married to the composer Antony Scott. The old affection for 'Puss' had stayed completely intact, and it was pleasant to have this solid link with the past, so much of which seemed ghostly, including her past self in it. The future was more invigorating; Sylvia loved young people, for their youthful grace, ardour, candour and sincerity. During the Fifties there were a number of young girls especially who caught Sylvia's imagination and admiration in this way; Vera Hickson's daughter Rachel, Oliver Warner's daughter Polly, the Stones' daughter Phillida and Anne, the daughter of a Catholic friend of both Sylvia and Valentine, Jean Larson. These were 'nymphs' to Sylvia, just as the young Bea Howe had been. The magic tended to wear off: the nymphs fell from grace, or became bogged down in adult life, but while it lasted was potent. Here was another talent Sylvia did not want to give up, the talent for friendship. Sometimes it was frustrated, or seemed to be, as in the case of Phillida's elder brother Edward: 'I wish he would like me,' Sylvia wrote in her diary after the family had been to tea, 'I should be so good for him.'[40]

The garden was immensely important to Sylvia. On Good Friday 1957, she noted the things in bloom in it, which included polyanthus, clematis, bluebells, daffodils, narcissus, anemone, fritillary, rocket, tulips, strawberries, leopard's bane, forget-me-not, wallflowers, auriculas, hyacinths, laurel, lilac, crocus, rosemary, columbine, Solomon's Seal, violets, pansies, pear, apple and cherry blossom. One year, listing her roses, she named thirty-three varieties in flower, most of them old roses. The flower garden was informally planned and Sylvia was, in the words of a friend, 'unorthodox but inspired'[41] in her care of it. The vegetable garden, which lay behind a large bed known as the Massif Central, was run on stricter lines and provided many of the ingredients for Sylvia's cooking, which was also inspired and somewhat unorthodox. A summer lunch which she noted down in 1957 consisted of fresh sardines, olives, radish, cucumber with mint and chives, rye-biscuit, followed by sweetbreads in cream with green peas, followed by strawberries scalded with a vinous syrup and iced, with Frascati. She also excelled at curries and idiosyncratic soups.

Sylvia's translation of Proust, *By Way of Sainte-Beuve*, was published in the spring of 1958. Her title is not a literal translation of 'Contre Sainte-Beuve' but nicely captures the digressive nature of Proust's work, in which the critique of Sainte-Beuve's method forms the centre from which many other ideas branch, including much material later incorporated into *À la recherche du temps perdu*. Sylvia had been enthralled to be able to share Proust's mind for a while in the process of translating, 'And as, even at my best, I could never write like that, for I have not got that stuff of genius, that steady furnace, only a few rockets and Catherine wheels, I am grateful that I have had at least the experience of seeing, line by line, precept upon precept, how it is done.'[42] Her translation is remarkable in being both clear and fluent and true to the tone of Proust, able to convey his changes of register, pace and mood. George D. Painter, the distinguished biographer of Proust and Chateaubriand, wrote to Sylvia, 'I think your translation, besides being a true re-creation of Proust, is a new achievement in English prose.'[43]

Her translation was a great success, and when Chatto & Windus were planning a revision of the existing translation of *À la recherche*, they turned to Sylvia again. Scott Moncrieff's famous translation, completed after his death by Sydney Schiff (Stephen Hudson), had been shown by the scholarly 1954 Pléiade edition of Proust's works to be based on a very defective text – the only one available in the twenties. The new French text demanded a completely revised English translation and early in 1960 Sylvia was set to ascertain the extent of the discrepancies between Scott Moncrieff and the Pléiade. Even with the promise of a helper/collaborator later on, it was a daunting task, but, trained in *Tudor Church Music* methodology, Sylvia fell on it with relish; 'what one monkey can do, another monkey *bis*.' After a month at it, she wrote to Norah Smallwood listing the variants she had found in the first section, 'Combray': 'although I would not exactly call them Legion, they are numerous.'[44] In the summer she met her collaborator, Andreas Mayor, when he and his wife called at Frome Vauchurch. The arrangement for them both to work on emending the translation was slightly clumsy and constraining, with its own inherent problems. 'The Recherche can't just be divided between us like a carcase', Sylvia wrote to Norah Smallwood. 'In a work of this kind there must be some sort of editorial consultation, [...] Ideally, we should each of us go through the complete text, and then pool and adjust our findings. Even if this is too demanding for 1960, we must at all costs work jointly on each other's findings. Otherwise there is every risk that the revised translation will fall into Warner's half and Mayor's half, and all the value of two heads being better than one go for nothing.'[45] They worked on until October, when Sylvia went to London to meet Scott Moncrieff's executors, his nephew and niece, at dinner at the Garrick with Norah, Ian Parsons and George Painter, whom Sylvia admired greatly, 'a kind of infra-red intelligence glows from him, invisible but powerful.'[46]

There was a shock in store. The Scott Moncrieffs would not countenance any revision of their uncle's translation. This was baffling (Sylvia thought it not only stupid, but malicious), but against their refusal of permission, there was nothing to do but go home and wait for a possible relenting. '[It] is like having a corpse in the house,' she wrote, thinking of the piles of paper work in her sitting-room and mulling over what the real objections could be. Personal animosity was a likely one, she thought, and went as far as suggesting to Norah Smallwood that the executors, both Catholics, might have taken exception to her on religious grounds (a suggestion which Norah instantly dismissed). But the episode was never explained and Sylvia was left with the frustration of having done good work for nothing. The desirability of revising an out-moded text was, for her, not a matter for question, and when she found herself in a similar situation two years later – when O.U.P. wanted to revise some *Tudor Church Music* pieces in the light of new manuscripts – she agreed without demur.

All this was happening at a time when Valentine was recovering from a small operation to her right temple to remove a piece of artery. The headaches which Sylvia had lain at the door of 'Church' were in fact one of the symptoms of a condition known as temporal arteritis, an inflammation of the artery in the temple, diagnosed in March 1960. Valentine had been put on cortisone, a diet to counteract the cortisone, and a regime of rest in the afternoons. There was a risk to her eyesight, and a slight risk of having a stroke. Valentine began to learn braille and drenched herself in Lourdes water every morning. Sylvia was as fearful as Valentine during these months, and superstitious. She was alarmed by a comment by Lucy Powys, looking from her garden at Katie and Valentine cast in shadow indoors: 'Don't they look strange? said Lucy. As if they were behind a veil. [...] it was as blood-curdling as anything of T.F.P's.'[47]

At the end of June, when Joy Finzi was making a drawing of Sylvia (she wanted the effect of animation, and asked Sylvia to talk a great deal), Joy told her of the Oxford witches who had helped Gerald through his operations. Sylvia was intrigued, but dared not mention it to Valentine, for fear of a rebuff, so Joy broached the subject herself and left the house with a drop of blood, ready to put Valentine 'on the box'. Valentine's well-being came and went pretty much as usual, but the black box certainly comforted Sylvia, who believed in it quite irrationally, as was fitting. In the summer, they moved to a new doctor, Dr Hollins, who considered that cortisone was having no good effect on Valentine, and that a small operation and biopsy of the extracted tissue were necessary. She was admitted to a private nursing home in Weymouth, and had the operation on 4 August. When Sylvia went to visit, Valentine was propped up in bed, 'her head bandaged to one side, delicate fronds of hair rising above the bandage, like an exquisitely elegant Byronic brigand'. The biopsy showed that the artery had been completely blocked, but there was no evidence of enlarged cells, making a clot the more likely cause than arteritis. Valentine continued to have headaches from time to time, but also had periods of feeling entirely well, a rarity in her life.

Although the Scott Moncrieffs would not allow revision of their uncle's work, the part of À la recherche previously translated by Schiff was able to be given a completely new translation by

Andreas Mayor, who sent pieces of his work to Sylvia for her comments and advice. 'I am sincerely glad that he can sail on,' she wrote in her diary, but worried that, for her own part, the business might have checked the growth of her friendship with her publishers, Ian Parsons and Norah Smallwood. However, within two months they had asked her to undertake another translation, more of a distraction than a compensation, of a contemporary French novel called *La Côte Sauvage*, by Jean-René Huguenin. She accepted, for she needed a project to help dispel the sense of futility which was descending on her. She was writing well for the *New Yorker*, and earning a lot – in the year 1960–61 she earned £3,928 from writing – but she had never before felt less impetus: 'idle and unenterprising and *disinclined*, with pains in my spleen' is how she saw herself. She was feeling her age, too, and had begun to clear the decks towards feeling more of it, sending her manuscripts of *Lolly Willowes* and *Mr Fortune's Maggot* to an American buyer and throwing out many of her papers. She felt vaguely ill most of the winter, sometimes putting it down to pleurodynia (a form of fibrositis), 'my old February friend', sometimes to 'mors et vita duello-ing'.

The rift caused by Valentine's Catholicism, though no less wide than before, had ceased to infuriate Sylvia. She saw that religious observance was a great solace to Valentine, possibly the only solace. They had not shared a bedroom for some years, Valentine's back and Candy's fleas being two of the reasons. Sylvia had the old bedroom at the front of the house, and the double bed. Valentine had the room past her study at the other end of the landing, a pleasant room with two windows, one overlooking the river. Up early one morning and at the airing cupboard outside Valentine's room, Sylvia noticed the table loaded with oblateries and guessed that there was more to Valentine's recent visits to Buckfast Abbey than met the eye. Valentine had, indeed, been received as a novice-oblate of the Third Order of St Benedict just a few days before. In her diary, Valentine had written, 'It seems to me of immense importance: so immense that I find I am not telling anyone at all, and I am hoping never to have to – or at any rate until for some serious reason it has to come out.'[48] It is a mark of how far Sylvia had resigned herself to the inevitable that she did not take mortal offence at being kept in the dark like this, in fact she didn't take offence at all: 'It is her life', Sylvia sighed into her diary, 'and I am twelve years older than she – and it must seem very sad and hard to her that I cannot listen and rejoice.'[49]

Sylvia was sometimes able to rejoice – in her way. When they heard of the recovery from an accident of a friend's cat, Sylvia was so thankful that she lit all six of Blessed Martin Porres's candles at once. Unfortunately, she then went out to Dorchester to have her hair cut and forgot all about them, and an anxious dash home ensued. Valentine was particularly devoted to Blessed Martin Porres, and found his power of retrieving lost property superior to that of Saint Anthony, although it sometimes mystified Sylvia. She could not understand, for instance, why he replaced Valentine's cigarette lighter upright in the middle of the drive when he had finished with it.

Valentine was frequently away at this time, for Ruth was ill and sometimes the luggage was scarcely unpacked before another alarm put Valentine on the road again to her cousins' home, Apsley Farm. The sting had gone out of Sylvia's feelings for Ruth, too; Ruth was eighty-four, weakening fast and constantly in and out of a nursing home in Worthing. Sylvia and Valentine were at Apsley when Ruth returned there for the last time: 'Ruth dined downstairs, and was incited to sing in a family chorus, which she did most gallantly, and with such decision that she led us all astray like sheep into confusions of tonalities and a brief passage of consecutive fifths.' A fortnight later, when Valentine was in Sussex and Sylvia at home, Ruth died, quietly and without fuss. Valentine was at her bedside when she died, and was the last person she recognised. Valentine had not witnessed death so close up before, nor been so bereaved: '[Ruth] gave me (under God) the opening through which to touch, for the first time, the end of life. It is a gift far beyond any other she gave me, except my life [...] What guilt lies on people like me, who could have but did not bear a child?'[50]

The funeral was on 10 June 1961, but it was not until September that Sylvia and Valentine went to Winterton to bury the ashes and clear up Ruth's house, which she had left in 1959, thinking she would be back in a few months. Nothing had been seen to since that date, though Mr Pye, the eighty-four-year-old factotum, had been charged with its upkeep. As in the worst sort of fairy tale, Sylvia and Valentine found moth and mice and dust everywhere, bins overflowing, food mouldering in corners. On the floor by Ruth's chair was a bowl of 1959 sugar, now liquified. In the spare-room cupboard was a maggoty fox-stole in a chamber pot, beneath which was 'a miscellany of papers about the local Mothers' Union, and at the bottom was a framed photograph (glass broken, of course) of three nuns having tea in a garden.'[51] They spent a week cleaning up and sorting out. At the end of it 'Timbers' looked so tidy and bare that Sylvia felt 'as if I had broken into a strange house'.

Unlike Sylvia, Valentine missed her mother very much and turned for comfort to the company of her sister Joan. Joan's visits to Frome Vauchurch became so frequent (and, Joan being newly converted, so Catholic) that Sylvia was forced back on the expedient of escape, visiting friends such as Ian Parsons and his wife Trekkie at Juggs Corner, near Lewes, or Joy Finzi. Sylvia looked forward to these breaks: 'It unsours me after so much reluctant listening to church and family. When I reflect how I reprobate both, I think pretty well of my social talents. But nice to relax them from time to time.' Her cousin Janet was a congenial person to escape with. When Alyse Gregory left Chydyok in 1958 for a less remote house in Devon, Janet had taken the tenancy of the cottage, and used it as a bolt-hole. When she and Sylvia were there together in July 1961, a storm broke and the power failed just as they were going to bed. 'Janet cried "I've put my hand in a mug of milk" & I answered with "I've found my teeth by lightning."'

In August, run down by depression and mysterious aches and pains, Valentine visited a psychotherapist, but came back declaring it a failure: 'He told her it all stemmed from frustrated maternity – and was rheumatoid arthritis.' Valentine was dieting again, having become heavy on cortisone. There are no pictures of her at this date, for she refused to be in them, but at fifty-five she was said to be still remarkably young-looking. When Betty and Hope Muntz called on them one summer day, Sylvia was struck by how decrepit they looked by comparison, 'Strange that Valentine, whose health is so much worse than all these, should look so young, so stately, so elegant, with scarcely a grey hair or a wrinkle.'[52] The disappointment to Sylvia was that Valentine did not take her elegance into society more often.

Misunderstandings, rebuffs, inadequate response one to the other were increasingly frequent, and increasingly difficult to avoid, given their differences over politics and religion. A cold word or gesture would plunge Valentine into a 'fever of pain', 'something very much like despair – or illness.'[53] These things were lacerations, but not quarrels, borne privately by one of them and apparently unnoticed by the other, for there are no incidents of this kind reported by both women in their separate diaries. They did not realise how they hurt each other, only that they were hurt. Love and dependence had rendered them both extraordinarily vulnerable:

Scarcely any speech possible between us now, unless I insist on it (as I did about Pacifism the other day) & then it costs me, at any rate, so much strain that I am almost crippled by it for days afterwards. [...] Niou has just come into my sitting-room. I look at him with the most sorrowful love. He has taken my place completely now, and is her care and her love and her refreshment and her rest and her support. [...] But I know she does still love me – though now, I sometimes think, not loves me, but loves the fact of loving, and loyalty and fealty and quite a lot of stubbornness makes her firm in *that* love. But love for ME?

(Valentine, 27 September 1961)

I look in my heart and see only the shape and colour of events: all substance, all backing has vanished from them, they are like glass-pictures made from prints, they are bodiless. This is not sublimation, merely a process of time, actuality transformed to memory. It is no business of mine, I had no hand it it – so it cannot be sublimation which is a deliberate or sub-deliberate process.

(Sylvia, 1 November 1961)

Valentine was hardly writing anything except her diary and

letters. She found she could no longer complete a poem or a story, partly because she felt she had not the wit, but partly because there seemed no point in it: 'the pitiful scrawled beginnings in my books and on little scraps of paper are worse than blank would be.'[54] Her stories had been relatively successful, published in the *Listener* and *New Statesman*, broadcast on the radio, and were predominantly about states of mind rather than sequences of events, but the better she got at expressing the kernel of her ideas, the less inclined she was to expand them, as she wrote to Alyse Gregory: 'Lately I wrote three rather bare, perhaps bleak "NOTES" for stories; I am not sure why I wrote them at all, but once done they seemed to me complete as they were and that "working them up" into stories would be useless [...] I suspect they will turn out to be nothing.'[55]

The shop continued to prosper in its modest way but Valentine felt less enthusiastic about it than before and the chores involved – book-keeping, making and copying lists, sealing up parcels (about 300 a year) – were tiring. The many mortgages on the family estates, plus death duties, had left Valentine with more anxiety than money as her mother's legacy. It made no difference that this was no longer a pressing matter; Valentine was still very easily 'panicked with worry about money', although Sylvia earned so much that to herself she had to concede 'I am almost a wealthy woman, though I continue to behave as a poor one.'

IV

A great part of Valentine's melancholy stemmed from her concern over the state of the world. The Berlin Wall, the repression practised by eastern bloc regimes, the Cuban missile crisis, all frightened her deeply, and as usual, it was stories of individuals persecuted, killed and caught up in these larger events which hung on her conscience. Having given up the *Daily Worker* in favour of the *Daily Mail* in the mid-Fifties, she now changed from the *Daily Mail* to the *Daily Telegraph*, and cut out hundreds of entries from that paper and *The Times* on subjects to do with what we would now call human rights violations. Valentine could no longer believe that Communism as manifested in the Soviet Union and its satellites was anything other than evil, and occasionally challenged Sylvia with the latest atrocity. Sylvia, who heard Church behind all this, usually answered in as condescending a way as possible, and dismissed newspaper 'facts' as propaganda. After one of these *impasses*, as Valentine recorded, '[Sylvia] said What would she have if she were to lose her belief and hope in Communism? Nothing but despair, she said. (Earlier she had said I had no idea of what isolation was: think of hers, here among these people, and so cut off –) I did my best to explain to her that her hope is not, in fact, in political communism at all ... but I did not say this in so many words.'[56] But hanging on to Communism was in part Sylvia's way of holding out for their past together.

In 1962, Sylvia was in her sixty-ninth year and in excellent health. She had occasional bouts of her pleurodynia, but was always more than willing to go to bed with it. As she had written to Alyse some years before: 'I have had a small touch of rheumatism in my shoulder, a painful nuisance, but no more; and [Valentine] has tended and cured me with such exquisite delicacy and sureness of touch that I look back on it as a really happy experience, as a luxury. Other women may go to the opera. I had rheumatism.'[57] Sylvia was, if anything, a more active gardener than ever, though since the onset of Valentine's back trouble they had always employed someone to do the heavy work; first Mr Samways, then Mr True, and latterly a neighbour of theirs, Sybil Chase. A local boy called Colin House came in occasionally to help with the garden. He was one of several boys in whom Sylvia and Valentine took a fostering interest, encouraging them, and in some cases paying for part of their education.

Though Sylvia was seldom ill, Valentine was acutely aware of any intimations of mortality, and found them alarming. Talking of someone who was 'wonderful for eighty', Sylvia commented that she didn't wish the same on herself. Valentine became distressed, and embraced her lovingly. 'My God, it is embraces I still want,'[58] Sylvia reflected, having been put to bed early with supper on a tray.

Sylvia finished her translation of *La Côte Sauvage* (called *A Place of Shipwreck* in her version) early in 1962 and went straight into a long story, 15,000 words, intended for the *New Yorker*, 'almost certainly a piece of total unprofit. But writing it I have, after so many short stories, tasted the queer excitement of giving my characters enough rope to hang themselves.' After a month 'The Beggar's Wedding' was returned, and for the first time she was not stung into wanting to write something else, but felt completely deflated – 'I just wanted never to write again' – although she wrote to William Maxwell the same day with her usual sense of justice: 'The burden is unevenly distributed. You have to say the story won't do – with nothing to mitigate the painfulness of saying it; except a good conscience, and we all know how much comfort that is.'[59] He wrote immediately, explaining the rejection, but she was preoccupied by the failure of what she had thought her truer artist-self. 'Am I so clichéd,' she wrote in her diary, 'that it is only as a cliché they like me?' Three months' 'agonising interim of fret and complete drought' followed, until she began another story, 'Heathy Landscape with Dormouse'.

In 1962, Sylvia published another collection of stories, *A Spirit Rises*, the title story of which evokes memories of her father and his study at Radnor Lodge, the only story she ever wrote which draws directly on her own childhood experiences without making a joke out of them. The stories in *A Spirit Rises* deal with a remarkable variety of types of people and situations, 'an uncannily equable openness to human data',[60] as the novelist John Updike later wrote – from the composer exiled from his house by consideration for two illicit lovers in 'On Living for Others', to the charwoman preparing to kill herself in 'During a Winter Night' and the doctor in 'The Locum Tenens', a story which contains an evocation of the West Riding of Yorkshire remarkable in a woman who knew it very little indeed. There seems little justification, in the sympathy and restless energy of these stories, for Sylvia to have looked on herself as clichéd.

In the summer of 1962 Valentine faced an agonising decision when she was told that Candace had a brain tumour and would not live long. She chose not to have the dog put down immediately for the shock was too great: 'It is not that C. is affectionate to me: but she LOVES me: and she clings to me.'[61] By the end of the month, however, Candy had to be killed. Valentine was so desolate that she immediately ordered a new puppy, which arrived in September and was called Fiddle, but the next month she died too, this time while being spayed at the vet's. A few months later, and against her better judgement, Valentine took charge of a third puppy, a brown miniature poodle bitch, whom she called Fougère.

Fougère arrived in the middle of the bad winter of 1963. At Frome Vauchurch, never a warm house at its best, the cats' peat trays froze – indoors – and washing stiffened with frost before Sylvia could even peg it up. The only place where things were not likely to freeze was the refrigerator. 'Bitter frost and savage wind', wrote Sylvia, 'scarcely a bird moving, or able to move'. Maiden Newton under snow was 'like the Switzerland of my youth: frozen, *scentless*, deadly pretty-pretty in its colouring of painted houses and white ground and background.' Sylvia hated cold weather and felt herself drain away under its influence: 'I feed the birds every morning and afternoon, I feed the animals, I feed Valentine, I do the fire (bless it) and the cats' trays; and little enough – but by the evening I am so tired I can hardly put one foot in front of another.' Niou was also miserable with the weather, but not only the weather. Sylvia noticed with desolation that his health was failing. Valentine's health was the more immediate worry, though. In February her ankles swelled enormously and she was put on some new drugs for oedema, which did not work. Her legs swelled, and her heart was racing. High blood pressure, the doctor said, and then, in April, he diagnosed TB of the pericardium and told Valentine she would need a major operation or submit to 'a long gathering invalidism'. This diagnosis was scotched by a Harley Street specialist to whom Valentine was referred for a second opinion. He said that there was no need for an operation but that Valentine needed to spend a fortnight in the Brompton Hospital having her blood thinned and undergoing tests. Meanwhile, completely overset by the implications of all this, Valentine had asked to be put on the 'black box' again, this time by a friend they had made through the Stones, and the next day her ankles were 'definitely less swelled'. 'I try not to think of what's to come,' wrote Sylvia. 'How shall I manage not to go to pieces, even if things go well.'

Valentine emerged from her fortnight in hospital on 9 May,

vastly thankful to be going home, although she was still taking Warfarin, and another drug for her continuing oedema. The blood-thinning treatment had been a course of pills to which she had reacted violently, and on her penultimate day the specialist had mentioned that she might have a benign lump – he did not say where – which would need to be removed at some later date.

When they went to pick up the cats from the Hicksons' farm on the way home, Vera confirmed that Niou was dying. He pulled himself up the stairs every night to sleep on Sylvia's heart 'as ownerly as ever' and by day he sat for hours and watched the river, as Thomas had done. Before the month was up, Niou was so weak that Sylvia called the vet and he was given his quietus. They buried him in the garden in a basket lined with sweet hay and catmint. 'I don't believe stoicism improves with age. Body goes out of it, as out of a wine.' Sylvia was, in a self-contained, tearless way, quite unhinged by the death of Niou and had a dream connected with him 'along the edge of madness'. Valentine bought her a new kitten in October, a Siamese called Quiddity, whom she grew to love, but five months later he was found dead in the river on a cold February morning.

Sylvia was not writing well, and knew it. 'Total Loss', the story she wrote immediately after the death of Niou, was returned by the New Yorker. Looking over three sets of proofs sent to her in one lot for correction, Sylvia saw a falling-off in her work and resolved to improve: 'I must acclimatise myself to Decline and Fall, and try not – if I do still write – to become a gay grandam, frisking beneath the burden of fourscore. I must study to be plain.'[62] She had begun her series of stories about Mr Edom, the antiques dealer, trying to keep her hand in while she recovered herself, but found that she couldn't take control of 'a nonsense piece' as easily as before. A month later, she set out on 'a nice calm story about incest'. '[It] must be flat as flat,' she warned herself, 'and dry as dry – WITH NO FRISKS OR QUIPS, my old girl.' The story, called 'Between Two Wars' at first, later 'A Love Match', flowed along so satisfyingly that Sylvia felt it must be doomed to failure, like 'The Beggar's Wedding', but by the time she finished it (only a couple of weeks later) she was in a trance-like state. She had not been so involved in a piece of writing of her own since The

Flint Anchor. At about 10,000 words, 'A Love Match' was longer than her usual *New Yorker* sprint, and weightier. The central theme, the incestuous relationship between a man broken by the First World War and his sister, bereaved by it, is a powerful but unobtrusive allegory for the condition of England between the first war and the second. The story was very compactly told, with the scope and leisure of a novella, and the themes of village life, wartime conditions and illicit love were ones Sylvia warmed to easily. The *New Yorker* cabled their acceptance without hesitation.

While she was writing 'A Love Match', Sylvia had a series of letters from Michael Howard, of the publishers Jonathan Cape, inviting her to write the biography of T.H. White the novelist, who had died only two months before, in January 1964. Sylvia agreed provisionally, but as a series of legal complications threatened the book, she gave it little thought for the time being. She had never met White, though he admired her books very much and had sent her his poems early in 1963 inscribed 'From an unknown worshipper'. She had noted in her diary at the time 'Some of them I like very much; partly no doubt because they are of my own way of writing.' On 17 January, she had written, 'T.H. White is dead, alas! – a friend I never managed to have. He sent me his poems, I wrote out of my heart to thank him. That was all.'

By the middle of May the project seemed to be viable and Michael Howard suggested that he take Sylvia to Alderney, White's home for the last seventeen years of his life, so that she could see his house, talk to his friends there and decide whether or not to do the book. In the bookroom at the top of White's tall house on Connaught Square, St Anne's, Sylvia felt herself quicken to her subject and went out to tell Michael Howard that she had decided in favour. White's suitcases, which had come home from White's last sea-voyage, stood unpacked in the hallway. His clothes and books and the accoutrements of his many enthusiasms lay about the house; half-finished projects, and, Sylvia noticed, an uncompleted hawk-hood in the sewing basket. 'I felt it intensely haunted, his angry, suspicious, furtive stare directed at my back, gone when I turned round.'

Sylvia took the plane home from Alderney with eight cartons of annotated books from White's library, a growing fascination with White himself and several new friendships; with Carol Walton and Harry Griffiths, friends of White, and with Michael Howard and his wife Pat. It was flattering to be sought after as a writer, admired as a woman and amicably squabbled over by Cape and Chatto & Windus, who agreed to a temporary joint-ownership of her: 'I never thought to become a Helen of Troy in my old age,' she said. Sylvia was disappointed, though, that Valentine did not seem very interested in the project: 'Everything loving met me, but no interest; and again I realised that I should not come home having got drunk at the party.'

Sylvia received the contract for the book two weeks later, having already planned chapters and an experimental beginning, and on the heels of the contract came the Howards in a car 'like the great bed of Ware', full of manuscripts and notebooks belonging to White. Valentine cleared part of the shed, but White spread himself all over it, and flowed into the house. Undaunted by the mass of paper, Sylvia set to, reading his books first, then his diaries, then the notebooks. By the end of the year she was well into her first draft, getting up early most days to secure some hours of undisturbed writing. As she finished each section she posted it to Carol Walton to be typed and to either Michael Howard or William Maxwell or David Garnett – White's and Sylvia's mutual friend – to be read. It was a remarkably overlooked first draft, and being overlooked ran up against criticism occasionally. Garnett wrote 'vehemently denying' any link between White and Turgenev and putting forward various amendments, none of which Sylvia used. 'No one will believe my book,' she wrote, 'because it is drawn from his diaries not from what is called life.'

She set out intending it to be White's *White*, 'a self-portrait', and in her first letter to Michael Howard had stated grandly that 'the essential in biography [...] is that the subject of the biography should have known himself; and this T.H. White certainly did.'[63] When she had laboured her way through his papers (one of her surviving notebooks for *T.H. White* is numbered '89'), it became less easy to say whether he had 'known himself' or not, there were such extremes in his character – child and man-of-action, swashbuckler and scholar, do-er and dreamer – that White seemed sometimes to have slipped down the gaps and disappeared. Eight months after her letter to Michael Howard, she was writing to William Maxwell, 'I find I am writing this book from the standpoint of an Aunt',[64] but that changed too. A biographer is both master and servant to his subject, and the servant can be extraordinarily possessive. After two years work on her book, Sylvia wrote in her diary: 'Sometimes as I handle these mss, notebooks, letters, the sense of his existence – that he handled them, knew the look of them – almost overwhelms me, and I think, I shall die when they are withdrawn: they are mine, he bequeathed them to me.'

Over this period, Valentine's health did not improve and she was forever being plied with new medicines. In April 1965 she was put on cortisone again to combat what appeared to be her main problem, 'thyroid trouble'. A few months later her head began to ache in the old place and all her fears of arteritis, blindness and incapacitation crowded in. She was given sedatives. But even more depressing was the car accident Valentine had in June 1966, which led to her licence being endorsed after forty blameless years on the road. What actually happened is unclear. Sylvia dismissed the other party's evidence as a pack of lies, and it was never decided whether Valentine's brakes had failed, or whether she skidded on oil – or mud – in the narrow lane outside Mappowder, or, having drawn in to let the other car pass, turned the wheel the wrong way. At the impact, Valentine threw herself sideways to protect Fougère and thereby hit her head against the dashboard instead of through the windscreen. Sylvia was not in the car at the time, but, alerted by Lucy Powys on the phone, reached the Dorchester hospital just as Valentine was being taken out of the ambulance. She had a broken nose, two black and swollen eyes, a bruised temple, and was bleeding profusely. After examinations in Dorchester and Weymouth, Sylvia managed to take her home. A night in hospital, she maintained, 'would have been as ruinous as the accident – and far more prolonged.'[65]

Valentine hired a car while their five-month-old Renault was being repaired (they replaced it with another new one), and got some of her old confidence back, but never all of it. Sylvia looked on, horrified, one day in October as Valentine completely lost her nerve manoeuvring out of the King's Arms garage, fell, grazing her knee, and cried out repeatedly, 'No one helps me!'

The day-to-day running of the shop was getting too much for Valentine, and in May 1966 she spoke of closing it down except as an agency to supply customers with specific items. And she was deeply melancholic – though she said little of this to Sylvia – about the state of her beloved Church since the changes initiated by the second Vatican Council. The foundation upon which she had re-built her life seemed to be giving way, and hearing the new English version of the Mass every Sunday was almost beyond her capacity for mortification, although Sylvia, when asked her opinion, could only muster 'a scholar's distaste'. At the same time, Valentine felt isolated because of all the emotional energy Sylvia was pouring into her book on T.H. White.

In the summer of 1966 Sylvia had embarked on the painful business of reading White's intimate diaries, bequeathed to Michael Howard with strict instructions that they should stay in his care. As a compromise – so that Sylvia could read them – Howard entrusted them to the Dorset County Museum. In the peaceful atmosphere of the Museum library, she went through the contents of the yellow tin trunk as if she were going 'deeper into dungeons'. 'Perversions like his are like a goblin child that will not quit the grown man's being. I would like to present the whole series to Cheltenham College.' She did not put any sexual 'revelations' directly into her book; as she noted, White's aberrations were 'so puny in fact, so overwhelming in feeling' and it was the feeling she represented. 'There is a kind of ill manners about such discussions *with strangers*: and that is what the printed page means.' There were people who did not want their names mentioned in connection with White and one of them turned up on the doorstep at Frome Vauchurch, ready to harangue. 'Oh poor Tim, what awful friends you made,' Sylvia exclaimed in her diary, adding afterwards, 'N.B., however; the anguish, dull to searing, of persons who from their desire for higher things, make friends with Tims.'

Sylvia finished the book on a Friday evening in mid-December, a few days after her seventy-third birthday, and wrote in her diary, recalling the *envoi* at the end of *Mr Fortune's Maggot*: 'Goodbye, my poor Timothy!':

> Valentine was out churching. The house so cold and silent, and I longed to rush into a congenial debauchery, to boast, moan, be praised and pitied.
>
> So I fed the animals and cooked smoked haddock and drank a little solitary whiskey. Then Kit [Kaoru] saw my state and said with large clear eyes that life has a lot of partings. I don't think he will live much longer. He is becoming profoundly wise.[66]

The letting-go of White was extremely difficult. Each diary to be returned, each parcel of manuscripts to be tied up, was a severing of the bonds of intimacy she had formed between herself and him. She felt she had never been at a lower ebb, and though the acknowledgements and notes were diversions, she dreaded everything being *done*, 'For suppose I don't want to write anything further? Or try, and it is dead.' White's friends had become her friends; she knew him better than he had known himself, more comprehensively, with her biographer's god's-eye view of his life, and foreknowledge of his death. It was hard to hand him over to whoever might care to read her book.

> The lights are going out all over Sylvia [...] as I walked to the kitchen to eat after finishing the preliminaries I said to the air, O Tim, I don't like to lose you; and could have sworn that a large shape – much too tall and too broad for the passage – was following me. It has been a strange love-story between an old woman and a dead man. I deliberately say love, not friendship, nor intimacy. One cannot have friendship or intimacy without some foothold in living memory.[67]

V

T.H. White was published in November 1967, and was Sylvia's greatest critical success since *Lolly Willowes*, praised as 'sympathetic', 'shrewd', 'splendidly intuitive', 'elegant'. She was gratified as much on White's behalf as on her own. At the end of the book is a rather badly-reproduced photograph (a late addition) of White's gravestone in Athens, with its epitaph 'who/from a troubled heart/delighted others/loving and praising/this life'. In a letter to Eric Hiscock, Michael Howard revealed that this was Sylvia's work, 'although she shrinks from taking credit for it. But David Garnett wrote to me the other day – "It is a most unusual epitaph – because it is strictly true."'[68]

Sylvia emerged from *T.H. White* overdrawn on her current account, probably because her output of *New Yorker* stories had been so much reduced by it. She was exhausted in spirits, but forced herself to work. And, with less effort, she threw her threescore years and ten around the garden in a series of ambitious remodelling schemes, often staying out all day, which, as always, revived her vitality. One day in July 1967 she noted the garden 'all roses, the tall and the Stourhead syringas, delphinium, crimson single pinks, Valentine's sweet peas, canterbury bells. I sat on the old stump dangling a coffee cup and opened my senses to this small earthly paradise.'

The stories Sylvia was writing at this time were collected in *The Innocent and the Guilty*, which was published in 1971. *A Stranger with a Bag*, Sylvia's eighth collection of short stories, had been published in 1966 while she was still working on *T.H. White*. It included 'A Love Match', which was awarded the Katherine Mansfield Menton prize in 1968, and a selection of pieces, mostly from the *New Yorker*, which had been written between 1961 and 1965. The two collections contain some of her very best stories and show how her manner had become less polished over the years, and all the more powerful for it. 'She has the spiritual digestion of a goat,' wrote John Updike (an unexpected champion), reviewing *A Stranger with a Bag*, and added, 'her stories tend to convince us in process and baffle us in conclusion; they are not rounded with meaning but lift jaggedly toward new, unseen, developments.'[69] Part of this effect was achieved by Sylvia's sudden dropping of one point of view in a story and picking up another, as in 'Heathy Landscape with Dormouse' when, having established our sympathies with Leo, the husband, the focus switches to his wife Belinda and everything is re-cast in the light of her view of events. Not only does this further the narrative by default, as it were, but demonstrates, as Sylvia's stories often do, that no motives are wholly knowable, particularly our own.

John Updike was able to write about Sylvia Townsend Warner in a familiar and unapologetic way because he was writing for an American magazine. In England, Sylvia's stories still 'dropped imperceptibly' into the book market, and the tone of reviewers had become ominously respectful, as if they were talking of a valuable but useless family heirloom. Something of this tone must have crept onto the Chatto & Windus jacket for *The Innocent and the Guilty*, for Sylvia wrote back to Norah Smallwood with evident irritation: 'The blurb's second paragraph is like getting a presentation electro-plated teapot. So here is an alternative, which says something about the book instead of some kind words about a retiring Cub-Mistress.'[70] The printed version of the blurb reads as follows:

> *The Innocent and the Guilty* is a title with intention. These stories explore the perplexing frontier between innocence which can steal a horse and guilt which cannot look over a wall – a frontier which has nothing to do with Goodies and Baddies, and lacks the reliability of classical Calvinism, since it is constantly shifting. Only in one of these stories does a character achieve total innocence, and then only by going out of her mind.

The story she refers to is 'But at the Stroke of Midnight', a disturbing and unsatisfying tale which is, even so, among Sylvia's best. It is structurally quite odd, with a series of confusing time changes, appropriate to the progress of the narrative, which is about schizophrenia. Lucy Ridpath, 'middle-aged, plain, badly kept, untravelled', leaves her home and husband suddenly and for no apparent reason. Adopting a dead cousin's name and assertiveness, she becomes Aurelia Lefanu and wanders from place to place, struggling to retain her new identity and evade her old husband. Freed by irrationality she lives purely for herself and the moment, inspiring in those she meets a sort of awe. She is 'a nova':

'A nova is seen where no star was and is seen as a portent, a promise of what is variously desired.'[71] She befriends a broken-down, cringing tom cat, whom she names Lucy, and it is the death of this animal which 'dislocates' Aurelia back into her former self and propels her towards her death. 'But at the Stroke of Midnight', which was written in 1967, was one of Sylvia's last 'conventional' short stories, and with its otherworldly heroine forms a bridge between those stories and her later development as a writer about elfindom. It is also a story with many oblique parallels to *Lolly Willowes*, and a comparison of the two works gives some measure of Sylvia's tremendous scope and breadth of feeling.

Late in August 1967, Sylvia and Valentine heard of the death of Alyse Gregory, a suicide cautiously and carefully approached across many years. 'I can scarcely believe it,' Sylvia wrote. 'People so seldom get the end to crown the work. She has, dying unvexed and solitary as a blade of grass. Not a familiar voice nor a familiarised fuss round her deathbed [...] As for me, I think sadly that my stock of congenial minds is running very low. Never mind, so am I.'[72] Valentine watched Sylvia's health like a hawk, and found it difficult to be reassured about it. Sylvia was very robust. She never took exercise, smoked and drank black coffee continually, sat for hours writing then worked in the vegetable patch regardless of the weather, and never came to much harm. Recovering from a viral infection which she had passed on to Valentine, Sylvia wrote, 'I try vainly to convince V. that I am well and spry again. This is one of the two hundred things she worries about. They are partly fever worries, partly habitual: Ruth coming out. I realise that it is as one ages and loses one's natural force that one is at the mercy of heredity, the young are themselves: the ageing, their parents' children.'

On 12 January 1968, they celebrated the thirty-seventh anniversary of their marriage:

It was a cold night like this:
Midwinter, motionless,
We had come back from a concert.
The singer, still wrapped in her music, had greeted us

– A general blessing and a nuptial, though
She had no thought of such and we did not know.
The hall where we listened, the substantial
House we returned to, toppled into the abyss,
The instruments of music were burned to ashes
This, too, was long ago.
Times change and disconcert:
The frail promise
Made on that winter night holds true on this.[73]

Two weeks later Valentine was told by Dr Hollins that, despite the
odd coloration over the lump on her left breast, and the pain in it,
there was no sign of cancer. A week after this, he said she ought to
have the lump removed, for she was tense, and the lump was an
agitant. Anxiety seemed a likely cause to Valentine, remembering
the lump she developed during the summer of 1949, and she told
Sylvia forthrightly that she was in despair about the Church, and
feared she would have to leave it. This concerned Sylvia deeply, for
Valentine seemed 'pinched in half' by the decision ahead: '12 years
ago, how my heart would have welcomed this: But now I can only
hope she will somehow reconcile herself and stay in. She would be
desolate without it.' They were both, by this time, very frightened
about Valentine's health, and their fears seemed justified when on
6 March a surgeon in Weymouth said he thought the lump was
cancerous. She was to have a biopsy, and, if the carcinoma was
malignant, an amputation.

'She is truly brave, I am not. I have only good manners to
depend on,' wrote Sylvia. The weary business of informing people
began, and choosing a surgeon. They plumped for Sir Hedley
Atkins on the recommendation of two friends, not knowing that
he was President of the Royal College of Surgeons. They tried to
continue as normally as possible until the appointment with Sir
Hedley in London, but for the first time, Sylvia had to consider the
prospect (she did not *face* it yet) of Valentine's death. 'A life
without her seems inconceivable: *physically* inconceivable, like
trying to conceive walking without a sense of direction, a flow
without a bed to flow into, an aimless plenitude of time.' Valentine
passed Sylvia's room one day and heard her saying to their cats

Pericles and Titus (Kaoru's successors, both Siamese), 'The days are gone.'

The appointment in London was complicated by Sylvia developing a high temperature and being ill at Farnham, where they had broken the journey. Valentine had to leave her raving in a fever – 'I have never felt so *drenched* in ignominy,' Sylvia said – and go on alone to be told by Sir Hedley Atkins that it was certainly cancer and that she must have an operation within weeks. Peg Manisty, a Catholic friend of Valentine, met through a correspondence in the *Tablet* in 1962, fetched Valentine and took her to Waterloo, whence she returned to Sylvia still flat out in her Farnham hotel. 'Not only had I totally failed her,' Sylvia lamented, 'I had become an alarm and an encumbrance. Not only had I become an encumbrance, I had become a senseless, unspeculative log.'

Valentine's operation took place on 10 April at Guy's Hospital. The surgeon removed a lump 'the size of a golf-ball',[74] and felt it had all gone 'cleanly'. Valentine convalesced for a while at Peg Manisty's house in Mayfield with Sylvia, and then went home, hopeful that the worst was over, bar the twenty-five sessions of radiation treatment she was prescribed over the next two months. Sylvia cast herself upon the garden again. She had written one story for the *New Yorker*, though it took her four months on and off, and had made two more dolls. Otherwise it was nothing, nothing but the garden.

Valentine was desperately concerned to put herself on a right footing with God, for she felt her private debate about the Church was threatening her faith. She had a tape-recording machine which she loved (she loved all such gadgets) and used to record birdsong, cat-song, herself speaking favourite poems and Sylvia's conversation (hopeless, for Sylvia immediately fell silent). Onto this machine she spoke some of her thoughts about the changes in the Church and whether she could live with them. She had lost respect, she said, for the Roman Church, and would have loved to rejoin the Church of England if it were not for 'schism, the Martyrs, Dame Julian'. And there were many practical considerations which made her reticent to leave Catholicism: small but important matters such as the effect her leaving might have on the faith and peace of mind of others. She inclined further and further towards Quakerism (except insofar as she was not a pacifist). It alone seemed to allow some room for the working of the Holy Ghost. On the tape her voice is truly beautiful, 'a viola voice' as Sylvia said, melancholy and resonant, with a correctness of pronunciation, phrasing and breathing so unusual now it sounds 'trained'. There are almost inaudible sighs, a long pause for thought, then another flow of speech.

In June, Valentine was told that she was healing well, and that the outlook was good, although she still had pains near her scar and felt crushingly tired and devitalised: 'If only I could feel interested in something again. This bewilders me: to be so heavy and so tired and so dull and so unloving! All my love is inside me but it is tears and weeping and parting and regret and dread. God – restore me to myself! If I can only find myself again I shall be free to love and live, even if it's only a month or so, and live in praise and joy, not as a lumpish burden.'[75] But a check-up in London in December indicated that the cancer had spread and a second operation was arranged immediately, at Guy's again, for the removal of her breast. This operation, coming so soon after the other, weakened her considerably. Her scar was very painful, her arm swollen and weak and her left shoulder ached continually. When she got home in the middle of January 1969, she had more determination than ever to return to 'ordinary' life, and drove the car, even though it was only as far as the pillar-box, by the end of the first week's convalescence. The same desperate desire to be doing things revived Valentine's interest in the shop, which Sylvia thought too much for her, but did little to stop. 'As for the further future, I don't intend to look at it till I have to,'[76] Sylvia wrote to William Maxwell. In the meantime they hung, unillusionedly, on every small possibility of a recovery.

After the second operation, Valentine spoke at length to an elder of the Society of Friends in Dorchester, and by the spring was attending Quaker meetings regularly, though she had not given up going to Mass. By the summer she had lapsed from Catholicism and had applied to join the Society of Friends. Writing to a priest she had known for some time, Valentine tried to explain why, in honesty, she felt she could no longer attend Mass:

I have had to stop going to Mass, & Holy Communion: quite simply because for some long time I have realised that I no longer believe that there is one true Church – except in the widest possible sense [...]

I found that the Quaker way of thinking exactly matched the point I had reached, and their way of worship enabled me again to pray *with* my fellows, which I had not been able to do because the changes in the Mass completely distracted me and I had found no way of making it, for myself, an act of worship or of fellowship.[77]

Valentine was accepted as a member of the Society of Friends on 11 September. Sylvia went with her to meetings, for Quakerism was a form of worship she could understand and approve. She went as an observer and did not speak. It was a pleasure and a comfort to attend because she did it with Valentine, and if Sylvia did not go as far as praying, she did have much to think about, and much to hope, though her mind was inclined to wander during the silences. There was a geometrically patterned carpet at the Meeting House which set Sylvia off on Euclid, or simple reveries of Miss Green's cottage and once 'a strange vision of a short hairy neolithic man peeping in; and recognising a *circle.*'

Sylvia wrote to Joy Finzi on 8 August: 'This miraculous summer still embraces us: the river flows gently and the moorhens converse and the enormous trout rise like explosions; we have never had such roses and the raspberries went on and on like Schubert and the figs are ripening. We have not slighted it, but we have been held back from it.' 'It is *almost unbearable* to LOVE things so much,'[78] Valentine wrote in her diary.

During the summer Valentine's shoulder hurt her so much that she had more treatment at a hospital in Yeovil, where the doctor thought her cancer may have spread to the lungs. She tried to give up smoking, and was put on hormone pills to contain the disease's advance, but they only made her feel worse, exhausted by any exertion, swollen and melancholy. 'She felt ill after lunch,' Sylvia wrote on 1 September. 'I gardened. While I was clearing up, she came out and gave me a skeleton leaf off the rainy tree, then picked some raspberries saying she could only totter – it is true –

and went to bed.' At Guy's a fortnight later, Hedley Atkins told Sylvia plainly that things were going badly. Valentine had a growth in her neck. She was on too many drugs, he thought, and should go into Nuffield House for tests. There was to be no more radiation treatment and no further operation; clearly they were leaving the disease to take its own course. '[Valentine] began to realise that she had been cheated: that nothing was done or suggested to help her oedema, that the series of tests is to ease the medical mind, not her. And she raged. And I could do nothing.'[79]

The next day their G.P., Dr Hollins, put off the idea of 'tests' and took Valentine off the hormone treatment. She had several pronounced growths on the lungs and a swelling in the neck. He wanted to try a new drug for a fortnight before taking last-ditch measures. 'She said if she could not be cured, then she would prefer to be killed – and quickly. My heart assents; my hope still holds out.'

On 1 October Valentine became breathless while shopping in Dorchester – for 1970 diaries – and Dr Hollins put her on yet another medicine. She had to spend a great deal of time in bed, getting her strength up, but rose whenever possible, dressed with great care and did some small job before collapsing into bed again. They bought a new grey kitten, Moth, to sit on her bed and be played with and Valentine watched the birds and trees she loved through a pair of mother-of-pearl opera glasses, lighter to hold than binoculars. Although she was very ill, she looked immaculate and kept very clean, a fastidiousness which Sylvia admired greatly.

At the end of October, her health took a sharp downward turn; she could still walk along the landing, and sometimes downstairs to the kitchen, 'but bent, crouched under her pain, with how slow steps. Her lovely gait, her proud carriage.' That day, in bed and bleeding, she folded Sylvia's hands over her own. 'It is sad,' she said. On the 26th, Fougère was taken away by Mr King, the garage man, and a night-watch began, shared by Sybil Chase and another local woman.

On the 27th, Sylvia wrote in her diary, 'This morning the swans flew over. She wept silently. This world so lovely, and she with such quick eyes for its loveliness. [...] I knew I had given up all hope. Panic descended on me at the thought of watching her die, then living half-dead without her.' Sylvia sat with Valentine all day, much of it in silence. She kept visitors away, but let Father Weekes in, though Valentine told him emphatically that she did not want the Last Rites. By 6 November, Valentine was wretched; alternately drowsy and in pain and bringing up a grey froth. That evening she was given her first morphia injection. They were stronger the next day, doubled the day after that. 'She is as strong as a horse,' Hollins said to Sylvia, for Valentine's pulse was steady although she was unconscious most of the time. In the small hours of 9 November, Sylvia sat holding Valentine's unresponsive hand, and 'though she could not have heard me' repeated her favourite poems and her marriage vow over and over. 'When the first light sifted into the room I knew she was beginning to die':

A gale raged round the house: a torn cloud let through the low sun. I saw a tall rainbow standing there. Hollins came. By now her breathing had changed – slow, harsh, like a tree creaking. His part was over, he went away. Sibyl and I stayed by her, wiping her lips, I still holding her hand. The intervals between her creaking breaths grew longer, longer. Then, no more. The silence seemed to solidify, like hardening wax. We cleaned her face and Sibyl took away the soiled towels. Sibyl spoke of calling old Mrs Stewart to lay her out. I said at once that we would do that. So between us we cut away her red silk pyjamas, and washed her beautiful, beautiful long body, so smooth, so white, and re-dressed her. The pliability, the compliance of her dead limbs – the last token of her grace and affability and obligingness. And we bound up her jaw.

Soon after her death, I saw all her young beauty flooding back into her face. It was the Valentine of forty years [ago], Valentine I first loved. Binding her jaws slightly changed this. She had the tragic calm beauty of the dead Christ we saw carried in the Good Friday procession at Orta.

I put her wooden cross and rosary in her stiffening hand, and some sprays of wet rosemary and the remaining white cyclamen from the garden.

Later that day I rang up Joy Finzi and asked her to come and do a drawing of my dead beautiful love.[80]

Sylvia had laid Valentine out very simply and beautifully, Joy thought, when she arrived to do the drawing. A pillow supported the head in such a way as to conceal to some extent the largeness of the growth on her neck. The bedroom window was open, and the wind lifted Valentine's hair slightly. But after about an hour, a trickle of blood began to run out of Valentine's mouth at the right side.

Joy left on 11 November, the day Valentine's body was taken away in a forget-me-not blue van, a detail Sylvia felt she would have liked. 'We always rejoiced when people went and left us alone together,' Sylvia wrote. 'So we are now.' The cremation took place on the 15th. Sylvia attended, against Valentine's written wishes.

> I unmake the death-bed, I remake the marriage-bed I said. And as I lay thinking of all the beds we had lain in, she came and pulled aside the sheets and leaped in beside me. And so I slept all night with her ashes in a respectable little fumed oak tabernacle beside me.[81]

In a letter of instructions dated 20 June 1969, Valentine had stipulated that she wanted to be buried in St Nicholas's Church, East Chaldon, in the south-east corner of the churchyard, 'with the regular C of E Burial Service [...] *no changes and no cuts*'. 'The funeral should be *as cheap as possible*: flowers, if people want to give them, but don't let them just die on the ground ...'

In her diary, Sylvia made the following entry for the day of the burial, 22 November:

> [...] it was a pearl-coloured morning, pale colours through a watery mist, a pearled morning such as she loved. Strange interval to fill up between waking and burying the ash-remains of the treasure of my soul. [...] Janet Stone, Sibyl and the car at 1.30. By now it was clear, fine, arrayed in light. [...] The wooden box lay on my knee. At Chaldon, Steven was in the road, looking at 24. 24 is empty, gutted, staring black windows. We were too early. People came up the road like deformed ghosts. Betty shrunken, André limping on two

sticks. At last, without any stage-fright, I followed Mr Tate
up the steep path into the church, holding my Love and my
mate in my arms. In the darkish church, Betty Pinney's face,
dead white and small. I put the box on a little table. He took
off his long black cloak, and read the two funeral psalms,
verse about with the congregation. The first wrung my heart:
it was as though her sadder self had written it, 'Let my young
grow up'. He read the epistle extremely well; as if it were
meaning something to him as he read it. Then the prayers and
the blessing; and he came out of the chancel and I picked up
the box and followed him into the brilliant green world, and
to the pit. There was a hassock beside it. I knelt, and lay the
box in the pit (such good earth) and settled it, and put the
knot of rosemary and married myrtle on top. And the sexton
threw the first handful of earth. I turned my eyes to High
Chaldon above the low stone wall, and knew she was there
beside me, looking the same way. Not comfort, but acceptance. I was loth to come away. But I drove back with Janet
[Machen], who looked so *young* with grief: and near
Owermoigne we stopped for old old Dr Smith on his bicycle.

Our queer impromptu tea of crumpets and red wine and
prawns. She stayed till dusk had fallen, and went away again
in tears. [...]

And so I began my widowed estate, with three cats and a
book about Scotland by a man called Smout.

Sylvia did not cry. On the 25th, she wrote that her eyes were 'arid
with unshed tears'. Three weeks after Valentine's death, when she
was still sorting out small bequests and legacies, she went into
Dorchester to find 'the burly broken-nosed stallkeeper' in South
Street, to whom Valentine had left £10.

[He] had known about her operations and had always
encouraged her and kept his fingers crossed for her. He was
there today, looking detached and philosophical and drinking out of a large white mug. I stopped. Did he remember the
lady with the poodle? At first, not. I coloured the poodle.
Yes, of course he remembered her. I told him she was dead,

and had left him a parting present with her love. He stared at me, all woe and incredulity.

'She was a lovely lady,' he said. 'We shall never see her like again,' said I. His eyes filled with tears. The reality of his words and mine broke into my composure. I began to cry. With tears on our old cheeks we patted each other sadly, while a woman who wanted to buy a cabbage stared at us.

7

1969–1978

I

Who chooses the music, turns the page,
Waters the geraniums on the window-ledge?
Who proxies my hand,
Puts on the mourning-ring in lieu of the diamond?

Who winds the trudging clock, who tears
Flimsy the empty date off calendars?
Who widow-hoods my senses
Lest they should meet the morning's cheat defenceless?

Who valets me at nightfall, undresses me of another day,
Puts it tidily and finally away,
And lets in darkness
To befriend my eyelids like an illusory caress?

I called him Sorrow when first he came,
But Sorrow is too narrow a name;
And though he has attended me this long while
Habit will not do. Habit is servile.
He, inaudible, governs my days, impalpable,
Impels my hither and thither. I am his to command,
My times are in his hand.
Once in a dream I called him Azrael.[1]

'One cannot grow out of a loss; one cannot grow round it. The only expedient is to grow *with it*, for the loss persists, develops, amplifies.'

[Sylvia to Samuel Menasche, 22 December 1974]

Valentine had said she would never leave Sylvia, and to Sylvia that assurance was everything; not a statement of intent, but a statement of fact. She constantly sought, and found, indications of Valentine's presence; a flight-feather lying by her chair, a letter in a book, a passage marked for her to read, Valentine's scent, suddenly, sharply, on the air. 'Her love is everywhere. It follows me as I go about the house, meets me in the garden, sends swans into my dreams. In a strange underwater or above-earth way I am very nearly happy.'[2] Even before the funeral, Sylvia had begun to collect up and order their love letters. She was transported by them to the 'amazing euphoric reality' of the past, their years at Miss Green, at Frankfort and at '24' which were so happy and unanimous. Sorting through the letters was not a comfort, but a wild excitement; she went to them 'as if to an assignation' and through them entered into a life parallel to her daily shadow-life, a brilliant real world in which she and Valentine existed together, where their love lived. All losses were restored in that world: it was not the anxious, ill Valentine of later years who dominated it, but Valentine glorified, imperious, suave. Sylvia, too, appeared in a cleansed form, disburdened of her ageing body and her scepticism.

'Ordinary life' persisted underneath the other, and in ordinary life Sylvia was a desolate lonely old woman, who despite whisky, friends and endless jobs to do – dismantling the shop, sending off keepsakes and legacies, writing letters of business – could hardly drag herself from one day into another. 'I creep on broken wing,' she wrote, expecting to die at any moment from sheer lack of momentum. She went to Quaker meetings, but fell asleep in them; friends rallied round her, but she could only respond with good manners: 'they wrap warmth round a stone'.[3] In mid-December she went to stay with Ruth and Tony Scott, and was at the Stones' house for Christmas Day, where Walter de la Mare's poem 'Autumn', in a book she was given as a present, struck her so forcibly she thought she would die then and there from 'the shock of this sudden assault of the truth', but being in company, she did not die. 'Total grief is like a minefield,' she wrote in her diary. 'No knowing when one will touch the tripwire.'

The turn of the year in which Valentine died was very hard; 'It is a formality of time: but it rends my heart.' In the first week of January, though, Sylvia found her diary of 1930, the time when she and Valentine first fell in love, their early days at Chaldon, Winterton and Lavenham. The diary not only complemented but corroborated the world of the letters, and Sylvia sat wrapped in it all evening: 'such happiness burned in me, such reality and such confident love that I was sure she was with me, followed me out of my room, watched me do the evening routine, followed me to bed (but was there already, waiting for me).' As if in acknowledgement of the two separate worlds she lived in, Sylvia kept two diaries in 1970.

Her dreams were vivid and in the main happy; Valentine with her at the King's Arms, Valentine waiting for her in a London taxi, Candace at the front door and the sounds of Valentine's return, but it was when she was awake that Sylvia had her strongest impressions of a presence, could feel Valentine watching her, sense her exact height in a doorway and, occasionally, very matter-of-factly, see her:

> I was sitting in the kitchen, looking at the deepening sky, and she appeared, stately and happy, cradling a child in her arms – lost Tamar. And I rejoiced to see that loss restored to her.[4]

Sylvia felt she was 'not so much haunted as possessed', guided and watched over; *Non omnis moriar*, as Valentine had chosen for her epitaph. 'This continuity is at once my only joy and my sharpest stabbing,' she wrote in her diary. After a day of sorting Valentine's room, when she had re-read Valentine's autobiography, 'For Sylvia', and some melancholy letters, 'It was time to go upstairs and draw the curtains round this empty house. On the stairs, in the narrow window, *she halted me* to look at the two birch-trees in their lacework, the moon shining over them, a mist, a mermaid mist, rising through them. I felt her then, her compassion. So I went out and walked the drive and came [in] chilled and drank whiskey and caressed the cats. I know nothing, nothing.'

As the second diary shows, Sylvia continued to write, though with the utmost effort and no pleasure. In her clearances, she found several half-finished stories which she decided to re-work, but the results were not satisfactory: 'Considered re-hashing Mr Dalrymple,' she wrote in February 1970, 'but it is just an itch, a psoriasis, and while I scratch, absorbing; and when the scratching is over I come back to my solid widowhood.' She undertook a number of book reviews for the *Spectator* at this time, and an introduction to *Northanger Abbey*. Although she did not expect to flare into artistry again, she found that 'on the whole, harness is supporting wear'.

'I have had my whole raison d'être sent out of my bosom,' she wrote to Jean Larson, 'and when I turn to any familiar occupation, trying to write, cooking my boring meals, listening to music, their familiarity catches me in the illusion that she is still here, I shall hear her tread, her whistle; or else that she is away and I am waiting for her return.'[5] She was unsteadied by having no one to care for and support. A few weeks after Valentine's death, Sylvia had had a visit (not a visit of condolence) from Betty Pinney's daughter Susanna, 'a nymph in ragged jeans' recovering from an unhappy love affair. Sylvia quickened immediately to the candour and melancholy of the young woman's tone and noted that as well as being intelligent and lonely she could also type. Unwittingly, Susanna did what little else had succeeded in doing: 'she raised my head because I felt I could help her.' Similarly, when an American writer and academic, Garold Sharpe, was recovering from influenza, Sylvia was pleased to have him convalesce at her house. 'It is so strange to have no-one to love,' she wrote.

By Easter 1970, she was incredulous that she was still alive, and wept for loneliness on seeing the first white violets.

A week later, she was sorting stories listlessly for a new book when she came across a poem by Valentine, 'This is the world exactly as Adam had it', written when Valentine was still the stalking solitary glimpsed from afar in Chaldon. It fired Sylvia with the desire to write a preface to the first section of their letters, telling the history of how they fell in love. All her energy flooded back as she set about this task – 'Tore up and tore up – but wrote on', she wrote on 9 April. Two days later she had worked her way to Miss Green's cottage: 'I bleed from every limb from cutting my way out of thickets. But I live – and can bleed.' It became clear that the letters themselves needed to be copied, for some were almost illegible with having been carried round, slept with, loved, and that they did not need a preface so much as a series of narratives, linking section to section. She asked Susanna Pinney to make a start on the typing, and realised with pleasure that she was preparing something for posterity. To William Maxwell she wrote, 'It is far the best thing I have ever written – and an engrossing agony. I am terrified that I should die before I have finished this. A month ago, it was the only thing I had the least inclination for.'[6]

Reading the letters of the troubled years, and her corresponding diary entries, Sylvia was accosted by remorse and regrets, and wherever she felt she had failed Valentine, was utterly woebegone. 'I WAS WRONG,' she wrote in her diary, thinking back sadly on the two episodes of Elizabeth: 'Either way it seems I was wrong to her, whom I loved with my whole heart, having made that primal mistake in 38/39. And yet I did it to please, or thought so; and to succour her renewal of life by lust: or thought so. But not for a moment do I doubt the truth of our love. It shed the dear pleasures of the flesh; it carried heavy burdens of doubt, care, calamity, disappointment. It never failed. It does not fail now.'[7] It was imperative to Sylvia to convey that truth, at whatever cost to herself. Overcome by the narrative of their stay at the Kibbe house in America, Sylvia had to break off and recover from it, but she wrote and re-wrote scrupulously in her determination to be both honest and accurate. It had to be the truth – 'it *must* not be dichtung.'

Valentine's birthday came and went, so did the stonemason with sketches for the gravestone – both women's names and only Sylvia's death date left blank. As often as she was elated and assured, Sylvia was downcast and desolate. On 27 June she wrote: 'melancholy, I was haunted by the *till you came to me* letter. When I read it, after the first caress of her assurances, I was overwhelmed by knowing how I had lost all that love, that no other love meant more than a dead leaf to me. I almost lost all sense of her, my sense of what I had lost was so vehement.' Before Valentine's death, Sylvia had looked elderly. Nine months after it, she looked ineluctably old; stooping, lined and bewhiskered. 'Till Valentine's death I never noticed that I was growing older,'[8] she wrote to Joy Finzi. The house was 'haggard with removals' and with inattention. Even the garden was neglected, although the enormously hard work of the previous two years showed in it still – the summer was 'jewelled with flowers – *unbearable*'. Lying in the bath and looking at her own arm, Sylvia remembered how often Valentine had kissed it: 'I bethought me that I inhabit my body like a grumbling caretaker in a forsaken house. Fine goings-on here in the old days: such scampers up and down stairs, such singing and dancing. All over now: and the *mortality* of my body suddenly pierced my heart. For of that, there is *no* question; no marrying or giving in marriage.'[9]

> The gifts remain, and I
> remain and love on
> But the hand of the loved one is gone.
>
> The gifts remain, the light-
> hearted, the love-freighted,
> The useful, the trivial, the
> remembrances of past pleasure, the
> promises of pleasures to come,
> the gifts remain
>
> And on them is the sheen
> Of their moment of giving, the
> hand of the giver, the lover,
> The summer hat hanging by the garden door,
> The sharp knife in the kitchen drawer,
> The shell and the feather.
>
> But I myself remain, and live on
> All else being gone,
> The chosen, the cherished,

The longest meditated,
The kept to the last, the most sadly relinquished.[10]

II

In September 1970 Sylvia wrote to David Garnett, then in his late seventies and living in the South of France: 'How old we both are, my dear. Alike in that, if in nothing else. In a way, I am now like the Sylvia you first knew, for I have reverted to solitude. I live in a house too large for me, with three cats; and when the telephone rings and it is a wrong number I feel a rush of thankfulness. I was grateful to you for your letter after Valentine's death, for you were the sole person who said that for pain and loneliness there is no cure. I suppose people have not the moral stamina to contemplate the idea of no cure; and to ease their uneasiness they trot out the most astonishing placebos.'[11] The passage of time did nothing to heal Sylvia's grief, in fact it made it worse, for her sense of being alone gained in mass and substance as Valentine receded into the past, as her presence was overlaid, even slightly, by changes in the house. Sylvia could no longer enjoy any part of being ill, for it was simply illness, ungraced by Valentine's ministrations, and she in turn had no one to cherish. 'That is the worst thing,' she wrote to Bea Howe, 'by far the worst thing: not to please, or comfort, or support, or enliven, or amuse. Not to give. To have, and not to share.'[12] 'I can't live for myself, it's not worth it,' she wrote, coming back from a visit to Ian and Trekkie Parsons in Lewes to her dishevelled house and the sheer tiresomeness of looking after herself. Even her sturdiest pleasures failed her: 'An interval of sitting in the garden, but the flourish of May overcame me and I cowered in again. Then, talking to Pericles, I said a truth: Only two things are real to me: my love and my death. In between them, I merely exist in a scatter of senses.'

Sylvia had been going through Valentine's notebooks and manuscripts slowly over the year, but early in 1971 began to read the diaries, and was overset by them: 'I had not realised how *soon* she began to lose hope of our love, to be ravaged about her poetry, to *feel the cold*.' She felt unequal to Valentine's melancholy, and gripped by remorse for the times when she had been insensitive or unnoticing. At about the same time, a radio broadcast vindicated Kurt Geisen, a man they had quarrelled over, who had been persecuted by the Russians. 'I listened frozen with shame,' she wrote in her diary, 'remembering how Valentine had bade me believe against my loyalty to USSR. Alas! Alas!' Having to admit that a hole had shown up in her bullet-proof Stalinism was nothing now to the thought that she had disbelieved her love.

She continued across the minefield. One day in March 1971, sixteen months after Valentine's death, Sylvia was suddenly released into 'real, unhinderable *free* weeping', remembering how she had lifted Fougère from Valentine's dying bed. The Kings were moving to Malta and taking 'Fou' with them, and when Sylvia went to say goodbye, she was greeted rapturously by the dog, 'a real contact with the past, and that is over.' 'It is the body which grieves, grieves for the body of the lost one,' she wrote, after sorting some of Valentine's clothes for a jumble sale. 'I took up her gloves, her paws, her little paws – and looked at her bedroom slippers. I do think her soul survives; but my body grieves and grieves for hers. My courage at the time has shredded away. I have none left. I am an old woman, and crave for comfort and protection like a child.'[13] She parted with Valentine's clothes stoically, as she had parted with all the mementos of their expeditions to Spain (sent to an Oxford college archive) and other treasures such as Valentine's poetry books (sent to the Arts Council Library), the car, the Craske pictures (given to the Snape Maltings). Part of this was her instinct to clear the decks, preparing to leave with a clean pair of heels, but part was pure Roman matron.

By the end of 1971, Sylvia had almost finished the narrative links and notes to the love letters, although it took her so long to compose five hundred words in the final section that she began to fear she was becoming senile. This intimation was less pleasant than the intimations of death she felt from time to time, which disappointingly came to nothing. She felt herself walking 'crouched forward and shambling, *like an old woman*', saw herself looking like Nora in age and feared the path down into decay. She had very little interest in herself and her own doings; she was phlegmatic about being made an Honorary Member of the American Academy of Arts and Letters and virtually ignored the publication of her stories, *The Innocent and the Guilty*, late in 1971. It was Valentine's doings which excited her deepest concern. After the love letters, Sylvia turned to Valentine's poems and submitted a selection of them to Chatto & Windus. They were accepted, and published in 1973 under the title *The Nature of the Moment*. This, together with the pamphlet, *Later Poems*, which Sylvia had privately printed in 1970 as a keepsake for friends, represented more than Valentine had published in her lifetime. But there was no escaping from the old trouble. The Chatto & Windus catalogue entry about Valentine harped on Sylvia, and neither Ian Parsons nor Norah Smallwood understood why Sylvia was deeply affronted by it.

During 1971, Sylvia began to write with more ease again and inadvertently made so many dollars from her short stories that she found herself '*much* too wealthy' and gave away large sums – 'pre-legacies' – to friends and relations who needed them. She appreciated fine things, good food, good wine, but spent little on herself. Old habits die hard; even in her wealthy old age Sylvia was more likely to put on more and more layers of clothes in the winter than light another fire. A friend of hers wrote that 'Sylvia, with an air of boasting, sometimes said she liked luxury, by which she often meant no more than clean sheets or a hot water bottle.'[14]

Ironically, a life insurance policy which Valentine had struggled to pay to provide for Sylvia's old age had matured in the autumn of 1969 and yielded £6,000, but even such a large sum went almost unnoticed in the general flow of income from Sylvia's writing and investments and the income from the money she had put by for Valentine in the fifties. She still prided herself on the ingenuity which could make an old pair of curtains into a tablecloth, or a tablecloth into a dress, or a dress into the appliqués on a cushion cover. A garment of hers survives in which one can almost see her train of thought in composing it: in front of her was a thick old Paisley cloth, in her head the idea of the warm dress it would make. Launching in with scissors and a needle (she never used a pattern and always sewed by hand), she arrived at her goal; a winter dress with panels in unexpected places, superlative darns where there had been holes and an elaboration round the collar which is the essence of afterthought.

Towards the end of 1970, Sylvia had written a story for the *New Yorker* called 'Something Entirely Different', a departure from her usual sphere, as the title suggests, and the forerunner of a series of stories about elfindom which provided her with a challenge and a diversion in the last years of her life. 'Something Entirely Different', which was not published until 1972, told the story of an elfin child, a changeling, planted in a Scots Presbyterian cradle and the parallel history of the human child taken into elfindom. The transposition allowed full reign to Sylvia's gift for social satire and she revelled in it. When Mr Shawn, the editor-in-chief at the *New Yorker*, saw the story, his comment was simply 'Remarkable!'[15]

Susanna Pinney, who had typed many of the love letters, was also typing Sylvia's stories for her. She would come to the house regularly, converse, share one of Sylvia's meals – planned and cooked with real artistry – and work. Their growing friendship had a congenially practical basis. The oppressive concern of friends for Sylvia's bereavement had begun to wear off – at one time Sylvia had likened it to being a tree every dog lifted its leg against – and she was able to regain some privacy and quiet, seeing those she chose to see, mainly the Scotts, the Parsons and Michael and Pat Howard, to whose grand new home, Boughrood Castle, Sylvia went for Christmas 1972. In the same year, Sylvia took up a long-standing invitation from Paul Nordoff to visit him in Denmark; a surprising decision, for apart from being seventy-eight, Sylvia disliked leaving Frome Vauchurch. 'The truth is,' she wrote to William Maxwell, 'I was growing rather alarmed by the way I was acceding to routine; compliance with it felt increasingly like madness. "Now I hang up the tea-cup on the 3rd hook. Now I put the blue plates in the rack."'[16] She planned to be in Denmark only one week: 'it will be easier for me to make a short stay – *because of the return*. The return to myself, I mean, to the shape of my thoughts and the pattern of my days. I have found it hard enough to return even after a few days – to the accumulated emptiness of this house and the accumulated familiarity of it. I daren't stretch the continuity too far, or for too long. I live with an old woman, Paul, and have to humour her.'[17]

Sylvia enjoyed her week in Scandinavia and was pleased to be involved in Paul's latest project, the book he was writing with Clive Robbins on their method of music therapy for handicapped children. 'In the mornings we disentangled the knots and in the afternoons went out to play.'[18] Photographs taken on this holiday include one of Sylvia in a Kensal Green attitude of woe before a piece of metal sculpture. In an unbecoming fur hat and coat she looks grey-faced, wrinkled and surprisingly small.

Some of Sylvia's most highly valued friendships were founded and maintained by her transatlantic correspondences. She loved, and needed, the uncluttered intellectual intimacy which depended on distance and separateness and which such correspondence allowed. 'A correspondence kept up over a length of years with never a meeting is a bridge which with every letter seems more elastically reliable,' Sylvia had written in her biography of T.H. White, 'but it is a bridge that only carries the weight of one person at a time. When the correspondents meet it collapses and they have to founder their way to the footing of actuality.'[19] Sylvia never met Leonard Bacon, met Anne Parrish very infrequently and George Plank, the American artist and illustrator, only once, yet she exchanged letters regularly with all three until their deaths. Her important later correspondences with William Maxwell and the sisters Marchette and Joy Chute were also nurtured by the Atlantic, and it was to these three friends she sent the love letters when complete. These were the most intimate and personal documents Sylvia possessed, the autobiography of her heart. Susanna Pinney had read most of them in the typing, but no one else had, and it is interesting that Sylvia entrusted copies to the very people with whom she was rarely, if at all, on 'the footing of actuality'. To the Chutes she wrote:

> I am so glad you have read those letters – for now you know us. As I grow old and cold, sometimes I feel as though she and I were being whirled away from each other like leaves on an autumn wind; it restores, it reassembles me to know that we still exist to you, in our exact truth, in our reality; and that

reading her letters you will know the phoenix that I loved in life and reality: that we were truly so ... 'so well completed in each other's arms'. A strange thing is, that we took the miracle almost for granted; heaven was our daily wear, at times, hell, too, but never completely; there was always, even in our worst afflictions and perplexities, a lining of comfort in each other.[20]

Valentine's love letters and Valentine's poems were all that could comfort her now. Posting the poems, after agonies of choosing and arranging, seemed to Sylvia another milestone 'in my long journey towards my dear death'. She was keeping the old anniversaries again – finding Miss Green, moving in to the cottage, becoming lovers – and read her 1930 diary day for day in 1972, like a breviary. She felt feeble and lonely, stuck in 'this cellular prison of time', with Valentine's presence waning and herself the prey to folly. One evening she heard footsteps overhead – light, intermittent. They were not Valentine's footsteps but 'with some such thought' Sylvia ran upstairs. Moth was in a corner with a dead vole. 'Weeping for my foolishness, my childish old age foolishness, my loneliness's credulity, I came down and went on with the poems.'

The intimations, when they came, were much more unworldly and real, so vivid that she felt sure of imminent death.

> [...] somewhere about 3 a.m. I woke in my sleep and there she was beside me in actuality of being: not remembered, not evoked, not a sense of presence. *Actual.*
>
> I was sitting in the kitchen and she standing beside me, in a cotton shirt and grey trousers, looking down on me, with love, intimately, ordinarily, with her look of tantalising a little, her easy amorous look. She was within touch of my hand. I looked at her and felt the whole force of my love for her, its amazement, a delighted awe, entrancement, rapture. We were familiar, ourselves to ourselves. I was withheld from speaking. I looked. I gave myself. I loved with my whole being. No words occurred to me. I knew I must not try to touch her, and I was wholly an embrace of her. And then

without ending, it was at an end. I was conveyed into another layer of sleep.[21]

And again, on 9 November, the third anniversary of Valentine's death, Sylvia dreamed 'with total distinctness' of Valentine in a long dress of brilliant rose colour, a dream of reunion. Walking up to Maiden Newton post office later that day against a brisk wind, Sylvia considered the odd duality of her life: 'an old woman lopsided with parcels, looked at kindly as come down in the world, inwardly alight with my dream.'

In the summer of 1972, Susanna Pinney left Dorset to take up a job in Italy, and in her absence Sylvia made friends with the young widow of an Austrian count, Gräfin Antonia Trauttmansdorff, who lived in the same village as Reynolds and Janet Stone. Antonia was widely and eclectically read, with a wayward imagination masked by gentle manners. This delighted Sylvia, as did Antonia's taste for the eighteenth century and Europe, and her combination of a disillusioned, mischievous mind with one that was also searching, ardent and open. What began as a slight social acquaintance grew rapidly to mutual liking, love and an alliance based on frivolity and diversion. One of Antonia's talents was for pen-and-ink drawing, and she entertained herself and Sylvia by creating 'surrogate holidays' through pictures. These 'holidays', in which Sylvia often appeared as an owl, and the many other private jokes they shared were very liberating, as Antonia has described:

> The games which Sylvia used to play with me were the games of a disillusioned mind. If one believes in nothing, one can pretend to believe in everything, the whole ragbag. I used to draw cartoons for Sylvia and she often contributed ideas. Our God could sometimes be an old Edwardian roué, who had become tired of philandering, or a family doctor or, on occasion, a Jethro Tull looking over the fields as Satan wrought havoc with the wheat. Satan on the other hand might be an Italian puppet master or a decadent French poet. In such diversions of fantasy the next door neighbour can become St Paul and the mouse in the larder can become Hercules.[22]

The advent of Antonia marked a significant change in Sylvia's life; her loneliness was eased, her imagination challenged, and as a result she was livelier than she had been in years. The opportunity to be flippant and to exercise the more acid and malicious side of her wit had presented itself and Sylvia took it willingly. It was not so much that the wound of her bereavement had healed as that she was exasperated at living so long. The letters and poems had been attended to, her business was done. She gave herself over to *divertimenti*.

Sylvia gave up writing realistic stories and turned back to the subject of 'Something Entirely Different', written three years before. Elfindom and its anarchic, amoral inhabitants suited her mood exactly: she was herself set outside ordinary human society by her bereavement and the parallel elfin world with its ruthless rationality and freedom from sentiment appealed strongly. In an interview she said, 'I suddenly looked round on my career and thought, "Good God, I've been understanding the human heart for all these decades. Bother the human heart, I'm tired of the human heart. I want to write about something entirely different."'[23] The stories drew on her knowledge of the Border ballads and fairy lore; her material an intriguing mixture of *Legends of the North* and the memoirs of Saint-Simon:

> The mysterious tribe of fairies are erroneously supposed to be immortal and very small. In fact, they are of smallish human stature and of ordinary human contrivance. They are born, and eventually die; but their longevity and their habit of remaining good-looking, slender and unimpaired till the hour of death have led to the Kingdom of Elfin being called the Land of the Ever-Young. Again, it is an error to say 'the Kingdom of Elfin': the Kingdoms of Elfin are as numerous as kingdoms were in the Europe of the nineteenth century, and as diverse.[24]

This extraordinary departure seemed calculated to irritate and confuse a great many readers, which probably added to Sylvia's pleasure. Speaking of these stories in an interview she said, 'I hope some of it will annoy people because that is the surest way of being attended to.'[25] She used Elfindom as a mirror to society, although all the satire in her elfin stories is very casually arrived at; she seems too *uninterested* in human dealings to aim at them with any care. She adopted a heartless, detached narrative style for the purpose and invented a great many sociological facts:

> Elfhame is in Heathendom. It has no christenings. But when a human child is brought into it there is a week of ceremonies. Every day a fasting weasel bites the child's neck and drinks its blood for three minutes. The amount of blood drunk by each successive weasel (who is weighed before and after the drinking) is replaced by the same weight of a distillation of dew, soot, and aconite. Though the blood-to-ichor transfer does not cancel human nature (the distillation is only approximate: elfin blood contains several unanalysable components, one of which is believed to be magnetic air), it gives considerable longevity; up to a hundred and fifty years is the usual span. During the seven days, the child may suffer some sharpish colics, but few die. On the eighth day it is judged sufficiently inhumanised to be given its new name.[26]

To write about elfindom, Sylvia 'inhumanised' her prose; the rhetorical equivalent of the blood-to-ichor transfer. The results are peculiar, both brutal and amusing, with not a moral guideline in sight. Many people considered the elfin stories to be Sylvia's most original work: to others they were little more than an old woman's folly. She threw herself into them with all the relish of a self-indulgence, and, propelled by curiosity and 'passionate' excitement, completed seven of the stories in 1973 alone. 'I never want to write a respectable, realistic story ever again,'[27] she said.

On 6 December 1973 Sylvia's eightieth birthday was celebrated at the Garrick Club by a select group of friends which included Bea Howe, Ian Parsons and Norah Smallwood. 'I never thought to drink such wines again – nor to eat a more superlative fish soufflé with prawn sauce. There was no one there I had not known & liked for a long, long time; & by the end of the evening I felt that the waiter and waitress were also dear old friends, they looked on our decent mirth with such kindness.'[28] The next morning she rose 'with octogenarian energy' and went to the Chinese exhibition at the Royal Academy. Her vitality was as boundless as her devotion to pleasure; she was determined to make the best of age, and extract amusement from it whenever possible. 'I am cultivating a new Vice for my old age,' she wrote to Joy Chute. 'I go to bed early – 10.30 or so, eat half an orange, read about the Tractarians and go to sleep. The cats flock to bed with me, & see how much of them can sleep on my face. By compression and involution they manage quite a high quota. There are not enough poems in praise of bed – and rather too many of them are taken up with epithalamiums.'[29]

Suddenly, two years afer Valentine's death, Sylvia had started to garden passionately again, and put enormous energy and love into it, although she no longer felt very interested in the state of the house. In 1972 she found the perfect char, Hilda Cleall, a Cockney married to a local man. Sylvia enjoyed Mrs Cleall's voice and company quite as much as the fact that the house was tidied. Bea Howe recalls how on a visit to Frome Vauchurch she heard a noise downstairs very early in the morning and went to investigate. It was Mrs Cleall tidying the kitchen, because, she said, Sylvia never remembered to do it and she wanted to get things straight before her 'official' entrance later in the day.

Drives out on sunny days, fireside conversations on chill ones and, from 1974 onwards, Christmas, were all undertaken by Antonia. 'Every difficulty can be overcome by having an Antonia,'[30] Sylvia wrote. Antonia came to the house several times a week and brought things to show Sylvia or give her: a basket of pears, books, figs, an item of gossip, a piece of meteorite. Once they had a 'truly Addisonian morning', eating strawberries and discussing Antonia's illustrations to Crabbe, and when Antonia went to China in the summer of 1975, Sylvia missed her much more than she expected to.

Although Sylvia still found herself 'craving and craving' for Valentine to appear to her, the peculiar intensity of the early apparitions had gone. On the seventh anniversary of Valentine's death she wrote in her diary and marked with an asterisk: '*rainbows* an inherent possibility: the sun – so the cloud – so. The rain-washed transparency of air in between. So *apparitions*.' It is as if she was waiting for something to happen. A later entry for the same day is 'Sea-Symphony – my love in the doorway. Her exact height,' but though this sounds comforting, it had not the intimate quality nor the actuality of before.

In the spring of 1976, Sylvia appears to have been preparing a larger, probably collected, edition of Valentine's poems, but found it intensely difficult to write the foreword and epilogue. Going back through Valentine's diaries and notebooks was a melancholy business, and on Valentine's Day, reading her own careworn diary of 1969, Sylvia was struck by 'a false thought', that she was happier than then. 'False and flimsy and soon dismissed,' she wrote, no doubt appalled at the imputation of infidelity that being 'happier' implied, but there must have been something in it, if only a nagging sense of guilt at enjoying an ostensibly jovial old age. The joviality, as she knew, was part of her 'despicable hold on life'.

As she wore down physically there was less to find amusing in old age. During Antonia's absence in China, Sylvia suffered some back trouble which led her to invoke the help of her friend with the black box. 'I feel as if I've been rolled on by passing cart-horses, but they have passed,' she wrote in her diary. To David Garnett she wrote: 'Do you ever feel the childishness of old age? I don't mean second-childhood, but the particular childish excitement at being able to do things dexterously? – to pour out milk without spilling it, to put things back in their proper places, to be capable and responsible? It is a pure pride, as it was then. I only get it occasionally, and it lasts like morning dew.'[31]

A bleak short poem she wrote in 1973 has a similar theme:

Learning to walk, the child totters between embraces;
Admiring voices confirm its tentative syllables.
In the day of unlearning speech, mislaying balance,
We make our way to the grave delighting nobody.[32]

III

Sylvia had lived long enough to see the reprinting of her early novels and a certain growth of interest in her as a writer. *Lolly Willowes* and *Mr Fortune's Maggot* were being reissued under the umbrella of feminist works and she was pleased to have *After the Death of Don Juan* sought after and *The Corner That Held Them* reprinted by Chatto & Windus. Norah Smallwood planned to publish a collection of Sylvia's elfin stories, *Kingdoms of Elfin*, early in 1977 and in America, where the *New Yorker* had made them known, the stories subscribed 6,500 copies before publication. Sylvia herself suggested to William Maxwell, whom she appointed as one of her literary executors, that a selection of her letters could be made after her death and there was interest too in her poems, which surprised her, as she wrote to the publisher in question, Michael Schmidt: 'It is the most astonishing affair to me to be taken notice of in my extreme old age.'[33] Peter Pears, a friend of her later years, proposed to put on a Sylvia Townsend Warner day at the Aldeburgh Festival. At first the prospect seemed rather alarming, but when she realised he meant 1977, not 1976, Sylvia was pacified: 'I might well be dead by then.'

Her flow of elfin stories was checked in the spring of 1976 when Mr Shawn let it be known that he thought the *New Yorker* had published enough of them. They had taken fourteen over the previous three years and rejected only a handful, but all the same Sylvia felt disappointed and wrote to Mavis Gallant that Mr Shawn 'doesn't like me [...] Vieux singe ne plaît à personne.'[34] Though she had lost her appetite for any other kind of story, she set herself to tease it back to life, the impulse in her to *work*, even aged eighty-two, was so strong. Money was not a consideration, for she had more than enough and gave much away, especially to friends faced with medical expenses or divorce suits.

1976 was the summer of drought when even Sylvia, who was devoted to heat and sunshine, found herself wilting and needed all her reserves of stoicism to witness the ravages wrought on the garden. 'The only creatures that thrive are moths and butterflies,' she wrote to William Maxwell, 'but they prefer it indoors, and flit about the house as though it were woodland.'[35] The drought was followed by floods in the autumn and the river in full spate, 'violently flowing towards me, breasthigh, as I walked in the squelching garden. Flood water all round the house.' Sylvia's physical strength was considerable: in the winter the house was hardly heated at all and the door often left wide open. 'The temperature of the rest of the house [apart from the heated rooms] was the same as outdoors,'[36] William Maxwell noted. But in 1977 Sylvia's stamina decreased noticeably. In March she had a fall, and though she claimed to feel better for it next day, it was the first of a number of similar incidents. She dropped a bottle of milk and felt 'weak and silly' – next she broke a plate. In May she fell on all fours on the river path. 'I am deplorably the worse for this last year's wear and tear,' she wrote to David Garnett, 'and a prey to vain regrets – that I shall never see the Aurora Borealis again, or listen to larks – too deaf; or walk up hills, too lame, or re-read *Clarissa* in small type.'[37]

Antonia came every Tuesday morning to wake Sylvia with coffee. She was impressed by Sylvia's instant alertness on the point of waking: Sylvia often began to talk before her eyes were open. Similarly, when she fell asleep, she did so very rapidly. There was no grinding in and out of consciousness. Antonia was a Quaker and in March Sylvia began to go to Meetings with her, where, she said, she played music to herself in her head. In the summer Sylvia gardened hard, but in spates rather than swathes. In her diary she made a note on fatigue: 'Things remembered, one by one, and at intervals [...] each involving a gymnastic of going off to do, to make a note of it: Continuity has to be powered by a working-order battery.'

On 20 June she set off for Aldeburgh with Antonia to the festival's day in her honour. It included a reading of her 'Twelve Poems', xeroxed and stapled for the occasion, a short story, 'The Cold', and settings of her poems by Alan Bush and John Ireland. There were also settings by Paul Nordoff, a melancholy reminder of his death by cancer earlier that year. On that familiar east coast, haunted by her own and Valentine's younger selves, Sylvia was cast down by thoughts of times past:

Hoisting my misshapen fat clumsy body with constipation

and bad toes out of my bath this morning, I thought of past love and pleasure and wished it dead, so that I could escape it.

But all the wings of my spirit, love and beauty and the sea and music and art and all knowledge and enlightenment and sorrow and pleasure and joy ALL came to it via the body I was wishing dead. *My body was the hostess.* And even now my sight totters to my eyes to see the wind and the sunlight on the sea.[38]

And on a separate page she wrote: 'By dying I shall lose my loss. The final bereavement? The reconciliation.'

She went on into the winter exhausted much of the time, and with bad legs. 'An atrocious night', she wrote on 14 October: 'Combatted legs with cigarettes and Wordsworth.' Nevertheless, she gardened vigorously the next day. On the 17th she fell against the tool-shed 'with a loud clang'. She felt 'deboshed', and though she still sat down to write, wrote 'fatuously'. 'Frost fading. So am I.'

Her eighty-fourth birthday passed quietly with Bea Howe at Frome Vauchurch and she spent Christmas Day at Baglake, Antonia's home. Her right foot had started to give her pain, and the district nurse was coming regularly to bandage it, but bandages posed problems of their own, such as how to bathe with one leg. Snow was coming from the north and the Rayburn had gone out twice in one month.

One preoccupation was off her mind, for in November Antonia had accepted her offer of the use of the house after Sylvia's death. With that settled, Sylvia made her final will at the end of November. In it she gave £36,000 in bequests and willed her residuary estate (valued at £165,000 after her death) to five organisations: the London Library, the National Trust, the University Federation for Animal Welfare, the National Council for Civil Liberties and the Musicians' Benevolent Fund. Antonia was to be allowed to live rent- and rate-free in the house for as long as she liked. The trustees of her estate were her solicitor, Peg Manisty and Joy Finzi. Her literary executors were Susanna Pinney and William Maxwell.

While she was still mobile, Sylvia devised a very efficient system for the sending out of bequests after her death, to spare whoever undertook it unnecessary bother. She made a card index of recipients and on each card wrote what they were to have and exactly where it was to be found. She then wrote another card to be sent with the object in question. All that remained to do was the parcelling.

The new year of 1978 began badly. 'My legs are like ancient monuments, they ache and give way, and my cats look at me deploringly, and say privately to each other that I am a shadow of my old self, a shadow even of what I was before Christmas. Belatedly, old age has clawed me in its clutch.'[39] On the same day, 6 January, her diary entry read 'Fell several times – not at my best' and the following day Antonia proposed that Sylvia should go to bed and stay there, with a joke that they both enjoyed – that Sylvia had always been good in bed.

After a few weeks, she still found walking difficult: 'I can only walk very slowly, and cling to whatever is near for a support.'[40] She was convinced that an improvement in the weather would cure her, and held out for that. Meanwhile, she was virtually bedridden.

'I am grown very old, dear William,' she wrote on 17 February. 'And I have grown so small, I scarcely know myself. And so slow. But really I should congratulate myself that my wits are still about me. When my mother was my age, she was senile. And I am not that, and I can still see to read, & hear to talk; and if the weather were not so biting and blighting I might not feel so like a dead leaf … de ça, de là, comme le vent n'emporte.'[41] In the latter half of February, though, the winter really showed its teeth: heavy snow fell and a violent east wind lashed it about: 'The garden, the fields beyond, the hills beyond the fields were all made of snow in the most extraordinary shapes – shapes the wind had blown them & frozen them into, so that nothing looked like itself. And there was Mrs Cleall's son, snow up to the waist, helping his mamma over the fence on her way to dig me out. The lane was solid snowdrift, so they had walked here on top of a hedge.'[42] Dozens of animals died in the cold and wind. The trains stopped, so did the post and the milk. Antonia, unable to drive through the snow, walked the six miles from Litton Cheney to make Sylvia hot meals.

In January, Sylvia had written to William Maxwell, 'the worst of my sufferings is the amount of care, solicitude, visiting that I provoke among my friends. I have almost forgotten what silence sounds like.'[43] To combat the lowering effects of last respects, Sylvia and Antonia played sardonic games with visitors to the deathbed, to see how far death and sociability could mix. It was a heartless pursuit, and not indulged very often. It was also strictly conspiratorial, which may indicate these games were undertaken in part to ease Antonia's own feelings.

One person Sylvia asked to see was the friend with the black box, who emerged from Sylvia's room after about an hour saying there was nothing she could do – Sylvia was simply old. It is interesting that Sylvia asked to see her, though. She was giving herself every possible chance to recover.

On 5 March she wrote: 'Today I have sat in the sun without an attempt of bravery. It *shone*, & crocuses came into bloom all round, exploded into bloom.'[44] But the spring came too late to do her any permanent good. She was sinking towards death. By the end of April a nurse was in the house almost all the time, and a sporadic night-watch in operation. The last thing Antonia recalled Sylvia saying was 'What *is* the meaning of all this, Antonia? They assure me there is one.' Her death, when it came on the morning of 1 May 1978, in the presence of an Irish nurse she disliked and Colin House, her former garden-boy – who had asked to be there – was prosaic and confused, as she had once dreamed it would be.

The funeral took place on 4 May at St Nicholas's Church, East Chaldon. Sylvia had requested the Prayer Book service, no music and no flowers. An envelope marked 'V.A.' had been cremated with her body. Sylvia also requested the Thanksgiving for Rain to be read. It had been Theodore Powys's choice on Sylvia's first visit to Chaldon church in 1922, as she may or may not have remembered. She chose it as 'the nearest P[rayer] B[ook] thing I can find to a Thanksgiving for Death':[45]

> *O God our heavenly Father, who by thy gracious providence dost cause the former and the latter rain to descend upon the earth, that it may bring forth fruit for the use of man; We give thee humble thanks that it hath pleased thee, in our great*

*necessity, to send us at the last a joyful rain upon thine
inheritance, and to refresh it when it was dry, to the great
comfort of us thy unworthy servants, and to the glory of thy
holy Name; through thy mercies in Jesus Christ our Lord.
Amen.*

Bibliography of Works by Sylvia Townsend Warner

Unless otherwise stated publication in London is by Chatto & Windus and publication in New York by The Viking Press.

The Espalier, London, 1925; New York, The Dial Press, 1925.
Lolly Willowes, London and New York, 1926.
Mr Fortune's Maggot, London and New York, 1927.
Time Imported, London and New York, 1928.
The True Heart, London and New York, 1929.
Some World Far From Ours, London, Woburn Books, 1929.
Elinor Barley, London, The Cresset Press, 1930.
A Moral Ending and Other Stories, London, Furnival Books, 1931.
Opus 7, London and New York, 1931.
The Salutation, London and New York, 1932.
The Rainbow, New York, Alfred Knopf, 1932.
Whether a Dove or Seagull (with Valentine Ackland), New York, 1933; London, 1934.
More Joy In Heaven, London, The Cresset Press, 1935.
Summer Will Show, London and New York, 1936.
After the Death of Don Juan, London, 1938; New York, 1939.
The Cat's Cradle Book, New York, 1940; London, 1960.
A Garland of Straw, London and New York, 1943.
The Portrait of a Tortoise, extracted from the Journals and Letters of Gilbert White, with an Introduction and Notes by Sylvia Townsend Warner, London, 1946.
The Museum of Cheats, London, 1947.
The Corner That Held Them, London and New York, 1948.
Somerset, London, Paul Elek, 1949.
Jane Austen, London, Longmans, Green & Co., 1951.
The Flint Anchor, London and New York, 1954.
Winter in the Air, London, 1955; New York, 1956.
Boxwood, London, The Monotype Corporation, 1957; enlarged edition, London, Chatto & Windus, 1960.
By Way of Sainte-Beuve, translation of *Contre Sainte-Beuve* by Marcel Proust, London, 1958.
A Spirit Rises, London and New York, 1962.

A Place of Shipwreck, translation of *La Côte Sauvage* by Jean-René Huguenin, London, 1963.

A Stranger With a Bag, London, 1966; New York (under the title *Swans on an Autumn River*), 1966.

T.H. White, London, Jonathan Cape and Chatto & Windus, 1967; New York, 1967.

King Duffus and Other Poems, Wells and London, Clare, Son & Co. Ltd., 1968.

The Innocent and the Guilty, London and New York, 1971.

Kingdoms of Elfin, London and New York, 1977.

Azrael & Other Poems, Newbury, Libanus Press, 1978.

Twelve Poems, London, 1980.

Scenes of Childhood and Other Stories, London and New York, 1981.

Letters, edited by William Maxwell, London and New York, 1982.

Collected Poems, edited by Claire Harman, Manchester, Carcanet Press, 1982; New York, 1982.

One Thing Leading To Another, edited by Susanna Pinney, London and New York, 1984.

Selected Poems, Manchester, Carcanet Press, 1985; New York, 1985.

Selected Stories, London and New York, 1988.

References

Where the date is made clear in the context, or is of no immediate importance, I have left quotations from Sylvia's diary unmarked by a reference. Unless otherwise stated, unpublished letters are in the possession of the recipients or their executors.   C.H.

Abbreviations

1   Unpublished Sources

ACKLAND	The diaries of Valentine Ackland, 29 volumes, 1925–1969. In the Sylvia Townsend Warner and Valentine Ackland collection, Dorset County Museum.
DORSET	The Sylvia Townsend Warner and Valentine Ackland collection in the Dorset County Museum, Dorchester (excluding diaries).
PUREFOY	Dorothie Purefoy Machen, Memoirs. In the possession of Janet Pollock.
READING	The Chatto & Windus archive in Reading University Library, Whiteknights, Reading.
TEXAS	Letters from Sylvia Townsend Warner to Nancy Cunard and Alyse Gregory, in the collection of the Harry Ransom Humanities Research Center, The University of Texas at Austin, Texas.
WARNER	The diaries of Sylvia Townsend Warner, 38 volumes, 1927–1978. In the Sylvia Townsend Warner and Valentine Ackland collection, Dorset County Museum.
YALE	Letters from Sylvia Townsend Warner to George Plank, from Valentine Ackland to Alyse Gregory, and the journal of Alyse Gregory 1931–1949, in the Beinecke Rare Book and Manuscript Library, Yale University.

2 Published Sources

(i) Works by Sylvia Townsend Warner

ADJ	*After the Death of Don Juan.*
Blackwood's	'Behind the Firing Line: Some Experiences in a Munitions Factory', *Blackwood's Magazine*, February 1916.
CCB	*The Cat's Cradle Book.*
CP	*Collected Poems.*
CTHT	*The Corner That Held Them.*
Espalier	*The Espalier.*
FA	*The Flint Anchor.*
IG	*The Innocent and the Guilty.*
KE	*Kingdoms of Elfin.*
Letters	*Letters.*
LW	*Lolly Willowes.*
MC	*The Museum of Cheats.*
MFM	*Mr Fortune's Maggot.*
Opus 7	*Opus 7.*
OT	*One Thing Leading to Another.*
Salutation	*The Salutation.*
SC	*Scenes of Childhood.*
Somerset	*Somerset.*
SR	*A Spirit Rises.*
SWS	*Summer Will Show.*
TH	*The True Heart.*
THW	*T.H. White.*
TI	*Time Importuned.*
TP	*Twelve Poems.*
WDS	*Whether a Dove or Seagull* (with Valentine Ackland).

(ii) Miscellaneous Works

Ackland (FS)	Valentine Ackland, *For Sylvia: An Honest Account*, Chatto & Windus, 1985.
Ackland (NM)	Valentine Ackland, *The Nature of the Moment*, Chatto & Windus, 1973.
Elwin	Malcolm Elwin, *The Life of Llewelyn Powys*, John Lane at The Bodley Head, 1946.

Frost	*The Letters of Robert Frost to Louis Untermeyer*, Jonathan Cape, 1964.
Garnett	David Garnett, *The Familiar Faces*, Chatto & Windus, 1962.
Graves	Richard Perceval Graves, *The Brothers Powys*, Routledge & Kegan Paul, 1983.
Harrovian	*The Harrovian*, vol. XXIX (1916), pp. 92–99.
Hartley	L.P. Hartley, 'The Conformer', in *The Old School*, ed. Graham Greene, Oxford University Press, 1984.
Hewett	Christopher Hewett (ed.) *The Living Curve: Letters to W.J. Strachan 1929–1979*, Taranman/Carcanet 1984.
Humfrey	Belinda Humfrey (ed.), *Recollections of the Powys Brothers*, Peter Owen, 1980.
LR	*Left Review*.
Morgan	Louise Morgan, *Writers at Work*, Chatto & Windus, 1931.
Partridge	Frances Partridge, *Julia. A Portrait of Julia Strachey by Herself and Frances Partridge*, Victor Gollancz, 1983.
PNR 23	'Sylvia Townsend Warner 1893–1978: A Celebration', ed. by Claire Harman, *PN Review* 23, 1981.
PR5	Sylvia Townsend Warner, 'Theodore Powys and Some Friends at East Chaldon, 1922–1927: A Narrative and Some Letters', *The Powys Review*, number 5, Summer 1979.
Quiller-Couch	Arthur Quiller-Couch, *Memories and Opinions*, Cambridge University Press, 1944.
Reynolds	Aidan Reynolds and William Charlton, *Arthur Machen*, The Richards Press, 1963.
Spender	Stephen Spender, *World Within World*, Faber, 1977.
Untermeyer	Jean Starr Untermeyer, *Private Collection*, Alfred A. Knopf, 1965.
Warner	George Townsend Warner, *On the Writing of English*, Blackie & Son, n.d. [1915].
Warner, O	Oliver Warner, *Chatto & Windus. A Brief Account of the Firm's Origin, History and Development*, Chatto & Windus, 1973.

3 Names

AG	Alyse Gregory.
BH	Bea Howe.
CP	Charles Prentice.
GP	George Plank.
GTW	George Townsend Warner (1865–1916).
GTW1	Rev. George Townsend Warner (1815–1869).
GTW2	Rev. George Townsend Warner (1841–1902).
JF	Joy Finzi.
NC	Nancy Cunard.
NS	Norah Smallwood.
PN	Paul Nordoff.
SC	Steven Clark.
STW	Sylvia Townsend Warner.
TFP	T.F. Powys.
VA	Valentine Ackland.
WM	William Maxwell.

Chapter 1: 1893–1917

1 PUREFOY, p. 6.
2 *Harrovian*, p. 97.
3 The quotations in this paragraph are from three letters of GTW1 to GTW2 – 23 March 1861; n.d. [1863] and 18 May 1862 – all of which were copied by STW into her 1962 diary.
4 *Quiller-Couch*, p. 46.
5 *ibid.*, p. 48.
6 DORSET: GTW to Nora Hudleston, January 1889.
7 WARNER, 17 August 1929.
8 YALE: STW to Leonard Bacon, 23 June 1952.
9 Copied into WARNER, 17 August 1929.
10 PUREFOY, p. 35.
11 STW, 'The Way By Which I Have Come', *The Countryman*, July 1939, p. 472.
12 WARNER, 2 February 1952.
13 'Sylvia Townsend Warner in Conversation', *PNR 23*, p. 35.
14 *SC*, p. 39.
15 *ibid.*, p. 40. This story is also referred to in notes on her childhood by STW, taken down in dictation by VA, 1965 (DORSET).

16 *ibid.*, p. 37.
17 *ibid.*, p. 60.
18 YALE: STW to GP, 24 May 1960.
19 *Letters*, p. 263.
20 *ibid.*, p. 180.
21 Thomas Carlyle's journal for 12 March 1828, quoted in WARNER, 20 February 1954.
22 DORSET: GTW1 to GTW2, 11 March 1863.
23 quoted in YALE: STW to GP, 5 January 1960.
24 WARNER, 20 January 1954.
25 DORSET: 'The Sylvie Book', a collection of verses written for STW by GTW, with contributions from Nora Warner and Frank Hudleston.
26 DORSET: Notes on STW's childhood, taken down in dictation by VA, 1965.
27 YALE: STW to GP, 7 July 1958.
28 *ibid.*
29 *Letters*, p. 251.
30 *ibid.*, p. 192.
31 *Times Literary Supplement*, 12 September 1936.
32 *Harrovian*, p. 96.
33 *Hartley*, p. 81.
34 *The Times*, 25 September 1916.
35 *Harrow School Song Book* (1974 edition), p. 103.
36 *Harrovian*, p. 96.
37 *ibid.*, p. 94.
38 *ibid.*, p. 99.
39 *SR*, pp. 153–4.
40 *Letters*, p. 263.
41 STW to BH, 3 June 1924.
42 *Harrovian*, p. 95.
43 An unnamed colleague of GTW, quoted in *T.P.'s and Cassell's Weekly*, 15 January 1927.
44 *Warner*, pp. 156–7.
45 DORSET: 'Pianos and Pianolas', unfinished article by STW.
46 Letter to *The Harrovian*, 15 October 1947.
47 *LW*, p. 26.
48 YALE: STW to GP, 22 December 1961.
49 WARNER, 24 May 1950.
50 *ibid.*, 25 April 1951.
51 *ibid.*, 20 December 1952.

52 *ibid.*
53 GTW, 'The Spirit of the War at Harrow', reprinted in *The Living Age*, 18 September 1915, pp. 731–5.
54 GTW, 'Improvised Armies', *Blackwood's Magazine*, October 1914, pp. 547–62.
55 DORSET: GTW diary, 1 January 1916.
56 DORSET: Eric Milner-White to GTW, February 1915.
57 DORSET: GTW diary, 22 April 1915.
58 *ibid.*, 25/26 August 1915.
59 *Blackwood's*, p. 198.
60 *ibid.*, p. 202.
61 *ibid.*, p. 196.
62 *ibid.*, p. 195.
63 Advertisements in *The Times*, September 1916.
64 PUREFOY, p. 138.
65 *The Times*, 25 September 1916.
66 DORSET: GTW diary, 26 April 1916.
67 *ibid.*, 3/4 April 1916.
68 *ibid.*, 26 August 1916.
69 *Harrovian*, p. 92.
70 STW to VA, 24 March 1931.
71 YALE: VA to AG, 16 March n.d.
72 WARNER, 28 January 1966.
73 *Letters*, p. 251.
74 *ibid.*
75 DORSET: Warner family papers.
76 *Harrovian*, pp. 92–9.
77 STW to VA, 25 March 1931.
78 DORSET: STW, an unfinished piece of writing about thrift.
79 *ibid.*
80 WARNER, 24 September 1958.
81 *ibid.*

Other sources include: F. Hudleston, *Hutton John* (privately printed, n.d.); *The Harrow Register*; *Reynolds*; DORSET: Flora Warner's memoirs; conversations with Ruth and Antony Scott, Vivien Elgood and Antonia Trauttmansdorff.

Chapter 2: 1918–1930

1   *SC*, p. 138.
2   *ibid.*, p. 141.
3   *Letters*, p. xxii.
4   STW, 'The Point of Perfection in XVI Century Notation', extracted from *The Proceedings of the Musical Association*, 11 February 1919, p. 67.
5   *ibid.*, postscript.
6   *Espalier*, p. 10.
7   *SC*, pp. 140–1.
8   *Hartley*, p. 79.
9   *Letters*, p. 114.
10 *Garnett*, pages 12 and 2.
11 *PNR* 23, p. 39.
12 PUREFOY, p. 141.
13 *Letters*, p. 251.
14 By BH.
15 STW to BH, 12 August 1921.
16 *PRs*, p. 13.
17 TFP, *Soliloquies of a Hermit*, Andrew Melrose, 1918, p. 1.
18 *PRs*, p. 14.
19 *ibid.*, p. 16.
20 *ibid.*
21 *ibid.*, p. 17.
22 *ibid.*, p. 19.
23 *PNR* 23, pp. 41–2.
24 DORSET: an account of STW's discovery of the Essex marshes (incomplete). Other unmarked quotations in this passage are from the same source.
25 STW, 'The Way By Which I Have Come', *The Countryman*, July 1939, p. 476.
26 *Garnett*, p. 8.
27 *Espalier*, p. 81.
28 John Cowper Powys to Llewelyn Powys, quoted in *Graves*, p. 156.
29 *Garnett*, p. 62.
30 *Humfrey*, p. 128.
31 *ibid.*, p. 129.
32 *ibid.*, p. 130.
33 *Garnett*, p. 5.
34 *Humfrey*, p. 130.

35 STW, 'Bathrooms Remembered', *New Yorker*, 11 January 1964.
36 *ibid.*
37 *Reynolds*, p. 140.
38 *ibid.*, p. 141.
39 This account of his visit to Little Zeal was related to the author by
    Hilary Machen.
40 Note on *LW* in WARNER, 1 December 1963.
41 *ibid.*
42 *Letters*, p. 168.
43 Antony Scott to the author, 24 August 1988.
44 Peter Austin Jones to the author, September 1988.
45 *PNR* 23, p. 36.
46 *Espalier*, p. 88.
47 Denis Donoghue, 'Ten Poets', *London Review of Books*, 7
    November 1985.
48 *PNR* 23, p. 42.
49 *Letters*, p. 3.
50 READING: STW to CP, 5 January 1925.
51 *Quiller-Couch*, p. 51.
52 *Letters*, p. 8.
53 *LW*, pp. 234–6.
54 READING: STW to CP, 15 February 1926.
55 *Newcastle Daily Journal*, 26 June 1926.
56 *Westminster Gazette*, 6 July 1926.
57 STW, 'Modern Witches', *Eve*, 18 August 1926.
58 *Letters*, p. 9.
59 I have been unable to trace the source of this.
60 READING: STW to CP, 4 June 1926.
61 *Warner, O.*, p. 20.
62 Norah Smallwood in conversation with the author, 13 July 1984.
63 *Warner, O.*, pp. 19–20.
64 *Ackland (FS)*, p. 108.
65 STW to JF, 3 February 1970.
66 *Partridge*, p. 108.
67 *ibid.*, p. 129 and p. 126.
68 Anne Olivier Bell (ed.), *The Diary of Virginia Woolf*, vol. 5, p. 47.
69 *Partridge*, pp. 127–8.
70 Note on *MFM* in *Letters*, p. 11.
71 *ibid.*, p. 10.
72 *Letters*, p. 9.
73 *MFM*, pp. 112–13 (Viking Press, 1st edition).

74 *ibid.*, p. 186.
75 WARNER, 27 April 1928.
76 TFP in an interview in *John O'London's Weekly and Outlook*, 23 October 1936.
77 *PRs*, p. 26.
78 *Garnett*, p. 6.
79 BH in a BBC radio broadcast, 'The True Heart', 15 March 1986.
80 *Ackland (FS)*, p. 98.
81 STW, Introduction to STW/VA letters.
82 *ibid.*
83 WARNER, 26 August 1929.
84 *TI*, pp. 28–9.
85 STW, 'Bathrooms Remembered', *New Yorker*, 11 January 1964.
86 *Morgan*, p. 27.
87 Oliver Warner, 'Sylvia Townsend Warner', *Bookman*, October 1929.
88 *TH*, p. 293.
89 WARNER, 8 March 1929.
90 DORSET: Anne Parrish to STW, 31 October 1948.
91 *TH*, p. 227.
92 *PNR 23*, p. 43.
93 WARNER, 20 January 1928.
94 *ibid.*, 20 April 1929.
95 *CP*, p. 12.
96 VA to STW, 2 January 1931.
97 WARNER, 5 August 1929.
98 *ibid.*
99 *ibid.*, 23 October 1929.
100 *ibid.*, February 1930. Later included in *WDS*, p. 89.
101 *ibid.*, 5 March 1930.
102 STW, Introduction to STW/VA letters.
103 *ibid.*
104 ACKLAND, 4 August 1930.
105 *ibid.*
106 *ibid.*, 25 August 1930.
107 *ibid.*, 5 August 1930.
108 *ibid.*
109 WARNER, 25 September 1930.
110 *Ackland (FS)*, p. 125.
111 WARNER, 11 October 1930.
112 *ibid.*

Other sources include: PUREFOY and conversations with Bea Howe, George Howe and Norah Smallwood.

Chapter 3: 1930–1937

1 *Ackland (FS)*, p. 51.
2 ACKLAND, 27 December 1952.
3 *ibid.*, 16 February 1948.
4 Obituary of R.C. Ackland in *The Times*, 31 August 1923.
5 ACKLAND, 27 December 1952.
6 *Ackland (FS)*, p. 75.
7 *ibid.*, p. 79.
8 *ibid.*, p. 80.
9 *ibid.*, p. 89.
10 *ibid.*, p. 115.
11 This and the other information in the paragraph comes from VA, 'Diary of Episodes June to October 1928' (DORSET).
12 *Ackland (FS)*, p. 119.
13 *WDS*, p. 131.
14 STW, Narrative 1, STW/VA letters.
15 WARNER, 23 October 1930.
16 *ibid.*, 19 October 1930.
17 STW, Narrative 1, STW/VA letters.
18 *Ackland (FS)*, p. 126.
19 STW, Narrative 2, STW/VA letters.
20 ACKLAND, 7 May 1930.
21 *Ackland (FS)*, p. 124.
22 Norah Smallwood in conversation with the author.
23 By NS.
24 ACKLAND, 7 August 1930.
25 Reported in VA to STW, 29 March 1931.
26 DORSET: 'Notes by V.A.', appended to 'John Craske: Notes on his life by Laura Craske'.
27 *ibid.*
28 STW, catalogue note, 'John Craske, Fisherman and Artist', Aldeburgh Festival exhibition, 1971.
29 WARNER, 7 June 1931.
30 *ibid.*, 18 June 1931.
31 *ibid.*
32 ACKLAND, 12 July 1931.

33 *ibid.*, 14 July 1931.
34 TEXAS: STW to NC, 26 July 1944.
35 *WDS*, pp. 116–17.
36 Antonia Trauttmansdorff in conversation with the author.
37 ACKLAND, 23 July 1931.
38 DORSET: from brief notes on her early books by STW.
39 *Salutation*, pp. 80–1.
40 DORSET: notes on her early books by STW.
41 *Letters*, p. 40.
42 STW, Narrative 7, STW/VA letters.
43 ACKLAND, 3 October 1932.
44 *ibid.*, 21 October 1932.
45 Bea Howe, Foreword to *Ackland (FS)*, p. 20.
46 *Ackland (NM)*, p. 13.
47 ACKLAND, 14 December 1933.
48 YALE: Alyse Gregory's journal, 26 February 1933.
49 *Letters*, p. 24.
50 *ibid.*
51 *CCB*, p. 9.
52 *Ackland (FS)*, p. 129.
53 ACKLAND, 14 December 1933.
54 READING: STW to CP, 9 November 1933.
55 Austin Clarke, *New Statesman and Nation*, 21 April 1934.
56 Humbert Wolfe, *Observer*, 8 April 1934.
57 *Frost*, p. 238 (23 February 1934).
58 *ibid.*, p. 240 (19 March 1934).
59 *Untermeyer*, pp. 157–8.
60 *ibid.*, p. 166.
61 *ibid.*, p. 145.
62 Llewelyn Powys to VA, n.d., copied into ACKLAND, November/
    December 1933.
63 ACKLAND, 10 January 1934.
64 *ibid.*, 23 January 1934.
65 *Letters*, p. 28.
66 *ibid.*, p. 30.
67 *ibid.*
68 STW, Narrative 4, STW/VA letters.
69 DORSET: VA, 'I always knew we had only come to stay', last
    stanza.
70 WARNER, 9 May 1972.
71 *Ackland (FS)*, p. 131.

72 ACKLAND, 21 July 1935.
73 *ibid.*, 14 October 1933.
74 *PNR 23*, p. 35.
75 STW, Narrative 5, STW/VA letters.
76 STW to Julius Lipton, 3 May 1935.
77 DORSET: STW notes for an introduction to VA poems (unfinished).
78 *SWS*, p. 256.
79 *PNR 23*, p. 35.
80 VA, 'Country Dealings III', *LR*, I, 2, September 1935.
81 ACKLAND, 17 September 1935.
82 *Letters*, p. 35.
83 *Untermeyer*, p. 167.
84 *PNR 23*, p. 36.
85 *ibid.*
86 *LR*, I, 10, July 1935.
87 *ibid.*, I, 7, April 1935.
88 *Letters*, p. 37.
89 ACKLAND, 14 November 1935.
90 *News of the World*, 15 March 1936. Some of Sylvia's unease about Brennand may be inferred from the characterisation of Ernie in 'The Snow Guest' (*SR*), whom she claimed to have modelled on him.
91 *News Chronicle*, 17 August 1936.
92 Unidentified newspaper clipping in ACKLAND, 1936.
93 *Letters*, pp. 41–2.
94 STW, 'Barcelona', *LR*, II, 15, December 1936.
95 *Letters*, p. 42.
96 STW to SC, 6 September 1937.
97 *LR*, II, 15, p. 140.
98 *Letters*, p. 42.
99 WARNER, 9 May 1972.
100 STW interview with Simon Blow, *Guardian*, 5 January 1977.
101 *Times Literary Supplement*, 23 January 1937.
102 *Listener*, 13 January 1937.
103 STW, Narrative 6, STW/VA letters.
104 From an account by the Belgian writer Denis Marion of 'Three Days in Madrid', *Combat* (Brussels), 31 July 1937.
105 VA, 'Writers in Madrid', *Daily Worker*, 21 July 1937.
106 *ibid.*
107 *Spender*, p. 243.

108 *ibid.*, pp. 241–2.
109 *ibid.*, pp. 244–5.
110 *Letters*, p. 49.
111 *ibid.*, p. 47.
112 Corpus Barga, 'El II Congreso Internacional de Escritores. Su signification', *Hora de Espana*, no. 8, August 1937.
113 DORSET: VA, 'Congress in Spain' (7-page ts, incomplete).
114 YALE: VA to AG, 14 October n.d.
115 *Letters*, p. 47.
116 YALE: VA to AG, 19 July 1937.
117 STW, Narrative 6, STW/VA letters.
118 *Spender*, p. 246.

Other sources include: *Elwin*; *Graves*; Vincent Brome, *The International Brigades: Spain 1936–1939* (London, Heinemann, 1965); *II congreso internacional de escritores para la defensa de la cultura (1937)*, 3 vols. (Generalitat Valenciana, 1987); conversations with Elizabeth Wade White and Hilary Machen.

Chapter 4: 1937–1947

1   *Letters*, p. 51.
2   *ibid.*, p. 49.
3   DORSET: STW to VA, 29 October 1937.
4   VA to AG, 29 July [1937].
5   DORSET: STW to VA, October 1937.
6   DORSET: STW notebooks.
7   STW to Edgell Rickword, 10 October 1937.
8   WARNER, 2 December 1937.
9   *ibid.*, 9 December 1937.
10 *Letters*, p. 303.
11 *ADJ*, pp. 23–4.
12 *Letters*, p. 51 (footnote).
13 *PNR* 23, p. 36.
14 STW, Narrative 7, STW/VA letters.
15 *Letters*, p. 54.
16 *ibid.*
17 *Ackland (FS)*, p. 134.
18 STW, Narrative 7, STW/VA letters.
19 STW to David Garnett, 14 June 1976.

20 WARNER, 6 February 1970 (i).
21 *Letters*, p. 258.
22 WM, Introduction to *Letters*, p. xv.
23 *Letters*, p. 55.
24 CP, pp. 44–5.
25 *Letters*, p. 55.
26 STW to VA, 31 July 1949.
27 *Letters*, p. 62.
28 STW, Foreword to Ilya Ehrenburg, *The Fall of France Seen Through Soviet Eyes* (Modern Books, n.d.).
29 WARNER, 17 June 1940.
30 *ibid.*, 20 June 1940.
31 YALE: VA to AG, n.d.
32 DORSET: draft poem in WARNER at 11 July 1941.
33 *Letters*, p. 64.
34 STW to NS, 14 June 1967.
35 ACKLAND, 29 August 1941.
36 YALE: VA to AG, 18 September 1941.
37 *Letters*, p. 203.
38 *ibid.*, p. 81.
39 STW to Elling Aanestad, 14 February 1942.
40 *Letters*, p.80.
41 STW, Narrative 8, STW/VA letters.
42 WARNER, 23 January 1943.
43 *ibid.*, 7 March 1943.
44 DORSET: STW, Notes on NC.
45 DORSET: STW notebooks.
46 *Letters*, p. 84.
47 *ibid.*
48 TEXAS: STW to NC, 9 May 1944.
49 ACKLAND, 5 May 1944.
50 STW, Narrative 8, STW/VA letters.
51 Reported in a letter from John Cowper Powys to Dorothy Richardson, 4 September 1939. See *Graves*, p. 305.
52 DORSET: STW, 'Notes on three Day-Books, Dorchester Rural District WVS'.
53 *Letters*, p. 88.
54 *ibid.*
55 YALE: VA to AG, n.d. [1944].
56 ACKLAND, 19 April 1945.
57 *ibid.*, 1 May 1945.

58 *ibid.*, 14 May 1945.
59 *Letters*, p. 91.
60 YALE: VA to AG, 9 October 1945.
61 YALE: VA to AG, n.d. [1946].
62 ACKLAND, 3 August 1947.
63 *ibid.*
64 *Ackland (FS)*, p. 35.
65 ACKLAND, 5 November 1947.
66 *Ackland (NM)*, pp. 39–40.

Other sources include: P.C. Buck, *Psychology for Musicians* (Oxford University Press, 1944); Anne Chisholm, *Nancy Cunard* (London, Sidgwick & Jackson, 1979); conversations with Norah Smallwood and Hilary Machen.

Chapter 5: 1947–1950

1   ACKLAND, 8 March 1948.
2   TEXAS: Arthur Machen to Colin Summerford, 17 January 1940.
3   STW/VA letters, footnote to letter 138.
4   *Letters*, p. 99.
5   YALE: VA to AG, 19 December 1947.
6   *ibid.*
7   Reported in VA to AG, 17 January n.d. [1948].
8   STW to SC, 19 May 1948.
9   STW to Walter Strachan, 14 August 1946 (*Hewett*, p. 65).
10 *MC*, p. 119.
11 *ibid.*, p. 138.
12 *Opus 7*, pp. 18–19.
13 *Letters*, p. 96.
14 *Somerset*, p. 8.
15 ibid., p. 53.
16 *PNR 23*, p. 36.
17 *CTHT*, p. 61.
18 STW inverviewed in *Guardian*, 5 January 1977.
19 STW to NS, 15 March 1971.
20 *Somerset*, p. 50.
21 Donald Davie, *Under Briggflatts: A History of Poetry in Great Britain, 1960–1985* (Carcanet, 1989).
22 YALE: VA to AG, n.d. [1949].

23 ACKLAND, 23/24 January 1949.
24 STW, ts inserted in ACKLAND, January 1949.
25 *Letters*, p. 112.
26 ACKLAND, 11 April 1949.
27 *ibid.*, 16 May 1949.
28 *Letters*, p. 112.
29 *ibid.*
30 STW, Narrative 10, STW/VA letters.
31 ACKLAND, 11 June 1949.
32 *ibid.*
33 STW, Narrative 10, STW/VA letters.
34 *ibid.*
35 *Ackland (FS)*, p. 132.
36 WARNER, 15 August 1949.
37 YALE: Alyse Gregory's journal, 12 September 1949.
38 WARNER, 9 September 1949.
39 YALE: Alyse Gregory's journal, 12 September 1949.
40 WARNER, 12 September 1949.
41 *ibid.*, 17 September 1949.
42 STW to BH, 6 September 1949.
43 WARNER, 30 September 1949.
44 *ibid.*, 6 October 1949.
45 *ibid.*, 24 October 1949.
46 *ibid.*, 7 November 1949.
47 YALE: STW to GP, 30 December 1960.
48 ACKLAND, 11 December 1949.
49 WARNER, 19 January 1950.
50 *ibid.*, 16 February 1950.
51 *ibid.*, 9 March 1950.
52 ACKLAND, 17 March 1950.
53 Reported in WARNER, 23 March 1950.
54 WARNER, 29 March 1950.

Chapter 6: 1950–1969

1 WARNER, 19 July 1950.
2 *Letters*, p. 108.
3 TEXAS: STW to NC, 21 April 1947.
4 ACKLAND, 25 May 1950.
5 *ibid.*, 10 September 1951.

6 *Letters*, p. 129.
7 *ibid.*, p. 128.
8 YALE: VA to AG, n.d. [1952].
9 YALE: STW to AG, 13 November 1951.
10 ACKLAND, 19 January 1952.
11 *ibid.*, 26 September 1951.
12 *ibid.*, 17 August 1951.
13 WARNER, 19 November 1952.
14 *ibid.*, 10 October 1952.
15 ACKLAND, 6 March 1953.
16 *ibid.*
17 WARNER, 7 January 1954.
18 *ibid.*, 4 September 1953.
19 *Letters*, p. 145.
20 ACKLAND, 1 December 1953.
21 FA, p. 78.
22 *Sunday Times*, 26 September 1954.
23 WARNER, 12 December 1954.
24 OT, p. 108.
25 ACKLAND, 8 January 1956.
26 *ibid.*, 17 February 1956.
27 *ibid.*
28 *ibid.*, 15 February 1956.
29 WARNER, 28 February 1956.
30 ACKLAND, 1 March 1956.
31 WARNER, 28 March 1956.
32 *ibid.*
33 ACKLAND, 24 April 1956.
34 *ibid.*, 9 December 1958.
35 WARNER, 10 January 1957.
36 *ibid.*, 15 March 1957.
37 STW to PN, 27 March 1957.
38 YALE: STW to AG, n.d.
39 WARNER, 14 October 1958.
40 *ibid.*, 14 August 1957.
41 Peg Manisty to the author, 4 September 1985.
42 WARNER, 8 April 1956.
43 DORSET: George D. Painter to STW, 5 March 1957.
44 STW to NS, 16 February 1960.
45 *ibid.*, 2 March 1960.
46 *Letters*, p. 179.

47 WARNER, 17 June 1960.
48 ACKLAND, 28 February 1961.
49 WARNER, 5 March 1961.
50 ACKLAND, 31 December 1961.
51 *Letters*, p. 228.
52 WARNER, 9 July 1961.
53 ACKLAND, 27 September 1961.
54 *ibid.*, 19 May 1962.
55 YALE: VA to AG, 3 December n.d.
56 ACKLAND, 24 August 1961.
57 YALE: STW to AG, 23 January 1950.
58 WARNER, 29 January 1962.
59 *Letters*, p. 199.
60 John Updike, 'The Mastery of Miss Warner', *New Republic*, 5 March 1966.
61 ACKLAND, 13 July 1962.
62 WARNER, 21 September 1963.
63 *Letters*, p. 211.
64 *ibid.*, p. 215.
65 STW to AG, 14 July 1966.
66 WARNER, 16 December 1966.
67 *ibid.*, 21 February 1967.
68 READING: Michael Howard to Eric Hiscock, 3 August 1967.
69 John Updike, *New Republic*, 5 March 1966.
70 STW to NS, 15 March 1971.
71 *IG*, p. 58.
72 WARNER, 28 August 1967.
73 DORSET: STW papers.
74 ACKLAND, 13 May 1968.
75 *ibid.*, 30 June 1968.
76 *Letters*, p. 237.
77 VA to an unnamed priest, 18 July 1969 (copy in the possession of Peg Manisty).
78 ACKLAND, 25 July 1969.
79 WARNER, 17 July 1969.
80 *ibid.*, '9 November 1969', though probably written not on, but near, that date. This entry, and those for 22 November 1969 and 3 December 1969 appear in the back of STW's 1965 diary.
81 *ibid.*, 20 November 1969.

Other sources include: conversations with Joy Finzi and Peg Manisty.

Chapter 7: 1969–1978

1 STW, 'Azrael', *TP*, p. 13.
2 *Letters*, p. 244.
3 STW to Jean Larson, 27 December 1969.
4 WARNER, 18 January 1970 (i).
5 STW to Jean Larson, 30 January 1970.
6 *Letters*, p. 246.
7 WARNER, 4 March 1970 (i).
8 STW to JF, 7 December 1970.
9 WARNER, 18 September 1970 (ii).
10 WARNER, 1970 (i).
11 *Letters*, pp. 247–8.
12 STW to BH, 15 December 1973.
13 WARNER, 14 June 1971.
14 From notes on STW by Antonia Trauttmansdorff (in the possession of Angela Pitt).
15 Reported in WARNER, 21 December 1970 (ii).
16 *Letters*, p. 255.
17 STW to PN, 16 January 1972.
18 *Letters*, p. 257.
19 *THW*, p. 219.
20 *Letters*, p. 257.
21 WARNER, 24 September 1972.
22 From notes on STW by Antonia Trauttmansdorff (in the possession of Angela Pitt).
23 *PNR* 23, p. 36.
24 *KE*, p. 15.
25 *Guardian*, 5 January 1977.
26 *KE*, pp. 1–2.
27 *PNR* 23, p. 36.
28 *Letters*, p. 272.
29 ibid., p. 273.
30 *ibid.*, p. 285.
31 *ibid.*, p. 287.
32 *TP*, p. 14.
33 STW to Michael Schmidt, 30 January 1978.
34 *Letters*, p. 289.
35 *ibid.*, p. 290.
36 *ibid.*, p. 305 (footnote by WM).
37 *ibid.*, p. 297.

38 WARNER, June 1977.
39 *Letters*, p. 302.
40 *ibid.*
41 *ibid.*, p. 303.
42 *ibid.*, p. 304.
43 *ibid.*, p. 302.
44 *ibid.*, p. 306.
45 STW to JF, 10 January 1970.

Other sources include: conversations with Susanna Pinney, Antonia Trauttmansdorff and Bea Howe.

INDEX

Note: Works by Sylvia Townsend Warner appear directly under title;
works by others appear under the name of the author